Louis XVI

This genealogy is only intended to show the relationship of the main Bourbons mentioned in this book: there were, of course, a great many others

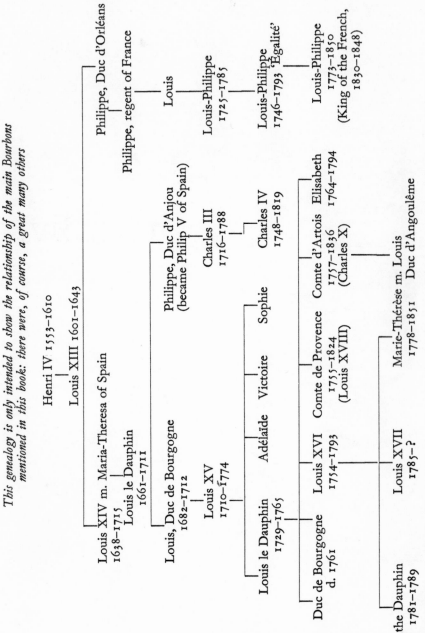

Henri IV 1553–1610
Louis XIII 1601–1643

Louis XIV m. Maria-Theresa of Spain
1638–1715
Louis le Dauphin
1661–1711

Philippe, Duc d'Orléans

Philippe, regent of France

Louis

Louis-Philippe
1725–1785

Louis-Philippe
1746–1793 'Egalité'

Louis-Philippe
1773–1850
(King of the French,
1830–1848)

Louis, Duc de Bourgogne
1682–1712

Philippe, Duc d'Anjou
(became Philip V of Spain)

Charles III
1716–1788

Charles IV
1748–1819

Louis XV
1710–1774

Adélaïde   Victoire   Sophie

Comte de Provence
1755–1824
(Louis XVIII)

Comte d'Artois
1757–1836
(Charles X)

Elisabeth
1764–1794

Louis le Dauphin
1729–1765

Duc de Bourgogne
d. 1761

Louis XVI
1754–1793

Louis XVII
1785–?

Marie-Thérèse m. Louis
1778–1851   Duc d'Angoulême

the Dauphin
1781–1789

Louis XVI

or

The End of a World

BERNARD FAŸ

Translated by
PATRICK O'BRIAN
from the French

W. H. ALLEN
LONDON
1968

Printed in Great Britain by
R & R Clark Ltd, Edinburgh for the
publishers W. H. Allen & Company,
Essex Street, London WC 2.
Bound in Edinburgh by
Hunter & Foulis Ltd.

491   00040   5

Contents

A section of illustrations appears between pages 218-219

PART ONE

Louis-Auguste the Ill-Beloved

Chapter I

A not very public birth

LOUIS XV'S SON, THE DAUPHIN LOUIS, AND HIS WIFE, Marie-Josèphe of Saxony, held aloof from the court. The leading figure there was Mme de Pompadour, and they did not approve of her morals or her way of thinking or her influence. They only made duty-appearances in the king's apartments, and for the rest of the time they stayed in their own quarters, spending their days among their books and their friends. Ever since they had come to love one another (for they had managed to do so, in spite of everything that should have kept them apart) they found that this kind of life had its own delights. It had its unpleasant sides, too.

One of the most disagreeable was their isolation just at those very moments when witnesses were called for – in the case of royal births, for example, which had to be duly verified, or else there would be very serious trouble. Now as it happened the Dauphin was so ardent a husband that the Dauphine could never be sure when the happy moment would come; and the obstetricians of those days, even the famous Jard, were quite at sea. It passed off well enough with the eldest daughter, the Petite

Madame,[1] but what difficulties there were over the birth of the Duc de Bourgogne, the Dauphin's eldest son!

Jard arrived in his bedroom slippers after the delivery had taken place. Since there were no witnesses the child had to be kept in the bed out of sight for some time, but there he kicked his mother violently, and she protested. At last the Dauphin appeared in his dressing-gown, and he rushed out into the corridor to bring in anyone he could find. Around the bed he gathered Mme de Lauraguais' chairmen, who were waiting for their mistress, the sleepy guards on duty, and the sentry, who was terrified of leaving his post. 'Come in, my good fellow,' he said to each of them, 'come in quickly, and see my wife brought to bed.' Presently the room was full and the baby was produced from under the sheets.

On 23 August 1754 things went better than that, although the birth was hardly any less unexpected. At half past three in the morning, when the labour-pains began, the Dauphine was able to send a message to Jard. The king was at Choisy, with the royal household. But the Chancellor and the Keeper of the Seals, the Marquis de Puisieux, could be reached, and they took the place of the absent family, being present for the whole process; it was not too painful, and at twenty-four minutes past six in the morning it ended happily with the birth of a prince, a small but well-formed baby.

While the labour was going on, the Dauphin told Binet, his first valet de chambre, to write a note to tell the king of what was happening; he gave the letter to a groom from the private mews and sent him off at once. As soon as the child was born the Dauphin despatched one of his equerries, M. de Montfaucon, to give the king an account of all that had taken place. As Montfaucon rode along he came upon the groom, who had taken a bad fall and who was lying across the road; Montfaucon took his message and gratified King Louis XV with a double packet of news – twice as much and twice as happy.

This was the third grandson the Dauphine had given the king. Between 1750 and 1764 this courageous woman had eight

---

[1] Madame was the title of the Dauphin's wife or of the king's eldest daughter or the wife of Monsieur, the king's eldest brother.

children – five boys and three girls – and she also had eleven miscarriages. She did not spare her time or her strength or her pains to give the house of Bourbon a numerous posterity! Yet she was by no means unaware of the danger: the Dauphin's first wife had died in childbirth.

The king was grateful for her devotion, and he was much attached to her. He came galloping back to Versailles to congratulate her and to see his new grandson, but he arrived after the private baptism, which for a child of the royal house was carried out at once. The ceremony had taken place in the Dauphin's council-chamber, with the king's chaplain, the Abbé de Chabannes, whose turn of duty it was, officiating in the presence of M. Le Roux, the curate of Notre-Dame at Versailles. At his father's wish, the baby was named Louis-Auguste.

As soon as he came in Louis XV gazed at the child, then at the Dauphine, then back again at the child, whom he created Duc de Berry, a very splendid name for the little sweating, squalling slobbering creature that wriggled there in the arms of the Comtesse de Marsan, the governess to the Children of France.[1] At last, when all the ceremonies were over, the Duc de Villeroy, the captain of the guards on duty, led Louis-Auguste to his apartments, according to protocol, together with Mme de Marsan.

The king devoted himself to the wearisome task of informing all those who had to be told in such cases, of being present at the Te Deum in the chapel, and of receiving the congratulations of all the court ladies. Meanwhile the Marquis de La Luzerne was galloping to tell the city of Paris, and then M. de Dreux, the Master of the Ceremonies, took a letter from the king to inform the city authorities. Another officer went to fetch the Archbishop of Paris, while still others set off for the King of Spain, the Elector of Saxony, King of Poland, the Infante of Parma, the former King of Poland Stanislas Leczinski, and all the friendly rulers, without forgetting the Holy Father. In Paris the guns were booming, and throughout the city the bells began to ring.

They did not ring very much. Paris was disturbed by the

---

[1] This is a literal translation of *les Enfants de France*, whose more exact, but somewhat cumbrous, rendering is Princes and Princesses of the Blood.

quarrels of the Parlement[1] and afraid that a new war might break out: neither the friendly sovereigns nor the guilds nor the king rejoiced for Berry as they had for his elder brother Bourgogne. Louis XV confined himself to giving La Luzerne the red ribbon of the order of Saint Louis and ten louis[2] to the injured groom; then at nine o'clock in the evening he lit a pretty little firework display in the Place d'Armes, setting it off himself from his balcony by means of a fuse. It was exceedingly showy for a quarter of an hour: then it all went out and prudent people went home to bed; nobody thought about Berry any more.

For its part, the city of Paris did not display much enthusiasm. There was discontent about the taxes; the cost of living was rising, and the government was blamed for it. So the king took care not to order the three days of holiday and illumination that he had called for when Bourgogne was born. At that time, in 1751, dis-affected people had been so bold as to put a parcel of flour and another of gunpowder in the baby's cradle, with the words 'If we go short of the one, we know where to find the other.' One of the nurses was instantly sent to the Bastille, but no one ever got to the bottom of the plot.

In 1754 the money the city authorities had to spare was being kept to welcome the returning members of the Parlement, who were coming back from exile. Louis XV had banished them be-cause of their systematic opposition, but he called them back on the occasion of his grandson's birth. There was eager competition between the young men of the law-courts and those of the university in seeing who could shout 'Vive le Parlement!' the loudest. Not a single cheer for Berry. Yet the town was in a kinder mood when the very popular Dauphin and Dauphine came to Paris to give thanks to God for the birth of their third son. Preceded by the governor, the Duc de Gesvres, they went first to Notre-Dame, where the archbishop welcomed them and chanted the Te Deum, and then to Sainte-Geneviève, where there was another Te Deum

[1] The Parlement was a high judicial court: there was one in Paris and others in many of the provinces, and they were in frequent conflict with the Crown because of their power to refuse the registration of decrees, which was necessary to give them the force of law.

[2] A louis was twenty-four livres, approximately a guinea.

sung. A vast concourse of people thronged round the coaches of the royal pair with that inquisitive, friendly and rather sceptical air that is so typical of Parisian crowds.

The people did not fail to make fun of the entertainment given in honour of Berry at the court theatre at Fontainebleau. In the courtier's world everything, even babies, was looked upon as the raw material for a show. The autumn season of 1754 was particularly brilliant: one after another there appeared Quinault and Lulli's *Thésée*, their *Alceste*, Fontenelle and Colasse's *Thétis et Pélée*, which was much applauded, and then Rameau's *Naissance d'Osiris ou la Fête Pamylis*, which was mocked by one and all, particularly by M. le Baron de Grimm.

> It is an Egyptian festivity [he said] in which the people dance minuets and rigadoons and sing choruses and commonplace remarks. Suddenly the heavens darken, the thunder roars, and everybody is terrified at the prospect of being pulverized. Not at all: the high priest of Jupiter assures them they have nothing to fear. Thereupon Jupiter himself appears and tells them of the birth of the prince in question – although there never had been any question of a prince at any time. After this everyone dances and everyone is happy, except for the spectators.

Louis-Auguste-Osiris was not happy either. A child at the breast cannot be happy when his nurse has no milk. This was known at Versailles: it was the talk of Paris. But nothing was in fact done about it. Yet it would have been easy to find a more plentiful supply among the five or six women chosen to deputize for the official wet-nurse. (Whenever a child of the royal house was born several nurses were brought together at Versailles, and there they stayed in reserve, well fed and well housed.) Mme de Marsan made a fuss, but in vain; and it was in vain that the Dauphine, the queen and the king tried to deal with the situation: no one could do anything, for the nurse was the mistress of the Duc de La Vrillière,[1] the minister in charge of the royal household and the only person empowered to dismiss her.

[1] Louis Phélypeaux, Comte de Saint-Florentin, Marquis (and from 1770 Duc) de La Vrillière: he was Secretary of State from 1725 to 1775, and from 1749 he was minister in charge of the royal household.

And that was the reason why Monseigneur le Duc de Berry was bawling in his cradle! How could he survive in this Versailles reeking all summer through with its stagnant pools and silted-up water-works, in the middle of a park that swarmed with mosquitoes and disgusting flies? The autumn brought freezing fogs, and in the winter the palace was filled with draughts that whistled through the rooms, coming in through the open doors and the ill-fitting windows, while in the immense fireplaces the blazing logs sent out an infernal heat. Never was there a moment of respite or of true peace at court, not even for the babies. All the courtiers and the gentlemen who were presented at the king's levee took a delight in going on to see the Children of France; on the days of audience the ambassadors invariably appeared, for they were anxious to pay their court to the Dauphin; the rulers who were passing through vied with one another in their attentions, the most outlandish being the most eager; and the baby had to smile at each one of them, unless he happened to be roaring.

Never did the procession come to an end, winter or summer, morning or evening: when the great feasts of the year came round, beggars made their way into every room in the palace and the guards could not keep them out: even in the middle of the night, when everything seemed quiet, a door might open and a dark form lean over the sleeping child – was it a Swiss guard from his post in the Hall of Mirrors, seized with homesickness at the thought of his own sons growing up without him among the peaks of the Grisons, or the King of France who had come along the secret passage to forget the wearisome difficulties of the day and to dream about the future of his race? All the hopes, all the anxieties and all the foul exhalations of the court, the town and the world flowed towards these cradles.

Mme de Marsan was governess of the Children of France, but for all that she was very much at a loss. Whenever the situation became really dangerous she quite lost her head: she would be overcome with a fit of the vapours and faint away. In quick succession there came the death of the Duc d'Aquitaine (born 8 September 1753) on 22 November 1754, and then that of the Petite

Madame on 2 September 1755, while Berry was coughing and gasping for breath.

A happy fate brought the famous Dr Tronchin from Geneva to Versailles in April 1756. This was an event of national importance. The Duc d'Orléans, on the advice of his regular physician, had desired him to come to Paris; but Louis XV, who was always inclined to be jealous of Orléans, took advantage of his arrival. He received him first in the gallery, as he received all his visitors, and then led him into his study, where they talked for a long while.

The king loved his family and he supervised its health with a closeness that was sometimes despotic and that was always well-meaning and far from useless. When he ordered a purge or a blood-letting the patient obeyed. Furthermore, he kept abreast of developments in medicine. When the interview was over, he entrusted M. Tronchin to the Dauphin and the Dauphine, who asked him questions for an hour on end. They talked about the children, and showed them to M. Tronchin. He examined Berry with particular care. Then he nodded, looked grave, and ordered a fresh-air treatment, at Meudon.

The Genevan's decision saved Berry. Meudon, upon its hills, with its two châteaux among the woods and its beautiful park laid out by Le Nôtre, was a peaceful spot. The court did not go there, and the turmoil of Paris scarcely reached it at all. Yet it was close enough to Versailles for the Dauphine (a devoted mother) to hurry over every day to see her three boys, the Duc de Bourgogne, the Duc de Berry and the Comte de Provence, who was born on 17 November 1755 and who was a fine, thriving child, thanks to an excellent nurse. For some months these little children were able to behave like children, and this gave them a liking for life and the habit of it. Berry put on weight, grew, and decided to live.

The pomps and vanities of the world still had to seek them out in this shelter. Three cardinals who had been named at the last conclave paid their court at Versailles and then wanted to do the same at Saint-Cloud. Bourgogne (aged five) received them, listened to their speeches and addressed them in his turn, while Berry (twenty-two months) and Provence (six months) sat solemnly in armchairs in their robes and their little caps, copying their elder brother's movements.

According to the Duc de Luynes everything passed off very well. Berry was bored, but he had been dressed in his frock trimmed with swan's down, which he loved, and it is to be hoped that that was a consolation to him.

What a life for a child! No sooner was he born than he had to share in the ceremonial life of the court. There was not a single royal funeral or marriage in which he did not have to take his place and play his part. There was no important betrothal that he did not have to grace with his presence. Before everything else, before living, moving or thinking, a prince was a supernumerary actor on the stage – an extra. The nearer he was to the throne the more arduous was his task.

Chapter II

The foil

THE POSITION HAD GROWN WORSE SINCE LOUIS XV CAME
to the throne. Under Louis XIV the courtiers attached to members of the royal family were there permanently: from the time
of the Duc de Bourbon's ministry they appeared only for
three months' service – for a quarter of the year. For them the
court was a theatre. They spoke their parts on the stage and then
withdrew: it was only the king and his children who had no
rest.

Some of them managed very well. This was the case with Mgr
le Duc de Bourgogne, the second of that name, a child who, in
1756 and 1757, gave rise to hopes no less than those his illustrious predecessor, Louis XIV's grandson, had inspired. He was
a fine, well-built, fair-haired boy with deep blue eyes. The whole
court was delighted with him, and the king never tired of watching him in his pink and silver hussar's uniform that the Dauphine
had just had made. At the age of five he possessed dignity, elegance and poise.

Kissing his hand, a courtier said, 'You look very well, Monseigneur: you will live until you are eighty at least.' He instantly

replied, 'Why not a hundred?' And when, because of the bad news (and the news was often bad in Versailles between 1756 and 1762), he saw long faces all around him he reproved the courtiers and the servants, saying, 'What are you looking sad for? I am very well!' Nattier has left us a picture of him at four years old – a baby still and already a king. He is wearing a blue velvet dress, and crosswise over it the gold-embroidered green ribbon of the order of the Holy Ghost: under his square cap with its waving plumes his childish eyes have the habit of command. The contest between him and Mme de Marsan had been violent and strenuous. Even at this age there was nothing of the silly child about him; he broke only what he meant to break and he answered compliments and greetings with pert replies.

His sallies delighted the Dauphin, and they spread hope and high expectation throughout Versailles: there was an intuitive feeling that Bourgogne was a budding despot; and the violence, selfishness and love for domination that he displayed in everything, even his virtues and his prayers, seemed a charming surprise – so, indeed, did his unconcealed pride.

One day he dropped a paper down a flight of stairs at Versailles. A footman suggested that he should go and fetch it. 'No,' said Bourgogne. 'It is a petition and it has a great deal of praise of me in it. Leave it to be found and handed about.'

The child had an instinctive grasp of the situation. When he heard people whine about the French defeats in the war he said, 'I shall bring England down. I shall take the King of Prussia prisoner. I shall do everything I want.' And then, in the midst of the servants' frightened silence, he added, 'Why was I not born God?' He had at least been born an actor.

Nothing of this applied to Berry. He knew nothing of his elder brother's overflowing vitality, cheerfulness and mischief. He was one of those whom illness had marked early in life: disease makes a compact that spares them; but it remains with them, and for this reason they seem cut out by fate to look inwards rather than outwards. This was all the more so since from his earliest days he had been short-sighted. He saw things near at hand clearly enough, but the rest was nothing but shadowy mystery. And royal children could not wear spectacles. So the pleasures that Bourgogne took such delight in meant little to him.

When he was three he went with his elder brother to the entertainment that the ladies of Saint-Cyr gave in honour of the Children of France. On the lawns there were ducks, turkeys, swans, pheasants and peacocks, with long strings tied to their legs. The children were to catch them by these strings, and the one who caught the biggest won the game. The happy Bourgogne dragged a whole poultry-yard behind him, while the poor Berry, pushed about by swans he never saw and bullied by angry turkey-cocks, had as miserable a time as if he had been at a court ceremony.

The strangest aspect of Berry's lot was that he never had anyone to turn to. Everyone was delighted to help Bourgogne. But not Berry. Even his father showed his affection by denying himself the pleasure of coming to his rescue. That was the effect life had had upon M. le Dauphin's nature. At the beginning he had seemed headstrong, quick-tempered and selfish, though not without charm. Then came piety and the far-reaching influence of his mother, Marie Leczinska. He remained her closest and most confidential friend; he shared her principles, he had adopted her friends, and he spent a considerable part of his evenings with her.

But it was another woman, a Spaniard, who completed this education that had been begun so strictly by his Polish mother. In a few weeks Marie-Thérèse de Bourbon taught him the lesson that the Bourbons always learnt so quickly and carried out so well. With him love for women took on that masterful and demanding form that had been seen in so many of his ancestors, starting with the good King Henri. He and his young wife plunged into an extreme intimacy, both sensual and at the same time mystical – an intimacy that was suddenly broken by death. Never did he forget his first companion.

When custom, the requirements of family interest, and the king's authority obliged him to marry again and to take the daughter of that very Frederick-Augustus of Saxony who had ousted his grandfather, Stanislas Leczinski, he agreed, since it was the king's wish and since she had been chosen by his hero, Maurice de Saxe. But at the beginning he did not conceal from her the fact that he did not love her; then later, although he loved her, he betrayed her with wenches who came early in the morning so that the queen should know nothing about it. Yet he still made great demands upon her, ploughing her as he might have ploughed a field – to such a degree, indeed, that sometimes Louis XV forbade him his wife's bed.

In 1752 it was thought that he would die of the smallpox: he was saved, thanks chiefly to the Dauphine's heroic self-sacrifice, for she nursed him through it at the risk of her life. After that his esteem for her reached the point of love; though not to the point of remaining faithful to her. In order to overcome this conflict he wanted to take part in the war; but the king, who was exceedingly fond of him and who feared very powerful emotions, would have none of it. Reduced to living at court, he behaved himself very well there: his dutiful regard for his father never diminished, nor did he ever lose that charming manner towards all he came into contact with—a characteristic said to be peculiar to the Bourbons. But the result was a deeply-concealed disproportion, a lack of measure that affected his whole personality, a veiled hardness and an essential want of balance that went hand-in-hand with an instinctive self-distrust.

He who did not care for field-sports at all and who only went out of a sense of duty, shot and killed one of his equerries: this happened in the summer of 1757. He never forgave himself, and he never got over it. He who adored the king his father never ceased opposing his policy and his mistress, whom he contemptuously named La Pompom – a disguised, secret opposition, but exceedingly eager. And he who wanted to turn his children into Christian heroes encouraged Bourgogne's infant pride and left Berry, who ought to have been helped and brought forward, alone in his corner. The Dauphine could have done it. She was intelligent, open-hearted, well-educated, and very proud of her rank; and she loved her children deeply. But she put her husband first – that husband who was so hard to hold.

By dint of humility to begin with, then of patience and then of self-sacrifice and moral superiority she had acquired an influence over him. She had succeeded in winning that ascendancy which a nurse has over a patient, and in retaining it. After the ordeal of the smallpox they seemed to be a perfect couple, and happy; and indeed they were very closely linked. Yet they were partners rather than lovers: he dominated her by his demands – exhausting, though complimentary – by his family and by his authority as a husband: she dominated him far more by her patience, which she pushed to the verge of contempt, by her motherly care and anxiety, and by her acute, vigilant understanding.

What with her husband and her pregnancies, there was little time and little energy left to her to devote to those children who were just managing to get along. From 1765 onwards she entirely lacked both time and strength, for the war had begun, and the first stroke was Frederick of Prussia's invasion of Saxony – he occupied it without firing a shot. The Dauphine's mother was a prisoner; her country was being held to ransom; her father had been crushed. The burden was too great for her to bear.

Is it necessary to say that the children's best and most attentive guardian during these disturbed and anxious months was the man they called 'Papa-Roi' and who was none other than Louis XV? The king often saw his grandsons. When he was returning from one of his châteaux – Fontainebleau, Choisy, Compiègne, Saint-Hubert – he would come back by way of Meudon to talk to them and play with them for a little while; he looked them over with great care, predicting their illnesses and doing his best to ward them off. He overwhelmed them with presents and kindness. He used to take them hunting, well aware that they delighted in it. He gave them little firework shows, such as the one he arranged at Meudon on 13 September 1756 for Bourgogne's birthday. Sometimes very strange notions came into his head: during the summer of 1757 he thought it would be a good thing to make Louis-Auguste, who was then two and a half, grand master of the order of Saint-Lazare. The long and incomprehensible ceremony was a torture to the child.

Louis XV was somewhat given to tormenting: he brought his grandsons into the pomps and splendours of the court against their will, yet he refused to teach his son the rudiments of governing, though he was longing to learn. Between 1754 and

1758 the war that England had savagely unleashed spread throughout the old world and the new. France, betrayed by Prussia, was
obliged to ally herself with her old enemy Austria: but Louis XV
would not allow the Dauphin to join the army or to attend the
council.

Damiens' attempt on his life kept Louis XV in his bed for a few
days, and this obliged him to make use of his son. He appointed
him Lieutenant-General of the Realm and required him to take
his place at the head of the councils. But as soon as the king was
well again he took everything back into his own hands.

The Dauphin then devoted himself to the bringing up of his
children, the hope of his family and of France. Yet even in this
field it was the king, the supreme head of his own family and of
all the families in France, who had the right to choose the tutors,
the servants and the gentlemen in waiting for his grandsons. He
agreed to transfer this privilege to his son.

As early as the beginning of 1758 the Dauphin began to look
for tutors and a preceptor. The choice was as important as it was
difficult. The greater part of the literary world and of high society
were then taking up the maxims of the *philosophes*,[1] maxims that
had their origin in England; and they were fighting a ceaseless
battle against Catholicism, the old ways and the monarchic traditions. The Dauphin was aware of this current of opinion and he
even admired some of those who supported it – the Baron de
Montesquieu, for example, whose acquaintance he had particularly wished to make. But he was also aware of the danger these
principles represented for his children's throne. The *philosophes*, to
be sure, were by no means insensitive to the flattery of those in
power, as they showed very clearly by their servile attitude to
Frederick; but for all that they were a danger to the established
order, even when they uttered fulsome praise of sovereign
princes.

A wise and far-seeing policy would arm the young princes
against the errors, the hallucinations and the charms of the new

[1] The *philosophes,* in this particular eighteenth-century sense of the word,
were usually deists or free-thinkers of a liberal, egalitarian, enthusiastic,
reforming turn of mind, and of course they were opposed to the Establishment.

teaching. To this end the Dauphin at first thought of making use of the illustrious Marquis de Mirabeau, the famous Friend of Mankind, the great upholder of the old ways and of knightly traditions. But the Marquis' excessive demands and his indiscretion caused this plan to fall through. Louis fell back upon a gentleman whom he had known for a long time and whose courage he had admired at Fontenoy – Antoine-Jacques-Paul de Quélen, Comte de La Vauguyon. He claimed descent from the Bourbon-Carency princes and from the ruling dukes of Brittany, and his wife was the daughter of the Duc de Béthune-Chârost, Louis XV's former preceptor. To the cheerful ways of a fat man he united the grave looks of one who was deeply concerned with religion. He was not known to have a mistress or any other kind of weakness; he was outwardly friendly, obliging and useful; and lastly he was there, on the spot, at the right moment, which is the secret of great careers at court. The Dauphin, who was haunted by his longing for the war and by his memories of Fontenoy, had brought him into his household as a *menin*, an appointed companion of high rank; and now he settled him there permanently as preceptor to the princes of the blood.

Then the other appointments were made. As tutor the choice fell upon Monseigneur de Coëtlosquet, the former Bishop of Limoges, who was renowned for his virtue and his zeal; the deputy-preceptor was the Marquis de Sinety; the deputy-tutor the Abbé de Radonvilliers (who had been recommended by the Cardinal de La Rochefoucauld). Mgr de Coëtlosquet brought with him one of his relations, the Abbé d'Argentré, who was appointed reader; and lastly, on 16 March 1758, there were presented at court MM. de Marbeuf, de Montesquiou and de La Haye, gentlemen in waiting. M. de Luppé, who had also been chosen, was not introduced to the king until somewhat later.

Such was the team that the Dauphin appointed after a careful search: the king confirmed his choice and the family approved; the Paris and the *philosophe* salons declared that La Vauguyon was a profoundly ambitious Tartuffe, Coëtlosquet a worn-out old man, and the others mere supernumeraries. They pitied the princes of the blood for having to live under their rod; they were even more sorry for the people of France, who were fated to be ruled by the pupils of such a worthless crew.

The person most immediately concerned was Monseigneur le Duc de Bourgogne, dressed in his pink and silver hussar's uniform. He was happily getting ready for life. On 22 May 1758 he moved on to the care of men. Surgeons and physicians examined him naked in bed and then drew up a report. From this moment on, the responsibility passed from Mme de Marsan to La Vauguyon. Then the captain of the guard on duty led Bourgogne to the king's study, where His Majesty, in the presence of two ministers, delivered him into the hands of La Vauguyon, not without thanking Mme de Marsan, who was, of course, in tears.

The Dauphin reserved the right to oversee this bringing-up. Twice a week Bourgogne was brought to him, and the Dauphin heard the boy his lessons. He was a very tolerant father to this son he admired, and he excused him all his faults. Bourgogne was a boisterous child, and so that he might play as hard as ever he liked the walls of his play-room were padded to head-height. He was given the finest toys in Europe, and everyone talked of his delightful little coach with its six miniature horses, its little coachman and its twelve-year-old postillion.

Bourgogne was enchanted, and in his own opinion he was superior to all other children: he wanted to be superior to his father and his grandfather the king, too. He talked, he darted about, he lived a very full life. How did it come about that unknown to anyone he took a heavy fall? The mysterious thing about courts (as it is about prisons) is that although everybody is perpetually watching everybody else, the really important happenings always pass unseen. In the end it was noticed that he was limping. He was questioned. He would not reply.

He had to be put to bed with a rising fever. The physicians found a swelling on his hip. There had to be an operation. For an hour the surgeons cut into the young body that twisted and writhed but did not utter a sound. After this torture the fever abated. The medical men thought he was cured. Yet the extremity of pain had broken the Duc de Bourgogne, and from then on he was an invalid, dominated by sickness.

His parents were exceedingly unhappy, for the occupation of Saxony, the repeated French defeats on land and sea, and the king's increasing unpopularity wounded them to the quick. For themselves they had given up any hope of a brilliant future, but they concentrated all their dreams and longings upon this child in whom, as it seemed to them, Henri IV's good fortune and Louis XIV's soul had come to life once more.

They did not refuse to see the danger, but they did refuse to accept the failure. They increased the number of medical consultations and treatments of every kind. Above all they tried to give Bourgogne back his love for living and for play; and this was how they came to think that it would be a good idea to give him his brother Berry, as a companion in life, or rather in misery. It could be said that they delivered up Berry to him. At that time Louis-Auguste was not six years old. He was beginning to grow and to come into his strength. Mme de Marsan and the quasi-solitude in which he had been left since Bourgogne went to live 'among the men' had let him open out, as it were: it was acknowledged that he had a loving and sensitive heart, but he did not seem to be a forward child. A report submitted to his father in March 1760 was of the opinion that it would be pointless to hurry on his education: the Marquis de Sinety and the Abbé d'Argentré would be enough for him, together with two gentlemen in waiting who were yet to be appointed. It was foreseen that when Provence joined his two elder brothers among the men in two years' time, he would be on a level with Berry.

So it was by no means a question of breaking the rule that fixed seven as the age when a prince of the blood should be brought up by men, nor of pushing on a precocious child, but of giving Bourgogne a companion and a support. Yet they had some notion of his distress and his unhappiness at leaving Mme de Marsan, and they made use of various artifices to bring him to it without too much conflict. He was given a firework display for his birthday, on 4 September 1760, a pleasure that he delighted in; they dressed him as a man for the first time and he was presented with his first shoe-buckles – silver, with diamond knots. Then early on the morning of 8 September they came to hand him over to M. de La Vauguyon.

It was not easy. The medical examination was not too bad, because he did not know what it was all about and because he was biddable. But he could not be unaware of the meaning of the ceremony in the king's presence, and it left him trembling and roaring. He did not want to leave 'Maman Marsan'. The embarrassed La Vauguyon tried to soothe him: he gave him a miniature cannon that (almost) shot real balls, and a variety of alluring toys. Something dark and powerful in Berry understood that he was being committed to a bitterly unpleasant adventure.

He was still crying when his father came to see him: La Vauguyon apologized for it. After two days he sent Coëtlosquet to tell the Dauphin that Berry would not be tamed. 'Really, now, Abbé,' said the Dauphin, 'are you worried by a child's tears? As for me, I find them charming. I look upon the fact that your fireworks could not influence my son's heart as a certain proof that he has one and that he will keep it sound.'

The Dauphin saw Bourgogne as the future Dauphin and the future king: he wanted to do everything to save him and to help him save himself; he thought it right that the rest of the family should sacrifice itself for him, especially Berry, since he had 'a kind heart'. A kind heart had necessarily to be of some use in a family. Was that wise? If Bourgogne were to die Berry would become the Dauphin, and the Dauphin would have been sacrificed for an empty dream. The father did not think of this: for him his eldest son and successor was always Bourgogne. It was Berry who was to pay for this mistake. He paid dearly. The disease was gnawing deeper into Bourgogne every day, and his lungs were affected; he turned his childish heroism towards his brother and appointed himself his honorary preceptor, so that the unfortunate Berry had two, who never left him in peace. Of these preceptors, Bourgogne was the more zealous: he watched all Berry's doings, he gave him advice about each one of his actions, he weighed his lightest words and supervised the lessons he prepared.

He had a still more touching idea. From his earliest childhood, when he could scarcely write at all, he had kept a 'spiritual diary'.

Every week he noted down all the good and evil that he had done, the faults that he had overcome, those that were still with him, and so on. He kept all these little volumes together in a case.

Some days after Berry had joined him he made him sit down by the bed, and in the presence of La Vauguyon and Sinety (they had been summoned for the occasion) he said, 'Come, brother, and learn how I was taught to correct my faults. It will do you good. Read everything.' Berry read it out in that gasping voice that children have when they are feeling shy. Sometimes Bourgogne blushed, but he urged his brother to go on when he came to the most humiliating details.

Berry had come to his brother strong and healthy, but living this kind of life he soon began to go backwards; yet it seemed so right and proper that nobody took any notice. Bourgogne was the only person who minded about it: was he stirred by that secret jealousy which had been usual with him in earlier days, or was it his own better side that was sorry for his brother?

He experienced those ups and downs which make up the rhythm of a prisoner's life – for no one is more of a prisoner than a sick child. Sometimes he believed and asserted that he was well again, and he would insist upon being allowed to return to his lessons: he got up and received a deputation from the city authorities from Paris standing – he always liked seeing them, and they brought him charming presents. In the court almanac he noted down the names of those who came to see him and those who neglected him. Then he had a relapse.

Visitors from the outside world, who could see him more objectively than his family, noticed that he was growing more emaciated every day. Now his piety increased twofold. Every morning he had a chapter from the Gospel read to him, listening with the keenest attention and kissing the book after the reading. He had lost all the skin from his back and he could not move without exquisite pain; he could not bear it any longer, and he prayed God aloud that He might let him find ease in some posture or another. The fever increased, and he showed an ever greater affection for his family, for Tourolles his valet and all the servants, whom he urged to go and rest, leaving him to himself. No one who came near him for a moment could doubt that he was a saint. No one who lived with him could fail to be tormented almost beyond endurance by the long death-agony of this cruelly tormented child who was nevertheless so rich in life that he could not relax or give himself up to death, which is peace.

Berry could not withstand it. At the very moment when his brother's state grew worse, on 20 March 1761, he was himself seized by a violent fever, with a racking cough and the spitting of blood. It is not in the least surprising that after six months in the sick-room of a patient with tuberculosis of the lungs and at the same time of the bones the younger brother should have been infected. His parents looked upon this as a fresh blow of fate, and they did not fail to wonder at Bourgogne's astonishing abnega-tion: he asked for news of his brother every hour. Nobody took much notice of Berry, in any case, for there was no one whose anxious mind was not wholly turned towards the next room, where his elder brother was dying.

The end was coming: an unceasing cough deprived Bourgogne of all his strength. Coëtlosquet warned him to make ready for death. It did not surprise him. He asked his father's permission to receive the viaticum and the extreme unction. He slept better that night and the next morning he was able to bear the ceremony – an agonizing experience for those near to him. Then pain took hold again, all through that day – it was Holy Saturday. During the night he coughed a great deal of blood. They hurried to bring the confessor. Then with a gasp he cried, 'The moment has come. Give me the crucifix.' Then again he cried, 'Mama, Mama!' and died. It was half past two on the Easter morning of 1761.

La Vauguyon at once hurried to the king; then together they went to the Dauphine. La Vauguyon said to her, 'Berry is im-proving, but . . .' She could not withstand the news and she fainted in Louis XV's arms. Then Provence and Artois were brought, their sorrow being as it were a nourishment for their parents' grief. The Dauphin himself, staggering under the cruel emotion, leant upon La Vauguyon's shoulder. Sometimes he looked into his wife's eyes, and there he read his own mind's thought – 'Now indeed our life is lost and over.'

Chapter III

The difficult parents

THE DUC DE BOURGOGNE WAS DEAD. BERRY HAD BEEN
settled into his room, and the same preceptors, gentlemen and
servants who had waited on his brother now served him as though
they had always done so. At court the trace left by a child fades
quickly, for it is not deep. But never was it to fade from the
heart of the Dauphin and the Dauphine; for them Bourgogne
was always the most living of their children, the family's hero.
He had been their only hope, and their hearts longed for him
for ever.

The funeral was splendid. But that did not prevent the courtiers
from tattling. Some talked about poison, others blamed the
physicians, and everybody was astonished that Vauguyon, responsible for not having watched over his charge properly, was
not punished. The blame reflected on to the father.

The Dauphin was criticized. The courtiers whispered that he
was never seen at court; that at church he made genuflexions like
a Capuchin; and that at home he shut himself up to learn music
and to sing matins. 'They say he is always among the monks and
that he hears as many as three masses a day. They also report that

he says his breviary to the best of his abilities', wrote Joseph Teleki, a Hungarian gentleman who visited Versailles in 1760, and who, judging by the gossip in the corridors, came to the conclusion 'He has even less wit than his father.'

Mme de Pompadour encouraged these rumours. She had done everything she could to be on good terms with the queen and the Dauphin, even to the point of feigning piety, of going to vespers and of giving a party to celebrate the Dauphin's recovery (1752), but then she grew tired of being snubbed, and, vexed by the Dauphin's insults (he never called her anything but La Pompom or Mother Whore), she declared war upon him. One after another she caused all the ministers he supported to be dismissed – the clever Maurepas, the wise Machault and the honest Argenson, and she thrust her own accomplice, M. de Choiseul, into office. She put all the power into his hands, and she turned him into the Dauphin's sworn enemy.

The Dauphin was a handsome, straightforward man: Choiseul with his star-gazing look and his gaudy clothes had the air of a performing ape. The Duc de Choiseul-Stainville was in fact an exceedingly witty coxcomb, with a mind as keen as it was unmethodical and a heart as generous as it was arrogant. He was kind to all around him, but he hated anything superior to him. He therefore assumed the highest possible degree of disrespect with regard to God. He built a new chapel in his château of Chanteloup, bigger, more beautiful and more richly adorned than the old one; he had his arms put up all over it, and he went to mass there every Sunday in great splendour, surrounded by his vassals and his household, carrying a missal with his blazon. Inside the covers of the missal there were La Fontaine's *Contes* or the works of Aretino. Furthermore, he did not eat fish on Friday or fast during Lent.

The *philosophes* looked upon him as their protector, and they poured out noisy propaganda in his favour; so he was able to tell the king that he had France behind him. Louis XV listened with pleasure: Choiseul's self-confidence and the clarity of his mind made him extremely valuable to his master, who was grateful to him for having wound up the Seven Years War and for having, by means of rapidly-concluded treaties, surrounded France with an impressive group of allied powers. All this was true.

But it was also true, as the Dauphin pointed out, that Choiseul's open-handed ways and his lack of method were increasing the muddle in the country's finances just at a time when they should have been set in order. And it was true that Choiseul was a present help in de-Christianizing France and in installing *philosophes* in every branch of the administration. The condemning, the pro- hibition and the expulsion of the Jesuits was a dirty job got up between him, the Pompadour, the Parlement and the *philosophes*. The Dauphin did his best to prevent it and to rally the forces of those who loved the ancient ways. But he was not well supported and he was inexperienced; he committed a blunder, and Choiseul made the most of it to humiliate him before the king and to insult him in a private interview. Although Louis XV shared his son's views, he decided against him. Choiseul triumphed. In the council the Dauphin was unable to do anything against the vote on this iniquitous law, and he solemnly declared that 'in honour and con- science he was unable to support such measures'. After this he attended all the meetings in silence.

Choiseul was busy. He overlooked nothing that might lessen the Dauphin's standing: and he attacked his children, those 'Dresden knick-knacks' who could never be ridiculed too much. Now it so happened that Louis XV asked Charles III of Spain to be the Comte d'Artois' godfather, and the Spanish king wanted Berry to be his proxy at the christening; Choiseul tried to dissuade him in favour of Orléans, with whom Choiseul was linked by a hidden web of understanding. To his great humiliation Charles sent a flat refusal. (For a Spanish Bourbon the natural position of an Orléans was between the Devil and the Antichrist.) Berry stood in for the King of Spain, and to this honour he owed that of writing his first official letter.

> Sir, Your Majesty was kind enough to send me a com- mission to stand proxy in Your Majesty's name at the baptism of my brother the Comte d'Artois, and I accepted it with the utmost gratification; having obtained permission from the

king, my lord and my grandfather, I have just executed it. And according to Your Majesty's wishes I have given him the name of Charles, which has been rendered illustrious by so many of our common ancestors and which is now receiving fresh glory in the person of Your Majesty. All that remains for me to do is to beg Your Majesty to believe in the warmth of my affection; it is a sentiment that I feel with the greatest force, and nothing could be more sincere than my wish to be wholly attached to Your Majesty throughout my life. I am, Sir, Your Majesty's loving brother and nephew,

LOUIS-AUGUSTE

Versailles, 19 October 1761.

Such was the beautifully written diplomatic epistle that Berry, aged seven, sent to his uncle Charles III; and such was the lesson that Choiseul received. It did not prevent the minister from working against the child, from trying to wipe him out, as it were; nor from beginning with his father.

The Dauphin was in no position to retaliate. Bourgogne's death had taken from him any desire for life. He shut himself up at home, writing to his many friends, giving up his afternoons to work and to the Dauphine, and his evenings to his mother. He scarcely hunted any more; still less did he go to the play. But he was often in Paris, and he walked about, alone, with no escort, in the Tuileries and the boulevards, anxious to know the state of mind and the views of the capital. There, at least, he was thoroughly popular and his face was well known.

There he kept watch on the current of public opinion, and he was shocked to see how the hatred for his father was mounting. People called out to him, 'Monseigneur, it's not your money we want, it's bread. We are very fond of you: get them to send away that whore who is ruling the country and bringing it down.' Then there were shouts of death against her. A placard was posted up on the Porte Saint-Denis in broad daylight, threatening the king and his family.

Bachaumont began his *Mémoires secrets* with a great eulogy of the 'Revolution' that was in progress, and Grimm praised 'that general weariness of Christianity ... that uneasiness which is exercising a hidden influence upon men's minds, urging them to attack religious and political abuses . . . and which foretells an imminent and inevitable revolution.' He added, 'It may be said that France is the centre of this revolution, which will at least have the advantage over its predecessors of being carried out without any bloodshed.'

They knew that since 1750 the greater part of the Académie Française had been won over to this Revolution, whose Trojan horse was the Encyclopedia, whose prophet was Voltaire and whose high priest was d'Alembert; they knew that Malesherbes, in charge of the censorship, among other things, was effectually protecting it, that Saint-Florentin, the minister of the royal household and a Freemason since 1733, was in favour of it, and that Choiseul, the all-powerful minister, was its patron. They reckoned that it would go as far as possible, that it would become the doctrine of the state, that it would change the customs of the nation and replace worn-out Christianity by wise and sound philosophy.

Opposed to them, in the years from 1762 to 1765, they had little more than a few scattered, powerless enemies – Fréron, Palissot, Le Prévôt d'Exmes and a few papers that not many people read. These sheets would soon have perished if the Dauphin had not given them the support of his protection. He subsidized *La Religion vengée*, a periodical brought out by Soret, a lawyer, and Father Hayer. He did his utmost to raise up other defenders of the traditional way of life; he kept the king's conscience and his remorse alive; he stirred up resistance in the higher clergy; and by his far-reaching correspondence he tried his best to awaken the zeal of the more pious bishops.

Above all he sought weapons for the future. When he was about thirty he realized how ignorant he was, and he set himself to read everything that might help him to build up a doctrine that he could oppose to that of the *philosophes*.

He read the Latin classics and the English writers, and he drew up accounts of what he read. He came to the conclusion that he and all he loved were fated to die and had no reality except in God. Like his father he had a deep awareness of death and he was

B

attracted to it. From this feeling he derived a basic faith as well as the foundation of his system.

'A monarch, the image of the Godhead upon earth,' he said, 'must take the Divinity as his model when he wields his power; the Divinity offers men the highest reward and the most dreadful punishments; the monarch, as unchangeable as the Divinity in the wonderful order that it has set up throughout the world, must submit to the laws, although he is their chief master.' The Christian monarch, the image and the message of God, reigned as such; but he must never be a tyrant. 'The monarchal state is ruled by a single man, but intermediary subordinate powers are necessary to it. The first and the most natural is that of the nobility, not to separate the prince's power from the people's but to be the link between the two. The power of the clergy is very right and proper; it sets limits to tyranny without physically resisting it. In a monarchy there is also need for a body that acts as a repository for the laws, the Parlement.'

Monarchy was hereditary, for that was the best way of handing it on, since it came from God, whereas all other systems rested upon human wisdom alone. (Is it not curious to recall that for similar reasons the democratic Athenians appointed their officials by drawing lots?)

The king was to maintain the intermediate bodies, but he was to keep them under his own authority. Without intermediate bodies there was despotism, which was horrible. 'When there is despotism, once the people rise they always take things as far as they can possibly go.' The only result was revolution. In a monarchy, on the other hand, the prince and the intermediate powers restrained the mob. 'Our history is therefore full of civil wars without revolution, whereas those of the despotic states are full of revolutions without civil war.' The prince must never forget that he had the supreme authority so that he might maintain order. 'No prince on earth exists except by means of his authority.'

He meant to take Saint Louis as his example for clemency and piety, and Montesquieu for love of the people. He asked the clergy to preach religion rather than 'the foolish notions of the day'. He reproved the *philosophe* priests, the worldly abbés and the bishops who haunted the court. Above all he censured the *philosophes* and their morality based upon self-interest.

> According to the principles of our new philosophers [he said] the throne no longer bears the divine stamp; they have made up their minds that it was the product of violence, and that what strength had the right to set up, strength has the right to bring down and destroy ... that the people can never entirely hand over authority but can only lend it; that they always have the right of giving it for a while and of taking it back according to their personal interest, the sole master ... But if this law of personal interest, that is to say of the whim of human passions, were to be generally adopted – adopted to such a degree that it caused God's law to be forgotten – then every notion of right and wrong, of virtue and vice, of moral good and evil, would be wiped out and annihilated in men's hearts, thrones would have no stability, subjects would become discontented and unruly, and masters would lose their benevolence and kindness. The nations would therefore be in a perpetual state either of rebellion or of oppression.

Behind these sometimes awkward formulas, what the Dauphin was looking for was a living force that could fight against the worldly philosophy of the time: against theoretical reasoning based upon physical sensation and looking solely towards self-interest, he wanted to erect a system made up less of ideas than of instincts. The need for the holy, the awareness and the love of spiritual dignity, family habits and family interests, the love of peace and the instinct of self-preservation – these were the motives upon which he counted, just as his ancestors had counted on them for the last eight hundred years.

What he had to do to start with was to bring up and form his children, the corner-stones of his work. As a beginning, the Dauphin had recourse to a solemn ceremony: he had Berry and Provence publicly christened – there had only been the private baptism at the time of their birth. Then, as everybody had to sign the parish registers, he pointed out the list of names to them, a list that ended with an artisan's son. 'As you see, my dears,' he said, 'on the plane of religion distinctions vanish. The only true superiority is that which is given by virtue. In men's eyes you will one day be greater than this child; but if he is morally better he will be greater than you in the eyes of God' (18 October 1761).

The Dauphin put religion and the practice of religious principles in the forefront of any education. It seemed to him that this discipline was equally necessary for all his children. Yet as they differed very much among themselves, each was to be given, apart from this basis, the kind of instruction suitable for his particular case. In 1761 and 1762 the courtiers noticed how sad and poorly Berry looked. His own disease and the after-effects of Bourgogne's illness explained it easily enough. Provence, on the other hand, who had only seen Bourgogne's death-bed from afar, still being among the women and under the rule of Mme de Marsan, displayed a lively, cheerful, wide-awake mind. Furthermore, he was an exceptionally pretty child. Artois was at this time no more than a noisy, undisciplined, jolly urchin of three.

La Vauguyon always attempted wit whenever he could, and he called the four brothers *le Fin*, *le Faible*, *le Faux* and *le Franc* – the subtle, acute Bourgogne, the weak Berry, the sly Provence and the open Artois. These names tell one more about the preceptor and his ideas than they do about his pupils: Bourgogne may have been intelligent, but his first quality was strength; and if Berry had been as weak as La Vauguyon said, he would never have withstood the long and harrowing trial of Bourgogne's death-bed. He did survive it; but he had contracted his brother's pulmonary disease, and he had to struggle with it all through his youthful years.

The Dauphin had so little notion of any intellectual weakness that he insisted upon a very elaborate education. Although Berry had more or less the same masters as Bourgogne, the atmosphere was quite different. The Dauphin had agreed that Bourgogne should be brought up on modern lines, with his work made easier by amusement and stimulation. He wanted Berry to learn with toil and effort; his labour was not to be spared, and the dryness of the subjects was not to be hidden from him. During

Bourgogne's education the pupil was the centre of everything and everybody: after a few months Provence was brought in to share Berry's lessons and the two were made to go along together, for there was little hope that Berry would live.

The work was carried on chiefly by correspondence: the masters sent the subjects for exercises or for work; one of the readers saw that they were carried out and then sent them off for correction. Twice a week, on Tuesdays and Saturdays, their preceptor took the children to see the Dauphine, and there their parents heard them their lessons and put them through a very searching kind of examination. The Dauphin had no hesitation about punishment, above all for Berry, with whom he was particularly strict. The Dauphin's special field was the teaching of languages: his wife supervised the teaching of religion and history.

The main teachers were M. Leblond, for mathematics; the Abbé Nollet, who was very well known for his experiments to do with electricity, for physics; M. Rousseau (subsequently called M. de Beauplan) for fencing; M. Laval, for dancing; M. Silvestre, for drawing; M. Gilbert, for writing; Victor Bourdon, to play the violin during the dancing lessons; and M. Buache, for geography.

For the teaching of religion, the Dauphin consulted Father Berthier, one of the most learned of the Jesuits, who had been his librarian until the banishment of the Society, and then he drew up several treatises upon morals and politics for Berry's use. As for history, Vauguyon invited Maître Moreau, a barrister, to write a whole series of surveys designed to make the young princes understand the formation of the empires and the present situation of the world. His pupils found this very long and exacting work unusually interesting. Buache spurred them on even more: he made use of blank maps that they had to fill in, and he went so far as to show them how to chart a given piece of ground. Berry took a liking to his work, and as he grew older so he became more and more diligent.

In that period of the applied arts, with its taste for mechanics and handicrafts, the Dauphin did not omit to give his sons some knowledge of this kind of work. Berry was put to carpentry, but he did not care for it at all. He was obliged to go on with it, ever, and they wanted to stop him doing metal-work, in which he delighted.

Lastly, La Vauguyon undertook the preparation of his pupils for the art of ruling as early as April 1763, and he had a series of talks with them – talks that had been carefully prepared between La Vauguyon and the Dauphin. Their object was to give Berry the necessary bases and the most useful knowledge for the exercise of the supreme power. Their accent and their orientation were religious. Above all, the Dauphin desired that his sons should never forget that they held their crown from God and that they should exercise their power only in the people's favour. Speaking to La Vauguyon in 1761 he said, 'Take my children into the peasants' cottages: let them see the poor man's bread with their own eyes and let them touch the straw of his bed with their own hands. I want them to learn to weep. A prince who has never shed a tear cannot be good.'

These were excellent intentions and aspirations worthy of all praise; but the Dauphin was mistaken in thinking that the Duc de La Vauguyon was well chosen for giving these young princes an exact notion of the people and the kind of life they led. He was scarcely less mistaken on the role of tears in character-formation, since they are a better weapon for hypocrisy than a wise discipline for an upright man. Yet it must be confessed that he knew the taste of his period, that he conformed to it and that he tried to make his children conform, wherever it did not offend against religion or morals.

Such was the basis of this education. Apart from a more deeply-felt religious zeal, it differed little from the education of other children of the time. Berry, Provence and Artois led the life of boys of their time and their generation, with more exercises in etiquette and public appearance, a stricter supervision, and a few additional pleasures, if pleasures they could be called.

Although they lived at the court, the princes of the blood saw nothing but its boring side and none of its delights: their parents did not allow them to go either to the balls or the plays. Their role was to take part in the wearisome routine of the daily receptions, in which the countless motley visitors treated them as curious animals, and to attend all the great ceremonies. To be sure the Dauphin did try his best to give them amusements suitable for their age: he had a little theatrical company of his own that acted sometimes at Trianon and sometimes in his quarters at Versailles; but the plays that were put on were moralizing proverbs, written for the children by Palissot, Sedaine or some other Christian author, and they were so dreary that they sickened Berry of the stage for the rest of his life.

Sometimes they went to Saint-Cyr, where the ladies gave parties or performances for them. On 22 April 1762 the Children of France watched *Esther*. But the three boys, put down in the midst of this gaggle of inquisitive and coquettish little girls, had no time for fun, so conscious were they of being stared at. Artois was the only one to enjoy himself heartily, and this he owed to the artless impertinence of youth and his precocious insolence. The three of them were only really happy when Papa-Roi persuaded the Dauphin to take them hunting: the fine clothes, the horses galloping through the undergrowth, the sound of the horns, and then the sudden, shadowy, magical passage of the quarry – all these things filled them with feverish excitement and gave them inexhaustible subjects for conversation.

From 1761 to 1765 the Dauphin never looked at his sons with anything but a sad and frowning face. He could never see them without being bitterly reminded of Bourgogne. With the queen it was even worse: she was a pious and extremely orderly woman, and children upset her.

Only one person seemed to understand their sad lot: this was the tomboy Madame Adélaïde, Berry's godmother; no doubt she was sorry not to be a man and no doubt she wanted to help her godson not to regret the fact that he was one. She took him home and said, 'Go on, my poor dear Berry, you are in your own place here: have fun, make a din, knock things over, break anything you want.' Upon this he burst out, for within him he still had that somewhat primitive, savage force that he must have inherited from his Saxon ancestors or from the good King Henri. He was the least tamed of the three, and he looked strangely out of place in the gorgeous surroundings of Versailles, among all the orders, the gold lace, the wigs, the bowing and scraping. The flattery, the double-dealing and the empty formality that his brothers took in their stride vexed his spirit, and sometimes he could not hide his anger, which suddenly broke forth.

One day without thinking he used the expression *il pleuva*, an incorrect way of saying 'it rained'. His brother of Provence, the good pupil of the family, gave a start and cried, 'What a barbarism! Really, brother, that is not right at all: a prince ought to know his own tongue.' All this was in the loud voice that children use, and La Vauguyon could not have been far away, for he told the story afterwards. Berry instantly replied, 'And as for you, brother, you ought to hold yours.'

At about this same time, in the winter of 1763, the Duc de Chartres, the Duc d'Orléans' son, a young man of sixteen, one of the best looking and best dressed at Versailles, came to see his cousins and to make his court; but at the same time he could not refrain from lecturing them. Artois listened open-mouthed, and Provence with his little smile: but Berry cut in. 'Monsieur le Duc de Chartres,' said he, 'you treat me in a very offhand fashion: you always call me Monsieur. Should you not say Monseigneur?' Chartres was utterly nonplussed, but Provence quickly intervened, 'No, brother: it would be better for him to say Cousin.'

The tale was handed about until it reached the newspapers, and of course it aroused the comments of those who were trying to make out the nature and character of the young princes. Everyone agreed in admiring Provence. But it was acknowledged that Berry could be charming when he chose. In December 1763 David Hume came to Paris and had himself presented at the French court. Now he was one of the Dauphin's favourite British authors, particularly because of his *History of England* and the way he did the Stuarts justice. So when Hume was brought to the reception of the princes of the blood and introduced to the Duc de Berry, the boy stopped immediately in front of him and told him he had a great many friends and admirers in France, adding that he himself was of the number because of the pleasure he had taken in the reading of several passages in his work. Hume was charmed; he bowed, and he was getting ready to make a polite

reply when the Comte de Provence, aged eight, spoke up and said
that for his part he looked forward to taking a deep interest
in Hume's splendid history. All these well-spoken compliments
delighted the historian; and when he came to Artois, who was
then four, the child in his turn began a compliment of the same
make, but he bogged down in the middle with a charming little
grimace – he had not been able to remember all the phrases. Hume
recognized in all this a particular attention on the part of the
Dauphin, and he was much touched.

This was how the three brothers' life went along, in a pleasant
companionship with the spur of emulation; it was a life that their
parents' isolation assured of an affectionate sobriety, and one in
which there was a continual contrast because of the presence of
M. de La Vauguyon.

Yet one fine day the Dauphin wanted to be informed about the
results of this education. He summoned one of his own friends,
Father de Neuville, a former Jesuit. He begged him to watch the
children closely and to question them while they were playing.
The priest found that Berry had less liveliness of mind and less
physical beauty than his brother princes, but he added, 'As for
soundness of judgment and the qualities of his heart, he promises
to be in no way inferior to them.' This delighted the Dauphin,
who cried, 'Your opinion of my eldest boy pleases me more than
I can say. I had always thought that in him I could detect one of
those natural, unaffected minds which at the time show only a faint
promise of what they will one day give in profusion; but I was
afraid that my heart might mislead me about the child.'

He also wrote to his intimate friend M. de Nicolay, the Bishop
of Verdun,

> My children are my solace; their manners are good and they
> learn all their lessons. Berry is making great advances in
> Latin and astonishing progress in history; he retains it by
> facts and dates, the right method for him, and he has a
> wonderful memory. Provence's is even better, for it comes
> more easily to him; and to put it briefly, you would never
> believe the number of Latin words he has crammed into his
> head. All I hope is that enough will stay there to be useful

one day, and that not all will be lost before the end of their education (end 1762).

This long period of distress for the Dauphin came to a sudden end: the death of La Pompadour (15 April 1764), delighted him all the more as for some months Louis XV came closer to his children, showing more feeling for religion and closing the Parc-aux-Cerfs.[1] Even the philosophic tide seemed to be receding. In 1764 Palissot brought out his *Dunciade*, a successful comedy in which he made game of the *philosophes*. A few months later he produced *Tom Jones*, a translation and adaptation of Fielding's novel: the mediocrity of his play and the intrigues of the *philosophes* caused it to be a failure on the opening night.

When they heard this the princes of the blood, wounded but not disheartened, bestirred themselves; they did it so heartily that all their officers and all their friends took tickets for the second performance, and so did their friends' friends. The theatre was full and the play appeared to be a success. This was the young princes' first triumph over public opinion. The hand-written and printed news-sheets did not fail to talk about it; and in this triumph the Dauphin could see a success for the education he had provided for them.

So during those two years 1764 and 1765 he was seen to be more cheerful than he had been since 1747: the thinness that had alarmed his whole family had given way to the glow of health and a fresh plumpness. He turned once more to an active life. In the summer of 1765 he had the longed-for occasion of being with the army again. The king had summoned several regiments to the neighbourhood of Compiègne so that he could see them go through their evolutions: it was called a pleasure-camp. The Dauphin took it in hand. He was in the saddle at dawn, and he went out to meet the regiments, taking them to their cantonments, settling them in and talking with their officers and men. When his own regiment, the Royal Dauphin, arrived he put on their uniform and went on wearing it throughout the manœuvres. He always commanded it at drill. He was the most zealous of all the colonels, the most

[1] A notorious establishment, little removed from a private brothel.

conversant with the movements and the nearest to the private soldiers. Sometimes he would take supper under canvas with the other officers. He by no means avoided contact with the visitors, and he was not at all displeased with them for not recognizing him.

In a few weeks he thus made himself a reputation throughout the army. No one had ever seen a prince, a Dauphin, fraternizing so with the men and behaving with such open simplicity with the officers; from his earliest days he had reserved these qualities for his intimate friends – now they suddenly became apparent, and they made him into the most popular leader in the kingdom.

Fate was kind enough to prove this to him. One day when Louis XV was to review the whole gathering the Dauphin had gone to the camp at dawn. His children, who did not want to miss such a splendid sight, set off early in an open carriage that drove across the front of the assembled Royal Dauphin. When they saw their father and his regiment they stood up in the carriage and began to skip up and down for joy. The Dauphin cantered over to them and picked them up one by one to kiss them. Then he rode back to the ranks. The soldiers and the officers cheered, shouting, 'Long live our good Dauphin! How he loves his children!' The French army too had a tender heart. The king appeared a little later and heard of the incident; he felt that strange, deep pleasure that he experienced at each of his son's successes, all the more so since he would not allow himself to make them easy for him.

This was an important success. A crown prince who knew his army and who could count upon it was a personality whom Europe respected and French public opinion admired. The Dauphin might have rejoiced in having scored a point against Choiseul. He did not have the time. One day, when he was going to see the abbey of Royal-Lieu, he was caught in the rain; he came back with a heavy cold; by the evening he had a high temperature and he began to cough. This fresh assault broke him. He was seized with a galloping consumption. By dint of looking after himself and taking medicine he managed to hide the ominous state of his health from his father.

The time for going back to Versailles had come: he followed

the court. He had barely reached Versailles before the most threatening symptoms made themselves apparent: the fever rose and he had a coughing or rather a strong vomiting of blood. The physicians could not be unaware that the patient was doomed. Horace Walpole saw him at this time and said that he looked like a ghost. For his own part, the Dauphin was no longer deeply concerned with anything but his own death. But others were still living, and he had no desire whatever to be a hindrance to them, particularly the king, whom he had never crossed in his whole life. The king made his task easier: he kept up his custom of never showing the deep affection that he really felt for the Dauphin, and of accepting all his sacrifices.

On the grounds that a change of air would do him good, the Dauphin insisted that the court should move to Fontainebleau, as it did every autumn. Now the château of Fontainebleau was very beautiful, but it had neither been repaired nor put in order since the time of the Valois. It was impossible to protect oneself against the cold and the dampness. After a short spell of apparent improvement, the Dauphin relapsed and had to take to his bed: he never left it again. The Dauphine stayed at his side from seven in the morning until late at night; Madame Adélaïde helped her, and between them they kept up an atmosphere of life in the over-heated room. When they were too worn out, they would go on to the landing and cry. He remained quite calm. He had always been interested in the face of death, and its approach did not frighten him. It was making an entity of him: it seemed that thanks to death he had found himself at last. The tide of anxious care and affection that flowed towards him from the whole country touched his heart, but it did not deceive him: he said, with a laugh, 'Six months ago a good many people loathed me; I had not deserved that any more than I do the love they show me now.'

He carried on with his usual life as he lay there in bed, and he went on giving his children their Latin lessons. The only difference was that he brought more firmness and zeal to his task. It was Berry who suffered from this: when his grandfather wanted to take him to the Saint Hubert meet on 2 November 1765, the finest and the most ceremonious hunt of the whole year, the Dauphin replied that it could not be, for Berry had just forgotten one of his lessons. It was in vain that the king insisted, saying, 'When you punish your children it is I who feel the most pain,' and it was in vain that Adélaïde, the queen and the Dauphine pleaded for him: the Dauphin would not give way.

And the dying man was stricter about the Latin than he had ever been before. It was a distraction for him, and it was the one hold on life that he still had: his children were aware of this, and they too took a kind of strange delight in it. Berry plucked up his courage and said to his father, 'The time that goes by the fastest is the time we spend at lessons.' The Dauphin was unable to withhold his affection; he called him close, kissed him, and said, 'Oh, my boy, what pleasure you give me! Since you find that lesson-time goes by quickly, it proves that you work hard.'

When they were in the room he let his mind drift. They alone were able to catch some echoes of his conversation with death. 'Look, children,' he said, showing them his emaciated arms, 'you see what being a great prince amounts to. God alone is immortal, and those who are called the masters of the world are subject to disease and death, like everybody else.' Berry was never to forget this.

The courtiers did their utmost not to think about it. The entertainments arranged by the Duc de Richelieu, the First Gentleman of the Bedchamber on duty that autumn, filled the palace with noise and uproar, until one day Louis XV burst out and stopped it all.

Then the court, Fontainebleau, the whole of France and Christian Europe seemed to be turned towards that room in which the Dauphin lay upon his death-bed. During this period the clergy caused prayers to be said in all the churches throughout France, above all in Sainte-Geneviève, which was always full, day and night. Prayers were organized in the army, too: the Royal Dauphin decided to fast for its prince-colonel. Messages came in from Italy and Spain. The only one who did not pray for his life was the Dauphin himself. His religious director required him to do so as a duty. But he refused the king's physician.

Yet he was surprised when his physician in ordinary, M. de La Breuille, warned him that he had not much longer to live. He sent for his confessor, therefore, the Abbé Collet, and told him once more that he did not long either for life or for the throne. On 13 November 1765, at eleven in the morning, before the whole royal family, the great men of the kingdom, the foreign ambassadors and his servants, Louis, Dauphin of France, received the viaticum and the extreme unction. The Duc d'Orléans and the Prince de Condé held the communion-cloth. The king, who until then had succeeded in not shedding a tear, fell on his knees at the door, covered his face, and wept. The long ceremony passed off with all its sublime magnificence, and the Dauphin never faltered: the old Cardinal de La Roche-Aymon, officiating as Grand Almoner of France, forgot one of the anointments; the Dauphin told him of it.

He had at last found that happiness towards which he had been feeling his way for so long. The queen was radiant with joy: she cried, 'How happy he is! He is dying like a saint. But how we are to be pitied!' When the priests had left and the room was empty, the king came to the dying man and took his hand. Seeing his look, the Dauphin said, 'Your pain is the only thing that hurts me at this moment. I have always been useless to you, and I am leaving you burdened with my children.'

Then he turned to his last duties: he made his will and he destroyed a great many of his papers; those he kept he sent to the Bishop of Verdun, Nicolay, so that he might one day hand them on to Berry, his eldest son. He had meant to have Berry brought to his bedside, together with his two brothers; but he no longer felt that he had the strength to withstand such a scene, nor the right to inflict it upon them. So he called for La Vauguyon. 'Monsieur de La Vauguyon,' he began, 'I charge you to tell my children that I wish them all kinds of happiness and blessings . . .' Then he had to stop. He begged the confessor to go on for him. 'Monseigneur le Dauphin,' said the priest, 'urges his children to fear God above all, and to love religion . . . to have the deepest respect for the king and the most entire submission, and all their lives to give Madame la Dauphine the obedience and trust that they owe to so honourable a mother.' Then he saw the Comte de Muy, his most faithful friend, and begged him as a last kindness to preserve himself for his sons – 'But above all do not ever let their youth put a distance between you.' His feelings overcame him.

The end was approaching. On the seventeenth and eighteenth of December he weakened: the prayers for the dying were read for him. Then, as he was officially on his death-bed his wife and his nearest relations were kept away, according to the rule in the House of France: a man must die alone, face to face with God.

At last after twenty hours he died, without any convulsions, praying to God for the kingdom. This was Friday, 20 December: it was six o'clock in the morning.

Chapter IV

The school of death

FOR A LONG WHILE THE DAUPHINE WAITED IN THE KING'S room, together with the queen and Madame Adélaïde. Then she went to bed.

Early in the morning her first chaplain, the Cardinal de Luynes, came to her and said, 'Madame, let us give thanks to the Lord, for we have another saint in heaven to honour . . .' She could not bear any more, and she fainted away.

The king too had kept up hope. He had even made a vow to God for his son's recovery. La Vauguyon came to his room with the Duc de Berry. According to the custom, when they were brought in there was the announcement, 'Monseigneur le Dauphin.' Louis XV rose: he kissed his grandson affectionately, and in a choked voice he said, 'Poor France! A king aged fifty-five, and a Dauphin of eleven!' Several times he repeated 'Poor France!'

Then he led Berry to his mother's rooms. Here again there was the announcement, 'His Majesty the King and Monseigneur le Dauphin.' The child threw himself into his mother's arms, and at last the two of them let themselves go in those violent tears that tire the weeper as much as they calm him. Louis XV gazed at them with the deepest melancholy. At last he told the Dauphine that he would look after her like a father and that he would give the direction of her children's education into her hands, since that was the natural order of things and since he had promised it to the Dauphin on his death-bed. He also gave her precedence over all others – a rare honour. Then he wrote to his grandson the Infante of Parma: 'This date will tell you the extremity of my grief clearly enough. Forgive me if I do not speak of it any further.' And no longer able to bear the court, he left for Versailles with the Dauphine, and from there he went to Choisy so as not to be obliged to endure the compliments of the first of January, nor all the cheerful ceremonies of the end and the beginning of the year.

The Dauphin was buried magnificently in Sens cathedral, according to his wish; solemn speeches praised him, and his disconsolate widow devoted herself to his memory.

Berry merely suffered. Ever since he had caught pulmonary tuberculosis in Bourgogne's room the greater part of his physical strength had been given up to struggling for his life: he was a tall, gaunt boy with a sickly look, and he did not give the impression that he could ever reach maturity. Provence's handsome appearance and Artois' ebullient charm made a strange contrast with Berry's weariness. The courtiers were convinced that he would never reign, and they were less inclined to conceal their views from him since his mother was of the same opinion. So he found himself deserted. His inner life was all the richer for it, but it was a life that belonged to him alone; his father had never known how to win his confidence, nor his mother, nor his preceptor. He did feel closer to his grandfather, however, for they both loved hunting and the open air.

But there was a wall that separated them – the king's haunting grief for his son. Louis XV wrote to Ferdinand of Parma, 'You have formed a true opinion of my sorrow; I distract myself as much as I can, having no other course; but I cannot get used to having no son any more. And what a difference there is for me when they call my grandson, above all when I see him make his entrance!'

His remorse for never having shown his affection to his son and for never having given the Dauphin's talents the opportunity to develop made him kinder to his daughter-in-law. He had summoned her sister Christine of Saxony, the Abbess of Remiremont, to her side, and he did his best to help the queen, Adélaïde and the Dauphine's ladies in waiting, who were trying to give her back a taste for life. Xavier of Saxony, the one she called 'the brother *par excellence*', also had this very much at heart. As early as the end of 1765 he wrote to her:

Madame, my very dear sister, I shall not attempt to describe the state into which the terrible news that we have just received has thrown me. Am I to add my pain to the sorrow that is overpowering you? ... You know that despair and dejection are contrary to the submission and trust we owe to God. You must take care of yourself for the king, for your children, and for a very unhappy brother who thinks only of you and who looks forward to everything that is pleasant in life from your friendship. In the name of these beings who are so dear gather all your strength, call a noble fortitude to your aid, and do not let sorrow make you forget the good that you can still do, nor the duties that you have yet to fulfil. My dear sister, you must seize upon these all-important first moments; make the most of the king's kindness and of the affection he shows you. The ministers see the king's feelings for you and they will not make any attempt at limiting their effects if they do not believe you to be their enemy. The king's sorrow and the tenderness of his heart are indeed providing you with the most favourable moment. Make the best of it to establish yourself on the footing that you would like to live for the time to come. I am sure that you will succeed, so long as those who now have the king's confidence do not suppose that they have a vital interest in working against you. In order to do away with this supposition, my dear sister will be able to forget the past and even if necessary to put it right; she will know how to make sacrifices for the sake of dear and sacred interests. Your future situation, the maintenance of your prestige and your influence in affairs, your peace of mind, your happiness and the happiness of those you love will all depend upon this beginning.

The appeal did not fall upon deaf ears. She did her best to play the most important part she could at court, combining craft and prudence.

This was seen in the question of Berry's marriage. The king was haunted by the thought that he no longer had a son: Choiseul took advantage of this fact to suggest that he should set up his grandson in a separate establishment earlier than usual. He showed him the advantage that would arise from supporting the French monarchy, at a moment when France had been brought low by the Seven Years' War and was in a disturbed and anxious state, with the strength of the Austrian empire – the advantages of marrying Berry to an archduchess. Louis XV allowed himself to be persuaded. On 24 May 1766 Prince Stahremberg, the Austrian ambassador in Paris, wrote to Maria-Theresa: 'Your Sacred Majesty may from now on look upon the marriage between the Dauphin and the Archduchess Marie-Antoinette as fixed and settled.' The king himself had told him so. He added, 'I owe this success, which I had very much at heart, chiefly to the good offices of M. de Choiseul.' Choiseul's plan thwarted the views of the party whose chief was henceforward the Dauphine, which was working to bring about the Franco-Saxon marriages. This was the great idea of Xavier of Saxony and his factotum, the Comte de Martanges. Madame Adélaïde supported them with all her might. It was a question of marrying Berry, if he lived, or preferably Provence, to Amélie, Xavier of Saxony's daughter, and Madame Adélaïde to the Elector of Saxony. The Dauphine, an able tactician, did not attempt to oppose Choiseul directly. But he had been imprudent enough to suggest that Marie-Antoinette should come to France at once, and the Dauphine made the most of it.

On the day Louis XV told her of his decision to marry Berry to one of the archduchesses, giving as his reason the necessity for 'making sure of the Viennese government's good will', she acquiesced, but added, 'I should have thought that the best way of making sure of the good will of the court of Vienna was to keep it in alternate hope and fear. Once the archduchess is at Versailles the Viennese court would certainly never be afraid that there could be such an affront as to send her back, and the

Austrians would therefore be far more difficult about the returns of kindness the king might require.' This thought pleased the king, who considered it both subtle and intelligent. Marie-Antoinette stayed in Vienna and the Austrian marriage remained in suspense.

This triumph was little known at court, but it was accompanied by a degree of favour for the Dauphine that was obvious to one and all: the king asked her to do the honours at Compiègne during the summer. In spite of her fatigue and the bitter memories that the place continually brought back to her, she succeeded in facing up to her task and in taking the unquestioned lead. She did not neglect her children either, for she was determined to carry on with everything that she and the Dauphin had formerly done together. She took his place in teaching them Latin; she studied Italian with Berry and history with all of them; and she went on with their scripture lessons. In order not to make any mistakes, she went over the lessons with the Abbé Collet before she gave them, and she based herself upon the advice her husband had left in a manuscript entitled *Papers for the instruction of my son Berry*. But she was found to be stricter than the Dauphin had been, particularly in the matter of reading, where she let nothing escape her. She read all the books her sons were to read: she read them first and she would allow nothing with the slightest trace of the *philosophes'* doctrine. She spoke to her children about the Dauphin every day; and she relied much upon the advice of Father Berthier.

All this left Artois unmoved, for he was entirely absorbed in himself and his own fun; Provence took it with that subtle, fleeting spirit that he had always possessed and that allowed him to bow without in fact submitting. Besides, she spoilt him, having transferred her affectionate preference for Bourgogne to Provence. Berry bore the whole burden of his suffering, and he would have found it heavy indeed if his grandfather had not had the excellent idea of letting him start riding that summer. He derived a curious pleasure from it, and the healthy tiredness gave him the strength to withstand all the rest. For it was an exercise that had the delightful advantage of solitude.

As soon as he was back at court there was the harness of etiquette waiting for him, the burden of unhappiness and the oppression of La Vauguyon's perpetual supervision. So it was also noticed that the Dauphin's liking for the applied arts had much increased. They allowed him to vanish into the forest of Compiègne, which he was mapping, or to disappear into his attic at Versailles, where he had set up his workshop.

Working with his hands was the only way he could reach what he lacked most in this court – relaxation and self-communion. While he was working at his locks and hinges nobody came to worry him. He was safe from La Vauguyon's pomposity, Provence's spying and the impertinence of servants. When he came down again from his attic he was calmer and stronger. His mother seemed to understand this and she took to teasing him kindly, calling him 'her little Vulcan' and drawing closer to him.

The end of 1766, which brought his first communion and his confirmation (the day before and the day after Christmas), gave them the opportunity for knowing one another better and for pooling that basis of love which made up the child's essential being and which had also been his mother's nature when she was young, in the days when she was called Pépa. In her youth she had been all ardent enthusiasm. Her husband's character and her life at court had turned her into a virtuous but hard woman, who required from others what she insisted upon from herself, that is to say, too much. Now, at the end of this month of December in 1766, Fate gave it to her: what she had never yet found in anyone at Versailles she found in her own son.

Berry was upright and humble before God, but he was capable of deep spiritual impulses. What remained mere words and gestures with others became real with him. In a world of dealers in false coin he alone offered the true gold. His mother discovered it at this time; and the ever-watchful courtiers saw the discovery reflected in her, a mysterious joy that she could not hide. But it was already very late. Life was allowing them only a little time. It thrust upon him all the onerous duties that were part of a Dauphin's existence: on 1 February 1767 he was installed as a knight of the Order of the Holy Ghost in the midst of a vast crowd, all curious to see the new prince, to know what he looked like and how he behaved. It was seen with alarm that he was thin, pale and awkward, and that he was so short-sighted that he seemed to be groping his way; at the same time enough was learnt about his natural goodness, the kindness of his heart and the quality of his mind for people to be afraid that presently they would have to mourn for another prince who could never be replaced.

Death seemed to be striking at the royal family everywhere at once. In February 1766 Stanislas Leczinski died in a ridiculous and pitiful fashion, from the burns caused by his dressing-gown catching fire. Now, at the beginning of 1767, both the queen and the Dauphine seemed doomed: the queen was overwhelmed by her son's death, in spite of all the care that Louis XV took to visit her more often, and she was sinking into a decline which no physician could heal. The Dauphine continued to lose weight and to cough and spit blood.

The king consulted Tronchin, but the great physician was unable to provide him with the hope that he did not feel himself (January 1767). Yet he did assert that in her case it was not the lungs that were affected. These ambiguous words caused a great deal of speculation at Versailles, where a great many people, including the Dauphine herself, began to wonder whether, behind all these deaths and all these illnesses, there might not be poison at work. La Vauguyon spread the rumour. According to him all this was Choiseul's doing. The wretch had never ceased criticizing the Dauphin and thwarting him; now he was persecuting him by means of his remaining family. The preceptor of the princes of the blood considered the chief minister capable of suppressing all who stood in his way. Moreover, Choiseul's intention was perfectly obvious: he wanted to rule himself under a child-king whose wife was to be an Austrian devoted to his cause. The Dauphine was so ready to believe this that she had her kitchen watched and she wrote a detailed will in which she reminded Berry that he was never in any circumstances to employ Choiseul as a minister. And now, at the beginning of 1767, the court was filled with the smell of death, with whisperings and denunciations.

Tronchin came back in January; he found nothing particular to worry about with the Dauphine, and it was hoped that she would live. Yet the French physicians, headed by Sénac, insisted that her lungs were affected and that her death was not far off. This battle between the doctors took up all the court's attention and distracted it from its anxiety, for the human mind has a need to busy itself about events that it cannot comprehend. The days of this harsh winter, full of mist and extreme cold, came one after another, bringing sometimes an improvement and a little pale joy, and sometimes a relapse. At last, faced with the incessant coughing of blood, Tronchin had to warn the Dauphine that she was weakening. He advised her to see her confessor; and the priest told her she was going to die.

For a few moments she rebelled against her fate: it was not that she clung to life any longer now, but she was naturally a fighter and it seemed to her that by going she was giving way to her husband's enemies, delivering up her children to Choiseul and their future to people who hated them. She could not submit to the thought that her disappearance would mean the definitive end of all the Dauphin had wanted and planned, and of all that he had been. Her only resource against all these misfortunes was her passionate soul. But this resource was her triumph.

On 4 March 1767, surrounded by a great crowd whose gravity contained as much alarm as it did sorrow, Mme la Dauphine received the last sacraments at the hands of her confessor, the Abbé Collet, in the presence of the king, her sons and all the princes of the blood. Berry stood first, behind Louis XV. He was following his mother's journey towards death step by step. But then for some days she seemed a little better. On 13 March she got up to eat her dinner, and she had a good appetite for it. At about four o'clock the king came to see her and they talked together. Suddenly he saw her face change. He hurried from the room and warned the servants that the Dauphine was dying. A few hours later, without having been able to speak again, she expired.

Chapter V

A lonely child

SO SHE DIED, AT THE AGE OF THIRTY-FOUR: MARIE-JOSÈPHE of Saxony, Dauphine of France, who would have held the fate of the kingdom in her hands if she had lived, for she was the shrewdest and most spirited woman in the court, the one who had best managed to comply with the king's whims without losing his esteem, and who had made him respect her without giving him offence.

Berry, distressed and unhealthy, was overwhelmed by a sea of troubles: in April Madame Louise had a serious attack of measles and Madame Victoire a terrible diarrhoea; all through the year Marie Leczinska grew weaker, and it was thought that she would die at the beginning of December, though on this occasion she recovered. On 3 September there was the service for the Dauphine at Notre-Dame, where Berry had to do the honours, together with Mesdames Adélaïde, Victoire and Sophie, and his brothers, surrounded by an immense, oppressive pomp. In the same month the court went into mourning for the Princess of Savoy. And the whole of 1768 was also marked with deaths. The Prince de Lamballe, the Duc de Penthièvre's son, died in May; and the

queen, who had received the viaticum in March 1768, died on
24 June of the same year. The king had never ceased to love the
queen, although he put many others before her, and he gave her a
magnificent funeral on 17 August at Saint-Denis, followed by a
solemn service at Notre-Dame on 6 September. Berry, as Dauphin
of France, presided over the ceremony, with Mesdames de France.
'It was a terrible day for them' wrote Louis XV (who did not go)
in a letter to the Infante of Parma.

It was indeed a 'terrible day' for this fourteen-year-old boy, sick,
weary and often shivering with fever, who in these great ceremonies had to bear the whole weight of the family mourning and
the boredom of the royal splendour; others could find distraction
in watching the display, but his weak sight, which closed him in
upon himself, turned each of these services into a dialogue with
death and with the dead. The king took care not to attend them;
he was protected by etiquette. And although he did feel a great
deal of sorrow he was good at evading it, and at deadening it,
when he could not forget it. He did nothing at that time to help
Berry. Far from it: his acts much increased Berry's pain and his
loneliness.

The Dauphine had bequeathed her finest ring to her son; she
had begged the Bishop of Verdun, Nicolay, to take the casket containing her papers, those that her husband had left her and which
she called her treasure, and to give them to her son later. When
Nicolay came the Comte de Saint-Florentin had already seized
everything in the name of the king, who kept it. He even had the
Dauphine's property sold. In these matters the king was hard: the
year before he had caused the Château de Commercy to be
demolished and its furniture to be sold at auction – it had been
left to the queen by her father, Stanislas. Louis XV had the right
to do so, since as head of the family and as king he could dispose
of anyone's possessions; and his uneasiness of mind before God
and men filled him with an insatiable urge to read his relations'
papers.

When Berry was present, the king could not overcome his grief
for the loss of his son. Although he saw the boy often, and although he took him to the sittings of the Parlement, the military

reviews and all the official receptions, it was all merely symbolic: there was no intimacy whatever between the two of them. There was even less now than there had been before, when Louis XV used to take a pleasure in playing with his grandchildren. His real affection remained a tormenting, hidden anxiety.

He was also haunted by other and more urgent anxieties with which Berry was well acquainted, for his father had told him of them long ago. Louis XV could see public opinion drifting away from him; the religious party and the great body of good people for whom France was still the realm of the Most Christian King disapproved of the banishment of the Jesuits, the 'good fathers', and the closing or the handing over of their schools to other and ill-prepared priests, so that the young generation ran the risk of being engulfed by the errors of the time; they resented the way the king allowed Choiseul to encourage the *philosophes*, and they resented his allowing the decline of moral standards in the court and the city by giving an example of shamelessness and adultery; for their part the *philosophes* despised the king and allowed him only one single merit – that of having delivered himself up to a right-thinking minister. Choiseul took little pains to hide the fact that he felt far superior to his sovereign, whose want of vigour, whose listlessness and dull mind were but a poor match for the outstanding qualities of a minister who was civil enough to accept office under him. Nor did he conceal his pleasure in wielding power and his intention of holding on to it by all possible means. His brilliant imagination, his perpetual ebullient activity and his cleverness had allowed him to stand out in the first place as the only man who could win the Seven Years' War for France by means of the multiple alliances; then, when that was hopelessly lost, as the only diplomat who could wind it up at the lowest possible cost; and lastly, when this disagreeable operation was over, as the only minister who was capable of re-establishing the nation's strength and restoring its prestige, at the same time maintaining the necessary stability and providing the king with the security that he longed for.

In 1767–1768 M. de Choiseul was omnipotent, and with ten years of supreme power behind him he felt that he was safe from

surprises: he knew Louis XV so well that he could play on him as
a skilful fiddler plays on a violin. He had looked for a mistress for
the king to amuse him; the king had taken another who was not
of Choiseul's choosing; but at least the minister had had the double
satisfaction of seeing the king grow so infatuated that he could
not do without her and of being able to reveal to His Majesty
the fact that the girl was a worthless drab. This had gratified his
feeling of contempt; and his prudence had thought it was pur-
suing his own interests in doing so, since this prevented a fresh
marriage between the king and an archduchess – a marriage which
was desired by the Church, the nation and the Austrians, but
which might have entailed changes among the king's servants.

So, as it often happened, M. de Choiseul was pleased with himself, and he went on governing according to his usual maxims: he
took a pleasure in disorder and contradiction, for he looked upon
it as the atmosphere in which a man with a brilliant mind like his
could show to his best advantage; the bitter struggle that the
Jansenist Parlement continued to wage with the clergy over the
billets de confession,[1] the open emnity between the Parlement of
Brittany and the governor, even the shouts of the poor and the
threatening placards that the people of the capital stuck up on
every corner to protest against the rise in the price of bread – all
these could not but raise Choiseul higher still. He had never given
finer suppers; he had never been so witty. But the king was still
uneasy, and the Dauphin felt fury rising within him.

But what could he do? The man his father had chosen, the man
approved of by his grandfather – his preceptor, in short, filled him
with utter disgust, even at this very time when he claimed to be
waging a holy war against the scoundrel Choiseul. No doubt La
Vauguyon would not have been an evil man if he had remained a
colonel in some distant garrison; but court life, which arouses
every unclean desire, the Dauphin's and the king's favour, which
had shown him his talent for flattery, and lastly the discovery of
his skill in assuming a Christian joviality – all the things that in

[1] It was forbidden to take holy communion without a *billet de confession*
signed by a non-Jansenist priest.

courtiers are called double-dealing, had turned him into a sanctimonious plotter.

In conjunction with Madame Adélaïde and Prince Xavier of Saxony he was carrying on an underhand war against the Austrian marriage: he was in favour of the other arrangement, the marriage of Adélaïde with the Elector of Saxony and of the Dauphin's children with the Saxon princesses, so as to counterbalance Austria's preponderance and Prussia's ambitions in Germany. Yet he was less preoccupied with this plan than he was with the return of the Jesuits, and above all how he could bring them back by gaining an ascendancy over the king.

Madame Adélaïde was deeply concerned with the eternal welfare of her father, whom she knew to be incapable of doing without a female companion, and she hoped that he would remarry; she would have agreed to an Austrian princess or any other bride, but she wanted to hear nothing more of any mistresses, for she very rightly thought that the time had come for Louis XV to settle down. M. de La Vauguyon was ready to be even more submissive to Providence, if it decided that Louis XV should take another mistress.

As soon as the king's choice had fallen on the Du Barry, La Vauguyon intrigued to get into her good graces; before this he had made an unsuccessful attempt at doing the same thing with the Pompadour, but the Du Barry was a good-natured creature and she still had certain religious inclinations. She came to an understanding with La Vauguyon all the more readily since the king had not concealed Choiseul's manœuvre from her. La Vauguyon was enchanted: he already saw himself in command. He attended upon the Dauphin more zealously than ever, never leaving him for a moment and doing all that he could to draw him into his scheme, although at the same time he harangued him upon morals, religious conduct and the struggle against the *philosophes*. Another boy might have lost his faith under this kind of treatment. Louis-Auguste was wise enough to do nothing but take a lesson in the nature of disgust.

The most disagreeable thing was that he had no ally at all. Madame Adélaïde, his godmother, had such spirit and such courage that she seemed a strong woman – one might almost have said a dashing fellow; but she lacked singleness of mind; she lost heart, and she gave up all idea of playing a political role. The sadness of the frequent bereavements and the court's immorality caused her to enter into an exclusive friendship with the Comtesse de Narbonne-Lara, her mistress of the wardrobe, and she devoted the greater part of her time to her. Berry could no longer look to her for support or advice.

Even less could he look towards his brothers. He was very fond of Provence and Artois, but he could not rely upon them. Provence was too subtle by far, and he had already learnt the lesson of court life; he was given to intrigue; he thought it enough to please the king, who thought him adorable in his robes of the Order of the Holy Ghost, and to get along with La Vauguyon, whose hopes he encouraged; and he cared precious little about his elder brother, whom he despised as a blockhead. As for Artois, he was a charming talkative boastful child, who said 'I shall be the king' to everyone, and whose charm had made him king already. Berry was alone.

One day he told them so straight out. It was a day when M. de La Vauguyon wanted to give his pupils a handsome treat: in agreement with Mme de Marsan he took them to her pleasant house at Andrézy, near Versailles, where they were often invited in the summer. It was a delightful afternoon, and the open air, the freedom, and the affection between the charming Mme de Marsan and the three boys added to it. 'Maman Marsan' was an excellent hostess. The climax of the party was a lottery: La Vauguyon had invited some court nobles and he had invented rules, not without a certain piquancy, that catered to the 'flow of heart' so fashionable at the time – whoever won had to make a present of his prize to the person in the company he loved best.

It was a very lively game, and in front of Artois and Provence the prizes piled up, given by the lords, who were well practised in flattery. Then it happened that Berry won. He put his prize in his pocket. This was noticed. The Duc de La Vauguyon, half in fun and half scolding, called upon him to obey the rules and give his prize to the person he loved best. 'Well, Monsieur,' answered

Berry, pointing to the emptiness in front of him, 'whom do you expect me to love most here, where I see that no one loves me?' A little shiver ran through the courtiers, and there was a marked drop in the temperature. Mme de Marsan did her best to smooth over the incident with kindnesses.

The court did not fail to talk about it. The members of the royal household discussed it among themselves. What would he be like, this ill-loved but apparently courageous child, if he were to become king? Another remark of his was repeated. A little before this several courtiers were talking about the characters of the kings his predecessors and the appellations they had been given or they had taken. One was polite enough, or curious enough, to ask the Dauphin what he would like to have added to his name. Without hesitation he replied, 'Louis the Strict'. People began to see that although he was not good at the polite small-talk Provence and Artois managed so well, he was better than his brothers at finding straightforward words that drove his point home directly.

From the way he spoke it became clear that he had judged both others and himself: when anyone asked him a question to do with books, paintings or any other artistic subject he would reply quite simply, 'You must ask my brother Provence: he is the clever one.' Furthermore, the three brothers got along very well, each having his own particular sphere – charm belonged to Artois, subtle intelligence to Provence, and strength of character to Berry. One day in 1767 they were arguing about how they would punish Marmontel who, in his *Bélisaire*, delighted in telling kings how to behave. Artois said, 'If it depended on me, I should have him whipped through the streets of Paris.' 'And I should have him hanged,' said Berry. He had thoroughly grasped that it was force alone that could solve certain problems. When it so happened that Provence indulged in intolerable foolery, Berry beat him. And this preserved a healthy intimacy between them. He also beat them when they played unkind jokes or practised little cruelties upon their servants or their companions – and Artois and Provence were somewhat inclined to do so.

He behaved in the same way when some great person's insolence became intolerable. Mesdames de France and he particularly wished to have Mme Thierry appointed First Woman of the Bed-chamber to the Dauphine (whose household had been kept together, being meant for Marie-Antoinette), for she had nursed the queen devotedly during her illness. The Noailles brought forward another candidate and intrigued cunningly in her favour. Berry sent for Ménars, the head clerk of the household, and said to him, 'If M. le Duc de La Vrillière causes the king to appoint anyone but Mme Thierry I promise to dismiss her as soon as I am married.' After this Mme Thierry was given the post. This strength, this directness of character, and the fact that he was not known to have any vicious tendency or perverse habits alarmed the court. What sort of hold did he offer, if any? No one knew. Meanwhile they spoke ill of him and they said that he was a fool.

'If it is possible to judge by appearances,' wrote the Austrian ambassador to the prime minister in 1769, 'Nature seems to have refused all her gifts to M. le Dauphin. The prince's face and what he says bear witness to but a limited amount of sense, to a plentiful lack of charm, and to no sensitivity at all.' And the conclusion of Carraccioli, the Neapolitan ambassador, was, 'He seems to have been brought up in a wood.'

Nothing could have been less true. There were few men at the court of Versailles as well educated as Berry. At fourteen he had a good knowledge of Latin, he could read Italian and translate English, and he was acquainted with German. Thanks to the Abbé Nollet's lessons he knew something of physics. As for mathematics he had asked to be taught more, and he did not want to stop at being able to solve an algebraic equation with two unknowns. He was not considered a born mathematician, as Bourgogne had been, but he had a good understanding of bases of the exact sciences and he had made himself familiar with their basic proofs. Unlike Provence, he had no claim to wit or taste, yet he wrote a correct, firm, varied French in an elegant and decided hand. But his chief excellence was in history, where his tutor had been Jacob-Nicolas Moreau.

As early as February 1764 La Vauguyon, on the Dauphin's orders, had invited this barrister – a well-known champion of Catholicism – to write *Leçons de morale, de politique et de droit public puisées dans l'histoire de notre monarchie* for the princes of the blood. The Dauphin's idea had been to impress their duties upon the minds of the young princes by means of examples drawn from the acts of their most famous ancestors. Moreau completed this work by a series of essays dwelling upon various aspects of the royal vocation: the *Traité de la justice*, the *Traité de la fermeté* and the *Institutions politiques et morales*. It was a matter of instructing Berry in all his rights and all his duties. In compliance with eighteenth-century taste these works were drawn up in the form of question and answer, so as to make it easier to absorb them.

The Abbé Nollet also wrote a treatise upon *Les Devoirs des princes*; and at Vauguyon's request, in June 1766, Father Berthier produced an essay that he entitled *Directions pour la conscience d'un roi*. It was very simply written, and it taught the art of examining one's heart, of loving work, and of learning how to reason logically. The aim of this teaching was essentially moral; and although it did appeal to the intelligence it did so only in order to reach the highest and most difficult part of the being.

It therefore had far more influence upon Berry than upon his brothers: Artois was bored and Provence, whose free-ranging mind set a great distance between words and actions, principles and practice, derived only theoretical lessons of wisdom from it. For Berry alone it was a direct message from his father and a concrete reality. As his mind was less well stored with words than his brothers', those that he did possess had more vitality, and they were more intimately connected with his life.

He liked doing the things he could do well; and he liked being true to himself. He drew his own maps, under the direction of Buache; and he was one of that geographer's best pupils. His first map, which shows the neighbourhood of Versailles, dates from 1769–1770. Indeed, as early as 1766 he had brought out two little works, the first a *Guide de la forêt de Compiègne* (he was too much attached to this forest not to do something for it), and the second *Maximes morales et politiques tirées de Télémaque sur la science des rois et le bonheur des peuples*. It was a pretty little book, meticulously printed and bound in twenty-five copies to be given to members of his family. Papa-Roi was the first to be served. He read the

book; he recognized certain extracts from Fénelon, certain remarks of the late Dauphin and some of that youthful severity
which had so irked him. He read it again, and then said to Berry,
'Monsieur le Dauphin, your book is finished: break up the type.'
That is why there is no copy to be found either in the Bibliothèque
Nationale or in the library at Versailles; and that is why the
Dauphin found it so difficult to resume the dialogue with his
grandfather during those years from 1766 to 1768. The teaching
that they had wanted him to absorb seemed to have turned
against Louis XV.

Yet the Dauphine had taught him too zealously for him to forget. 'My son, Heaven is preparing the finest crown in the world
for you', she had warned him. 'Providence has caused you to be
born so that one day you shall rule a nation that is as sure of the
true principles as it is attached to its masters. What a dazzling
future! But what duties it entails! And what great knowledge it
calls for!' Her chief aim was to 'settle his way of thinking'; she
required him to think first and always as a Christian, for what
mattered was not brilliant and superficial ideas but 'the proper
exercising of the qualities of your soul, and the directing of the
qualities of your heart towards what is right'.

She begged him never to forget that he belonged 'to the most
illustrious family on earth' and she urged him to follow the
examples of the thirty-one kings of his line, particularly that of
Louis XIV, the true founder of modern monarchy. She desired
him to reflect upon the great king's writings, so that their message
should sink deep into his mind. 'Respect yourself and you will be
respected.' 'Nothing is so dangerous as weakness.' 'When you
have made a mistake, put it right as soon as you can.' 'Love each
one of your plans . . . do not prefer those that you find most
gratifying.' 'Treat your servants well, but do not permit them to
become too familiar.' 'Do not allow yourself to be ruled.' She
advised him to follow all these maxims, without ever forgetting
his father, who 'combined all the qualities that are the mark of a
great man'. 'On his death-bed he left you the rule of your life: fear
the Lord, love religion, know the limits of your authority exactly,
and, in the period before you reign, display an entire submission

C

to the king. Meanwhile, do not forget that the anxious nation is already turning its eyes towards you. What transports of joy for this beloved people, when it is learnt that you are tirelessly learning how to rule well when the time comes!'

Following his mother's advice, Berry drew up a kind of political catechism for his own use, basing it upon La Vauguyon's conversations and upon all the essays and reports that had been written for him. He entitled it *Réflexions sur les entretiens avec M. de La Vauguyon*, and he began it with an examination of the duties of a king – piety towards God; benevolence towards men; humanity in government and even in war, which was to be avoided if possible, and in all events to be cut short; unceasing care for the people's happiness ('A good king ... must have no other aim than that of making his people happy'); and lastly the strict exercise of justice, not directly but through judges, for 'it is not right that kings should condemn alone ... the throne is too far from the people of low condition and too closely beset by the nobles.' The Parlements, which did not possess the slightest sovereignity of their own and which only represented the king, were nevertheless useful.

With regard to his people, the king must never forget his subjects' natural rights, which were 'there before the existence of any political or common law – the right to life, to honour, to freedom and the ownership of property ... The prince must therefore reduce taxes as much as he can: he needs wise counsellors, and he will attend carefully to what they say, though he will not rely upon them alone. The king must be firm and never descend into weakness. He must also know men, so that he may not be deceived.'

At this point Louis-Auguste summed up for his own use what was known of the characteristics of various nations. 'The Italians are crafty, vindictive, cunning and jealous; the Germans steady, full of endurance, and rude; the Spaniards proud, slow, bold in resolution, noble and free; the Swiss are faithful; the English vain, jealous and overweening; generous towards their friends, but stubborn enemies. Lastly the French are naturally flighty and fickle. They have a passion for new things; for them everything is a matter of fashion, and they follow the fashion blindly, even in the most serious and essential matters, just as they do in the slightest and least important.' The prince must take care of this. The French were also given to cavilling, and they were extremely touchy upon points of etiquette; they were mockers and scandal-mongers. The king should never give them an opening.

He should also pay great attention to the temper of his present age, in which there was a predominant sense of irreligion and independence, sloth and indifference to the public good. He must not escape from it, however, but live in his time in order to do good; and he must not allow himself to be hoodwinked. One of the greatest dangers of the time was women and the shameful influence they had upon the government of the country. 'It is a misfortune, but it cannot be prevented. Their reasoning is short-sighted, superficial.' Yet they were to be humoured, and it was worth listening to intelligent, keen-witted women; but they were all to be looked upon with caution.

In order to preserve himself from these dangers the king was to read Suetonius, Tacitus, Cardinal de Retz ('a most chaotic and dangerous mind, but an exalted one'), La Bruyère's *Caractères*, Richelieu's *Testament*, Clarendon and others; and this would help him to understand mankind. He was to beware of literary men 'whose endeavour is merely to entertain people'; he was on the contrary to look for good generals and to pick them with care, not letting himself be deceived either by flattery or affected zeal, nor yet by obliging civility. He was to listen attentively to words, to watch faces, and above all to take account of actions. A king's first duty among men was clearsightedness.

These pages show a young man with a direct, strong Christian faith devoid of illusions or bigotry, and with a spontaneous love for the French people: in this essay he speaks severely of the courtiers and he devotes little space to the nobles; he blames the clergy who misuse the wealth of the Church and he criticizes the pluralist abbés and the non-resident bishops; yet there is nothing but friendship for the people. 'Everything a father owes his children, everything that is due from a brother to a brother and from a friend to a friend, a prince owes to his subjects; and every action of the crown must be of benefit to humanity.' 'Doing good is the soundest way of keeping affection.' Rulers had to be benevolent; the French insisted upon that in their kings. 'What is only benevolence in private individuals is justice in kings; they are answerable for all the injustices that they have been unable to prevent. The king holds the sovereign authority from God, to whom alone he is responsible; but if he enslaves his people he is guilty in God's eyes,' and if 'through his fault, the nation under his rule is not as happy as it might be, then he is guilty.' And Berry ended with the words, 'All my plans must be directed by the feeling of tender affection for my people.' This sprang entirely from his own heart.

Even when he was still very much of a child he was following a hunt when the horns blew the mort, and he had to hurry if he wanted to be in at the death of the stag; but he stopped the coach-man taking a short cut across a sown field. Provence and Artois were thinking of nothing but their own pleasure, but Berry gave the order and the coach turned back. Thus when he was no more than twelve he showed his respect for the property of others and his concern for the humble. Later, when he managed to get away from La Vauguyon's supervision, he liked to walk through the fields and talk to the men working there. Once he even took a plough and turned a furrow that met with the approval of the peasant. He found it easier to talk to working-men than he did to courtiers. And then he loved the open air, movement and direct contact with men, creatures and things.

It was this that saved his life and brought him closer to Louis XV once more. Between 1766 and 1770 he was often ill, with the two chief crises occuring in August 1767 and during the autumn of 1768. The king was very much afraid indeed, thinking that Berry had the same disease as his father, his mother and his brother; Louis XV was probably right, and the courtiers gave Berry up for lost. Yet he recovered, and he began to grow and increase in strength, so that presently he became the most robust of the three brothers. As soon as he could ride he took to hunting with an energy and a zeal that surprised everyone. His *menins*[1] and his gentlemen in waiting – Bourbon-Busset, Montmorency, d'Angivilliers – were delighted, and they began to grow fond of him.

He first hunted on horseback in August 1769. His grandfather was enchanted with his dash and his courage. They began talking in an easy familiar way, and the king was astonished at finding so much warmth and deep affection in Berry. 'As for me, I could not live without air,' he wrote to Ferdinand of Parma, 'and I believe the lack of it had a great deal to do with the death of my son. Fate has given me another who seems likely to make me happy for the rest of my days, and I love him with all my heart, for he returns my love . . .' (16 June 1770). 'I am very pleased with my grandson because of the friendship he shows me, both inwardly and out-wardly; and it is the second that gives me the greater pleasure, for I was quite certain of the first . . .' (25 June 1770). When one remembers Louis XV's intense and somewhat remorseful attach-ment to his son's memory it will be seen how far Berry had travelled in three years. Through his own honesty he had at last come by a friend – the king.

It was a late encounter. Louis-Auguste was just about to come of age. And the king was growing old; when he passed the Gardes-Françaises and the Swiss guards in review in April 1769 the crowd was much struck by how he had changed and by how bent he was as he sat there on his horse. To tell the truth, he had had a bad fall hunting on 4 April; and apart from that he was feeling weariness gain upon him. That was why he hastened Berry's wedding.

Since the summer of 1768 work had been going on at Versailles to build a setting in which this marriage could be celebrated worthily. And Louis XV often gazed at the portrait of this little archduchess. She was called Marie-Antoinette: the picture was charming. But who could tell? Berry was well aware that the wife they were giving him was to be a fresh ordeal for him, for Choiseul had chosen her and he meant to make use of her to prolong his rule and to spy upon the court. La Vauguyon often told Berry

[1] Boys of noble family chosen as companions.

this, and Madame Adélaïde did not conceal it from him, either. Yet he made up his mind to obey his grandfather, for the king's new-sprung affection made him hope that he would not be abandoned nor flung into pointless adventures. The worst was by no means certain.

He asked the advice of his other friend, the only man apart from the king whom he could call by this name – the Abbé Soldini, once his father's confessor. In this essentially religious consultation, the Abbé reminded him that 'his first earthly duty was to obey and serve the king'. Then the Abbé traced out the path that he was to follow: he was 'to understand his religion; to struggle against the writings of the *philosophes*, without sparing their authors; and to protect the Church, without being over-gentle to bad priests or greedy abbés.' 'Avoid favourites', he said, 'keep close to the people; eschew empty show, wasteful spending and pleasures – it is known that you do not care much for them, anyway. You love work, but you must learn how to rest; you are frugal, and you must not allow yourself to be seduced. Be kind to one and all, but remember that you are the crown prince. And may you reign as late as possible!'

This was his old friend's last wish in 1770. Berry trembled at the prospect of the kingly duties the Abbé pointed out, and at the dangers that the sovereign power entailed. With all his heart he echoed the Abbé Soldini's wish, and meanwhile he hunted with all his might.

Chapter VI

The triumph of the Duc de Choiseul

AT THE AGE OF FIFTEEN LOUIS-AUGUSTE DE BOURBON, Duc de Berry and Dauphin of France, was a loose-limbed, clear-eyed youth with a high forehead; his slim body and strong limbs gave promise of more vigour than endurance; and his abrupt gestures, his swaying walk, his air of seeing nothing and of scarcely hearing the noise around him, made strangers think him aloof and remote; but those who were acquainted with him knew that he was full of integrity and affection.

Berry, standing in the highest place in France after the king, was the only man at court who did not belong to a party; he was the only man who possessed no party and who did not concern himself with any. At a time when all men were doing everything possible to appear to be what they were not and to make themselves what they were not, he alone did not even trouble to show himself as he really was; and his sole care – a care that he never abandoned – appeared to be to do everything necessary to be wholly what he was and what it was right that he should be. He needed all of himself, all the faculties he possessed; for the task awaiting him seemed enormous, and he was sick, hated, and alone.

There was still a total vacuum all round him. His grandfather was always busy and therefore neglected him; besides, the king's affection was too anxious and too closely associated with sorrow for him to show it much.

Berry's aunts always welcomed him kindly, but they loved gambling, which bored him, and gossip, which he found very tiresome, and intrigue, which he forbade himself. They loved him dearly, just as one loves a part of one's own being. But apart from that, all Adélaïde's power of affection was turned towards God in heaven and towards Mme de Narbonne on earth: her sisters' remained fixed upon the Lord and upon sweetmeats.

The Duc de La Vauguyon was supposed to act as his father, his friend, his guide and in general as his guardian angel; in fact his preceptor allowed him little peace and took his place for all acts in which authority or prestige were concerned. But the brother La Vauguyon had chosen as his friend was not Berry at all but Provence, whose subtle mind, prettiness and somewhat feminine wiles had seduced the fat and foolish duke. That was enough to set Berry and Provence in opposition to one another, without actually separating them: they liked one another without the slightest mutual trust. Artois seemed too self-centred for anything to be expected from him other than the pleasure of loving him and making him happy. Berry remained as friendless in his family as he did at court, where his bluntness, his want of health and the likely expectation of his death kept the courtiers from him, for they were careful not to waste time paying court to a prince incapable of granting favours. No one was interested in Berry.

Only M. de Choiseul was passionately concerned with him, for Choiseul hated Berry. The duke had never forgiven the Dauphin for believing in God more than in him and for not having entrusted him with the bringing up of his children, whom he, and he alone, could have turned into fine free-thinking minds. He was therefore preparing to take his revenge upon both the dead and the living Dauphins, by forcing Louis-Auguste to take a wife of his own choosing, so young and inexperienced that he would be able to mould and dominate her, thus managing the young household through the bride, just as he saw fit. So at this time, the beginning of May 1770, Berry was waiting with a heavy heart for the young woman his grandfather, M. de Choiseul and Fate were giving him as his life's companion.

Knowing nothing of the young man whose companion she was to be, and knowing nothing of life itself either, Antoinette of Hapsburg-Lorraine, Archduchess of Austria, was making her way towards her fiancé by short stages through the showers and the squalls of this rainy springtime, and through the sudden changes in her mood. To begin with she had thought it a fine thing to become the most powerful queen in Europe, to outdo all her sisters, and to be almost equal of her big brother Joseph. Then, overwhelmed by a tide of despair the day before her departure, she had thought that nothing could be worse than leaving her beloved, cheerful Vienna, leaving Schönbrunn, where every corner was familiar, leaving the court that she knew so well and over which her mother ruled quite as much as a matron as a queen, and leaving all her young friends in that heavy, sentimental, easy-going Teutonic world she had scarcely had time to enjoy, since she was so young – leaving all this to go and live in a distant country, so hard and proud. Maria-Theresa had to lecture her severely. She was packed into her coach after an immense party she had enjoyed so much that it had driven grief out of her head.

Now she was on the road for France. There was no wavering, for she was accompanied by the strong-minded princes Stahremberg and Schaffgotsch, and she knew that if her mother were told of any hesitation on her part she would receive a most unholy scolding. She resigned herself to the inevitable. She behaved charmingly at Strasburg, where she was given a charming welcome and where the Comtesse de Noailles came to receive her in the name of the King of France. She went on being charming all along the road, where the towns and the villages did their utmost to celebrate her passage. At fifteen she was already a woman, and she knew all about the resources of feminine power. She had a somewhat skinny look, and the delicate oval of her face possessed more charm than a real beauty; but when she stood up her elegant figure gave her a remarkable dignity, and the proud movements of her neck made her seem truly regal. Her spirit was royal, too. She came imbued with the grandeur of the Hapsburgs, determined to have that grandeur respected and to insist upon it even in France. The Abbé de Vermond, the reader Choiseul had sent to teach her French and to prepare her for the role she had to play, spoke to her of her future husband as a dull-witted fellow whom she would have to lead and dominate.

Her mother, who had her suspicions, thought it proper to read her a long lesson advising prudence, caution and deference towards the king, and friendship and good relations with the reigning minister, the architect of the Franco-Austrian alliance and of this marriage: everyone told her that it would set an everlasting seal upon the understanding between the two great empires and thus ensure the predominance of the Hapsburgs in Europe, if only she, Antoinette, were clever, prudent, well-behaved and biddable with their great friend M. le Duc de Choiseul.

M. le Duc de Choiseul had indeed no call for anything but rejoicing: this was the most splendid marriage of the century, and for him it was his apotheosis. It may be added that he did not make a conspicuous use of it, for he was a man of taste.

Everything was in the most delicate, the most noble taste. The eighteenth century and perhaps French civilization reached its highest point on this 14 May 1770, when, at the edge of the forest of Compiègne, with its great trees still fresh and green with the spring, in the presence of companies of the body-guard, light horse, musketeers and life-guards, and the whole court, Marie-Antoinette of Austria was handed over to King Louis XV amidst the sound of oboes, drums and cavalry trumpets, and when she met her fiancé the Dauphin. Smiling behind her there was M. de Choiseul, for the king had allowed him to be the first to see the archduchess, and he had gone out to welcome her five or six miles beyond the meeting-place. The look that revealed Marie-Antoinnette to Louis-Auguste de Bourbon also showed him Choiseul at her side.

After this Marie-Antoinette and Louis-Auguste were no more than docile supernumeraries in a magnificent and exhausting spectacle. In a few moments they were separated: the king took Marie-Antoinette to stay the night at the Château de Compiègne, while the fiancé, according to the established protocol, slept under another roof, the guest of the Comte de Saint-Florentin. On Tuesday the fifteenth he went back for the night to Versailles, where everyone was hurrying about to complete the vast preparations. Everywhere there were gardeners carrying flowers, pyrotechnicians putting splendid fireworks into place, tailors hurrying to deliver the blazing gold-laced, embroidered clothes that were the nobles' pride (how many gentlemen ruined themselves during those days!), and musicians rehearsing in every corner.

On the sixteenth, at ten in the morning, the archduchess went to Versailles for her robing and her marriage. All the Parisian ladies had deserted the town and now they were filling the stands and the seats that had been set out all along the suite of rooms. The weather was beautifully clear and mild. How far was Louis-Auguste aware of all this? There was the golden haze that danced in front of his eyes; there was the effort to carry out his duty to everyone, particularly to this young stranger, his wife; he stiffened his body to withstand the long weary hours, and he withdrew into his mind so as to offer a submissive heart to the fate that God had ordained for him.

He wore the heavy, beautiful gold-laced robes of the Order of the Holy Ghost. In the chapel he knelt at Marie-Antoinette's side. Motionless, neither awkward nor constrained, held up as it were by their robes and enveloped in a kind of glory by all the eyes that were fixed upon them, the Dauphin and the daughter of the Hapsburgs received the nuptial blessing from the Archbishop of Rheims. The most thoughtful of the spectators saw the fate of Europe conjoined in their persons; and the wisest said their prayers. At two o'clock everyone went away, to meet again in the gallery adorned with chandeliers and gilded busts.

Louis XV and the youthful pair made their appearance for the *jeu du roi*, at the king's card-table. At nightfall everything was lit up; diamonds blazed out everywhere, and everywhere gold, silver and precious stones shone with a brilliance made still more effulgent by the darkness of the night, a blackness that was thickened by the pouring rain. Then came supper in the new ball-room, freshly gilded and lit by thousands of candles. The royal table shone like a cluster of stars. The band of the Gardes-Françaises, dressed as Turks and making as much din as possible, reminded everybody that here below everything, even the most splendid feast, was but a masquerade.

At midnight, physically exhausted and with flayed nerves, Marie-Antoinette and Louis-Auguste were led to their marriage-chamber: the Dauphine's undressing was carried out in public, up to the point when the Duchess de Chartres passed her her nightgown; it was the same for the Dauphin, to whom the king handed his, whispering some words of advice: the young prince made no reply. When both ceremonies were over, all the courtiers walked into the bedroom of the Dauphine, who was thought very pretty in her night-time déshabillé.

She looked defiant and proud, rather than embarrassed; for she was never at a loss when it was a question of playing a part. The Dauphin seemed weary and bored. Once they were in bed the curtains were drawn back and everyone looked at them: the well-bred people present were exceedingly embarrassed; the others were delighted; and the king was pleased.

The France of former days was very fond of this sort of homely licence – a coarseness which had set the late Dauphin's teeth on edge because he was so much in love with his wife, and which now revolted his son Louis-Auguste because it made it harder for him to love this foreign woman who was henceforward his wife.

He was joined to her by a sacrament and he was separated from her by everything else – tastes, education, pleasures; and she did not like him. Yet he was drawn to her, for she seemed to him a child whose fragility, rashness and even mistakes had to be pro-tected so that she might live and thrive. He was the first Bourbon for many generations to wish to serve and to win love, rather than to assert himself by force. Louis XV too had just the same protective feeling when he was faced with Marie-Antoinette. He was charmed with her looks, but he did not think of her as a woman and she did not arouse any of the desires that he was only too apt to feel in women's presence: the more he thought of her the more he considered her as an adolescent, an expert charmer and a strong-willed girl, but devoid of balance and maturity – too delightful a creature not to be loved, too incomplete to satisfy a man, and too frail not to be in continual need of protection. And indeed he had to begin by breaking a lance for her.

In a somewhat rash and hasty manner the imperial ambassador, the Comte de Mercy-Argentau, had tried to make the most of this opportunity to emphasize the superiority of the family of Lorraine over the rest of the French nobility. He so managed things that at a ball given for Marie-Antoinette, Mlle de Lorraine, the daughter of the Comtesse de Brionne, was to dance a minuet immediately after the princes of the blood. As soon as this was known at court there was a general outcry, and it grew into a rebellion. Louis XV was told: he entered into negotiations, displayed a great deal of tact, caused the heads of the families and Aranda to intervene, and granted compensations all round.

In the end the ball took place in great splendour. Mlle de Lorraine danced her minuet, but Artois danced the next with the Marquise de Duras. Then came the dance called *la Mariée* with Lambesc and Mme de Duras, a quadrille with the Dauphin and various people of quality, and two other quadrilles; but as these dances were unknown to the Dauphine the ball finished with an allemande which she danced with the Duc de Chartres. It was noticed that she danced well, that the Comte de Provence had made progress, but that the Dauphin needed practice and that he danced badly.

Everyone was pleased: that is to say, everyone was rather dissatisfied. The French nobility had made the Dauphine understand that one needed tact and delicacy to be accepted. Louis XV, like a true King of France, tried to wipe the whole thing out by a dazzling display: at ten o'clock the ball came to an end and the fireworks began. The air was filled with blazing streams, cutting across one another in every direction and making an appalling din; fiery serpents rose up in battle, looking like satanic flowers, with a basso continuo of cannon, and an accompaniment of firebursts that shed a blinding light. The climax was the biggest, most beautiful fountain of golden fire mingled with dazzling explosions that had ever been seen. Of course, it seemed too short, like every one of life's pleasures.

Now came the illuminations, which made all the gardens and the park glow fiery red. Many-coloured Chinese lanterns filled the lower flower-garden; pyramids of lights blazed on the lawns; and on either side of the canal great triangular frames held still more lanterns whose light turned the water into a bronze sheet of looking-glass. A huge concourse of people filled the walks and crowded into the theatres that had been set up for them among the greenery. The heat and the light that rose from it all reached as far as the gallery, and it attracted the Dauphine. She made as if to slip away, but she was not quick enough. The king held her back. For all this was not so much pleasure as the exercise of the royal calling.

The King of France owed it to the queen-empress and he owed it to himself to make it clear that the union of the two greatest families in the world was a radiantly happy event; he owed it to his court and his people to associate them closely with it, giving them all the opportunity of seeing the Dauphine and of celebrating her arrival; and lastly he owed it to all the artists and craftsmen of France to give them the the chance of shining, so that Europe might be reminded once more that it was only in France that people could dress, adorn themselves, buy jewels, precious stones and diamonds, learn to dance, grow acquainted with the very best food and see the most magnificent spectacles. The fêtes went on and on, an endless flow; and every single one of them was splendid.

The Dauphin was virtually the only person to be bored: all this turmoil, all these monotonous, meaningless phrases sent him to sleep. Luck did give him a few good days of hunting towards the end of May and the beginning of June: on the sixth he killed two stags at La Croix-de-Perray, and on the sixteenth another at l'Etang de la Tour.

All these hollow words and lying compliments made a painful impression upon him, and this was rendered all the more unpleasant by the shocking loss of life at the entertainment the city of Paris gave in his honour.

Bad organization, the provost's stupidity, and a mob of people treading one another down in the middle of the night among the cuttings of the rue Royale (not then finished) caused a hundred and thirty-six deaths and spread the most dismal feeling throughout the town. Many people would have thought it proper to stop the wedding celebrations at once. But during the last ten years the king had seen a great deal of mourning; and since he wanted neither his young couple nor public opinion to be left with the taste of this disaster he particularly desired that the rejoicings should go on. Louis-Auguste had to endure them all, and he was obliged to wait with what patience he could summon until the end of the month before he could write this letter to M. de Sartine:

'I have learnt of the misfortune that has happened because of me, and I am very deeply moved by it. The sum the king sends me every month for my private amusements has just been brought; it is the only money I have at my disposition, and I send it to you so that you may do something to help those who are most gravely affected.'

The page who brought the letter to Sartine also handed over six thousand livres.[1]

But this was not the end of the misfortunes: on 5 June a gust of wind threw down the erection that had been set up for a firework display to be called the Temple of Hymen. As it happened no one was killed by the fall; but for a long while the memory of these dismal celebrations haunted the Dauphin's mind.

A few aged courtiers attached to the royal family had watched him closely throughout all these ceremonies; they had watched both Louis-Auguste and his young bride. It was impossible not to feel drawn towards them: they were so young – she had such charm and he held himself so straight. But on consideration the old courtiers, like the Duc de Croy, said, 'They are all married too young!'

Once a man is married he has to live with his wife: it is a duty,

[1] The livre was a little less than a shilling.

and a very delightful one when the pair are in love. Now Louis-Auguste was very fond of his wife. But since his mother's death he had lived alone: he knew all about solitude, all about the telling of secrets and the abuse of confidence. How could he be ignorant of the fact that his wife told the Abbé de Vermond about every one of their conversations – the abbé being the reader chosen for her by Loménie de Brienne, Archbishop of Toulouse, so that his friend M. de Choiseul should have all the satisfaction and all the information he might require? Nor was he unaware that M. de Mercy was also consulted and informed, so that he could, as was but natural, send an account to his queen and empress, and also – which was somewhat less natural – to his friend M. de Choiseul. Every word the Dauphin uttered to Marie-Antoinette was a dispatch for all the chanceries in Europe.

The Abbé de Vermond had many faults: he was a not very pious priest; he was an encyclopedist[1] and not very well-read at that; and he was a not particularly delicate courtier. He would have been nobody if he had not flattered Loménie de Brienne and if he had not been singularly attached to Marie-Antoinette. He suited Choiseul so well that at the beginning there had been a move to make him the Dauphine's confessor; but the Archbishop of Paris, who believed in God and who liked his priests to do the same, was against it. Choiseul was always well-bred and he yielded the point: the heart of the matter was that Marie-Antoinette should have a confidential friend beside her, a friend in holy orders who could hear and say anything. Indeed, perhaps it was better that he should not be her confessor ... it might give him a greater freedom with regard to his patrons. So the Abbé de Vermond was satisfied with his title of reader; but thanks to the favour of the Empress Maria-Theresa and of M. de Choiseul he could command his mistress' confidential trust and he enjoyed an intimate daily contact with her.

La Vauguyon, who was no well-wisher either to Choiseul or to the Austrian alliance, had succeeded in preventing Vermond from becoming the Dauphine's confessor. He now thrust on; he tried to have Vermond dismissed and a confessor of his own choice

[1] Diderot's great *Encyclopédie* was of course the organ of the *philosophes*.

provided for the young princess – a confessor who believed in God, a man of good character and one who did not associate with *philosophes*. It appeared to be a good moment for La Vauguyon's attempt. Vermond had come back from Vienna with the title of reader, and it seemed quite evident that the Dauphine did not read at all: she prattled charmingly; she danced quite well, though not in time; she played the harp with the best of intentions, and she sang, though not quite so well; but she never read. So it would be easy to take away her reader and it would cause her no distress.

Marie-Antoinette was not slow in scenting the danger. She at once warned Mercy, and Mercy told her how to arrange things so that Mme de Noailles should speak to the king. The king, naturally enough, decided in favour of his daughter-in-law. She kept Vermond; she could see Mercy at any hour of the day; and she was given the king's confessor, an exceedingly discreet ecclesiastic. Choiseul believed the game was won. Marie-Antoinette felt that she was in a strong position and that she was strongly supported; she therefore set about her husband, following the advice she had been given. She found him very frank. He told her that he knew all about marriage, that he wanted her to be his wife and to belong to him entirely, and that that was how things should be – furthermore he meant to prove it to her as early as their stay at Compiègne.

She thanked him and then went on, 'Since we are to live together in the closest friendship, we must talk quite openly about everything.' This seemed fair enough, and far from unskilful in so young a girl. The Dauphin retorted that he knew more than people imagined, but he had never discussed matters with anyone. She tried to start him talking about the du Barry; she was sorry for the scandal caused by the king and she regretted all the schemes which that vile woman set on foot to overthrow Choiseul, whom all right-thinking people must necessarily support. The Dauphin cut her short. 'You do not know all that Choiseul did to reach his present post, nor how he plotted with the Pompadour, nor how he worked to increase her influence. No: a right-thinking man would have to be very thoroughly deceived to defend Choiseul against the du Barry.' The Dauphine felt that she had been clumsy. She broke off the conversation and hurried away to consult Vermond about her difficult husband.

The crisis came in the days immediately after this. Whether it was all these ceremonies and the dust raised that stimulated his disease, or whether its development had taken a new line, Berry's illness broke out afresh. On Monday, 16 July, he was seized with a violent fever, a cough that nothing could allay, and a great spitting of blood. The rumour spread through Paris within a few hours; the physicians gathered round his bed hastily sent for the king, who was at Bellevue. After many learned observations they asked Louis XV's permission to bleed his grandson. The permission was granted and the king left again, full of care, for Bellevue, where Mme du Barry was waiting for him. As he travelled he could not help thinking of the brief life of his son, Berry's father. Had he married Berry only to urge him towards his tomb?

For two days the Dauphin's life seemed to be in danger, but after the blood-letting he took a turn for the better. On Friday, 20 July, Louis XV went to Compiègne, where the young couple joined him on Monday, the thirtieth. As early as the thirty-first Louis-Auguste was on horseback. Throughout the whole of August he gave himself up entirely to hunting, following the hounds until he was exhausted. He seemed to be driven on by an overpowering instinct – it was as though his life depended on it. The king, who was of the same opinion, and whose happiest hours were spent in the forest, encouraged him. Indeed, he sometimes kept him to dine at the place where he was to join the du Barry. On those days the Dauphine was abandoned to herself and her advisers.

She did not waste her time. These lonely periods were filled with talks with Vermond, interviews with Mercy in Mme de Noaille's room, or consultations with the Duc de Choiseul, either in the forest or in her own apartments if the Dauphin were hunting far away. Thanks to their good advice and to the counsel that was lavished upon her by Mesdames de France and Mme de Narbonne, she scarcely ever saw the king without asking him for something.

He agreed cheerfully, for giving was a pleasure to him. She induced him to let her have Mme Thierry as one of her first women of the bedchamber, both on her aunts' recommendation and because she had a child – Marie-Antoinette liked playing with little boys. She asked that the names La Vauguyon had struck from the list of those who had free access to the Dauphin should be put back. The king complied, but not without giving La Vauguyon the pleasure of making the announcement to those people concerned, which vexed the Dauphine. She begged the king to let Mercy have the same access to her as the 'family ambassadors' (from Spain and Naples), and he acquiesced. She wanted to ride: the king sent her a drove of well-trained asses, upon which she galloped about, accompanied by her ladies in waiting and her brothers-in-law.

So everything ran smoothly: she felt at her ease and she began to assert herself. She smote her enemies – that is to say Choiseul's enemies, beginning with La Vauguyon, whom one day she caught listening at her door: she did not deny herself the pleasure of calling him a rascal, even in the presence of her husband, who smiled, being better informed about the matter than she. She behaved with more circumspection towards her lady in waiting, the Comtess de Noailles, whom she called Mme d'Etiquette, but with no less off-handedness; she had men and women servants appointed without consulting her, and she habitually left her out of account.

Now that Marie-Antoinette was triumphing over one and all, she naturally tackled her husband. She tried to break him in. He appeared late for meals, worn out with hunting: so she took a pleasure in refusing the dishes and sending them away without his being able to get at them. But the game made the Dauphin laugh too much to be very amusing. She tried to return to her serious conversations with him: he was very close to his grandfather, and although he took no trouble about it and did nothing extraordinary, he was on good terms with the du Barry, thanks to those evenings at the Hermitage, where he used to meet her. The king was very grateful to him for this relationship. Once again the Dauphine attacked Mme du Barry; and the Dauphin took care not to defend her. She reproved him for going to see a person he respected so little and who was in fact so little worth respect. 'One has to be prudent; one has to yield for the sake of peace,' he answered, not choosing to say anything more. Then they talked about their journey, and on 31 August they returned to Versailles, stopping for dinner at Chantilly.

At Versailles Berry had another attack or fever, and once more the king grew anxious. What was going to happen to these young people? They had been married for close on five months and they were still not man and wife. He had spoken to his grandson about it in July, and he had told him that everything would be settled at Compiègne: yet nothing had been done. When he looked at them, the one so threatened by his illness and the other so young and child-like, he said to himself, 'Perhaps it would be better for them to wait.' So although the king treated her charmingly, Marie-Antoinette felt embarrassed in his presence: she was cut off from him by age, taste, appetites and above all by that du Barry, whose low origin and whose success she could not forgive. Everything brought her back towards her husband, for he seemed the most truly human being in the whole of this court and this Versailles existence.

So she began to speak kindly of him, using a patronizing tone that came straight from the Duc de Choiseul – a way of speaking that did not exclude affection but that did come very close to contempt. When she was with Mercy, Vermond, her ladies in waiting, Mesdames de France or even with others she said that she was pleased with the Dauphin; she attributed his shyness and his coldness to his bad up-bringing, but she acknowledged that he was good-natured.

She took pleasure in saying that she was gaining influence over him and that she was taming him with her charm and gaiety. From now on he talked to her confidentially about matters that he had never discussed with anyone. She even knew what he thought of his preceptor.

This was the way she spoke, and this was the way she let those about her speak. She already saw herself – and others already saw her – as the mistress of the Dauphin's mind, capable of ruling through him or in his place. Yet her mother and her advisers were still uneasy at the fact that Marie-Antoinette had not yet been able to gain enough ascendency over him to make herself his wife in the full meaning of the word.

Mesdames de France, who were worthy creatures and anxious for the family's welfare, discussed the matter at length among themselves; then they consulted various physicians in order to be better informed, one or two priests, so as not to make a blunder, and certain old friends – gentlemen – who could give them further enlightenment. Finally Madame Adélaïde, who had never ceased to take an interest in her godson Berry, volunteered to go and offer him useful advice and to encourage him. At the first word Berry turned his back and walked out of the room: that evening he did not appear in his wife's bedroom, and for some days he avoided her, all the more so since he could see the whispering of the courtiers who surrounded him.

Yet he bore no sort of grudge against her, for he was incapable of rancour; and Marie-Antoinette had enchanting ways of bringing him back to her. Now that she was allowed to ride they saw more of one another, for sometimes he went riding with her and sometimes she would join him in the field. At Vermond's advice she launched into ostentatious acts of charity. When they were hunting on 29 November 1770 she had a wounded postillion treated, and on another day she looked after an old woman. Everybody praised her, and the affectionate Dauphin was twice as attentive.

As she took a great delight in dancing he began to ask for balls to be held, and presently there was one every Monday in the Dauphine's suite at Versailles. The give and take between the young couple increased: he was exceedingly clean and she was sometimes rather careless; she made a real effort to return to the habit of baths, and to the wearing of corsets in the French manner, although the harsh whalebone hurt her. So there grew up an intimacy between them, an intimacy made of custom, kindness, mutual attraction, and reserve. She contributed more charm to this relationship, he more generosity: he did not cross her in anything, and although he had too low an opinion of the Abbé de

Vermond to speak to him – he had made it a rule never to enter into contact with *philosophe* priests – he was remarkably civil to Mercy. This was neither ignorance nor blindness: he was perfectly aware of the harm she was doing him, yet the very seriousness of that harm attached him to her.

Things were not working out as Choiseul would have liked. He turned to harsher methods. One day when he was working with the king he stated that his grandson's upbringing was lamentable and that if it went on like that 'the nation would come to hold the Dauphin in abhorrence'. He added that he could not be made a member of the Council of State.

Louis XV made no reply, but lowered his eyes.

Chapter VII

The 'Revolution' of 1771

AT HALF PAST ELEVEN ON THE MORNING OF 24 DECEMBER
1770 the Duc de La Vrillière, the minister in charge of the royal
household, walked into the Duc de Choiseul's appartments at
Versailles and handed him a letter in the king's own hand, a very
curt letter that required his immediate resignation from his two
ministries and that banished him to his estate at Chanteloup.
Choiseul was utterly stunned.

The king was aware of everything that went on at Versailles,
but he said little. All around him there was secret contention.
Although Marie-Antoinette and Provence seemed so friendly
they were bitterly opposed to one another. The Dauphine remained loyal to Choiseul, Provence to La Vauguyon: the enthusiastic followers of M. de Choiseul and the Parlement 'not only
loved Marie-Antoinette as a Princess Charming, but did her the
wrong of looking upon her as the leader of a faction'. 'From this,'
says Moreau, the lawyer, 'there arose the most improper and the
most absurd kind of gossip': it was the source 'of hypothetical

disagreements, stories devoid of common-sense that were fabricated and then handed about'. The Dauphine refused the place of mistress of the wardrobe in her household to Mme de Saint-Mégrin, La Vauguyon's daughter-in-law, although both the king and the Dauphin had promised it to the duke. Marie-Antoinette was a stubborn hater. Berry was wiser; he listened to everyone, watched everything and was silent; he spent all the time he could spare hunting in the forest, where he filled his lungs with fresh air and forgot the dirty tittle-tattle of the court. When his wife opened her mouth too wide he checked her; when his brother made a nuisance of himself he boxed his ears. Thoughtful observers approved of his conduct.

Not so the ladies, not so the young blades, not so the old beaux, who thought him by no means attentive enough to his wife. One of the most charming women at court, the Comtesse d'Egmont, who was born a Richelieu, said of him, 'M. le Dauphin does display a few barbarous qualities, but he has no wit, no learning and no reading – he does not even want to possess them; and he is as harsh in his principles as he is violent in his actions' (13 May 1771). 'If he had been civilized,' they said, 'it would have been self-evident; he would have proved it by providing the charming Dauphine with the delights of motherhood.' The gossip, coming from Marie-Antoinette's circle or that of Mesdames de France, ran briskly round the town.

The Dauphin took little notice of it. He was uniformly affectionate and kind to his wife, and her whims amused him. As early as the end of 1770 she organized little balls in her own part of the palace, and a young court began to form there. Her mistress of the wardrobe, Mme de Noailles, did not wish to be behindhand, and every week she too gave a handsome party for the Dauphine. These, together with the plays and the sledge-rides that were Marie-Antoinette's great delight – it was she who had introduced this custom of the northern courts to Versailles – made the winter pass very cheerfully.

So cheerfully, indeed, that towards Lent the Dauphin and the Dauphine could no longer stand the pace, and after the last ball on Ash Wednesday they collapsed into bed and did not get up for twelve hours, while Louis XV wrote to his grandson the Infante of Parma, 'Madame la Dauphine dances as much as ever she can, and from what I hear my grandson seems to take pleasure in it; I know nothing of it myself, not having been there, since I prefer hunting and my business . . . Here the carnival has ended for my children, fortunately enough. Monsieur and Madame la Dauphine have stayed in bed for several days, but they are quite well.' Berry could not avoid going along with his wife, and everyone would have blamed him if he had not done so; but the king was displeased with him for not insisting that Marie-Antoinette should lead another kind of life – he quite forgot that it was he alone who had chosen this young archduchess, against the advice of the late Dauphine-dowager.

Marie-Antoinette enjoyed herself at Fontainebleau, where the court stayed from half way through October to the middle of November. Balls were given there, great receptions, and those plays that she so delighted in. She even tried to bring her husband round to liking them, though he was strongly opposed to the stage.

When they were back at Versailles he was not above taking part in the little plays and charades that his wife, his brothers and sisters organized with the help of the subtle Mme de Marsan and the participation of the more quick-witted members of the young court. In these the Dauphin played one of the most useful of roles, and certainly that which suited him best – he constituted the audience. He was alone, for it would have been improper to allow other spectators to watch this too highly-born and too in-experienced company, in which the Dauphine's charm did not really hide her professional incapacity. Short-sighted though he was, her husband saw in these productions still another reason for condemning plays; and anyone who reads the insipid comedies of the time will agree with him.

He was quite right too in stealing away as soon as he could and escaping to work. That had always been his inclination and now it was becoming his duty. Whenever he had the opportunity he was always busy. He arranged the Dauphine's books on his library shelves, which rather shocked M. Moreau, the librarian. He helped the workmen who were repairing a lock in his apartments, which of course filled the courtiers with indignation; for although they were always eagerly praising 'the people', they were equally eager to avoid coming into contact with the subject of their praise.

Louis-Auguste, on the contrary, was like the French people; he loved highly-skilled manual work and the thorough, searching work of the mind. In that age of the Encyclopedia, when fashionable people admired crafts but fled from the craftsmen, he did not read the Encyclopedia but he did understand the workers; and, which was even better, he understood their work. He therefore went on with his watch-making in his attic workshop with the help of Gamain.

He did not neglect his geography, either. In 1769 he had drawn and carefully illustrated a large map of Versailles and he was now preparing another; he was making himself acquainted with the geography of the world, and he was very eager to talk about it with the Duc de Croy and his friend M. de Kerguelen. He returned to his studies with M. Moreau, who gave him a chapter every week, according to the plan that his late father had laid down and that M. de La Vauguyon had forgotten to follow. Set free by this timely death, Louis-Auguste was able to go back to his patient reading of the history of France, of his ancestors and of Europe. In 1771 he caused the Abbé de La Ville, a high official in the foreign ministry, to teach him the elements of international politics.

He completed his education by reading the papers. He sent to Holland for the best-edited gazettes and he followed their articles with all the more attention since outside France they formed the organ of the French *philosophes* and the supporters of the Parlement, together with their auxiliaries, the European Protestants. So he was at once the most silent and the best-informed of the princes at the court. Those who knew him, like Thierry, his valet, could not but smile when they heard the Dauphine, who never opened a book, assuring M. de Mercy that she would do anything to induce the Dauphin to take to serious reading. But that was the tone and the atmosphere of the court at that time.

These were bad habits: Louis-Auguste put up with them out of scorn, and Marie-Antoinette derived great profit from them. There were other games that were even less edifying.

She delighted in plotting. She plotted furiously against the La Vauguyons, the Broglies and above all against the du Barry, whom Choiseul pointed out to her as the chief target.

Now this campaign against the du Barry was the revenge of the men of the Parlement, helped by public opinion at home and abroad. The salons, the *Nouvelles à la main* and above all the pamphlets dragged her name in the mud.

Louis XV was perfectly aware of all this, for he too kept a watch over the gazettes and the broadsheets. He was therefore all the more eager to oblige the court and his relations to accept Mme du Barry, as a kind of compensation. But he ran up against the Dauphine's opposition. Her mother, her husband and Mercy all scolded her, but in vain. After innumerable threats and prayers she was at last persuaded to address a word to the du Barry on the occasion of the New Year's visits.

'There are a great many people at Versailles today', she said, looking elsewhere; and everyone had to be satisfied with that. By way of defending herself, she let it be understood that she was obeying her husband's wishes. Maria-Theresa, ever mindful of Austria's interests and prepared for any kind of complaisance, so long as it should prove useful, therefore insisted that the Dauphin should do his part. Mercy had to lecture both husband and wife. At Compiègne in August they succeeded in getting the Dauphin to promise to attend the suppers given by the king and Mme du Barry; and he did so. On her side, the Dauphine had the adroitness to say a few pleasant words to a woman close to the du Barry, who could understand them as being intended for her. Everyone was happy, at least for a few months. Louis-Auguste wanted no kind of scandal, and at the end of December 1773 he was unusually gracious when the favourite made her appearance: he spoke to her with marked politeness. Mercy smiled, charmed and surprised: he was even more surprised when he saw the Dauphine ostentatiously turn her back upon Mme du Barry.

A few weeks later there was a question of regaining the du Barry's goodwill by going to sup with the king and her in their private rooms: Berry took the bull by the horns: he went to see his grandfather and said, 'Sire, there can never be any limits to my affection for you, and you may put my obedience and my respect to any kind of trial; but Your Majesty will appreciate that my interest and my duty lies in seeing that no scandal of any sort comes near Madame la Dauphine.' The king made no reply; but he caused Adélaïde to tell Berry that 'it grieved him to see that M. le Dauphin took no pleasure in society and that he deliberately stood aloof from the fair sex'. The king begged his daughter to bring the Dauphin back to a more sociable kind of behaviour and to urge him to be polite to the ladies who were often in the king's company. The king did nothing more with regard to his grandson, who was too obviously in the right, other than adopting a sad and distant attitude towards him.

Chapter VIII

The Dauphin humiliated

MARIE-ANTOINETTE HAD HAD ENOUGH OF THE COURT. They did not pay enough attention to her there. She wanted to reign, to be the focus of all eyes and the most important person in the company. She wanted Paris to adore her.

It was her plan to carry Berry along with her – he was more lively now that his health had improved. She persuaded the king to allow them both to go incognito to the ball at the Opéra, and there they enjoyed themselves. The public knew about it after the event and took to filling the place in the hope that they would come back. She determined to make the most of the situation. She also wanted to make the most of Louis-Auguste's increasing self-assurance: he was proving more and more affectionate to-wards her, more and more affable towards all who served him, and – a striking phenomenon in this atmosphere of glum formality – more and more direct and open with any importunate person who worried him.

When they wanted to introduce the du Barry's niece to him at the time of her presentation at court he would not turn towards her but went on drumming a tune of his own composition on the

window-pane: when they tried to force a servant upon him whose
character he did not approve of he gave a flat refusal, adding, 'If
he gets the place he will have the double advantage of the office
and an exemption from ever appearing.' The minister yielded.
Indeed, it was even said that when Mme du Barry wanted a relation
of hers to enter his service, the Dauphin said to her, 'If your
nephew is given this post, let him never come anywhere near me,
or he will get my boot in his face.' Whether it was true or not,
the outburst pleased the public.

The young prince's somewhat barbarous harshness and his
wife's charm instinctively attracted the masses, who were drawing
away from the aged king.

Louis XV was wise enough to accept this: he allowed them
to make their entry into Paris in June 1773. On the eighth
the Dauphin and the Dauphine paid their first official visit to
the capital. They arrived from Versailles at about eleven in the
morning, coming in by the Porte de la Conférence, and the
corporation were there to meet them. The provost was at their
head, with the Duc de Brissac, the governor of Paris, and M. de
Sartine, the chief of police; and they were attended by the mounted
company of the watch. A deputation of six fishwives from the
Halles had the honour of presenting an immense bouquet of roses
and a basket of oranges. The fishwives kissed Brissac and Sartine,
who put up with it very well.

The Dauphin and the Dauphine changed into state coaches and
drove to Notre-Dame amidst a vast concourse of people. The
Archbishop of Paris received them in great splendour at the head
of his cathedral clergy. They said their prayers in the choir, heard
a low mass in the Lady Chapel while the choir-master played an
anthem of his own composition, and then went to see the treasure.
From Notre-Dame they moved on to Sainte-Geneviève, where
the abbot and all the monks welcomed them; there they said their
prayers, and according to custom, walked round the saint's shrine
before going on to the palace of the Tuileries.

As they went some of the fishwives called, out 'Monsieur le
Dauphin! Do make us a baby, now!' At the Tuileries a splendid
dinner had been prepared for them in the concert hall; and

hundreds of people were allowed in to see the royal pair, leaving a moment later by another door. After this the Dauphin and the Dauphine went for a walk in the Tuileries gardens, which were open to the public, having first given all the guards the most explicit instructions that no one was to be pushed or bustled. They ended their walk by going up to the gallery to show themselves for a good quarter of an hour, in spite of the sun, which was very oppressive on so hot a day.

The crowd showed their hearty gratitude by clapping and by outbursts of cheering interrupted by short intervals of the most profound silence as a mark of respect and admiration. At last the young pair withdrew, bowing very deeply to all the spectators. Tears of emotion were seen in the princess's eyes – 'most precious tears, for they were the mark of a beautiful soul'. The crowd was enchanted and so were the Dauphin and Dauphine; and there was no untimely incident to spoil their pleasure. As they returned they anxiously questioned the officers of the Gardes-Françaises and the Swiss Guard who assured them that there had been no incident nor even the slightest unpleasantness.

> How fortunate it is for people in our condition [wrote Marie-Antoinette to her mother] to win the friendship of a whole nation at such little cost. Yet there is nothing so valuable; I became thoroughly aware of that and I shall never forget it. Another point which gave great pleasure during this delightful day was the behaviour of M. le Dauphin. He answered all the speeches wonderfully well; he noticed everything that was done for him, and above all he saw the zeal and the happiness of the people, for whom he showed a great deal of kindness.

Mercy was no less eloquent in the announcement of victory he sent to Vienna: 'From the point of view of HRH's success upon this occasion there was nothing left to be desired: the public was seized with a kind of enthusiastic rapture for Madame the Arch-duchess . . . M. le Dauphin behaved admirably . . . This entry into Paris is of great importance for fixing public opinion.'

Together they had won their first battle, and they had gained the heart of Paris. They could not be in any doubt about this during the following weeks: they came to the Opéra on 15 June and the audience gave them an ovation; and at the Comédie-Française, which they visited on June 23 to see Belloy's play *The Siege of Calais*, the actors' patriotism had free rein, and every allusion was taken up with wild enthusiasm by the whole house. But perhaps the most agreeable performance was at the Comédie-Italienne, where the first production, *Arlequin et Scapin rivaux*, was lucky enough to make the Dauphin laugh, while the second, *Le Déserteur*, gave both the cast and the public the opportunity of showing their attachment to the king. The king did not fail to be impressed by the welcome his grandchildren received. He congratulated them upon it; and when the Dauphine prudently cried, 'Oh, Father, how they love you! If only you had heard how they cheered us because of you!' he smiled. He had always liked being deceived by women, and he was delighted that the French public should share his tastes.

People were astonished at the fact that the public liked the Dauphin as much as his wife, and that he was no less at his ease among these ordinary citizens than she, for at court he was thought most uncouth. They forgot that from his childhood he had been taught to love the common people, and they were unaware of his conviction that a king does not only reign over a nation, but by and with a nation, and that nothing can take the place of a people's love for its king. These days proved to him that he could be beloved by the people, and in his mind this increased the feeling of his own responsibility.

What would happen if he were suddenly to find himself king? He still knew nothing of the calling. When he tried to question his grandfather he got nothing but short and evasive answers. Out of respect for the king and hatred of intrigue he would not (unlike his brother Provence) allow himself to become attached to any minister. He therefore turned to his father's old friends, Muy and Maillebois, who found him a tactical instructor, with whom he carried on a correspondence that he kept entirely private. This was the son of a high official in the Duchy of Lorraine; his name was Jacques Masson, and he used the style of Marquis de Pezay. He had a quick, lively mind; he knew all about the new currents and the new men, and he told the Dauphin about a world that was as yet quite unknown to the young prince.

This was a difficult period, one in which the king seemed old and the Dauphin very young. Choiseul's propaganda described the prince as ignorant, unread and stupid. The noble duke did not think it beneath him to write a ludicrous and insulting piece with his own hand. 'The prince is half-witted,' it said, 'and it is to be feared that his imbecility and the ridicule and the contempt that it will entail may in the natural course of events produce a decay of authority that may deprive the king's descendants of the throne.' Marie-Antoinette, who was taking part in Choiseul's campaign and who refused herself to her husband, did the Dauphin serious harm: she spoke of his dull sluggishness and she allowed more to be understood, thus making him ridiculous to the court and the city.

Both Maria-Theresa and Louis XV became uneasy. Having spoken of the matter several times, without dwelling upon it, Louis XV arranged with Lassonne that Louis-Auguste should undergo a complete examination early one morning so that his physical constitution should be thoroughly understood. Lassonne's verdict was perfectly clear: the Dauphin was well formed, and as he was amorously inclined there was nothing on his side to prevent the consummation of the marriage.

This verdict in favour of Louis-Auguste was exceedingly embarrassing to Marie-Antoinette, who wrote to her mother, 'M. le Dauphin has answered Lassonne very well on the several occasions they have spoken together. He is very well made, he loves me and he is full of good will; but he is perpetually listless and unconcerned . . .' Of course this could not be made public, and what is more no good purpose would have been served by publishing it, for at court it was scarcely less absurd to spare a wife who did not choose to give herself than to be unable to satisfy one who did choose so to do. So the secret remained a secret, and Berry still passed as incapable of fulfilling his marital duties.

It was known that Provence was in the same condition, although he was far more sly about it. So the court looked forward anxiously to see what Artois would manage to do. The fishwives were already shouting 'Make us a baby!', and although Croy was well-disposed and very loyal to the dynasty he calmly wrote in his diary, 'If this prince, who was married too young, does not give us any children, and if the other two do not do so either – a most lamentable state of affairs for three boys – then it may prove all the more unfortunate since the royal house nevertheless costs so many millions!' (5 December 1773).

Aranda came to find out what was going on, and he wrote, 'M. le Dauphin has not yet revealed his talents nor his character. There is no doubt that he is upright, and a great friend to virtue. He has a good figure and he is strongly built; he is exceedingly fond of hunting and he rides so well that it is hard to follow him – indeed, it is thought that he exposes himself to dangerous falls. It is supposed that he had not consummated his marriage. Some assert that he has, but several of the Dauphine's ladies seem not to believe it: there is no lack of evidence to make one think so. Marks have been found on their Highnesses' bed-linen that show that the act has taken place; but many people attribute them to the outward ejaculations of the Dauphin, who, it would seem, has not succeeded in penetrating. It is said that this is not out of any lack of amorousness but because of a little ill-placed pain that hurts more when he is insistent. Others think that all has been accomplished because for some time now the Dauphin has been most affectionate towards the Dauphine; but in spite of its great importance there is still a great deal of doubt about this matter, and one cannot suppose that the desired end has been reached, otherwise there would have been a celebration.

'The Dauphine is beautiful and very Austrian at heart; until he has attached her to France it is natural that she should think little of the delights of this country. But she is very fond of jewels and ornaments and here she has many opportunities of obtaining all she wants; so she may find abundant satisfaction for the propensities of her sex ... The king is very fond of her and he looks for ways of giving her pleasure ... The Comte de Provence looks very well. But everyone unanimously asserts that he is impotent ...

'The Comte d'Artois is a fine-looking, sprightly young man; he has more intelligence than his brothers and a greater capacity for learning. Judging from his outward appearance, his liveliness and all his other qualities make him seem the preserver and the restorer of his family. The condition of this government and this monarchy is by no means an enviable one . . .'

Such was the Comte d'Aranda's summary. In his anxiety to serve his master well, the ambassador set about spying on the three young princes day and night, and he began turning the mind of his court towards the sending of a Spanish Infanta who might marry Louis XV – still young for his age – and give him children, thus relegating Marie-Antoinette to the second rank. In this way the Orléans would cease to be dangerous; France and Spain would be firmly united; and the Bourbon dynasty would receive fresh blood. The Comte d'Aranda's great mission depended upon the success of this plan.

The only one to retain common-sense and good-nature in all this was the Dauphin. He went on hunting, for this pastime, which was essential to his health, was the only one that brought him nearer to his grandfather. At the review of his regiment, the Dauphin Cavalerie, he was as gracious to the officers as he was kindly to the men; and he was seen to be skilful in putting them through their manœuvres. Everyone who was present at the meeting of the Order of the Holy Ghost for the installation of the young Duc de Bourbon was struck by the affectionate care with which he treated the new member. And lastly, on 23 November, at the time of his visit with his grandfather to Madame Louise at her Carmelite convent, everyone admired his quiet gravity and his noble bearing.

Chapter IX

'The King does not die'

WHEN THE KING WAS COMPLAINING TO HIS PHYSICIAN OF the decay of his powers, he added, 'It is clear to me that I am no longer young and that I must put on the brakes.'

'Sire,' was the reply, 'it would be better if you were to put off your harness.'

He often longed to do so, and he remembered how in former days he had wanted to abdicate and hand over power to the Dauphin; but his son was dead, Berry was not ready, and the position was still extremely difficult.

It is wearisome to live. It is not easy to die. Everyone succeeds in the end, they say, even the stupidest. But for some death is gracious and comes to meet them. For others she has to be coaxed and persuaded.

On 26 April the king was supping at Trianon with the du Barry. He was seized with a fit of shivering. La Martinière had him taken back to Versailles at once and put to bed.

On the twenty-seventh and twenty-eighth the illness developed: at eleven in the evening of the twenty-ninth the physicians announced that it was smallpox. The Dauphin and the Dauphine were kept away: they had to shut themselves up in their own apartments, for fear of contagion. The physicians did not yet dare to tell the king anything about his condition: they thought him very ill, but not hopelessly so.

At last on 4 May they grew frightened, and Louis XV, informed about his disease, sent the du Barry away. He confessed at three o'clock in the morning of the seventh and in a document that Cardinal de Beaumont read to the court he publicly asked God's forgiveness for the scandal he had caused.

On the ninth he saw his confessor again and received the last sacraments with the utmost piety. At times he said, 'I should like to feel more pain.'

His death was expected all night, while the forty-hours prayers were said in the churches of Paris and the Dauphin remained on his knees. At about ten o'clock in the morning the Bishop of Senlis earnestly admonished the dying king: he said, 'Yes.' At one o'clock the priests asked the courtiers who were still there to kneel and pray, for the death agony was beginning. It lasted two hours and a half.

Suddenly the doors of the room were flung wide open and an usher went down to the ante-chamber of the great hall of the palace, the room called the Œil-de-Bœuf, and there he cried, 'The king is dead.' Then everyone was required to leave and the room was shut up.

The reign of Louis XV was over.

Louis XVI was king.

PART TWO

Louis le Désiré

Chapter I

King at nineteen

LOUIS-AUGUSTE UTTERED A GREAT CRY WHEN THE MASTER
of Ceremonies came to tell him that his grandfather was dead – the
only friend he had had in his youth, a careless friend and remote,
but sincere. His only protection and his only guide had vanished:
suddenly upon his head there had descended the crushing weight
of the crown of France.

'Oh God,' he cried, 'I am the unhappiest of men.' They thought
he was going to break down and weep. But he regained control
over himself. 'Clearly it is God's will. He had decided it. All that
remains for me is to protect religion, which has great need of it;
to remove vicious men and knaves from me; and to comfort the
nation.' And when his sisters Clotilde and Elizabeth came in he
kissed them most affectionately, saying, 'Let us not be separated:
I will take the place of everyone for you.'

Then he left for Choisy, for it was essential to leave Versailles,
all pestilent with the malodorous death of Louis XV. The coach
moved off, and a tremendous roar went up from the people,
'Long live the king!'

They settled hastily into Choisy. Mesdames, Louis XV's

daughters, who had taken care of him throughout his illness, came too, and they were lodged in a separate building, the little palace, for fear of contagion. In his grief the king thought first of others: he comforted the queen, who was overwhelmed by these events, and then he received the Duc de Villequier, who brought him a note from the Duc de La Vrillière, minister of the household, who wanted orders upon various urgent questions. He wrote his replies in the margin: he would take the name of Louis and not of Louis-Auguste; he would be Louis XVI; the customary notices might be sent out; he would retain all the ministers and they might correspond with him by letter until they could see him on the ninth day; he also ordered that all the intendants – the administrators of provinces – and all the commanding officers should be kept at Versailles so that he might see them as soon as it became possible. Then, having signed this note, he sent to tell the queen that he was going to work, and shut himself in his study at his desk, alone.

For nine days he worked steadily, writing letters in his own hand, sending messages, reading long reports and only breaking off to pray and to eat his meals with his family, as he had done all through Louis XV's illness. Meanwhile, both outside and very close to him, the plots were being knitted, the rumours ran from mouth to mouth, the queen was busy or nervous and impatient, his brothers fell to their calculations, the courtiers intrigued, and the ambassadors searched avidly for any information.

He worked: and his first aim was to see clearly into himself so that then he might see clearly, if that were possible, into the matters of state in which he was to be the final judge. His first feeling – a feeling that he had been unable to conceal but that he was now mastering – was still dread: he was not yet twenty; he knew nothing about state business; he knew none of the men who were governing or who might govern.

The task seemed enormous. Straight away he had the 'deficit' thrown in his face. France, the greatest and richest kingdom in Europe, was short of liquid money, and this hampered the country in its policies.

Everything cost a great deal: the queen would cost a great deal (she loved precious stones and jewels); Monsieur would cost a great deal, because that was his policy; and so would Artois, because he was a natural spender. The court would cost a great deal. Yet a brilliant queen was necessary, so were the brilliant princes and a brilliant court – they were necessary to a country which held the highest rank in Europe, which set the fashions, and which had so many craftsmen who would lose their living if France ceased to stand out as the most elegant country and court in Europe.

Money was needed for the roads and the administration of France; and for industry, which was still behind England's. The population of France, which was continually increasing thanks to family fertility and the far greater well-being and better hygiene of the last thirty years, called for very expensive care. Twenty-four and a half million people filled the countryside and crowded into the great towns. Paris had close on seven hundred thousand inhabitants, the poorest of whom lived in revolting slums: the capital needed rebuilding and making beautiful.

All these outlays seemed necessary; but so did economy, for France was going through a crisis. The Seven Years' War had been followed by a period of ebullient expansion with everything rising and everyone working happily: but since 1770 the tide had turned; it was ebbing now, and prices were falling. The farmers, the wine-growers and the craftsmen complained, the taxes came in badly, and there was talk of terrible bankruptcies, particularly at Marseilles. There was a simultaneous call both for the spending of money and for the saving of money. Faced with the pile of Terray's reports and minutes – very well drawn up, it may be added – the king was terrified.

The reign of Louis the Well-Beloved stood out as one of France's great periods. His successor had to fear both those who would blame him for being inferior to his grandfather and those whose hatred would be carried on from the grandfather to the grandson. Still more dangerous would be those who would flatter him in order to lead him far from the traditions of his grandfather, his father and his ancestors. On every side he had to beware.

The first and the most pressing of these dangers was the public discontent at the bad condition of the finances. When the peasants were leaving their land in the Pyrenees, Dauphiné, the Limousin and the Cévennes because they were too poor to work them and to pay their taxes, then it was high time to be on one's guard. All these men drifted into the slums in the towns and into unhealthy workshops where they grew bitter in their discontent, or else they loitered about the streets, asking nothing better than to be re-cruited by rebels. The history of the League and that of the Fronde showed how far along the road of excess the wretchedness of the humble could be pushed when it was exploited by the ambitions of the great. The country was prosperous, but it was in the midst of an economic crisis: most of the people lived well, but they all owed money; it was a situation that was not intrinsically alarming (for most of the peasants had reserves), but it became so because of the contrast with the wealth and arrogance of the great men and the parliamentarians – a wealth and arrogance upon which they prided themselves.

The movement of the Parlements against the monarchy had been broken by Louis XV, but it was still dangerous. The parliamentarians were closely linked by ties of blood with the greatest families in France. These great houses had never forgiven the Bourbons for Richelieu's work in bringing down their power. The Rochefoucaulds and the Montmorencys refused to come to court, and they formed centres of opposition. At La Roche-Guyon the Duchesse d'Enville gathered around her the most republican of the parliamentarians and the *philosophes*. At Châtillon the Duc de Montmorency held assemblies of freemasons. The Noailles, the Duforts and the Uzès seemed less unruly, but they had to be gratified with continually-renewed favours. A few, such as Richelieu, Luynes and Croy, proved more loyal. They were called old-fashioned for their pains.

The most powerful were still the most dangerous. Louis XV had feared the Orléans, although the Duc d'Orléans was a kindly fat man: but Louis XVI knew that Chartres was dangerous. He had known it since they were both children. The Orléans family had sat on the throne together with the Regent, and neither they nor their dependants forgot it. Their vast wealth and their splendid palace in the heart of Paris gave them both the means and the opportunity for being in the closest contact with the vital forces of the capital. And during the last crises they had put themselves forward as the champions and the protectors of the Parlements. Versailles had heard the whisper 'William of Orange'. Chartres' reputation was sullied by his vices, but he was intelligent; and the queen did not dislike him. Artois thought him charming. Chartres therefore had supporters even among those closest to Louis XVI. Indeed he had them everywhere. The fishwives of the Halles loved him dearly, so did the gentlemen of the Parlement; all the whores in Paris were devoted to him, body and soul; the financiers bowed very low; and the foreign ambassadors prowled assiduously around him.

The Orléans factor – that meant the English alliance ... England maintained agents everywhere in France. The Masonic lodges in France corresponded with the lodges in England that had founded them. They formed a kind of republic within the realm of France, and in 1773 they had just chosen the Duc de Chartres as their sole head. At their meetings they preached equality, and they were preparing a new élite for the future, a chosen body intended to lead a new society without distinction of class and without dogmas of any kind.

For some months Chartres had also been doing his utmost to enter into contact with Choiseul and his party. Choiseul's party was one of the young king's greatest anxieties. The duke maintained a positive court at Chanteloup and discontented lords, parliamentarians and *philosophes* flocked to it like pilgrims to Mecca. Choiseul had detested him ever since his childhood and he was now spreading propaganda against the young king. Yet the queen set herself up as Choiseul's most ardent supporter, and Mercy, the imperial ambassador, never ceased hurrying from the one to the other.

Louis XVI kept his eyes upon this obvious danger. He suspected the existence of another: what was Aranda, that very anti-Catholic minister of the Catholic King, the apostle of absolutism and of the doctrine of the *philosophes*, doing in France, with his perpetual spying upon the royal family? The king could not penetrate the depths of Aranda's mind; but he knew very well that if ever he were to stumble, Aranda would spare neither him nor his country.

France, happy and rich in spite of these financial difficulties, was the first nation in Europe; but all the other countries were jealous of her, even her allies, and not one would excuse her the slightest weakness. Poland was a reminder of what happened to divided nations. Meanwhile the country was in the grip of the greatest spiritual crisis it had known for fifteen hundred years. French catholicism was trembling on its foundations. To be sure, as the religion of the sovereign and the nation it enjoyed the highest honours – there were priests to be found everywhere, the clergy formed the first of the three orders of the nation, and a fifth of the land in France belonged to the Church. In theory the twenty-four and a half million inhabitants of France were Catholics; the king was entitled His Most Christian Majesty; and it seemed that the Church ruled everything in France, even the throne.

But the Church of France was sick. Everything showed it: the churches were often empty: whole regions, such as the dioceses of Sens, Troyes and Albi, were losing all their practising Catholics. The number of priests, monks and nuns had dropped astonishingly since the beginning of the century – from the 1667 figure of 260,000 (180,000 men and 80,000 women) without Alsace, the Franche-Comté, Lorraine or Corsica, to 194,211 (129,944 men and 64,267 women). The moral crisis seemed to be even greater still. The clergy were no longer respected as they had been. They defended themselves against the rising impiety; yet many were the priests who had doubts about their mission – even more numerous were those who carried it out badly.

The *philosophes* led public opinion, and thereby the women, the upper classes and even some foreign rulers, such as Frederick II, Joseph II, Leopold of Tuscany ... What exactly did this motley combination want? Louis XVI could not tell; yet he had to bear in mind the fact that in France the *philosophes* formed a kind of international party, one that might show him a certain amount of consideration but that always looked upon him from a higher plane, as though the *philosophes* were not his subjects but his judges; and in fact a great proportion of the world and a great many Frenchmen would form their opinion of him from what they said.

The well-organized Encyclopedists, with their leaders, their watchwords and their agents everywhere, confronted the monarchy and preached the ethics of self-interest. Few indeed were those who were not impressed by their threats – or their flatteries. The most worldly of the bishops worked for them and with them. Among the clergy, in the ministries, at the censor's office, their friends kept watch for them. Even the humble parish priests, reduced to their 'adequate emoluments', were unable to withstand the praise the *philosophes* lavished upon them from 1762 onwards. It could not but please them to hear it stated that bishops were unnecessary, superfluous creatures, whereas they, remote provincial curates, represented wisdom and morality – that although they might have no standing in the Church, yet they ought to be of the greatest consequence in the community.

This was not a fickle, thoughtless age; it was impious.

The king, who served God and for whom this service was at the heart of his being, could neither hesitate nor compromise upon this point. Here he was at one with the mass of the ordinary peasants, with that handful of writers, that group of bishops and with the thousands of loyal priests: he knew that it was his duty to act, and he sought for the means of doing so. He had succeeded to the throne at the age of nineteen and a half, tolerably well-read in history and geography and with some notions of science; his confessor, the Abbé Soldini, had armed him thoroughly, and he was endowed with a great deal of courage: but he knew nothing of the finances nor of the administration, and what little he understood of military affairs was in no way practical. His experience of men filled him with a deep mistrust for most, except for those peasants and workmen to whom he always talked whenever he could, thus following his father's advice.

For them, for the French people, he felt himself prepared to make any kind of sacrifice. But what a task! He was the Most Christian King: France, the eldest daughter of the Church and the right arm of the Papacy ever since Clovis and Charlemagne, could not forswear this vocation without ceasing to be herself; he was therefore obliged to defend the country against itself as well as against all others.

From his earliest days he had taken a pleasure in work. Now he rediscovered the deep, diffused happiness that comes from steady toil. He had everything to learn, and he made up his mind to be a hard-working king. He had no wholly reliable allies, so he made up his mind to be a reticent, close-counselled king: neither the queen, nor his brothers, nor his aunts, nor his ministers were ever to make out his thoughts, his intentions or his plans. And lastly he did not believe that it was possible to do good work with men he disliked, so he determined to treat his ministers as friends. This discipline, which he adopted instinctively and without regret, appeared to him more a help than a constraint; but his essential support and stay was still his deep, humble, regular religious life, from which he never deviated.

What was to unite him to his nation and to sustain him in his crushing vocation of king was his attachment to the French people, an attachment made up of simple good-heartedness, pity, and a sincere spiritual love. Everyone in his immediate circle felt it. And they knew that all the time he worked as hard as he hunted – that is to say to the limits of his strength – and when he was staggering and faint with tiredness he was happy to say within himself, 'At least I have done all I can.'

Chapter II

The tender-hearted accession

HAVING CAREFULLY LOCKED THE DOOR BEHIND HIM AND having considered for a long while, the young Louis XVI took a piece of paper and wrote:

M. de Maurepas,

Monsieur, in the midst of the right and natural sorrow that overwhelms me and that I share with the whole kingdom, I nevertheless have duties to fulfil. I am the king; and many, many obligations are contained in this single word: but I am only twenty years of age. I do not think that I have acquired all the knowledge that is needed. What is more, I cannot see any of the ministers, for they were all closeted with the king during his illness. I have always heard your integrity spoken of, as well as the reputation that your deep knowledge of affairs has so rightly obtained for you. It is this that induces me to beg you to be so kind as to help me with your advice and your understanding. I should be grateful, Monsieur, if you would come as soon as you can to Choisy, where I shall look forward with the utmost pleasure to seeing you.

LOUIS-AUGUSTE

The choice was intelligent and gracious: it was the proof of a political instinct in the young sovereign that was not generally acknowledged but that was shown by his actions. Even before the death of his grandfather he ordered the parish priests of Paris, to distribute two hundred thousand francs to the poor, asking them to pray for Louis XV. To Terray, the Controller-General, he said, 'If you have not enough liquid money for this, you may keep it back from my allowance and from that of Madame la Dauphine.'

Now all the streets of Paris echoed with his praises. And the salons were very pleased with his appeal to Maurepas, drawn up in such modest, dignified and moving terms.

Maurepas, at the age of seventy-three, had neither enemies nor ambitions. He had been a minister at twenty-two; he had been in office for thirty years on end; and he had owed his disgrace to his stubborn insistence upon funds for the navy, as well as to the vexation of Madame de Pompadour, who disliked him for some ill-natured songs that were said to have been written by him. He was a wit and a man whom everybody liked, even his wife, although he had never been able to satisfy her (unless it was the other way around?).

The late Dauphin Louis had had a high opinion of him for his attitude towards the Pompadour, and in 1764, a little before his death, he tried to bring him back as Chancellor. The papers he left to his son and the advice passed on by La Vauguyon determined this choice. Louis XVI had to give up Machault, in spite of his esteem for him, in order not to displease the clergy at the beginning of his reign. Maurepas was not looked upon as particularly religious, but he did possess this disadvantage. He was La Vrillière's brother-in-law, Aiguillon's uncle, cousin to Maupeou and Richelieu, and he was related to the La Rochefoucaulds and the Maillys. And everyone thought of himself as Maurepas' friend. Everyone was delighted – except the queen.

They were still delighted when they saw Maurepas walk into Choisy like a ghost from the beginning of the century. He shut himself up with the king and they had a long conversation. Louis XVI began by thanking him; then Maurepas spoke. 'The Cardinal de Fleury was accused of having prolonged your grandfather's childhood in order to be master for a greater length of time' he said. 'I do not want to deserve such a reproach, and if you see fit, I shall be nothing, as far as the public is concerned. I shall be here for you alone: your ministers will work with you. I shall never speak to them in your name and I shall not undertake to speak to you for them. Only do not make up your mind upon matters that are outside the ordinary daily run: let us have one or two conferences a week, and if you have acted too hastily, I will tell you. In a word, I will be your man, yours alone, and nothing beyond that. If you choose to be your own prime minister, you can, by dint of hard work; and I offer you the help of my experience: but never lose the sight of the fact that if you do not wish to do so, or if you do not feel able to do so, then you must necessarily choose one.'

'You have grasped my meaning exactly', said the king. 'That is precisely what I hoped for from you.'

So they decided to have frequent conferences outside the Council of State, which met twice a week, and the *Conseil des Dépêches* which met once. Then the king began to speak about his ministers: Maurepas stopped him. 'I shall not say anything to you about the men who make up your ministry. Some are near relations; others I know only by what the public says of them. Let us not hurry your decision. That is all I shall say to you today.'

This sensible method, which gave the ministers in office the hope of retaining their places, was calculated to ensure steady, zealous work on their part; and at the same time it did not discourage the others.

Hope and happiness were the order of the day. This was obvious to the king and queen when they left Choisy for La Muette on 17 May. As they passed the barrier at Sèvres the king was repeatedly cheered by the people who had come from Paris and the nearby countryside to pay their respects. There was a universal atmosphere of kind-heartedness and affection. It seemed as though his goodness made the king handsomer – as though it surrounded him with an effulgence.

He took his meals in the queen's room together with his whole family; and as he had dismissed the special *service de la Bouche*, the royal catering department, everything was very modest. He used to say, 'I feed my family, but on plain food.' Above all he worked. On 19 May he saw the ministers and the great dignitaries; on the twentieth he held his first Council of State, and Maurepas attended it – a mark of his growing importance. From that time onwards he took part in all the councils, and everyone understood that he was the king's confidential adviser. The king wrote an enormous number of letters to his uncles and cousins of Spain, Naples and Parma, to Maria-Theresa, and to many others. The Controller-General presented his financial plans, which were approved: they forecast a surplus of sixty million in three years.

Meanwhile the delegations came flooding in from all sides. One day it would be the administration of the city of Paris. Then came the six merchant guilds. Occasionally one of the speakers would lose his way in his speech, and the king would have to stifle his mirth. Another time it was the fishwives, bringing some rather stale flour, and some rather heavy compliments, none of them very fresh: they also asked that the barriers round Paris should be abolished. The king received all these people, replied, kissed those who had to be kissed, and escaped to get on with his work.

The poor and middling sort of people liked him. He was in the fashion. But there were some who grumbled; already there was murmuring in the higher circles. Choiseul's supporters were growing impatient; making herself their mouthpiece, the queen put forward the duke's name. The king at once replied, 'That man? Never.' But he promised to allow him to return to court if he behaved properly.

Louis XVI's administration was beginning to take on a colour of its own, and his people to grow interested in their king.

This interest increased when it was learnt that he was going to have himself inoculated. He had made up his mind to it at the persuasion of his wife and his brothers: and the three brothers were all to be inoculated at the same time, which the young members of the court found 'charming' and the old foolish. 'Here are three lives that are of the greatest value to the nation', they said. 'What is the point of risking them all at one throw, particularly when we have no heir?' And M. d'Aranda grumbled, 'It is just handing France over to the house of Orléans.'

However, the matter was decided upon. Everyone was making ready to leave for Marly when the queen, profiting by these last cheerful days and the king's happiness, wrung Choiseul's return from banishment from him. 'How can I forget that I owe my happiness to him? It was he who married us', she said. The king could only smile and yield; but he granted no more than a first short visit to Paris and the court, to be followed by liberty if the duke did not make an ill use of it.

So as early as 12 June he came to pay his respects. He made his first appearance in the king's apartments. Louis XVI stared at him. 'Monsieur de Choiseul,' said he, 'you have lost some of your hair. It is growing thin in front.' Then he walked on. When his turn came Monsieur said, 'How is Mme de Choiseul?' And lastly when she saw him the queen cried in a transport, 'I owe you everything: you have made me the happiest of women!' M. de Choiseul went off with his head in the air as usual, but he was puzzled; and in the meanwhile the peripatetic court once more packed its trunks to go to Marly, where it settled in on 16 June for six weeks.

From 18 June to the twentieth, leading the secluded life that inoculation required, the young king worked and meditated. This was the last interval that he had before the decisions and the choices that were to fix the orientation of his reign. His head filled with hope and anxiety, he indulged in the re-reading of these lines written in his honour:

> *Go forward, on our hearts impose your yoke:*
> *We twenty million subjects long to hear*
> *The glorious words that you may utter soon,*
> *'I am but twenty, yet I make them all*
> *Happy, content, rejoicing in my rule.'*

As soon as he was better the conferences with the ministers and the great men of the realm began. During this month of July the Duc d'Orléans also made motions towards a reconciliation. He was unable to resist the current that was carrying the whole country towards the young king; he went to Versailles, and there he adjured him to take back the former Parlement. Louis XVI listened to what he had to say: he distrusted the house of Orléans, but he wanted to be at peace with everybody.

Unhappily Louis XV's funeral service at Paris, his *catafalque*, to use the exact term, set them at variance once more. Orléans agreed to attend, but not to bow to the new Parlement, which would be there. It was in vain that Louis XVI pointed out the impropriety of this attitude; Orléans, urged on by Chartres, was immovable. In reply, Louis XVI banished them to Villers-Cotterêts. Immediately there rose the murmur, 'Louis XV's reign is continuing'. And a cabal at once began to form.

M. de Maurepas seized upon this moment to induce Louis XVI to take a most important decision. In order to give the younger part of the nation and philosophic opinion a pledge of the king's favourable attitude, he suggested that M. Turgot, the Intendant of Limoges, should replace M. Boynes at the Admiralty. Boynes had not made a success of his post and at the last council the king had noted that he had 'mislaid' three million livres of naval funds. Louis XVI welcomed Turgot's name. This administrator of forty-seven had the reputation of an upright man and a tireless worker, the possessor of the most enlightened mind in France. A great number of influential women supported him, particularly the Duchesse d'Enville, the leader of the clan of the Rochefoucaulds, whom Maurepas was happy to call kin. There was general applause (19 July).

Then the court moved on to Compiègne; it was a beautiful place, full of game, and the king was very fond of it. In the intervals between hunting and going for walks, Louis XVI and Maurepas worked out the first full cabinet of his reign.

Louis XV had left him some great ministers – and some great dangers. By their coup of 1771 Maupeou and Terray had restored the traditional monarchy; but they had not done so in a legal manner – the parliamentary offices should have been dealt with by compensation, not by confiscation. The parliamentarians, with their countless followers and with even greater numbers who aided and abetted them, had been campaigning furiously; from every quarter there came denunciations of 'the revolution of 1771' and the attack upon private property. If Louis XV had reigned for another ten years, would he have managed to hold by his decisions, to have divided his enemies and to have overcome them? Heaven knows.

Louis XVI was a king of nineteen, unknown to the army, the police and the heads of the administration; he was threatened with defection by the nobles and with rebellion by a great part of the country; would it have been sensible of him to keep Maupeou, however intelligent and loyal he might be?

Maurepas thought it would not and he persuaded his master that the danger was too great to be defied.

Yet the making of this decision was most unwelcome to Louis XVI. Day after day he put it off. He also postponed it for the Abbé Terray, formerly one of the Jesuits' most violent enemies; the abbé was a libertine and as a minister he was extremely grasping; but he was intelligent, skilful and hard-working. He carried out his duties well, and the king could not bring himself to dismiss him.

That was where matters rested: but Maurepas, urged on by Turgot, wanted to carry it through. He would have liked to give the office of Keeper of the Seals to Malesherbes; but Malesherbes, afraid of the post, declined it in advance. What is more, no one else wanted this burdensome, dangerous ministry. Finally Louis XVI promised to dismiss the two ministers when the time came to leave Compiègne. He wanted to enjoy these beautiful days in peace: the gravity of the decision frightened him.

Yet when Terray was absent for a little while between 20 and 23 August, there was a rumour that he had been dismissed, and Maurepas spoke of it again to the king. Louis XVI admitted that he would not be sorry to send Maupeou away, but as for Terray he said, 'I regret it and I should very much like to keep him; but he is too much of a knave. It is a pity. It is a great pity.'

'I regret it too,' said Maurepas, 'for I thought highly of his work, as I have always told you. But even so it is impossible to keep him. We have his successor in M. Turgot.'

The place of Keeper of the Seals still had to be filled, as well as the ministry of the marine, which Turgot would leave. They discussed the men who might hold these offices. 'I shall go on thinking about it,' said the king, 'and on Tuesday I will let you know my decision.' During the afternoon he carried out some work on the navy with Turgot and for a long while they spoke of savings that could be made. They got on well together, both being straightforward men; but the king spoke no further on the matter.

On the morning of 24 August Maurepas came into the study at ten o'clock, carrying nothing in his hands. This surprised the king. Maurepas told him that he had an urgent matter to deal with, one that called for no papers. 'The doubt in which you leave public opinion is having a very bad effect on your present ministers: they flounder in uncertainty and they are not despatching their affairs.' He urged the king to reach a decision. 'Yes, I am determined to change them,' said the king. 'I shall do so on Saturday, after the *Conseil des Dépêches*.' But Maurepas pressed him still more urgently, saying that immediate action was essential. Too much time had been lost already. 'I am sorry,' said the king. 'I am overwhelmed by all this business and I am only twenty. The whole thing confuses me.'

To induce him to come to a decision Maurepas reminded him that his function was not to attend to details but to choose upright ministers. 'Is yours an honest man? If he is not, change him. That is what your function consists of.' Then, when the king stated that he had made up his mind, Maurepas questioned him about those who were to be appointed in the place of the dismissed ministers. 'Have you decided about the successors? For everything should be finished together. Uncertainty about offices are harmful to business and it brings intrigues into existence.' 'Yes, I have made up my mind: M. Turgot shall have finance. M. de Miromesnil shall be Keeper of the Seals and M. de Sartine is to go to the Admiralty: a messenger must be sent.'

As he left, Maurepas begged the king's pardon for having spoken with too much heat. 'Oh no, do not be afraid of that,' said the king, laying his hand upon his arm. 'I am convinced of your integrity and that is enough for me. It will give me great pleasure if you always tell me the truth with such force.'

Maurepas went to see Turgot at once, told him everything that had happened and sent him to the king, while he went on to speak to Terray. The king received Turgot with an affection that touched him.

'My words are all in a certain disorder,' he said to the king, 'for I feel flustered and confused.'

'I know that you are diffident, but I also know that you are determined and upright and that I could not make a better choice. I sent you to the Admiralty for a while in order to come to know you.'

'Sire, I must ask your permission to put my general ideas in writing – my general ideas or, if I may presume to say so, my conditions as to how you will have to support me in this office; for I must acknowledge that the slight knowledge that I have of it makes me tremble.'

'Yes, yes,' said the king, 'just as you please. But I give you my word in advance,' he added, taking Turgot's hands, 'that I will enter into all your views and that I shall always support you in the bold part that you will have to play.' The two men were so near to tears that they were obliged to separate.

And that was how the leader of the French *philosophes* became the financial minister of the most Christian of the Most Christian Kings who had reigned in France since Saint Louis.

The true affection that united these two men, the most straight-forward in the kingdom, could not prevent the clash between them when they reached the essential questions, those that affected men's hearts and souls. But they began by being on the best possible terms, since for the moment they were concerned only with practical matters in which their painstaking habits con-corded, each being devoted to hard work.

On 1 September the king returned to Versailles. From then onwards he preferred this palace to all others. Here he was at home; to some degree he could escape from the unceasing pre-sence of the courtiers, servants and spies. He could climb to his attic and work there at his bench; he could slip away to his library and his books; he could pay the queen a little visit, see Mesdames, be with his dogs . . .

Turgot was pleased, also. He installed himself high up under the roof in a quiet refuge where he could work, and he resumed his regular visits to Paris. He looked upon Louis XVI as a disciple and an admirer. They both of them had such scrupulous hearts that at first they neither of them noticed that they gave the same words opposite meaning, and that for each the same glow of enthusiasm had contradictory objects.

When it was contrasted with Maurepas' supple, feminine spirit, Turgot's direct bluntness could not but please the king; and although because of his meticulous ways and because he grew tired even Turgot's best friends admitted that he was a slow and tedious worker, Louis XVI took a liking to his method. The king was young, in a good state of health, and he had a great deal to learn: Turgot's schoolmasterly manner suited him. They spent long hours alone together, planning the country's happiness. Their first action was obvious – domestic free trade in corn. This was one of the basic ideas of economic doctrine of which Turgot was the patriarch (not undisputed, however). The late Dauphin had supported it in council in 1763 and 1764, and he had spoken about it in his son's presence. The decree was accepted by the council without any difficulties on 13 September 1774. Turgot received the ovation that he had expected. There were scarcely any complaints. Yet one anxiety haunted the king and Maurepas: the harvest had been bad. Woe to the government if prices climbed too high in the spring! But this was still autumn. And there were plenty of other things to worry about.

The great anxiety during this autumn of 1774 was the question of the Parlements.

Because he was an honest man and did not wish to lay violent hands upon private property nor force through a *coup d'état*, and because out of faithfulness to his father's memory he had taken M. de Maurepas as his adviser, King Louis XVI was led to re-establish the Parlement banished by Louis XV in 1771.

Chapter III

That upright man the king

THE KING WAS STILL ANXIOUS. HE HAD FOLLOWED THE
best advice and he had followed his own conscience; he had even
followed his father's counsels of long ago, for the late Dauphin
had been of the opinion the monarchy was not viable without the
great intermediary bodies. But Louis XVI was perfectly aware of
the weapons he was giving to unreliable subjects and blundering
magistrates. He tried to calm himself by reading the papers and
pamphlets that thought highly of him. In the *Nouvelles à la main*,
usually so irreverent and critical, he found articles of this kind:

> There is nothing more comforting at this painful time
> when the nation is lamenting the loss of its monarch, than
> the manner in which his grandson has behaved since his
> death – the manner in which he, together with the adorable
> princess who has succeeded to the crown with him, concerns
> himself with the duties of his great office. All the information
> that comes in minute by minute increases the nation's love
> for them. How can the French people conceivably avoid
> carrying their affection for their masters to idolatrous lengths!

Applause reached Paris from every part of France and Europe. It meant something, to have rallied a disunited public opinion in this way and to have brought Europe back to the view that France was a strong country, a nation led by a young and popular king!

He looked at the picture that Madame Louise had given him and that stood there in front of him. The inscription read 'For the eldest son of the Church, Louis XVI, by the grace of God King of France and Navarre.' Then came these words, an anagram of the inscription – an anagram, naturally, of the French in French. 'His reign, already determined by his uncommon virtue, will be that of the Faith.' And to this there was added these verses:

> *August, no: Louis. Better than Apelles' brush*
> *It paints your heart. It bears within itself*
> *A fortunate conjunction, the likeness true*
> *Both of the Christian and the mighty king.*

And that, to be sure, was just what he hoped to be.

There were songs to be heard everywhere, songs that sprang from cheerfulness and that were full of affection for him; and they were sung to applaud his happy accession. Art, craftsmanship and fashion all joined hands to celebrate it. Everywhere there was to be seen the shagreen snuff-box decorated with a medallion of Louis XVI and Marie-Antoinette and with the inscription 'Sorrow's Comfort' – shagreen and sorrow both being *chagrin* in French. The man who thought of this and who sold it made a fortune. Another had an even greater success: he had the idea of setting medallions of the Father of the People, Louis XII, and of the good King Henri IV on his boxes. The legend underneath read 'XII and IV make XVI'.

On the plinth of Henri IV's statue on the Pont-Neuf an unknown hand set a placard: Resurrexit.

Such a great many good omens for a youthful king!

The queen danced; and the king was glad that she danced. While she did so she was not busying herself with politics. She danced twice a week, on Mondays and Wednesdays. There never had been so brilliant a carnival as that of 1775. Entrancing quadrilles brought the royal family and the whole court together. Mourning was left off on Monday, 9 December 1774: to begin with the women had to appear in white taffeta trimmed with gauze and the men in blue velvet coats and white waistcoats edged with blue; then later everyone dressed in the manner of Henri IV's days. The men wore the clothes of that time, with tall plumes, and the women high stiff collars and feathered coiffures of an astonishing height.

On 23 January 1775 the king himself opened the ball, dressed in the style of Henri IV: a quadrille of thirty-seven men and thirty-seven women accompanied him. A second quadrille was made up of people dressed as mountebanks; the third, in which there danced the queen, was all dressed in Tyrolean costumes, and the fourth as Indians. The queen stayed until half past three in the morning. It was a dazzling spectacle. All Paris heard about it, and at the Opéra she received the ovation due to a queen and a prima donna. She found it quite intoxicating.

There was no kind of imprudence that she did not commit. She was far more anxious to be the queen of fashion than of France, and she surrounded herself with a frivolous, hare-brained set – Coigny, Lauzun, Ligne, Besenval, all of them irresponsible, flighty creatures.

She could not manage to receive her lumpish brother Maximilian, who was travelling under the name of Comte de Burgau, with enough discretion to avoid another open disagreement with the princes of the blood (beginning of 1775).

She became infatuated with the Comte de Guines, the French ambassador to England – and a most unworthy ambassador too, for he plotted with Choiseul and Spain in favour of war, and he amused himself by gambling on the London stock exchange.

Once again Louis XVI was well aware that strong feelings were mounting up and that the queen was compromising herself. She was too vain not to want to meddle with everything and too trifling to understand what it was all about: whenever she interfered she left everything in a state of hopeless muddle.

So the king was alone, and he took refuge in his workshop. He had ordered all the trophies of his hunting days as Dauphin to be arranged along the staircase that led to his private rooms. On the first floor, in a handsome drawing-room whose blue velvet gilt armchairs represented the only expenditure that he had ordered on settling in, he hung engravings of his kingdom and drawings of the canals of France; on the next floor there was his geography room, with his plans, maps, globes, armillary spheres and all his instruments – upon the table there was always to be seen a map that he was roughing out. On the third floor he had set up the wood-working lathe and all the ingenious tools that he had inherited from Louis XV; he used them when he worked with Duret. On the fourth floor there was his library, two rooms which contained everything published in his reign and his family papers. Above this he had had a forge installed, with two anvils and his blacksmith's tools. When he could not hunt he took great pleasure in this hard but delicate work. He hid it from the queen and the court, for they were of the opinion that it was stupid, and they preferred cards or racing.

Lastly, at the very top of the palace, the king had the delight of a little raised turret, where he could sit in an armchair with a telescope and see what was happening in every corner of Versailles. He was short-sighted and he had always been obliged to see things dimly, so it can be imagined how great a pleasure he took in being able to make out certain objects with clear precision. But this too was blamed, and held against him.

The habit of criticizing the king, which had been made fashionable by Choiseul, persisted among the grander sort of people in spite of his popularity. Only Maurepas, who saw him close at hand, began to understand the extraordinary mistake that everybody was making in their opinion of Louis XVI; but it was not in his interest to say too much about it, and he preferred to let his feeling in the matter hang like a veil of affectionate collusion between a youthful king and an experienced minister. This indeed was the chief source of the intimacy that had grown up between them and of the pleasant collaboration that brought them together in hard, painstaking work. But there was also another

source. Although Maurepas seemed no more Catholic, no more
devoted to tradition, no more attached to the ancient principles of
the monarchy than the mass of the courtiers, at least as an intelligent Epicurean he did understand that in order to live and die
contentedly he had to help the king save the monarchic and
Catholic France into which he had been born. Maurepas preserved
a wisdom that bound him to the king and that no one else possessed, not even M. Turgot.

Turgot had a lively intelligence and he was a very cultivated
man; he had a great deal of benevolence and administrative ability;
but he lacked common sense and a feeling for reality. He was passionately devoted to his principles and he was in a hurry to apply
them, thereby putting them into jeopardy. Without taking the
bad harvest into account he had decreed free trade for corn on the
home market at a moment when the poorer people, from one end
of France to another, were in the grip of an instinctive dread of
the high cost of living, of famine and of the cornering of stocks.
There were bitter complaints of the dearness and the scarcity of
wheat from many parts of the country. But Turgot was by no
means on his guard when at the end of April he was told in rapid
succession that the price of wheat was rising excessively at Paris
and at Rouen, that there were disturbances at Ervy, in Champagne
and at Metz, and that positive riots had broken out first at Rheims
and then at Dijon, where a mill had been pillaged of its corn.

By order of the king du May gathered considerable forces in
the neighbourhood of Paris – about twenty-five thousand men.
Biron, one of Turgot's supporters and colonel of the Gardes-
Françaises, was in command of this 'Army of Paris', and he had
strict orders: furthermore all the garrisons in central France were
warned to be ready for action. Thus the 'flour war' came to an end.

By recalling the Parlement and making peace everywhere the
king had parried the blow in advance. His authority emerged
stronger from the battle and his personal standing was much increased in the eyes of all who had seen his vigorous manner of
dealing with the trouble. Yet at court and among the public the
rumour was spread that he had been weak, that he had wanted to
harangue the rioters, that he had lost his nerve and had lowered

the price of bread to satisfy them. All this was untrue. Every one of these accusations was applicable to the Prince de Poix. But the slander, launched by Choiseul, was so hardy and long-lived that from that day onwards Poix' misconduct lay upon the shoulders of Louis XVI.

On the other hand, when they were speaking of Turgot, people said, 'What a ferocious man! In spite of the king's attitude he has punished the officials and the rioters most savagely. And what high-handedness towards the other ministers!' M. de Maurepas was deeply impressed by it. The night sitting of the council on 4 May struck his friendship with Turgot a deadly blow. Maurepas was of the opinion that it should be taken with a smile, that all this mere sound and fury should not be turned into an unduly grave affair. Turgot mobilized the troops of half the kingdom, wrote several hundreds of letters and committed himself entirely. The contrast between their nature and their methods thus became perfectly evident, and from that moment M. de Maurepas decided that he had made a foolish error in bringing this hothead into the council.

In the king's eyes Turgot was a righteous man, a good man to ask for advice and to employ because he was known to be wise and honest; but the king also thought him a man devoted to a system and to a party, or rather a clique. The Maréchal de Biron had not behaved any better than Le Noir at the time of the riot in Paris, but Turgot dismissed Le Noir at once, because he did not belong to his group, and he kept Biron. The king liked Turgot's energy, which helped him to appreciate his own; but he was beginning to know him for what he was, a 'reforming *philosophe*'.

After these events the older courtiers said, 'The Encyclopedists are reigning.' And in fact the Encyclopedists were trying to win over the king and to push him into a position that would be convenient for them.

A curious work that came out during these days, *The Life of Louis XVI since his Accession*, provides evidence of this. These dialogues between a Pole and a Russian speak in the highest terms of the 'great and righteous' king's philosophical labours and of the work of Turgot, 'that man of learning and of genius'. The 'great Choiseul' is not forgotten, and the Parlement is praised to the skies. 'How happy is a nation,' exclaims the author, 'when it is governed by a righteous king and when his chief wish is to win his people's friendship by doing all he can to make them happy!' The book also traces out his path for him: he is going to dismiss the farmers of the revenue and summon an assembly of deputies from all the parlements in France in order to make laws of an all-embracing justice and to sweep away abuses. In this way he will fulfil his ambition and become Louis the Just. The book ends with a piece of advice: he should have himself crowned in Paris; it would cost less and it would make a better impression.

This was Turgot's opinion also. He told the king that the coronation at Rheims would be very expensive and that it would be difficult to supply the town properly, whereas in Paris everything would be much easier; a coronation there would attract more foreigners, and it would delight the people of the capital. It would also be an opportunity for changing the oath, which was really offensively Gothic with its sections that obliged the king to exterminate heretics and never to forgive duellists. Louis XVI attended to what M. Turgot had to say, and took notice of the newspaper campaign against the 'expensive' journey to Rheims: he thanked Turgot for his frankness with a friendly good will that left no disagreeable feeling behind it. But he set off for Rheims, firmly determined to take the oath that his ancestors had taken before him, and to do so in the course of a ceremony like those his forbears had known for seven hundred years, whatever other people might think and whatever it might cause him to do or to suffer in later days.

E

Chapter IV

The Most Christian King

LOUIS XVI AND HIS SUITE LEFT VERSAILLES ON MONDAY,
5 June, for Compiègne, where he rested and hunted the boar for
two days. Then they went on to Fismes, where he supped and
spent the night of Thursday, the eighth. The weather was fine
and dry and all the relays were ready, thanks to the twenty
thousand horses that had been brought together for that purpose.
On Friday, 9 June, accompanied by the queen and in the greatest
splendour, he made his entry into the royal city of Rheims, all
hung with tapestry and flags, crowded with spectators and overflowing with delight. The weather was still perfect. A mile or so
from the town the king changed into his state coach, with its
gilding and its painted panels and its tall plumes at each corner;
the two grenadier companies, shining with gold, were drawn
up on either side of the door. Ahead of the king's coach there advanced other splendid carriages and the royal household.

At five o'clock they reached the cathedral in the midst of a
magnificent sound of trumpets, drums and the great bell ringing
its loudest. Standing there in the middle of the ancient square with
its Gothic houses this huge, strange and splendid coach had an

extraordinarily brilliant effect. The king stepped out, went into the empty church and knelt at the prie-Dieu in front of the altar, while his brothers and all the members of his suite knelt behind him. After saying a few prayers the king walked slowly up through the gallery that led from the cathedral to his rather cramped lodgings in the archbishop's palace. There he withdrew, having made a few friendly remarks to the courtiers he knew best. Everyone was impressed by his look of kindness.

At four o'clock in the afternoon of the tenth the king went to the cathedral for vespers and the sermon upon the coronation, which was meant to prepare him for the next day's ceremony. The Duc de Duras, the current gentleman in waiting, and the architects of the Menus-Plaisirs[1] had seen fit to add to the beauty of the cathedral by building a classical façade in wood with a gallery that connected it to the palace, where the king stayed; and in the nave they had also set up an immense gilt wooden construction with columns. This narrowed the choir and placed a kind of classical theatre within the most beautiful of Gothic churches; but the Duc de Duras thought it very fine. The Duc de Croÿ did not entirely approve, but he admired it. The king took no notice of it, for his thoughts were upon God and his destiny. They were still there throughout the long and pompous sermon that the Archbishop of Aix preached to him.

There was something sublime about the opening, and it evoked an applause more in keeping with the spectators' enthusiasm than with the time or the place. The rest of the sermon unfolded slowly: it dealt with the duties of a King of France and then with the perils that beset him. The speaker showed France as a country capable, if she did not give way to her faults, of being the universal arbiter and of bringing about the world's happiness. As he was a parliamentarian at heart he dwelt upon the respect due to the laws and upon their essential function in the state. All this time the king prayed. After the service he returned to his own quarters to rejoin the queen, who was present at the ceremonies but who took no part in them.

On the eleventh the church was full by four o'clock in the

[1] The department in charge of ceremonies and court festivities.

morning: it was full and overflowing with dignitaries and ladies in the most brilliant of robes, wearing the plumes that the queen had brought into fashion. At six o'clock the service began with prime: at half past seven the king appeared, dressed according to custom in the long robe with silver lace that he had slept in; and he was supported by the bishops of Laon and Beauvais. The clergy went out to meet him. Then they all came back into the cathedral to the sound of military fanfares. Louis XVI was followed by the Constable of France, represented by the Maréchal de Tonnerre, by the Chancellor of France, represented by Miromesnil, and by the Prince de Soubise, representing the Grand Master: all in full robes and wearing crowns. After them came the Chancellor, wearing his cap of office, the gilded toque. The very aged Archbishop of Rheims, M. de La Roche-Aymon, thanks to potions and to an extraordinary effort of will, managed to officiate throughout the whole service, which lasted six hours, although it had been shortened because of his age and because it was thought proper not to overtire the king in the summer heat.

It was a dream-like sight, the king there alone in the middle of the church beneath a great canopy, the nave filled with magnificently attired lords, the red robes of the bishops in the choir, the blazing jewels of the queen and the ladies in the galleries. The archbishop first gave the holy water and then chanted the Veni Creator; and then came the Holy Ampulla. Sext was said, and the archbishop robed himself for the mass. Then he came to the king and required him to swear to continue and to preserve the Church's privileges. When he had done so, two bishops raised the king, who faced the congregation. Formerly the people were asked whether they accepted the king and the crowd replied with acclamations: for Louis XVI this ceremony was left out. And many people were displeased by the omission.

The king read the oath in a clear, firm voice, in Latin, stressing each word and speaking with great earnestness. Everyone felt that as he spoke he was praying. He promised to maintain the peace of the Church, to prevent depredation and iniquity, to see that justice was observed, and to set himself whole-heartedly to the extermination of heretics. When this was over, he swore the oath of the Order of the Holy Ghost, and lastly the oath never to pardon any duellist. After these essential rites the Archbishop blessed all the regalia, girded him with the sword of Charlemagne, which was for the protection of the Church, the widow and the orphan, and put on his spurs and took them off again.

The king lay at full length on a square of violet velvet and the archbishop did the same at his side, while the litanies of the saints were said over them. When these were finished the archbishop, sitting at the upper end of the altar, recited a series of prayers over the king as he knelt before him; then the archbishop consecrated him, anointing him on the bare skin with six unctions that conferred upon him the first orders of the Church, but not the priesthood. This done, the gloves and the ring were blessed and the archbishop handed the king Charlemagne's sceptre, a great silver wand six feet tall, and his hand of justice, saying fresh prayers as he did so.

Then the coronation properly so called began: in the midst of the senior peers assembled the archbishop held the great crown of Charlemagne over the king's head, saying, 'May God crown you with the crown of glory and of justice . . . and you will come to the everlasting crown.'

He set the crown upon the head of Louis XVI, and the peers supported it a finger's-breadth above his hair. A wave of feeling overcame all those present, and it affected the king profoundly; meanwhile the archbishop, taking off his mitre, blessed him once more and honoured him with still more prayers.

After this came the enthronement. The king, who had been on his knees all the time, was raised, and they dressed him in the great royal-blue robe, sprinkled with fleurs-de-lis and ending in a long train. Wearing the robe and with the crown on his head, Charlemagne's sceptre in his right hand and Charlemagne's hand of justice in his left, he was solemnly led to his great throne, raised very high between four tall columns, visible from everywhere: at the same time the great doors were opened, the people crowded in, birds were set free, all the trumpets rang out, and the enraptured, overwhelmed assembly burst into tears and cries of 'Long live the king!' There was a universal transport of joy. It found its expression in loud, prolonged cheering when the archbishop, having prayed for the happiness of the king and his family, cried, 'Vivat rex in aeternum!' Then came the Te Deum, and the mass which completed the ceremony, the most splendid that had been seen for half a century.

Louis XVI's radiant happiness was apparent in all his movements. He took the air after dinner and allowed the crowd to approach him freely.

On the twelfth he rested. On the thirteenth and fourteenth there were fresh ceremonies, including a cavalcade. He touched four hundred poor people for the king's evil.

On the fifteenth, which was Corpus Christi, he walked in the procession with his eyes fixed upon the Host in an ecstasy of joy and gratitude, before a huge and admiring crowd.

After dinner he left for Compiègne, as delighted with his subjects as they were with him. He spoke of this in the regular letters that he continually sent Maurepas from Rheims, and of which this is the last:

> I have quite recovered from all my fatigue . . . I was grieved that you were not with me to share in the gratification that I have experienced here. It is but right and just that I should work for the happiness of a people that contributes to mine. I shall set about doing so. I hope you have reflected upon the means that we discussed together. For my part I have thought as much as I could in the press of the ceremonies. The task is formidable; but with a good heart and with your advice I hope to carry it through. Farewell until Monday evening, when we shall see one another. Louis.

These letters caused a sensation. It was thought that the queen would come back from Rheims defeated, and this view was not mistaken.

There was a continuing need for vigilance: although Europe seemed calm, this was not at all the case in America, where violent fighting was going on. The colonists seemed determined to carry their rebellion through to the end, and England was sending troops, stores and ships across the sea. If the French wanted to avoid a surprise like that of 1754 they would have to take precautions. It was decided in council to send fifteen thousand men to the French West Indies, so as to put them out of reach of any sudden attack: but the troops did not leave: the king remained in two minds. Spain, in the person of Aranda, urged war with England. Turgot would not hear a word of it. He insisted upon the urgent necessity for economy. Everything remained in suspense.

La Vrillière resigned at last, and the queen very much wanted Sartine to be given his place, with Ennery, a friend of Choiseul's, taking Sartine's post at the Admiralty. Turgot wished to fill the council with his friends: he wanted Malesherbes at once, to be followed by Francès, the brother of his great friend Mme Blondel.

The king listened to everyone, and then on Maurepas' advice he chose Malesherbes, whose independence he liked and whose wit he admired. There was only one obstacle left: this was Malesherbes, who, out of idleness, scepticism and prudence, had just refused the place three times running.

Louis XVI wrote to him:

> M. Turgot has told me of your dislike for the post I have offered you. I still think that your love for the country's welfare should overcome your repugnance; and you cannot believe how you would please me by accepting it, at least for a while, if you do not choose to make up your mind to it entirely. I think this is absolutely necessary for the good of the state. Louis.

All this vexed, flattered and worried Malesherbes to the edge of a nervous breakdown: he accepted, saying that he would never stop talking about his retirement, and that although he would be able to fulfil his legislative functions he would not be able to deal with 'administrative detail'. Sartine remained at the Admiralty and became a member of the council.

At Versailles the autumn came bringing with it rain, ill-natured gossip and intrigue. Mme d'Artois was so presumptuous as to have a son, although the queen had none. Marie-Antoinette wept with rage, and once more there were rumours of the king's impotence and the necessity for an operation. She was angry with him for his refusal to grant dukedoms to the Marquis du Châtelet and the Prince de Beauvau, Choiseul's protégés, and for expelling Durfort from the court, merely because he did not pay his debts. By way of revenge she continually visited Mme de Lamballe's Orleanist salon and the Princesse de Guéménée's dubious gambling-table.

Louis XVI hunted every day in the pouring rain and he went to the theatre three times a week, but he went on working hard, preferably with Maurepas or Vergennes. By a subtle manœuvre he brought the Comtesse Jules de Polignac into the queen's circle; she was the most moving beauty in Europe, and Maurepas knew her well – he was her secret adviser. In a few days the queen was overcome, and that left the king time for work.

Turgot gave him a report on the assembly of the clergy. At the end of its meeting it voted a 'free gift' of sixteen million, which satisfied the minister, and it railed furiously against the 'impious authors' upon whom it called down the wrath of the king. Could not the clergy itself do with a little reformation?

Chapter V

Louis the Strict, or the Puce-coloured Year

ONE DAY THAT WINTER THE QUEEN WAS CHOOSING material; she had an exquisite taste for these things, and the king delighted in watching her. She fixed upon a rather dark cloth with a charming gleam. 'Ha!' cried the king, 'that is the colour of a flea' – *puce* in French. The queen adopted both the material and the name. Everyone wore it that winter; and 1776 was a puce-coloured year.

The great excitements of 1775, the riots, the coronation and the ministerial changes were over; the weather had grown very cold; the queen went for long sledge-rides through Paris at night with the whole court, by the light of torches. It was extremely beautiful. The king hunted and worked with his ministers, particularly with M. Turgot, who was still confined to his room with gout. The effect of his disease was to make Turgot work all the harder; he felt that he was behindhand with his programme of reforms and he tried to double his pace.

At the beginning of January the king and the council accepted Turgot's draft decrees; but as early as 21 January 1776 the Parlement, incited to it by the Prince de Conti and using the fiery Duval d'Espréménil as a mouthpiece, condemned an essay on the corvée[1] by Condorcet and another entitled *Disadvantages of the Feudal Rights* by Boncerf. These pamphlets supported the Controller-General's work and they prepared the way for his reforms: they served as an opportunity for Parlement and the privileged classes to make it clear to Turgot that they would not accept them. All this occasioned a great deal of noise. But the king put an end to it by a solemn *lit de justice*[2] on 13 May which compelled the Parlement to give way. Louis XVI displayed a great deal of strength, calmness and courage. Everything passed off well.

Yet the Parlement would not accept defeat. And what was more important, the queen increased her manœuvres against him. She kept up a secret correspondence with Choiseul, and she even met him at the ball at the Opéra, as though by chance, during the 1776 carnival. It was he who dictated the main lines of her campaign.

The king knew Marie-Antoinette too well to pay attention to her plots. But Pezay, his secret adviser, came out against Turgot at the same time, and he showed the king his mistakes and errors.

In the course of this pamphlet-war it became clear to the king that Turgot was intolerant and ruthless. With the king's consent Malesherbes had just set up a commission to restrict the use of *lettres de cachet* – that is to say of arbitrary imprisonment – yet at the same time Turgot was shamelessly locking up pedlars, authors, publishers and printers. Rightly but ferociously he persuaded the king to recall Guines from London, where the ambassador's treachery was a matter of common knowledge, and he came very near to sending him to prison. Louis XVI was more prudent, and he avoided driving Guines and his protectors to extremities.

One of Turgot's choices caused the king a great deal of anxiety of another kind. As soon as he was in office Saint-Germain set about reforming the French army with such ardour and with such

---

[1] The peasant's unpaid feudal labour or their unpaid statute labour on the roads.
[2] When the king presided over the Parlement in person the sitting was called a *lit de justice*: on these occasions the court was unable to refuse registration of the decrees the king introduced.

uncompromising zeal that passionate protests arose from every side. Maurepas was in doubts as to his wisdom, and Vergennes grew uneasy.

The troubles in America were growing worse; and England and Spain were increasing their armed strength. The king wondered whether at this moment it was advisable to put himself into the hands of a reforming minister in a poor state of health, one who was undertaking so wide a reform that it must need ten or twenty years or more and exclusive attention throughout all this time. To be sure, Turgot had just drawn up a remarkable report for the king, who wanted to answer a question from the King of Spain: in this report he stated that all the American colonies would soon gain their freedom by themselves, and that there was no need either to intervene or to take precautions that might draw France into a war with England, since France could only gain by the destruction caused by England in her American colonies and by the triumph of the English crown over its rebellious subjects – England would in this way destroy her own power and the French would have the time to build their country anew in peace. The king did not believe that England wanted peace: he only knew that M. Turgot insisted upon having it, and that at a moment when it was least certain. It was impossible to ignore the dangers of this demand.

One day when they were talking confidentially, Maurepas told the king that the time had come for him to make up his mind about his government. If the king wanted a Turgot ministry then he ought to grant M. Turgot all he wanted – the choice of his fellow-ministers and the first place among them. If not, he ought to dismiss him without delay. Now the king did want Turgot as a minister; but he did not want a Turgot ministry at all, nor a Turgot revolution. Louis XVI felt esteem and affection for Turgot; but working with him had by no means increased his admiration. M. Turgot worked slowly, in a somewhat heavy-handed and a very schoolmasterish way.

Louis XVI's modesty would have accepted this if Turgot had not seemed to him ignorant of a great many matters. He had understood nothing at all of what went on at Rheims. He saw the ceremony as nothing but a series of fine words with a social meaning. With a satisfied gaze and his hair in disorder he wondered at it all. But for Louis the very basis, the prime mover, of his life as king lay in this – in communion with God and with his people in God. The coronation gave him the means of bearing the overwhelming burden of kingship without being either overwhelmed or terrified by it. Anyone who saw him take communion or touch the four hundred victims of the king's evil understood that for Louis XVI Christ was an immediate reality, a personal as much as an absolute fact. The divine presence was so clear to him that it preserved him from any kind of bigotry, just as it did from all anxiety. It was perfectly easy for him to put up with the prudent scepticism of Maurepas, who was dubious even about his own doubts. But every day it became harder for him to work with Turgot, a humanitarian materialist and the apostle of a social humanitarianism.

Turgot explained his plans of setting up municipalities to the king at length: it was a matter of bringing the people to understand, to formulate and to realize their wishes by means of a double education, both intellectual and political. Each parish was to have a municipal council, elected by the freeholders, to discuss immediate material requirements: these councils would send delegates to the canton to form an assembly made up solely of landed proprietors: this assembly would attend to the interests of the canton and would delegate some of its members to join the delegates of other provinces in a national assembly, empowered to discuss the material interest of the whole country (taxes, roads, police, and so on).

So that these men should have the necessary information, a lay schoolmaster was to be installed in each parish; he would teach the children and the adults that true science of economy and patriotism which must be the basis of all modern states. In this way, according to M. Turgot, there would be brought into being a truly modern and truly happy France, without touching the clergy, who could go on preaching the good word and singing vespers; or the nobles, who could still go to war and hunt; or the Parlements, which would continue to hand out justice; or the king, who would be the executive.

All this sounded very fine; but it meant the end of that kingdom of France, Catholic and hierarchical, which Louis XVI had promised to maintain at his coronation. Instead of an unruly but traditionalist Parlement, he would have to deal with a National Assembly, violent and hungry for innovation. Money would rule the country. After what had been seen in May 1775 the king was far from sure of M. Turgot's skill and sense of timing. If there had been such a fuss about a measure desired by the great majority of the country, what would it be like for a purely personal scheme that clashed with the interests of the clergy, the nobility, the parlements and virtually everyone who held a public office in France? Besides, if the work of this body were to depend upon the education of the people in civics and political economy, how long would the country have to wait before all was running smoothly? And would England, Austria, Prussia and even Russia wait all this time without interfering in French affairs?

Faced with a plan of this nature the king decided to dismiss Turgot. Here Louis XVI was applying the doctrine that he formulated a little later: 'It is easy to see what actually exists, but one can only have a notion of what does not; and one should not undertake dangerous enterprises if one cannot see where they are leading to.' As soon as Maurepas had introduced M. de Clugny, the naval intendant at Bordeaux, an intelligent hardworking man who was well acquainted with financial questions, Louis XVI sent Bertin to ask Turgot to resign and to let him know what the king could do to help him to live in comfort. It was a sudden measure (11 and 12 May 1776) but there was no harshness about it and everyone had foreseen it since January: Turgot was the only person to be surprised. He wrote a ten-page letter that the king sent back unopened; the barrier between them could not be explained if it had not been felt, and since Turgot had felt nothing at Rheims he would neither feel nor understand now. Talking the matter over could only wound him and waste time.

There was no time to be wasted. As soon as Malesherbes had been replaced by Amelot (a second-rate mind, it is true, but a prudent one, adequate for a post with no great problems) and Turgot by Clugny, it was decided that Maurepas should preside over the financial council, in order, with the king's consent, to oversee the doings of the Controller-General. The protests of Turgot's supporters were ignored; it was said among them that the dismissal was owing to Pezay's calumnies or to letters that had been forged by his enemies and then intercepted.

Louis XVI wanted to calm these strong feelings. He wanted to carry out the duties of his office in peace. There was the review of the Gardes-Françaises and the Swiss Guard on the Sablons plain on 9 May, and the memorial service for Louis XV on the tenth at Notre-Dame de Versailles. He also had to attend to his family. The queen was still committing imprudences. One evening as she came back from Paris he said to her, 'Did they cheer you heartily in Paris?' The queen replied, 'No. It was a cold welcome.' 'It would seem that you did not have nearly enough feathers, Madame!' said the king. The queen angrily retorted, 'I should have liked to see you there, Sire, with your Saint-Germain and your Turgot. You would have been thoroughly booed.' The king burst out laughing.

He could not content himself with laughing in the case of Artois, whose debauchery was going beyond all limits. He lay with his wife's maids; and in February he organized an entertainment for all the most lewdly-inclined young men at court. The king put a stop to it and had the door guarded by the police. No one came in, and the dinner was eaten by the poor. In June Artois caught measles and he was very ill: Monsieur had it after him.

Louis XVI wanted peace at home and in the state. As Clugny's successor he took the worthy M. Taboureau des Réaux, the northern intendant, and at the Treasury he installed M. Necker, the Genevan whom people cried up so. M. Necker entertained the *philosophes* and they approved of him; he flattered public opinion and it flattered him back: he had a big peasant face, the dignity of a man of wealth and the tact of a parvenu. But he was accommodating. And with him in charge there would be peace. It would be possible to get on with the work.

The news from America seemed so serious that it could no longer be overlooked: on 4 July 1776 the rebellious colonies declared themselves independent. They sent representatives to enter into commercial relations with France and to ask for discreet assistance (November 1776). The king did not want war with England but he certainly meant to take advantage of the United States' trade, and he saw to it that Mr Deane and Mr Lee should have talks, though with partners who could not compromise the French government. But on 24 December 1776 public opinion was much excited by the news that the famous Franklin, the man who had discovered the true nature of lightning, had just reached Versailles. 'What has he come for?' asked everyone in Paris; and the Comte d'Aranda camped in Vergennes' antechamber to ask 'What has he come for?' For his part Vergennes went to Louis XVI and asked, 'What are we going to do?'

1776 was over. A new year was beginning.

Chapter VI

King Louis XVI's great plan

THE WINTER BROUGHT QUIETNESS AND WORK BACK TO
Versailles. The rain fell and the high roads were empty: once New
Year's day was over the train of coaches dwindled away. Everyone stayed at home; and everyone, from the king to the humblest
footman in charge of keeping up the great fires, was busily at
work. Avoiding the misery of getting wet and seeing to it that
one was thoroughly, delightfully warm – these were the great
occupations of the season. This was also the time for casting
accounts, and the queen was vexed to find how deeply in debt she
was. And it was the time for making plans for the future: the king,
perfecting a lock in his attic workshop, pondered upon the
significance of the sudden arrival, in the midst of a November
storm, of this Benjamin Franklin, the grocer, journalist and
statesman, the master of thunder.

They tattled at court, they gossiped in the town: a singular man;
no wig, no sword, no clothes of the French kind at all – a brown
coat without any lace, long white hair falling each side of his face,
and on his head a fur cap like a Canadian trapper's! He excited the
liveliest curiosity in all quarters. M. le Comte d'Aranda's was so

violent that he could not bear it. It was his particular delight to explain things to people, saying 'You see what I mean? You follow me?' in a tone that was now domineering, now persuasive; but at present, with his desire to know frustrated, he grew sullen and glum. How could it possibly come about that he, His Catholic Majesty's ambassador, the masonic Grand Master, had not been the first to receive Brother Franklin's visit? How could it have occurred that this man who was said to be so knowing should in the first place have applied to these beggarly Frenchmen? Aranda could not understand it: he haunted Vergennes, who had received Franklin mysteriously at Versailles on 24 December and had seen him discreetly in Paris on the twenty-eighth. And he made an appointment with the American. Everyone came to see Franklin at his Hôtel de Hambourg, and they asked him innumerable questions: there was Caron de Beaumarchais who was later to trade with him; officers who wanted to try their fortune on American battlefields; and the Duc de Croy, who wanted to know Franklin's views on the North-West passage and the begetting of elephants. But the Sage was unswervingly prudent; without answering he too indulged himself in the asking of questions.

He asked the King of France, 'Would you like to be our ally?' And in his attic, filing away at his lock, the King of France pondered. 'What should be done about this Franklin? What should be done about the Insurgents? What should be done about America?' This was no doubt the most serious decision that he had had to make since he became king.

For he was king, this man who had seemed in no way ready for the crown and who had been so afraid of it. From now onwards he wore it proudly, since he did not feel unworthy of being king and since God had acknowledged him as such. These thirty-two months had transformed him. He was putting on flesh; he was growing stronger; he understood himself better. Whatever others might think, within himself he was still the same man that he had been before; he never ceased praying to God; at Christmas he was seen at vespers, at the three night masses, at matins, lauds, high mass again in the morning and then vespers once more. That was the source of his strength. And work was still his only companion.

He got up between six and seven in the morning and took some lemon-juice and a little dry bread. If the weather was fit he went out with the captain of his guard; at eight o'clock he came back for his official levee; then he went into his study and gave audience to those who had asked for it. After this he worked with his ministers. At eleven he went to mass, which lasted a quarter of an hour. Returning to his own quarters, he took his luncheon – a little pâté, a cutlet, some fruit, and a long glass of water to wash it all down. Often he would eat it standing, for Louis XVI was a frugal king. Then he went to see the queen and to visit his family: this done, he set himself to work or to read, and he lingered over it as long as he could. Often a member of the clergy would ask for an audience. If it was fine he would walk in the gardens or the park. And every evening, from seven o'clock until nine, he held a council – on Thursdays and Sundays the Council of State. At nine he gave his orders to the officers on duty and went to the apartments of Madame, the wife of Monsieur, where all the family supped together. At eleven o'clock exactly he rang and went to bed at once. He rarely slept more than six hours and often less, for he had so many duties. On days when he hunted (about twice a week in summer) or when there were banquets, the timetable changed. On Tuesdays he received the ambassadors.

Such was his life of work and seclusion. He had early grown used to secrecy, and he was the most reticent prince in Europe. No confidences with his wife, above all: that would merely mean confiding in Austria, the whole of Europe, Choiseul, and all the king's enemies.

The worst was undoubtedly the Abbé de Vermond, the queen's reader, Choiseul's agent and Brienne's confidential friend. He ruled Marie-Antoinette, and he often drafted her letters. He presumed to tell her confessor, the weak Abbé Mignot, what he should say to her. He handled Mercy skilfully and deceived him and through him the empress. He deceived everybody except Louis XVI, who would neither see him nor speak to him.

Louis XVI did his best to bring his wife to reason by kindness mingled with firmness. He showered presents on her, paid her debts and granted favours to her particular friends. And there he stopped.

He behaved in much the same way with Monsieur. A pleasant brotherly familiarity: Monsieur's gaiety and the king's jovial humour brought them together – that and their childhood. Nothing beyond that, however: Louis XVI saw an opponent in Provence.

Artois, for his part, was a real danger. Of the three brothers he seemed the only charmer, but also the only fool. He had an indiscriminating love for women, wenches, horses, houses and pictures. His taste was reliable only in the last two. And he instinctively chose the most undesirable men for his friends: Choiseul was his idol and Chartres his mentor. Those who had looked upon him as his family's hope changed their tune. Louis XVI never stopped scolding him and paying his debts. Most of the young men at court assiduously followed his example, and the king had nothing in common with them. Indeed, he had to make an effort to be civil to them; yet this effort had to be made, because he was the king and because they honoured him in coming to court. He therefore talked to them about hunting. After that he had nothing more to say.

He worked with his ministers, and that was the most important relationship. But now that he had been ruling for thirty-two months he knew that as soon as a minister was appointed he dreamt of becoming prime minister and of dominating the king, or else of pleasing his mistress by finding places for all her friends and overwhelming them with presents. Sometimes that did not prevent them from working well; but it did prevent the king from trusting them.

Yet he had a feeling of friendship for some of them: Maurepas seemed an upright man, and his wonderfully penetrating mind, his delicate discernment of character and his knowledge of business made him an unrivalled companion. Louis XVI admired him all the more since Maurepas loved France as she was and not a chimerical France of his own imagination. But Maurepas was worldly, and that prevented the king from reaching a complete understanding with him.

M. de Vergennes, in spite of his total lack of charm, pleased him more every day. He had a profound, serious mind that went thoroughly into each question and each man; he united discretion to reticence and even to affection, but for all that he was something of a great man. The king knew it. In the same way he would have liked to distinguish M. de Saint-Germain, for the old soldier's energy, his stern Christian faith and his uncompromising sense of discipline seemed to the king worthy of former times. But Saint-Germain was ill, much criticized and already half out of office. For the work in hand Louis XVI had to count chiefly upon himself.

What a task! The people were quiet, to be sure: what with the Christian religion and the great standing of the king, the few thousand men of the Maréchaussée, the mounted police force established by Louis XV, were enough to make the country and the roads the safest and the most peaceful in the world. Le Noir and his police kept such a good watch over Paris that there had not been a single murder recorded since 1769. Indeed, Le Noir had just found a criminal in Vienna whom Kaunitz had been looking for in Paris. The good and kindly populace was good and kindly still.

The danger lay elsewhere. The great nobles, the courtiers, the rich bourgeois of Paris and the great cities, and part of the clergy and the middling bourgeoisie were followers of the *philosophes*. They had an equal contempt for the king and for the common people, and they wanted to rule the country. Choiseul's government had given them both confidence and boldness, and they had plenty of effrontery too. They were not restrained by any form of morality. For them Christianity was no more than outward form.

It was at this time that Turgot and his political economists appeared, to set up a world founded upon expedient honesty. But the common people, who were still Christian, wanted nothing of it; and the fashionable people only did so in order to be able to profiteer and cheat. The abolished trade-guilds left chaos behind them: as soon as Turgot closed down the Poissy guild organization, which did exploit the poorer butchers to some extent, the richer butchers at once seized the whole of the market for themselves! In order to replace a morality based upon right and wrong that did not always work, and an aristocracy based upon birth – an aristocracy that was sometimes unfairly and wrongly used – Turgot brought forward an entirely vain morality based upon expediency, and an unfailingly vulgar supremacy of wealth.

Louis dreamt of saving that Christian France, the France of the masses, the ordinary people. To do this, it was necessary to recast a framework that was in many ways out of date; and at the same time it was necessary to maintain the unchanging true principles. But he could not do so all by himself. He needed helpers, a basis of support. This he could not find either in the upper clergy, who had joined the *philosophes*, nor the lower clergy, who were discontented with their wretched 500 livres a year and who were far from united.

In England, thanks to Whitefield's religious crusade, George III had the middle classes solidly behind the monarchy. There was nothing of the kind in France. In spite of shining figures here and there, Catholicism was half asleep.

Nor did the nobles provide any strength. The greatest among them, the families of Lorraine, Montmorency, Bouillon and so on, would not forgive the Bourbons their supremacy; and their hidden opposition in the parlements and the masonic lodges evoked still more opposition on the part of a considerable number of their fellow-nobles.

Even the lesser nobility stood aside: they were being squeezed between the peasants who were reaching up for wealth and the bourgeois who were reaching up for patents of nobility, and they were stifling. War was the only resource for this class, for war alone provided honour and money. But since 1763 there had been no war any more, and the king was disbanding his finest corps, the poor nobles' last refuge. Among many of them the king could make out a discontented, anti-government feeling; and this was encouraged by the Orléans, who gathered round them the most outstanding of the malcontents – Lauzun, Voyer, Guines, etc.

The French nobility no longer had leaders capable of leading, and they were blundering about aimlessly.

Parlement, which ought to have been a pillar of the state, was becoming the theatre for every kind of ambition, and it indulged in demagogy: it dreamt of being a sovereign power like the English parliament, and it declared that it represented the nation. By his prompt, mild action Louis XVI put it to silence, and Miromesnil kept it well under control; but the danger was still close at hand.

The common people were far more estimable; they were hard-working, cheerful, frugal and very thrifty; they hardly shared in any of the excesses of the richer classes, and they even seemed to be overcoming one of their worst faults, for the number of law-cases was falling throughout the whole country. They were still Christian and they were still deeply religious. But the confusion of the country's finances worried them. This was a danger to be watched closely. The riots of May 1775 had shown that the nobles and Parlement had their own ways of rousing the mob. In his talks with M. Turgot Louis XVI had learnt just how the factious nobles, ambitious parliamentarians and shameless pamphleteers could excite the scum of the towns and the drifting poverty-stricken rustics who could easily be dealt with by the police so long as they were scattered and unorganized, but who became formidable because of their numbers and their fluidity as soon as they had leaders and money. All these people had to be kept under control, and the financial question, now the key to all the rest, had to be solved without delay.

Turgot had laid this down. No one had denied it, but no one had been convinced: for a nation that is so taken up with internal affairs that it is incapable of any activity abroad is a nation in full decline, one that is given over as a prey to its enemies. Like Turgot, and even more than Turgot, Louis XVI wanted peace: ever since Louis XIV and his fateful words 'I loved war too much' the rulers of France had had a great longing for quietness. Vergennes knew it, and he represented himself to the king as the minister destined to preserve the peace of the world for him. He was one of those diplomats who love negotiation and who are remarkably good at it; no impulsive act was to be feared from him.

Yet his experience had shown him that in order to defend her own interests France had to be ready to make war, and that she had to be ready to seize a favourable opportunity if one should appear.

In one of his first reports to Louis XVI, one of those that bound the two men together in intellectual intimacy, he said, 'The utter contempt for the principles of justice and decency that is characteristic of the behaviour and the undertakings of some of the present-day powers must be a subject for the urgent consideration and indeed for precautionary measures on the part of those states that are guided by more salutary maxims and that do not set the righteous and the unrighteous upon the same level' (1774). And the minister concluded, 'The world respects any nation that is obviously in a position to put up a vigorous resistance and that, while not abusing its superior strength, desires only what is just and useful to all – peace and universal tranquillity.'

The king was in agreement with his minister upon all these points; he had placed Saint-Germain at the ministry of war to shake up the torpid French army and Sartine in the Admiralty to carry through its revival and to perfect its new organization. All this was expensive, but from henceforward the French navy was capable of holding its own with the fleets of any other nation whatsoever. If the opportunity were to come it would be possible to seize it.

Now here was M. Franklin appearing from over the seas with the offer of a treaty: was not this the opportunity that fate had in mind? This was the question that Louis XVI continually asked himself: he pondered upon it when he was working with his ministers, when he was alone in his study, and when he was in his workshop with the door closed behind him. Was this really the opportunity? Or was this the way to disappointment? M. Turgot's decision had not convinced Louis: the minister looked upon American democracy as too pure to be helped by France. The thought of such an outrage secretly shocked Turgot's Anglophilia. He wanted America to win as he might have wanted a geometrical problem to be solved, by the force of logic alone.

But M. Franklin did not see things in this light: he offered an alliance and he pressed to have it signed quickly. He did not hide the fact that if it were not signed the Insurgents might be reconciled with England, who, by way of a present to mark the remarriage, would not fail to deliver up to them that rich and succulent prey, the French West Indies. This was also what M. Vergennes was afraid of, and in a report for the king he wrote, 'We do not want to increase precautions and measures to such a degree as to alarm our neighbours, but on the other hand we must not be the victims of our own straightforward, disinterested attitude. The surprise attack we suffered in 1755 is one of those events in which horror ensures remembrance, although resentment may no longer exist.' Who indeed could forget that in 1755, in a time of complete peace, Admiral Boscawen fired upon two French ships that were carrying troops to Canada and that the English fleets took all the French merchantmen that they met with at sea – seven hundred of them, carrying ten thousand sailors and representing a value of a great many millions?

Certainly the French navy had never forgotten it, and the idea of revenge was very dear to the French naval heart. It was a factor that the king was always to bear in mind when he was making his calculations. Now in 1777 the French possessions in the West Indies were very wealthy and very vulnerable. There had already been discussions in council in 1776 as to the wisdom of sending troops and ships, and every time it had been renounced, in order not to provoke the English and in order not to bring on the disaster that the measure was intended to avoid. Now the worthy Franklin, in the name of a million and a half Americans, was offering an alliance that would be the best of protections for the French sugar islands and that would give France a youthful ally capable of helping her in her difficulties with the English.

There was another reason for looking most attentively at this aspect of the matter: Louis XVI was beginning to grow anxious about the country's alliances. He knew that Sweden was weakened and divided, a mere shadow of what it had been under Charles XII; France's great friend in the east, Poland, who had so often been so useful, appeared to be in the process of disappearing from the map of Europe as an independent power. Turkey seemed hardly any less weak or sick. The Austrian alliance, to be sure, was still extremely valuable. But it cost a great deal. With a flighty, ambitious sovereign like Joseph II there was the danger that it would draw France much farther than she wanted to go. Yet it remained essential for the maintenance of peace in Europe and for preventing Austria from following her natural bent – the English alliance.

The same had to be said about the Family Pact and the Spanish alliance. It was prudent and necessary for the maintenance of peace, but it was not very useful in time of war, for his Spanish pride, the slowness of his decisions and the habitual listlessness with which they were carried out made His Catholic Majesty a difficult ally. His disagreeable recollections of the Seven Years' War made him an even more difficult ally since they made him long for revenge. The chief supporters of this policy were the Comte d'Aranda and his minister, M. de Grimaldi. They dreamt of the annihilation of England, the sharing out of her colonies and the abolition of her fleet, and they never ceased preaching their doctrine at Versailles.

But Louis XVI proved stubborn. He said to Vergennes, 'If we are obliged to make war against England, it must be to defend our possessions and to reduce her power, not out of any idea of territorial gain for us; it must only be an attempt to ruin her trade and sap her strength by supporting the rebellion of her colonies and their separation.' This operation now presented itself in an even more favourable light – that of alliance with the Americans. M. Franklin, devoid of title, devoid of gold lace, devoid of wig, had arisen from the turbulent ocean to offer the oldest monarchy in Europe the friendship and alliance of the youngest republic in the world: his proposal seemed both extraordinary and alluring.

For this friendship to mean anything, it was necessary that the new nation should in the first place be viable. At that point in time, January 1777, no one could assert that this was the case. On thorough consideration it appeared that it would be to France's advantage that this new nation should succeed in living and that it should create a power in the New World that was independent of England. This deserved a great deal of attention and effort on France's part.

Several months earlier Sartine and Vergennes had authorized an elderly physician named Barbeu-Dubourg to organize a trading venture with the United States: the two ministers had also set up a considerable organization, disguised under the name of Roderigue Hortalez et Compagnie and managed by Beaumarchais, which was to supply the Americans with all the stores needed for their war. From now onwards Beaumarchais was very close to Franklin, to whom the king had advanced funds to help him settle in Paris, live there and carry on his business. Franklin was advised to be discreet, but the king was delighted to have such a considerable pledge.

Yet it seemed difficult to reconcile these negotiations with what was due to the allies of France. How could His Catholic Majesty fail to distrust these republicans, above all republicans so close to his own possessions? He feared them both because his subjects might be infected with their independent spirit and because of the Americans' territorial ambitions. Charles III sincerely wanted to make war upon England as France's ally, now that he had a splendid navy once more; but he could find no sort of worth or merit in the Insurgents. Grimaldi, who was very much under Aranda's influence, might perhaps have stomached them, so great was his desire for a war of revenge and for the utter defeat of Great Britain, but he had just been dismissed because of an expedition he had planned against the Barbary pirates – an expedition that had ended in disaster.

Aranda could not get over it. To fill Grimaldi's place Charles took Floridablanca, a freemason of long standing and, like Aranda a veteran of the struggle against the Jesuits. But Aranda and Floridablanca could not get on together at all: they were at daggers drawn from the beginning. Aranda reduced his dispatches to the minimum, and Floridablanca purposely told him nothing, carrying on all his negotiations through the French ambassador to Madrid, the Comte de Montmorin, who was already very much in favour with the king. However, it was by no means easy to reduce Aranda to silence. He made his way into every gathering and he ended up by knowing everything: he was an ever-present problem – one that Vergennes solved by making him play lotto with Mme de Vergennes, and Louis XVI by pertinaciously talking about horses and hounds. From Madrid, then, there was agreement as to the principles but perpetual reserve as to the means. It was essential to come to an understanding with the Spaniards and at the same time it was impossible to succeed entirely. At least their hatred for the English could be relied upon.

This was not at all the case with Austria, where the upper classes were unanimous in extolling England and the English cause. At Versailles itself the queen showed particular attention to the English ambassador, Lord Stormont. Maria-Theresa would say nothing, but Joseph II was much to be feared. He very much wanted his revenge upon the King of Prussia, for whom he had as much hatred as he had admiration, and he was anxious to pick up anything in the way of territorial possessions that lay within his reach; he therefore thought it most improper that the King of France, his ally, should consider making war by himself without worrying about Austria's interests. He was therefore wholly opposed to a war between France and England. If things were to reach that point, it would be necessary to take the greatest care of him.

M. de Vergennes and Louis XVI were in agreement upon the attitudes to be observed towards France's great allies, Austria and Spain. The king summed up his views in these words: 'All things being considered, Spain has taken unfair advantage of the Family Pact: it is necessary to support one's ally (particularly an ally that it is so reasonable and just for us to have as Spain) in everything that is right and in the common interest, but not in what is merely for that ally's ambition or vainglory.' He was of the same opinion with regard to Austria, and in this he was following his father's views as well as those of the majority of Frenchmen: when occasion arose he did not hesitate to tell the queen his mind.

Neither Austria nor Spain would prevent him from allying himself to 'Messieurs les Insurgents', as they were called then, if their cause seemed sound and if they gave guarantees of their fidelity. However costly such a war might be the chance was far too important to miss; besides, the acquisition of the American trade was well worth sacrifices. The king was not ambitious for any conquests, but he saw the population of France growing and he wanted to find outlets for his subjects; in the American trade he saw the prospect of immense prosperity.

He did not mean to be led any farther than that. He would have nothing to do with a life-and-death struggle with England. It would cost too much in lives and treasure, and he did not consider that he had the right to desire so much destruction and so much bloodshed. Furthermore England had a useful place in Europe, and he had no wish to turn the world upside down. What he wanted was to put France back upon that pinnacle of splendour and strength that she had occupied before 1760 and from which the Seven Years' War had cast her: he could not forget his father's outraged tears nor those of his heartbroken mother. Above all he looked upon this opportunity Fate seemed to be offering his country as a means for re-establishing the balance of Europe, which had been completely upset by the peace of Fontainebleau: and then he hoped that this victorious effort would rally the nation about him, and that by putting the financial question into its true proportion it would make the solution possible.

It seemed to him perfectly clear that the financiers were talking nonsense: France was rich enough to maintain her army, fleet and government – it was not money that was lacking, but patriotism. Nobody wanted to pay taxes, above all those who should and could pay them. Would not a military victory that aroused people's love for the country and that increased the country's trade overcome these individual selfishnesses and the plot that bound them all together?

Louis felt this plot all round him, though he could not manage to find its centre or its agents. The parlements? They had seemed to be the leaders; but now they were on their best behaviour, for they were firmly controlled. Orléans was still the most dangerous centre of opposition. But the attack was coming from farther off. The *philosophes*, with their war against Christianity, had called the tune; and since 1763 theirs had ruled supreme as the country's official form of literary expression. They had the women on their side. It was a patient, systematic struggle.

All the members of this conspiracy had one characteristic in common: they cried up England and they filled France with English ways and English clothes – English frock-coats, English horse-racing, English gardens. Children were dressed in the English manner; people read English novels and extolled Shakespeare; but above all there was an endless flow of praise for the English laws and constitution, such as they were seen by M. de Montesquieu. In spite of his strong and steady disapproval, Louis XVI's ears were continually filled with eulogies of English customs. He was perfectly aware that the Palais-Royal was the headquarters of this anglomania. Chartres surrounded himself with Englishmen, particularly a certain Forth, who did not disguise the fact that he was an agent of George III's.

Would not the Insurgents provide a way of counterbalancing this profoundly stupid fashion and of showing the country England's weak side? At this juncture it was clear that the much-praised British constitution was at fault: it was the requirements of this constitution that had raised the English of America against those of the home country.

The Americans railed far more savagely against the English parliament, the direct cause of the conflict, than they did against the king, who, if he had been a little less faithful to this famous constitution, might have worked out an agreement with the Insurgents. For a long time this was what Benjamin Franklin hoped, for he was convinced that the British parliament and its two parties were incorrigible. If the French public were to grow enthusiastic about the Americans, that would necessarily detach them from England. In any case, the long and carefully prepared plan of forcing a constitution based on the English model upon France was nipped in the bud. In the moral crisis that France was going through this was an unlooked-for chance to rally the fashionable people, the writers, the parliamentarians – the whole nation.

So the Americans had to be supported in their attempt at becoming a republic apart from England, a republic that would necessarily be England's rival. This republic would remain faith-

ful to a powerful France, not in the least out of a feeling of preference but because it would be anxious to have European ports
open to it and effective support that would allow it to trade, even
if England, eager to take vengeance on her former subjects, were
to close her harbours and try to close the seas.

Louis was accustomed to reflect upon circumstances, plans and
schemes at length; he examined the whole of this problem with
the clear-sighted Maurepas and the prudent Vergennes, and he
became convinced that nothing should be neglected that might
bring the American revolt to a successful end. He was perfectly
aware of the dangers that would result for the French colonies;
but he also knew enough to be of the opinion that the French
colonies, making their entire living out of their trade with France
and wholly turned towards that country, would behave in the
same way as the English islands in their fidelity towards the
mother-country; the danger existed only for continental colonies,
whose thoughts and hopes ran on different lines.

This reflexion kept him from desiring to reconquer Canada.
It was not that he did not feel the loss bitterly, but he recognized
the impossibility of keeping on good terms with the Anglo-
Americans (who had begun the Seven Years' War in the New
World) if he attempted to recover Canada, the neighbour upon
whom they looked with a jealous and an acquisitive eye. It
appeared to Louis XVI that the time had not yet come for retak-
ing Canada nor for looking towards any fresh territory: the
French nation was too deeply disturbed, its institutions were too
threatened and its very civilization was too unsteady on its
foundations. For the present France, though rich and happy, had
to try to establish her power and protect it, by war if need be,
but not by conquests.

Vergennes and the king both reached this same conclusion, for
they both had reflective minds and they were both working upon
precise data. Unhappily public opinion could not be told, for the
strictest secrecy was essential. To let the plan be made out too
soon would merely be offering England the opportunity of winning overwhelming victories, or at least of carrying out innumerable attacks on French trade.

Vergennes therefore urged Franklin to be close and secret; and Franklin, having taken a quiet little house in the depths of Passy belonging to M. Le Ray de Chaumont, the Intendant of the Invalides and Mgr le Duc de Chartres' secretary for masonic affairs, lurked there like a spider in his web. When people came to see him he talked of his health, his experiments, or his poor virtuous country, abandoned by one and all. At Versailles Louis was no less mute. He had long sessions of work with Maurepas, and long conferences with Vergennes; and he hunted.

Public opinion was behind Louis XVI. A print of him had just been published, with these verses:

> *Friend of wisdom and of clear-eyed truth,*
> *True virtue's lover, adulation's foe,*
> *Strive on: each earthly day that here goes by*
> *Is one step nearer immortality.*

Chapter VII

The lucky King

ALL THROUGH THOSE EARLY DAYS OF 1777 VERSAILLES WAS dull and dreary, and it remained so throughout the days of the carnival. The king scarcely ever left his study; the queen rarely went to Paris, and her balls at Versailles became less frequent and less well-attended. As she was seen to keep all her favours for her ten or twelve particular friends people no longer troubled to come. And then everybody had a cold. The queen was also deeply in debt, which she found very irksome, since it obliged her to turn to the king. She tried to cheer herself by reflecting that presently her brother, Joseph II, would be coming; but the reflexion was not really much comfort, for in her family Joseph was something of a Saint John Chrysostom, an eloquent and often most untimely preacher.

Everything seemed untimely. Just at this moment Cardinal de La Roche-Aymon died, the Grand Almoner of France. Few tears were shed for him: he was scarcely liked or respected at all. It was said that 'he had crawled all the way to the top'. But how was his place to be filled?

Louis XV had promised it to the Rohans, for Cardinal Louis de

Rohan, Archbishop of Strasburg. It so happened that the queen hated him. Urged on by Vermond, she begged the place for Loménie de Brienne, Archbishop of Toulouse. But Louis XVI would have none of him, for he was a bad priest, unprincipled and unbelieving. Nor did he choose to go back upon his grandfather's word and vex the Rohans, particularly his former governess, Mme de Marsan, who was of that family.

After a great deal of negotiation and a great many scenes with the queen Louis XVI conferred the office upon Rohan, warning him that if he did not behave well and that if the slightest unpleasantness arose he would have to resign in two years. The queen was displeased with the appointment, and displeased with her husband, whose 'weakness' she found blameworthy; what is more, she was quite dissatisfied with herself and with all these vapid young men, to whom she paid far too much attention.

The active, boisterous young men in question were more in quest of adventure than of love affairs. Who would ever have supposed that the somewhat foppish Marquis de La Fayette, always thinking about the impression he would make and always eager to model himself on his cousin the Vicomte de Noailles, his bosom friend the Prince de Poix or his particular friend the young Ségur, would one day leave the court and set off for America? He was very popular, but he did not seem gifted with a particularly lively intelligence nor with a strong character: besides, he danced badly. But it so happened that he spent a few months at Metz: there he met M. le Comte de Broglie, whose dream it was to be the king of the Americas, and the Duke of Gloucester, who railed against his august relation, the King of England; and within a very little while La Fayette was off.

To tell the truth ill-natured gossip asserted that he had begun by paying the most attentive court to Aglaé de Barbentane, Comtesse de Hunolstein, the prettiest girl at court and at the Palais-Royal, where her father was one of the Duc d'Orléans' principal gentlemen and Chartres' closest friends. She too was said to be very intimate with Chartres, and it was alleged that he had taught her many things that a young person would like to know. And she did in fact know a great deal. Ségur, Ligne and

F

many others had been smitten by her incredible beauty and they had wooed her, not without success; but they were very clearly aware of what it had cost them, for the fair Aglaé had her price-list. What is more she was much given to picking pockets, both men's and women's, and to shoplifting. She was the most expensive mistress in France. As soon as he was married, the first thing La Fayette was determined to do was to treat himself to her. She showed no more reluctance than was necessary to raise the tariff somewhat. But La Fayette, who had just come up from his native Auvergne, and whose head had been turned by his recent fortune, his splendid marriage with a daughter of the house of Noailles, the kindness of the queen, and certain appearances of success, chose to insist upon fidelity – a fantastical notion that the Duc de Chartres, who was very much at home there, would not have for a moment.

After a certain number of quarrels, a certain amount of weeping and various misunderstandings, Aglaé dismissed him; so the humiliated, infuriated La Fayette had no choice but to become a hero. As he was naturally simple-minded and scatter-brained, he set about it so clumsily that the king and Vergennes were obliged to forbid him to leave. Was it proper for a prominent courtier to hurry off to America with a great deal of publicity, in a ship charted by him personally, immediately after he had been staying with the French ambassador to London? Besides, the Noailles were indignant and they asked the king to stop him. Louis XVI therefore commanded La Fayette to remain in France; but Vergennes was cunning enough to send a messenger who arrived after the Marquis had left (from Pasajes, in Spain, on 20 April 1777). For three months on end it had not been known whether he was going or not – it is easy to imagine the prodigious flow of rumours.

Meanwhile, at ten o'clock in the morning of Saturday, 19 April, an unassuming, rickety four-horse coach, with no escort, drew up in front of the gate of the queen's apartments at Versailles, and with a single bound an exceedingly lively young man in a puce-coloured coat with steel buttons leapt out; he was wearing low boots and his hair had only one row of curls. This was M. le Comte de Falkenstein: for such was the name that His Royal and

Imperial Majesty Joseph II of Habsburg-Lorraine, the Holy
Roman Emperor and the Queen of France's brother, had assumed
to travel in her country. As soon as he was shown the staircase
he hurried up it and appeared at the queen's door; here he found
the Abbé de Vermond, whom she had posted there as a sentry,
to soften the first shock if necessary . . . and if possible. There
was no need for him at all.

Joseph II, standing in the just-opened door, gazed happily at
his sister for a moment before throwing himself into her arms,
and immediately afterwards he said to her, in German, 'My dear
sister, if you were not my sister and if you could be wedded to
me, I should not hesitate for a moment to marry again, to provide
myself with such a charming companion.' Upon this they embraced very lovingly and exchanged their news as fast as they
could speak. Their hearts were deeply moved; and the queen's was
still very much disturbed – she had been so very much afraid!
And what her brother was bringing back to her was the whole of
her childhood, all the charm of her young days in Vienna.

She was delighted: and she was even more delighted when
Joseph told her that if she were to be left a childless widow she
should want her to come back and live with Maria-Theresa and
him. The queen was charmed, and she fell straight into the trap.
Although Joseph II was continually on the move, and although
with his mother's permission he had undertaken this long and
difficult journey, his curiosity as a traveller and as an innovating
king was only one of his motives: the primary aim was to bring
Marie-Antoinette and her husband together, so that she should
become his wife in fact, so that she should have children, and so
that in the eyes of the French she should become their queen,
their king's wife and the mother of his children. It was only in this
way that Joseph could derive any profit from the alliance; it was
only in this way that the house of Habsburg could profit from
a marriage that might otherwise turn into a disaster. Joseph II
attended to the matter at once.

This was his first talk with the queen. She had some very awkward confessions to make and she was afraid of being horribly
scolded. She had privately told her faithful Mercy that she would

like to prevent too much confidential talk between her brother and her husband. But Joseph's compliments disarmed her. She candidly admitted her errors, or at least she told him enough about the situation for him, in a half-laughing, half-reproving way, to make her promise to abandon this abstention that she had persisted in too long and that was so dangerous to her interests.

Finding her brother tolerant and kind the queen told him all about her life. Joseph was amused to see how well he had succeeded and he was pleased with this sister whom he had managed to beguile; he was intelligent enough to maintain his benign, prudent attitude. He listened a great deal, spoke little, and had himself taken to the king's apartments.

On meeting the two sovereigns embraced one another, then Louis XVI greeted Joseph with kind and simple words that thoroughly pleased the emperor. From the outset each felt liking and respect for the other as a man. And throughout the time of the emperor's stay he and the king talked in the most cordial manner, though Joseph particularly desired his incognito to be respected, and did not wish to appear at Versailles except on the same footing as the courtiers.

But above all Joseph moved about like a whirlwind. On the nineteenth he saw all the ministers and then he lunched in his sister's bedroom with the king, all three on folding seats of equal size, Joseph wearing black, the king violet and the queen a half-mourning déshabillé. The king was on the top of his form there between the two of them, laughing, quite at his ease and happy, while the somewhat anxious queen cast furtive glances at the two men and Joseph preserved a consciously respectful air. The king of France, with his two extra inches of height and his air of taking the whole thing as an agreeable joke, gave the French courtiers the impression of being the most royal of the three.

Then Joseph, as a *philosophe* monarch and as a conscientious Teuton, went to see everything that ought to be seen and everyone that ought to be known – the convent of the Carmelites, the Invalides, the Hôtel-Dieu, the Opéra, the menagerie at Versailles with its she-elephant, the ministers' wives, Croy (who asked him about the male elephant at Vienna, and who, dear soul, dreamt of a marriage), the horse-racing, a royal review, high mass in the king's chapel at Versailles, the queen's card-party, a court banquet, M. Trudaine, the Arsenal and its libraries, the Gobelins and its tapestries, Sèvres and its china, the Abbé d'Espagnac and his dumb pupils, the pretty women of Paris, the beautiful ladies of Versailles, the city's whores and Mme du Barry, and then a host of ministers, diplomats, engineers, generals, officers, financiers, great lords, eminent citizens . . .

He saw neither Voltaire nor Franklin, the first because he had promised his mother not to, and the second because he was a republican whereas he, Joseph, was a king and one who 'was in active practice of that calling'.

Nor did he seek out M. de Choiseul. The expectant clique hoped that the emperor's arrival would provide the occasion for intimate and flattering conversations that would lead to more important things. Nothing of the kind happened. He met Choiseul at court and spoke to him in a friendly way, but no more; and he took care that this conversation should take place in the king's presence and that he should tell Louis XVI about it. 'Sire,' he said, 'M. de Choiseul is an old acquaintance, and one I have taken pleasure in seeing again: forgive me if I left you for a moment . . .' This was another occasion when the Duc de Choiseul went back to Chanteloup in a thoroughly bad temper.

The queen's importunity in favour of Choiseul and certain imprudent remarks of hers induced Joseph II to speak his mind at last. He took advantage of the occasion to lecture her severely upon her conjugal duties: she was not to go with the king if he visited Brest for 'she was of no kind of use'; he reproached her for her over-easy, unceremonious attitude towards her husband, 'the want of respect in her way of speaking', 'her lack of submission', and indeed he said all that he had intended to say. She was extremely upset; she called Vermond to her assistance and sent him to see Mercy, to cause that faithful servant to intercede and pacify the emperor. During one of the meals they took together he advised her to be meek and gentle. He might as well have been talking to the wall. Joseph could not hold himself in for long: he broke out again to tell his sister that it was wrong of her to hold back the king's supper during Lent, for the king fasted, eating nothing between the morning and his evening meal, whereas she had luncheon.

On another occasion he told her how sorry he was that her will was not subject to her husband. For indeed he was well aware of the danger that Marie-Antoinette represented both for the French and for the Austrian courts. She was too scatterbrained to acquire a thorough understanding of the current problems or to learn about people, but she nevertheless wanted to have her way in all the important appointments, and in this respect her influence could become very dangerous, if Louis XVI allowed it. Her rashness would endanger both her husband and her family. Why this foolish enthusiasm for Ligne, a gambler, a braggart, a freemason, a man of no consequence? Why this infatuation for the worthless Esterhazy? And so many others! And as well as all this there was her gambling and the countless follies that caused Maria-Theresa to say again and again. 'She will ruin herself, she will ruin herself!'

Before he left, Joseph II again told her of his anxiety for her, and above all he told her that it was her duty no longer to refuse herself to the king. Then by way of bringing his mission to its end, on 14 May he had a long and frank talk with the king, a conversation in which he gave Louis the benefit of all his varied experience of women and advised him how to treat his sister, both from the physical and the moral point of view. Lastly, to bring pressure to bear upon the queen, whose levity of mind he knew only too well, he drew up instructions that she was to keep and read over. 'Do you make yourself necessary to the king? Does he see your affections turned towards him alone? Do you check your frivolous pleasure in shining at his expense? Are you absolutely silent about his faults and weaknesses? ... The one aim of all your actions, your only goal, must be the king's trust and friendship ...' But above all he made her swear to become Louis XVI's wife: he insisted so strongly upon the importance of this and upon the terrible dangers of a continued refusal that there was real hope of a change in her behaviour. He also advised her to give up the Princesse de Guéménée, to leave off high play and to be often in the king's company.

She promised, she swore, she wept. On the last evening they dined together, and after a great many kind words, injunctions, promises, advice, plans, confidences and confessions they parted at midnight. The queen was in floods of tears: the emperor hurried away even faster than usual. He spent the night at the inn at Versailles. At dawn on 30 May he set off in his old coach without looking back, leaving as he had arrived, as fast as his horses would carry him.

He left a brilliant reputation behind him. He had been liked. In France being liked was success. M. le Comte de Falkenstein's lightness of tone – a lightness that was both supple and imperious – was thought charming, and an emperor masquerading as an ordinary person in order to come and see his sister the queen enchanted that age which looked upon the masquerade as the highest of pleasures. And then it is always flattering to be visited. The court praised him and so did the people. The *philosophes*, that is to say all the fashionable writers, were a trifle sulky, because they had not been thrust into the forefront of the scene; but so as not to be left in the background they set about praising him too. The king was very happy to have seen his brother-in-law close at hand and to have let him understand that he would not follow him in any adventure. As far as politics were concerned it would not have been right to say more than that, or too much might have been read into it; and Joseph had enough spies in his pay not to ask questions. But in Louis' opinion Joseph was flighty and unreflective; and Joseph thought Louis distinctly weak. For Joseph the right course of action was dissimulation and then sudden movement; for Louis it was caution and holding fast. M. de Vergennes, who had had long and affable conversations with Joseph, confirmed the king's views. That aspect was clear enough; but the essence of the matter remained. It was still a mystery. What was the queen going to do? She wept and wept, she wiped her reddened eyes: she was seen to be re-reading Joseph's advice. When the king hurt his leg with his knife out hunting she looked after him with particular kindness – this was on 10 June. She showed both affection and care for her husband (all the more so since it had been announced that the Comtesse d'Artois was pregnant again – a fact that seemed to her almost like a piece of downright disrespect). Her heart was deeply moved as she read her brother's last message once more: 'It was painful for me to leave Versailles, for I am sincerely attached to my sister; and I rediscovered a kind of delight in living that I had quite given up but whose taste had never left me . . .'

Delight in living, the charm of a life both luxurious and plain – a life in which it was possible to walk out of a gilded palace and ride into great forests full of wild creatures; a life in which two men talking calmly and serenely to one another in private could settle the fate of empires! The delight of feeling that one was French, a member of the most powerful, most civilized nation on earth, a people among whom intellectual refinement and wit were joined to delicacy of feeling and strength of character. In coming to see his sister the head of all the Imperial states had also come to pay homage to this nation and its leader: he prided himself upon having been able to make himself liked by them. This was the first time since Charlemagne that the head of the Empire had come to pay his respects to the King of France in his palace.

The fact was all the more striking since at this same period England was inextricably entangled in difficulties that caused Horace Walpole, then in Paris, to write,

> The country, where I now am, is, luckily, neither in a condi-
> tion or disposition to meddle. If it did, it would complete our
> destruction, even by only assisting the Colonies, which I can
> scarce think they are blind enough not to do. They openly
> talk of our tyranny and folly with horror and contempt, and
> perhaps with amazement, and so does every foreign Minister
> here, as well as every Frenchman. Instead of being mortified,
> as I generally am when my country is depreciated, I am
> comforted by finding that, though but one of very few in
> England, the sentiments of the rest of the world concur with
> and confirm mine. The people with us are fascinated; and
> what must we be, when Frenchmen are shocked at our des-
> potic acts! Indeed, both this nation and their King seem to
> embrace the most generous principles – the only fashion, I
> doubt, in which we shall not imitate them! Too late, our eyes
> will open!

Mr Franklin was not unaware of this – it was his best tool – and he did not fail to encourage these favourable tendencies as much as he possibly could. It was not always so easy in 1777, when the tide of the war often flowed against the insurgents, yet in February and again in April Paris was filled with the rumour of important American successes – the public could already see Stormont leaving for London, with war declared. Things had not reached that stage, however. Beaumarchais sent off three ships loaded with stores at the beginning of 1777 and nine others followed them in September of the same year; the minister needed a great deal of coaxing to grant any more, and England's attitude was threatening.

So Franklin increased his activities. He entered into contact with his neighbour, Mme Helvétius; she was old and widowed now, but she was still charming and she entertained all the most influential *philosophes* and the richest financiers, who were all old friends of her husband's. What is more she also received 'the charming young', that is to say the wealthy young, for she had pretty, very fashionable daughters with handsome dowries. Franklin paid her such assiduous and such successful court that he became king of this salon (thereby vexing Mme Helvétius' oldest friend, M. Turgot, a suitor whom she had rejected long ago but who had never grown discouraged).

Franklin's ambitious heart was not satisfied with this conquest, extremely useful though it was to the United States; he also became a close and indeed a tender friend of Mme Brillon de Jouy, the young and charming wife of a financier. He had women friends of every kind. He was looked upon with favour at the Palais-Royal, and he had himself made a member of the most influential masonic lodge in Paris, the Loge des Neuf-Sœurs. He did all this both for his own pleasure and for his country's good. Although it was quite obvious that he was trying to draw Louis XVI and Vergennes into a terrible war, he was at the same time doing his utmost to prepare public opinion for it and to support the king in everything – he was never weary of uttering his praises.

Praise flowed towards the king from all quarters; but it was often the precursor of some appeal. This was the case when Linguet dedicated a fresh volume of his *Annales politiques, civiles et littéraires* to Louis XVI and said, 'Sire, you love justice', but 'France, humiliated by catastrophes and losses abroad, uneasy at home, crushed by an enormous national debt' that never stopped growing and that prevented a skilful minister from restoring the country's fortunes, was in a very anxious state. 'The country's single and most precious resource lies in its king's youth and his good intentions.' Good intentions are never easily turned into reality. This was seen once more when Louis XVI, going back to a plan worked out by Turgot, announced an edict designed to alleviate the wretched condition of the former Jesuits.

Unhappily the Comte d'Aranda got wind of it, and this worthy diplomat, whose masterpiece had been the expulsion of the Jesuits, warned the zealots of the Parlement: the result was that the most violent Jansenists of that body set off on the war-path, led by Duval d'Esprémenil, and they cut the king's edict to pieces.

Louis XVI was furious when he was told of it. He suspected that M. d'Orléans was behind it all and he spoke to him very forcibly indeed, sending him away quite crestfallen: he spoke even more strongly to the Keeper of the Seals, who restored the edict to its first state and had it registered as it stood. In this matter the king displayed strength and activity – it was one that was particularly dear to him, for he thought it would put an end to a cruel injustice.

But one cannot always be angry, nor see to everything oneself. If the country were to make the most of the opportunity that the war in America seemed to be offering it, what was needed was money, a great deal of money; so this was no time to set about a far-reaching financial reform that the Parlement would delight in mangling. Now since Turgot's failure the whole question had remained in suspense. Two competent men had been appointed, M. Taboureau as minister of finance and M. Necker as Director of the Treasury. It seemed a reasonable arrangement, for since M. Necker was a banker and a native of Geneva and therefore a stranger both to the country and to the administration, he could not occupy a ministerial post, however able he might be, and M. Taboureau des Réaux, the former Intendant of Flanders, was a worthy man, perfectly honest and remarkably efficient –

one who was suitable for the post without being entirely adequate for it. Unhappily the two did not agree. It appeared to Taboureau that in fact he was being treated as his nominal subordinate's inferior and that this made work impossible; he resigned 'for the good of the service' . . . and 'for his own peace of mind'.

This suited M. Necker. M. Jacques Necker, a tall, burly man of forty-five, had begun life as a humble employee in the Thélusson bank in Paris, but he made such a success of it that he became a partner and the moving spirit of the enterprise. He made a great deal of money; and with the money there came a young, pretty wife, a Swiss too, but even more ambitious than he. She had no doubt that her husband was a genius, for the good reason that he was her husband. The outcome was a splendid town house with servants in gorgeous liveries, pictures, a famous chef, dinners for *philosophes* and writers and then gradually for the great nobles, for everyone needs money!

It was reported as a matter of fact that M. de Pezay, the king's correspondent, had profited by M. Necker's generosity, and had supported him when writing to the king; and Maurepas was behind him too. Yet as M. Necker was a Protestant he was not qualified to take the oath and he could not be a minister of the crown: he contented himself with the title of Director General of Finance, refusing both the honours and the salary of the post. The public was dazzled. A courtier muttered, 'Nothing is more expensive than servants who do not choose to be paid.' But the king wanted quietness at home and he wanted guaranteed resources; he was happy to take M. Necker, who promised him both the one and the other. For the moment there was nothing better to be done; and Louis XVI, having come to the help of the Jesuits, did not revolt at the idea of having a Protestant as minister of finance, so long as he understood his calling and provided the country with the money it needed.

Everyone must follow his own calling. A royal pair must have children. During this year of 1777 the attacks upon the king and his impotence grew more and more outrageous and disgusting. A certain Cahouet (he was paymaster to the servants of the royal household) had to be arrested for the vile pamphlet that he wrote and handed about, *La Coquette et l'Impuissant*: an even baser sheet called *Les Besicles* circulated in the capital. The people were indignant, but they read them, at the same time blaming the government for tolerating such filth. The best way of putting an end to it all was to have an heir. And since 20 July 1777 the king could hope for one.

The queen herself, moved and excited by the venture that she had recoiled from so long, wrote to Maria-Theresa,

> My dear Mother, Vergennes sends to tell me that he is about to send off Breteuil's courier. This is the happiest of times for me. I am in the most blessed state for the rest of my life. It is more than a week now since my marriage has been wholly consummated; the essay has been repeated, and yesterday even more completely than the first time . . . I do not think it is the case yet, but at least I can look forward to being pregnant at any time now . . .

Joseph II had succeeded in appealing to her pride: he had won. But the less the road pleased her, the greater was her hurry to reach what it led to. It seems that she soon tired of the pleasure of physical knowledge of her husband; and it is perfectly clear that no man before him had stirred her to the point of making her forget her duty. She was not so much frigid as indifferent. She was very near to the state of saying to her husband, 'Do it, but do it quickly.' With her own little circle, her confidential friends and her favourite maid, she was proud of having thus become a woman in the fullest sense. Yet for her there was still a certain awkwardness: she had always advanced her husband's malformation as the reason for her state; but it was plain to everyone that Louis XVI had never been operated upon. On none of the occasions when the *Nouvelles à la main* had put these rumours about had he left off hunting; and the operation in question is one that cannot be done without the patient's staying in bed for ten or fifteen days for the stitches to be removed and the wound to heal. The falsity of the pretence was obvious. Marie-Antoinette therefore passed quickly over the subject, merely observing, 'Up until now I have managed to hide my distress, but I often wept in secret.'

The king was delighted, and he took a candid pleasure in the situation. But he was so much taken up with work that he scarcely had any time to see the queen. He had not had leisure to go to Compiègne, in spite of the attractions of its splendid, game-filled forest, and by way of compensation he went more and more often to Choisy or Marly and stayed there longer and longer. The queen did not mind his absence; she took increasing pleasure in the Petit Trianon, which she had had built according to her own wishes, with a garden and a park arranged according to her own plan; and there, with a small circle of friends, she rested from the boredom of the great ceremonies at Versailles. The trap set by Louis XVI and Maurepas was successful, and as her particular favourite she had recently adopted the charming Yolande de Polastron, Comtesse de Polignac, with her velvety eyes, her silky ways and her secret, delicate tastes. Marie-Antoinette abandoned the Princesse de Guéménée and Mme de Lamballe, who bored her, and shut herself up with her new friend.

Through this channel the king could exercise an influence over his wife that he had never possessed until that time, and he was therefore enabled to concentrate upon current problems with a greater freedom of mind. When Marie-Antoinette wanted to give a party for him at the Petit Trianon at the feast of Saint Louis he felt uneasy and he made inquiries. He found that it was going to cost eight hundred thousand francs. He refused categorically and spent the time working with Vergennes, who submitted a plan for the renewal of the alliance with the Swiss cantons so that this time France could enlist soldiers from all the cantons, even those belonging to the 'allegedly reformed religion'. He saw a twofold advantage in this scheme: it would give a wider and more certain recruitment and it would strengthen the unity and the stability of Switzerland, which mattered a great deal to France, seeing that Switzerland protected part of her eastern frontier.

All the smaller cantons had signed, but the two large ones, Zurich and Berne, needed coaxing. Joseph II had the good idea of going to Berne on his way back from France, and there he spoke of certain rights he possessed in the neighbourhood of Bâle, rights which, in his opinion, had not been sufficiently respected

by the cantons. That was enough: two months later the men of
Berne and of Zurich, alarmed by Austria's intentions, signed the
treaty with France. Yet another good turn that he had done for
his brother-in-law! But Joseph II could not be everywhere, and
there were a great many other problems that grew steadily more
dangerous.

Above all in relation to England. The English were stopping
French ships, ransacking and confiscating them. The French protested. In vain. In return the French sent stores and weapons to
the United States: Stormont came to see Vergennes and asked
him whether France intended to support the American rebels.
Vergennes replied, 'The King of France has no aim but that of
ensuring the freedom of trade for all nations.' Finally, in agreement with the Spaniards, it was decided to send troops to the
West Indies. When Stormont expressed his indignation (July
1777) Vergennes retorted, 'Your publications, your pamphlets,
your public speakers, as well as ours, continually repeat that if
you do not win back your American possessions you must
necessarily fall upon ours. It may be that our precautions will not
save them, but at least we shall have done what ought to be done.
Furthermore, these troops cannot and should not cause you the
least anxiety; they are too far away from the theatre of war to
make you fear any diversion.' 'Just so,' said Stormont, 'but they
will be exceedingly close to Jamaica.' 'If you are apprehensive
about that island, you may rest easy. If you were to offer it to us
we should refuse it. We wish to keep what we have; but even if we
had a mania for making conquests, your example would be a
lesson to us.' Speaking in this way, telling him nothing but the
truth, Vergennes deceived Stormont; and for his pains he was
called a knave by all those who were used to falsehood, for they
are always shocked by the subtlety of truth, lies being so much
simpler and more credible than facts. Louis XVI and Vergennes
were truthful, reticent men: this created a firm bond between
them. Nevertheless they were unable to prevent English spies
from seeing ships of the line and frigates on the stocks as they
moved about the French dockyards; nor, in spite of Franklin's
care and shrewdness, could they stop the American delegates'

circle, which swarmed with informers, from being a plentiful source of indiscretions. Nothing could be done about it. But at least the fleet was being made ready.

The army was being made ready too; but here the king ran into great difficulties. M. de Saint-Germain was an intelligent man and one of great moral worth; he possessed the outstanding advantage of a thorough knowledge of the central European armies, which in 1777 were the best in the world, the most experienced and the most seasoned – and those which the French army was most likely to have to fight. M. de Saint-Germain understood the handling of great masses, those tactics which consist of concentrating the greatest possible number of soldiers, all used to manœuvring together, against one point at the most favourable moment, in order to overwhelm the enemy and then to exploit the situation thoroughly. He did his very utmost to teach these tactics and to inculcate order, regularity and uniformity in the French army. This was a task that had become necessary, and it was one from which his successors were to profit. But he came up against ancient traditions. Most men do not fight out of a desire to make money, but rather out of a kind of enthusiasm and emulation. A man in the Flanders or the Artois regiment, fighting under the standard of his own province, is likely to feel more strongly about his regiment and to be more zealous in upholding its reputation than a soldier of the 28th or the 87th; for these numbers do not stir the heart in any way.

In the same way he wanted to abolish the greater part of the king's military household (twelve thousand picked men) because it was too showy and too expensive. The king did not allow him to carry out the whole of his work of destruction, for the monarchy had to keep some ceremonial troops and some staunch supporters about the king's person. Furthermore, as Louis XVI told Saint-Germain, 'In great states like mine great favours have to exist, so that I may attract the great nobles to my service and retain them there.' For this reason he opposed the abolition of the great offices on the staff of the cavalry: more clearly than his minister he saw the danger that lay in setting influential men of high standing against the crown.

Saint-Germain yielded with a bad grace. Yet the king acknowledged his worth and thought highly of his work in regaining
control over all sections of the army. And to help him in his task
he appointed the Prince de Montbarrey as his assistant, an old and
exceedingly capable officer of the Seven Years' War, a relation of
Maurepas', a man whose fine open cheerfulness was combined
with the wily penetration of his native Franche-Comté. His
function was to avoid clashes with the nobles and the generals.
He carried out his duties so well that little by little he acquired all
the power. Saint-Germain's indifferent health and his exasperation
at having to come to terms with the other ministers in order to
carry out his programme brought him close to discouragement.
Yet he did want to execute some of the reforms that were dearest
to his heart – the setting up of an army council composed of the
king's best generals, the reorganization of the military hospitals
and of the military school. M. de Maurepas disliked the first plan
and caused it to be rejected by the other ministers. The second
was prepared with meticulous care: the third brought about Saint-
Germain's fall.

The minister had been educated by the Jesuits and he was a
very pious Christian; in his view a good army could only be built
up with good Christians, their leaders filled with a sense of duty
and of respect for human life. He wanted officers who believed in
God. He therefore reorganized the religious side of the service
and planned a military school in which the chaplains should have
the greatest influence over the moral formation of the young
officers. In order to avoid the risk of merely fashionable abbés or
philosophe priests he wished to have former Jesuits. In 1777 the
persecuted, oppressed Jesuits were among the best, the most pure
of the priesthood.

Saint-Germain felt this and Louis XVI was certain of it:
he approved his minister's plan. But at the council he found that
he was entirely by himself, except for Vergennes. All the others
had been taught their lesson by their wives or mistresses, who in
their turn had been indoctrinated by their *philosophe* friends, and
they would not hear of a military college with such a degree of
clerical influence. Saint-Germain was criticized on every hand:

there was not a single hand-written news-sheet that did not run him down nor a salon where he was not slandered. M. Necker accused him of increasing expenditure by his ill-conceived reforms.

After a bitter contest the plan was rejected. This failure made Saint-Germain decide to resign. He left without regret. It was the king who was the sorrier of the two: for in spite of all Saint-Germain's faults Louis XVI had a great respect for his earnestness, his zeal for work and the manly firmness of his character. The king was in favour of the plan for the military school. But he had made it a rule never, so long as he kept them in office, to go against the unanimous opinion of the counsellors in whom he trusted. Any other form of conduct seemed to him anarchy or despotism. He therefore gave way and allowed Saint-Germain to resign, but not without giving him a suite of rooms in the Arsenal and a pension of fifty thousand livres. The former minister went happily away, and the care-worn king turned back to his work.

He had little rest except during his stay at Fontainebleau, where the court arrived on 9 October 1777. The king took great pleasure in hunting in the immense forest, and he was very fond of the ancient, noble building, which had so many memories for him. The queen was bored at Fontainebleau, but she did like the plays that were performed there and she used the long rainy days of autumn as an excuse for the wildest gambling. She had forgotten her brother's advice and no one held her back. The Abbé de Vermond had refused to come, observing that since she would not attend to what he said his presence was useless. He could not bear seeing her so intimate with her husband, and he rebelled against the whole state of affairs. She made the most of it to indulge herself to the full. The faro-party to which she devoted her evenings became a gambling-hell.

The king put up with it, for he saw no other way of filling the mind of a woman who liked neither reading nor any serious way of spending her time. He would rather she was in the card-room than in the ministers' studies, or in his own, trying to extort favours. In this way he remained free to work and to think over his worries. One of the keenest of them, in this autumn of 1777, was the death of Pezay.

Louis valued this informant, who told him things that the ministers kept from him, sometimes adding intelligent observations. The ministers hated him and kept a watch over him, for Pezay had been unwise enough to allow his function to be suspected.

Maurepas, profiting from this, had granted him the place of Inspector of the Coasts, the excuse being that it was a due acknowledgment of his merits. Pezay was very proud of his official title, and he was puffed up by the twelve thousand livres that the king gave him every year; he wanted to throw his weight about, but it so happened that he came up against a highly-placed official who gave him a very brusque answer. Pezay complained to the minister, who carried the complaint right up to the king. Louis could not but say that his friend was in the wrong, and in order to teach him a thorough lesson he sent him an order to withdraw to his own place at Pezay and not to move from it. This unpleasantness, his vexation at having behaved like a fool, the winter's cold in a not very comfortable house, and Fate, made M. de Pezay extremely ill. He did not look after himself properly: he died of it. It was a great sorrow for the king, for he was fond of his remote, intimate correspondent – a youthful, dogmatic creature, both chivalrous and astute. Louis had so few friends that he grieved for Pezay a great while.

Another death that was expected day by day caused him still more grief. The Elector of Bavaria had it in mind to leave this world. It was said that he was on his death-bed, and already Joseph II was declaring, in too loud a voice, that he had to have Lower Bavaria; indeed, he displayed some fifteenth-century charters that according to him gave him a right to it. For his part the Elector of Saxony claimed twenty-two million florins' worth of allodial property, which he claimed on the grounds that his wife said he ought to have it. The old Prussian fox said nothing, but this did not mean that his mind was not very busy. Louis XVI was closely in touch with all this grisly activity. He was quite aware that during his stay in Paris Joseph II had made thorough inquiries about the negotiations between France, Spain and the Americans, and that Joseph thought France was too much taken up with these matters to pay attention to his wishes, his advice or his protests. And in fact Louis XVI did pass the best part of the summer and autumn in writing to the King of Spain and negotiating with Franklin through M. Gérard, a high official in the foreign ministry, in order to bring the views of the three powers into line and to set up a triple alliance, which alone could subdue England, and, by a short war, put an end to the Anglo-American conflict. He noted that whenever he made a step forward, the Comte de Floridablanca took two backwards, and that if he took one back, Floridablanca took one forwards. Charles III did seem to want a war against England; but he distrusted France, whose behaviour in 1756–1762 he thought blameworthy.

It was a different story with Franklin: the American, patient but stubborn, invariably called for the same things – an alliance, ships to ensure the freedom of the seas for the Americans, and a commercial agreement that was to come into force immediately. It was in vain to tell him that his country had as yet too little credit, stability or authority for France to be able to commit herself to such an undertaking: he went back to his old refrain and added, 'If you cannot make up your minds, we shall make peace with England.' Upon this Gérard promised him assistance, facilities and money; he produced them; and the dialogue began again. But it never reached a firm conclusion, and in spite of his philosophy Franklin was losing all patience, and the king, in spite of his caution, all calmness.

This was how matters stood for Franklin when at dawn on 4 December a post-chaise drew up at his door and Jonathan Loring Austin, an envoy from Congress, leaped out to tell him that General Burgoyne and his entire army, the best the English had in America, had surrendered to General Horace Gates at Saratoga on 31 October 1777. Galvanized by this news, the old philosopher sat down to his desk: he drew up a communiqué which he spent all night printing on his letter-copier and which, early next morning, his servants and his grandsons carried to all the embassies. He himself sent Vergennes a short message for the king. At last his country had 'stability and credit'. The news from London, where there was the utmost consternation and where everyone except the king thought that henceforward there was no possibility of bringing the Americans to heel, did a great deal towards deciding Vergennes and Louis XVI.

Franklin was breathing freely, looking upon the game as won, when on 5 December 1777 the messenger reached Paris with the news of the Elector of Bavaria's death on 30 November, and of Joseph II's warlike preparations for invading the duchy. Instantly the cry of war ran through the whole court. All the young men packed their baggage and furbished their weapons. Everyone foresaw a European war. Vergennes feared that they were right: but it would be one war too many.

The king did not want it. But with the Austrian alliance – and with his wife – would he be able to avoid this untimely conflict?

Chapter VIII

The daring King

NEVER HAD THE OLD COURTIERS SEEN A QUIETER NEW Year's Day at Versailles than that of 1778. Everybody was waiting for news and no one said a word.

From 5 January on the news came flooding in. Joseph II was assembling an army of twelve thousand men and he was making ready to occupy Lower Bavaria, which he had just acquired by a treaty that he had signed on the third with the Elector Palatine, the heir of the Elector of Bavaria. The whole of Germany was on the move. At Versailles the queen wrote to Mme de Polignac, 'I am very much afraid that on the present occasion my brother may be up to his old tricks' – an observation that M. de Mercy found extremely shocking. On his side Louis XVI did not hesitate to let his wife know his mind at once, speaking strongly and clearly, so that there might be no argument and no recrimination. 'Madame,' he said to her, 'the ambition of your relatives will throw everything into confusion! They began with Poland, and now Bavaria is the second volume. It grieves me, for your sake.' That was quite plain, and no one could be mistaken about it, not even those who considered the King of France a weak and timorous man.

He knew what he wanted and he had often spoken of it to Vergennes. 'I have not left the queen in ignorance of the fact that I think the house of Austria's acquisitions ill-founded and that I feel we are in no way required to help in retaining them.'

The king did not wish to go to the help of Joseph II because he did not want a continental war: Vergennes agreed, and so did Maurepas and Necker and all the ministers, as well as the country in general; but the young officers were strongly opposed to his opinion, for they preferred a war by land, in which everybody had honours and promotion, to one by sea, in which everyone was confined to boring garrison-duty, while the fleet spent all the money and the sailors got all the distinctions, decorations and valuable places.

Vergennes at once caused Breteuil, the ambassador in Vienna, to adopt a frigid tone, and all the other French representatives in other countries were ordered to show their disapprobation, particularly those at the German courts, which were in a great state of concern. A more disagreeable situation could scarcely be imagined. Maria-Theresa wept and blamed her son. 'My plan has not been followed and therefore the responsibility for the other must fall on the Emperor and Prince Kaunitz.' But she also blamed her daughter. 'It would be more to our advantage . . . and more necessary than ever that my daughter should put her influence over the king to good use; but how can one flatter oneself that she will do any such thing so long as she is utterly taken up with her usual frivolity and dissipation?' The queen did her best to obey, however. But the cause was already lost.

There was nothing to be done: Joseph II had behaved foolishly. Russia looked upon Austria's increase with an evil eye. Saxony, filled with anxiety, called upon the King of Prussia to come to the rescue. The Duke of Zweibrücken, the Elector Palatine's legitimate heir, joined forces with Saxony. The King of Sardinia uttered shrill cries of indignation; and England was delighted at the prospect of a general European war that would give her time to deal with her revolted subjects.

In Paris Franklin and his famous rebels were very active, and both the king and public opinion responded warmly. Since December 1777 the king had been working with Vergennes to perfect the Franco-American alliance. Unhappily there were continual hindrances that kept him from his task.

He lost an entire week in dealing with the foolishness that arose from the stupidity of the Comte d'Artois, perpetually amorous and usually drunk. This time the trouble arose over a pretty Auvergnate, Mme de Canillac, formerly lady-in-waiting to the Duchesse de Bourbon and then mistress to the Duc de Bourbon – so much so, indeed, that the Duchesse, vexed by such over-zealous conduct, dismissed her.

On the evening of Shrove Tuesday 1778 Artois was staggering about at the ball at the Opéra, propped up by Mme de Canillac. A masked figure went by whom he recognized as Mme de Bourbon: he insulted her. She wanted to know who the ill-bred fellow was and she raised his mask. With his fist Artois struck his cousin's mask and her face. There was a great deal of noise and fuss, and they were separated.

It was hushed up and Mme de Bourbon was forgetting the whole thing, when Artois saw fit to boast of his feat in the Polignac salon: the gossip ran round the court at once. All the princes of the blood began to stir. Condé insisted upon an exemplary reparation. Louis XVI wanted to stifle the whole foolish business. In his presence Mme de Bourbon was to say that she regretted her hastiness and Artois his violence. Artois stammered out some quite unsatisfactory nonsense. They left the study in a worse temper than ever.

This time there was no avoiding the duel, though Artois did not look forward to it very much. In the Bois de Boulogne Bourbon wounded him in the shoulder. The captain of his guards, the Chevalier de Crussol (whom Louis XVI had made responsible for Artois' life), stopped the fight. The adversaries embraced: Artois leapt into his coach and went to apologize to Mme de Bourbon.

Was it over? For months on end the whole of Paris cheered the Bourbons and shunned Artois. It was yet another success for the house of Orléans.

The Artois-Bourbon duel took place on 16 March: on the morning of the seventeenth the Parisians were astonished to see a placard posted up on all the walls of the capital and signed by the English ambassador, a placard which stated that he was leaving and that anyone who wished to be paid should apply without delay, before 20 March, the day of his departure. The bystanders gaped at this dramatic turn of events, but those who were in the know said that on Friday, 13 March, the Marquis de Noailles, the French ambassador in London, had handed the King of England a conciliatory and indeed a courteous note informing him that the King of France had signed a treaty of friendship and trade with the United States, which he had at the same time recognized as a free and independent power. The document was signed by the King of France and countersigned by Vergennes; there was no Spanish participation whatever. The King of England protested strongly, of course; and English public opinion seemed at once passionate, regretful and taken aback – how could France dare to behave so? Had she forgotten her disasters in the Seven Years' War?

This brilliant outcome was due to Franklin's skill, Vergennes' prudence, Louis XVI's courage, and to the English themselves. As soon as the surrender at Saratoga was known in England the British government saw that something had to be done; and they did something that never should have been done at all. In rapid succession they sent Paul Wentworth, the chief of the British Intelligence in Paris, to see Franklin; then Mr Dempster and Sir Alan Ferguson; and lastly, since these efforts were in vain, Sir Philip Gibbs, and the pious Mr Hutton, the 'pope' of the Moravian Brethren, an old friend of Franklin's. They all asked him, 'What are your peace conditions?' To all of them he replied, 'Independence.' And they all of them (except for the long-suffering Hutton) went away again, raising their hands in despair. Pointless approaches? Not as far as Franklin was concerned, for he took care that Vergennes should hear of them. So Louis XVI and Vergennes, who did not wish to let the American opportunity slip, made up their minds to go forward, in spite of the difficulties in Bavaria, in spite of Spain's reticence, and in spite of the court's opinion. On 6 December 1777 M. Gérard of the foreign ministry came to Paris to see Franklin and to collaborate with him in the drafting of a treaty of friendship and trade; it was signed on 8 February 1778 in the foreign ministry, on the quai des Théatins. This was the first international treaty ever signed by the United States. The Most Christian King was the first in the world to recognize the United States, to treat with them on equal terms and to declare them his allies.

This daring stroke of Louis XVI's surprised everybody. His great continental ally Austria had just committed herself to a war against Prussia and her satellites; his great Atlantic ally Spain would not follow him; and yet he went ahead! For his part he knew that the only way of proving to Joseph II that his presumptuousness had not overawed him was to act, and that the only way of drawing Spain along behind him was to march a long way in front.

The king's boldness, typical of a man of action, bore the mark of his personality. An arrogant sovereign would have attacked England without warning, as England had attacked in 1755; a cunning ruler would have said nothing and watched his opportunity. Louis XVI signed the American treaty, informed Charles III, telling him that he could be a party to it whenever he chose, and then politely warned England, without either bitterness or threats, like a well-bred man who is sure of himself and whose conscience is clear. There were some people in France who blamed him – the French are so bright that they do not often give themselves time to understand!

But the moral effect in the United States was prodigious. If it had been done with a view to gaining allies nothing could have been better imagined. In Europe it was thought that Louis XVI was either very simple-minded or else very strong to lay his cards on the table in this way, leaving the English the initiative to attack or to bide their time. Fontenoy came to mind, and the scene when the French officer invited the English to fire first – '*Messieurs les Anglais, tirez les premiers.*' In order to assert his determination, the king had Franklin and his colleagues presented to him. On 20 March 1778 he received them at Versailles. There had been a great deal of argument as to the protocol to be followed, but Franklin, having tried the regulation wig, found that his head would not get into it. 'He has a big head, and a great head,' cried his female admirers. He therefore went to Versailles dressed in his everyday clothes – a dark brown velvet suit, spectacles, grey stockings and a little grey hat under his arm: no powder, no sword, no wig.

That was how he appeared before the King of France at his levee, in the midst of a crowd of astonished courtiers who whispered, 'He is dressed as a Quaker!' The four other representatives of Congress who followed him, wearing their finest clothes, looked like footmen. While the drums beat the general salute, while the royal standard on the roof was dipped and the household troops drawn up in the court presented arms, the Americans walked up the great staircase, conducted by Vergennes.

At the top of the stairs the great door of the king's apartments opened wide before them and the adjutant of the Swiss Guards announced 'The ambassadors of the Thirteen United Provinces.' They made their way through the crowd with tears of emotion in their eyes and they found themselves before the king, who said to them, 'Gentlemen, I hope that this will be for the good of our two nations: I beg you to assure Congress of my friendship. I also desire you to let Congress know that I am exceedingly pleased with your conduct during your stay in my kingdom.' After this they went back to their quarters to rest. They did not present themselves to the queen, to Monsieur, to Madame, the king's sister, and to the ministers until the next day. Hardy, the bookseller, who was endowed with eloquence, wrote in his diary, 'In Franklin's person His Majesty was welcoming exceptional genius and merit rather than the luxury and brilliance that are as usual in our days as they are foreign to the talents of the mind. *Eripuit coelo fulmen, sceptrumque tyrannis.*' The tyrant was George III and the angel of liberty Louis XVI.

Like all angels, Louis XVI had a hard life and a very full one. But like them he had great compensatory joys. Heaven rewarded him for his generosity towards the United States by granting him descendants. With a cry of triumph Marie-Antoinette wrote to her mother on 19 April 1778, 'Madame, my dear Mother, my first impulse – one that I am sorry I did not obey a week ago – was to write to my dear Mama of my hopes . . . I believe I have good reasons for trusting in them.' The queen was in fact pregnant. Louis XVI's delight was almost unbelievable, and it showed in his every movement.

After all the insults and outrageous slanders that his wife had earned him Louis XVI was regaining the high standing that was his due; his long patience was rewarded, his loving subjects, to whom such very deep feelings bound him, were about to do him justice, for as he conceived it the French monarchy was the union of all the families that tilled the soil of France, fearing God and honouring the king, their protector, the head of the reigning family. A king without children could not be a real king, since the essence of the monarchy lay in the certainty of continuity, just as in other régimes it lay in the expedient of the moment. At last Louis could feel that he had fulfilled his duties towards his forbears, just as he had to his country and to the future generations.

This child might also save its mother. Marie-Antoinette now had the opportunity for pulling herself together and the means for doing so. This bond with her husband and with France might make a new woman of her.

Unfortunately her family was harassing her to make her compel Louis XVI to come to the help of Austria. Through Mercy Maria-Theresa sent to tell her, 'The king can be of the greatest assistance by firmly showing the friendship that he has for us and for the alliance.' For his part Joseph overflowed with lamentations. When Frederick declared war on Austria and threatened her with a hundred and sixty thousand men he wrote, 'Since you do not choose to prevent the war, we shall fight like brave men; and whatever may happen, my dear sister, you will certainly not have to blush for a brother who will always deserve your regard.'

The queen was overwhelmed, and she could not do less than badger Louis XVI and Vergennes. Joseph, having consulted no one before setting all this pandemonium in motion, now accused everybody, and above all Louis XVI! This time it was not the King of France who looked a fool, but his illustrious ally the Emperor of Austria. Maria-Theresa knew it: she wrote to Mercy, 'I do not touch upon current affairs at all. You are aware of the course of conduct that I have laid down for myself in this respect; I consider it the best, when one is forced to acknowledge that one can do no good.'

Meanwhile Louis XVI's position was very disagreeable and difficult: his wife, who was carrying his child, trembled for a brother very dear to her. Louis desired neither Joseph's downfall nor the ruin of the Austrian alliance; for if that were to happen Austria would at once fall back into the arms of England, and there would be the danger of terrible upheavals. It was essential that the queen should have her baby quietly, and that Joseph should learn his lesson without being hurt too much and without losing too much standing. And lastly it was essential that England should not be given the chance of a German war to divert France from her true aim. It was a difficult task, but the king thought he could carry it through.

He had to keep a continual watch on the queen. Paris was wild with enthusiasm for Voltaire, and his fame prevented her from sleeping. She wanted to receive him, at least in her own apartments and very quietly, if the king did not wish for more. But the king would not even have as much as that. She thought of a cunning stroke: she would go to the Comédie and there allow Voltaire to be presented to her in secret. The king heard of it and sent her a very firm note in her box. She was quite heartbroken. So was Voltaire. He wanted to see Versailles and this popular king. But Louis XVI refused. Nevertheless he did authorize M. d'Angevilliers to order a statue of Voltaire from Pigalle. Voltaire took advantage of it to write this sixain to Pigalle:

> *King Louis knows your skilful hand:*
> *Both in the little and the grand*
> *Your work fills all with joy.*
> *But now see contrast's giddy height,*
> *He bids your chisel bring to light*
> *No hero, but the drummer-boy!*

This was how Voltaire, with a smile, enrolled Louis XVI in his army; and the king could not prevent himself from smiling too. At one and the same time he had avoided paying a public tribute to the impious *philosophe* and he had avoided provoking the hatred of the most virulent pamphleteer that irreverent century had ever known.

Freed from Voltaire, he still had the queen to comfort and to help. Her state wearied her; she was bored. Vermond was not there – he was in a state of indignation against the coming child – and his absence made her more biddable. She gave up dancing, going to Paris, and playing billiards. To pass the time she sang or listened to music or gossiped with her favourites.

When she was with her husband she always came back to the Bavarian trouble. The Prussian and Austrian armies stood face to face in Bohemia, without engaging. Frederick was in occupation of parts of Bohemia and Silesia, rich territories that he was pillaging.

Joseph II was deeply grieved. He was angered by the tone of the French ambassador in Vienna and the French diplomats in Germany, who all said, 'This matter has nothing whatsoever to do with France.' He was worried about Frederick II's advances to Versailles, although Louis XVI had replied to Count von der Goltz, the Prussian ambassador, 'I do not wish to interfere in your master's affairs.'

Faced with the king's steadiness the queen turned towards Maurepas and Vergennes, who evaded the issue. Getting nothing from them, she came back in tears to her husband.

She asked him to make his ministers behave in a manner more in conformity with the alliance. He repeated the council's decision: 'Neither the part of Bavaria claimed by Austria nor her fresh acquisitions in Poland can be included among the possessions guaranteed by the treaty of alliance; but as far as the Austrian Netherlands are concerned, if they are attacked by Prussia, France will defend them.' She was obliged to say that she was satisfied with this reply. He was by far the stronger of the two, and he remembered Joseph's II's advice about being firm – Joseph had never for a moment supposed that one day it would be so useful in helping Louis XVI to withstand Austria's pressure. His brother-in-law's visit had certainly been most uncommonly valuable.

There are useful enemies, and they occur more frequently than is generally supposed; and there are useful friends, though they are far less usual. But Franklin undoubtedly belonged to their number.

In those very delicate first stages of a close alliance between the most ancient Catholic monarchy of the Old World and the youngest Protestant republic of the New the slightest error would have been fatal. Ever since they had been founded the English colonies in America had looked upon France as their prime enemy and the King of France as the Beast of the Apocalypse (unless indeed the Beast was the Pope: but in that case the King of France was the crowned head that was to be seen on the Beast's tail in the illuminated manuscripts). In order to make a reality of this alliance the good will of this nation and its leaders had to be gained.

Congress, which was largely made up of men engaged in trade, was well disposed; they depended upon France to do business with them and to bring in fresh money. This was one of Franklin's first requests. On that side Louis XVI's open-handedness ensured the future of the alliance. But the lawyers schooled in the English legal system, the anti-Catholic ministers of religion, the school-masters filled with the tradition of English supremacy, and the officers who had fought against the French colonists between 1700 and 1763 remained on the reserve.

What, above all, would be the attitude of this Colonel Washington, a former British officer and one of the guilty men of the Seven Years' War, since in time of peace he had caused the death of Jumonville, the commander of a French fort? There was much uneasiness about him at Versailles. This was mistaken. Washington was a good fighting-man, and he wanted to win this war against the English, just as he had wanted to win the last against the French.

Furthermore, Fate was kind enough to bring the young Marquis de La Fayette to his side, and La Fayette behaved with great tact and skill. La Fayette, Vergennes and Louis XVI had an intuitive understanding of the right line of conduct: plain, direct, straightforward behaviour was much more useful to the alliance than any devious policy, for it won the Americans' hearts.

There were intrigues that made this conduct necessary. At the last moment Charles III had drawn back, because Floridablanca hated Aranda, who supported the war; because the king remembered Choiseul's blunders between 1756 and 1762; because the fleet was not ready and an American convoy was expected; because Spain dreaded the Insurgents; and above all because Spain did not choose to be hurried.

So Louis XVI found himself thrown into the arms of the Americans, his only allies. In no circumstances must they be allowed to withdraw. Now as soon as Lord North learnt of Saratoga and the Franco-American alliance he put a bill through parliament allowing him to start fresh talks with the Insurgents upon a wider and more favourable basis. At the same time he sent his friend and banker William Pulteney, the member for Shrewsbury, to Paris, to urge Franklin to give advance approval of the offers of peace and reconciliation that the English commissioners were to take to America in the name of the king and parliament.

But Franklin warned Vergennes and said to Pulteney, 'Do you recognize our independence? No? Well then, there is no point in any further talk.' With this Franklin sent him away, as he had also sent away Hartley, another member of parliament, and George Hammond, who importuned him for his influence in pacification and who went so far as to suggest a triple peace-treaty; and as he had sent away Charles de Weissenstein, who proposed an Anglo-American reconciliation, together with the creation of American peers, among whom Franklin and Washington were to be numbered.

There was no danger in any of this, for Franklin was loyal both to his country and to France. He had feelings of personal regard and gratitude for the king, and of positive friendship for Vergennes, who felt the same for him. Had it not been for this bond the two men upon whom the whole alliance depended would have been driven mad, so complicated did their problems become.

They had to reckon with human moods, the variations of the wind, and the rates of exchange – things of which it may be said that each is more unstable than the last. Yet everything began well enough. The English recalled their ambassador; the French king's representative returned to Paris and most of the French left England, though no general order was made.

Still there were neither hostilities nor declarations of war. But there were provocations. The English seized some French ships that they accused of smuggling; they stopped others which refused to be searched, as was the case with La Motte-Piquet about 10 March. He replied to the English with a broadside, and they did not press the matter. Now all-embracing precautions had to be taken. The king had a squadron fitted out at Toulon: it was to be commanded by the Comte d'Estaing and it was to carry M. Gérard to America to take up his appointment as the king's minister plenipotentiary to Philadelphia; it was also, should need arise, to go to the help of the Americans and the French West Indies.

D'Estaing sailed with sealed orders that were to be opened only after he had left. It was when he was on the high seas, having passed through the straits of Gibraltar, that he learnt who Gérard really was and found that he was carrying the first French diplomat to America. He had with him eight ships of the line and five frigates in excellent condition. There was no finer fleet to be found anywhere in the ocean.

Like the waves of the sea when they have no settled direction and change according to every wind, so events remained uncertain: the King of France declared that he did not want a war; the King of England told his parliament that he would not take the responsibility of beginning a war; the King of Spain asserted that in the meantime he would wait and see what happened. And all the nations did the same.

In the morning of 22 June 1778 the waiting came to an end. Three couriers reached Versailles, galloping furiously: M. d'Estaing sent to say that on 20 May he had reached latitude thirty-four and that all was well; the king, who had been anxious for three weeks past, breathed freely, and M. de Sartine swelled with pride. The King of Spain had just told Montmorin, the French ambassador, that he was ready to act when the French king wished and when his galleons had come in; and they were expected at Cadiz from one moment to the next.

The third courier, coming from Brest, announced that the frigate *La Belle-Poule*, Captain de La Clochetterie, had sighted an English fleet cruising off the coast of Brittany; having learnt the *Belle-Poule*'s nationality, an English frigate had ranged alongside and had ordered him to come and speak with the admiral. La Clochetterie replied that he had no order from his court to that effect and that he had his destination to reach, which prevented him from complying. Upon this the English frigate fired her entire broadside into the *Belle-Poule* and battle was joined, almost within pistol-shot. It lasted five hours: at nightfall the English ship tacked and fled in the direction of her fleet without replying to the fifty remaining shots that the *Belle-Poule* fired at her stern. Aboard the *Belle-Poule* half the crew were dead or wounded. The ship had been shot through and through and she was obliged to run aground on the coast of Brittany. The English frigate was out of action.

The news flashed through Versailles like lightning: from one end of the palace to the other, in the salons, the gallery and the Œil-de-Bœuf there was only the one cry to be heard, 'War! War!' It was in vain for Maurepas to claim that it was a maritime accident: the events of the following days showed that the war had in fact begun. Keppel took two frigates and a French lugger that fell in with his fleet. The king at once sent orders to Brest for the fleet to sail. The thirty-two ships of d'Orvilliers' grand fleet were at single moorings, as near as possible to the channel: they weighed without delay. On 8 July 1778 the fleet stood out.

And so a new war began. For more than two years the king and his ministers had been making ready for it: there was none of the lack of preparedness that had been seen in 1755. The French fleet numbered two hundred and sixty-four men-of-war, seventy-eight of them ships of the line, as opposed to the twenty-five ships of the line and frigates that Louis XV had at his disposal in 1756. In 1778 France had well-trained officers and petty-officers, and the best technical services in the world, for Louis XVI concerned

G

himself with them and Sartine neglected nothing. The Académie de Marine had accomplished a great deal. The kingdom had never had a finer tool in better hands.

Louis XVI was determined to make a vigorous use of these men and this material, and not to allow himself to be distracted from victory by any person or any thing. Yet on 5 July Frederick II had just invaded Bohemia and Maria-Theresa was weeping: Marie-Antoinette shed rivers of tears. But once again the king told his wife that he would never go to war for Lower Bavaria. And Vergennes assured the king that this business could be successfully dealt with 'provided it was allowed to grow ripe'.

It is not easy to let a matter peacefully ripen when it is one that distracts your wife and excites furious reactions all around you. This was the height of the summer: from economy the king did without the journey to Compiègne and the court roasted first at Marly and then in the oven of Versailles. By way of relief the courtiers passionately discussed the events of the two wars. At last, at eleven in the morning of 27 July, the fleets met some seventy miles off Ushant. There was a furious cannonade and the English line began to waver and bend; but Orvilliers, hampered by the heavy sea and unwilling to risk everything with unseasoned crews, did not make the most of it. The gunfire lasted from eleven in the morning until five in the afternoon: the English fired too high, right into the rigging, and did little harm to the French ships, whereas the English ships were hulled. This arose from a traditional difference in gunnery between the two countries, for the English tried to take ships and the French to sink them.

As soon as darkness fell the English fleet stole away, whereas d'Orvilliers' spent the night where it stood, all lights lit, in the hope of a battle the next day. None occured. The fleet sailed back to Brest in good order. Twenty-seven French ships with 1,934 guns had prevailed over thirty English ships carrying 2,778 guns. D'Orvilliers brought back 126 dead and 413 wounded, Keppel 407 dead and 789 wounded.

The news spread at once, and the king hurried to congratulate Orvilliers, who had commanded with equal coolness and intelligence.

Versailles, 1 August 1778.

It is with much pleasure, Monsieur, that I have received the news of the battle that you fought with the English fleet. By your excellent conduct and your skilful manœuvres you have fully justified the choice that I made in appointing you. I desire you to let the gentlemen of the navy under your command know that I am very pleased with their behaviour. I am much concerned to hear of M. du Chaffault's wound. I hope that it will not be troublesome, and that he will soon be well and in a state to continue his good services. I have given orders that the utmost care should be taken of the wounded: tell the widows and the relatives of the dead how very much I am aware of the loss they have suffered. M. de Sartine will communicate my subsequent orders. Judging by the way in which they have been carried out hitherto, I am convinced that the navy will be successful.

LOUIS.

M. d'Orvilliers was much touched by this letter; so was the country in general. 'I know that it touched those I have spoken with to the heart', said the Abbé de Véri, one of the best-informed of the courtiers. 'Its disconnected style arises from a sensitivity that thinks of everything.' After all the defeats, failures and disappointments of the Seven Years' War this successful encounter with the British grand fleet filled the nation with enthusiasm. Sartine was vexed with Orvilliers for not having pushed on to victory; but Louis XVI acknowledged the admiral's wisdom in wishing first to season his crews before adventuring upon a naval battle in which everything might be lost.

Very soon confirmation of the French superiority arrived with the news that the English Admiralty was putting Keppel on trial for his conduct at Ushant. So when the Duc de Chartres, who had served aboard the 84-gun ship the *Saint-Esprit*, as lieutenant-general in the national forces, reached Versailles at two in the morning, he was rapturously welcomed by all the women who had been in love with him – that is to say, by all the feminine members of the court. At eight o'clock he gave the king an account of the battle, and then the Te Deum was sung. He was complimented by the whole royal family and after that he returned to Paris, where endless ovations awaited him. That evening at the Opéra the applause was so violent and so prolonged – it lasted twenty minutes – that it became unbearable. When he went home to sup the singers followed to the illuminated Palais-Royal and sang:

> *Honour the hero, true blood of your kings!*
> *Honour the hero, with glory crowned!*

Alas! While the freemasons were extolling their Grand Master and while the ladies were arranging entire fleets upon their heads in honour of Chartres, d'Orvilliers' dispatch from Brest brought the news that it was this prince who, by not carrying out the signalled orders, had prevented the admiral from cutting the English fleet in two and destroying it. At once everybody turned against him. There was a general outcry. So that the matter should be dropped, the king hurriedly appointed him a colonel of light infantry. The public said, 'Now Chartres is colonel of the light wits – it suits him perfectly!' Maurepas was more civil: not seeing him at the Opéra he hummed,

> *Jason set out, all bold and tall;*
> *But what did he do? Why, nothing at all!*

According to Louis XVI's calculations the returns from this one naval battle were excellent: for not only had the English fleet been repulsed, but at the same time Chartres had been taught a lesson!

In the course of this burning summer danger arose on every hand, and the king was obliged to defend himself on all sides: information came in so slowly and (when it did arrive) in so confused and contradictory a state that only the patience of an angel prevented him from going out of his head and only the wisdom of a serpent allowed him to work on such shifting foundations. Back in Brest the fleet repaired its rigging, then it set out for a cruise in the Channel that brought little result. The court looked for news from d'Estaing, but in vain; for the admiral, both out of prudence and out of a desire to proceed according to his own judgment, sent no information to Versailles, for fear that it should be captured and taken to London, or, if it reached Versailles, that more exact instructions should be sent back to him.

All that was known from America was that Congress had just enthusiastically ratified the treaty with France and that it was sending a new representative to Europe, Mr John Adams, a man with a most respectable intelligence, a most laudable character, and an utterly unbearable attitude towards his fellow men. Meanwhile the king and his ministers gathered together and prepared an invasion army to threaten England, and at the same time they saw to it that the French coasts were thoroughly guarded.

In spite of Maurepas' preference for other men, of Vergennes' lack of enthusiasm and of the plotting of Choiseul's faction, Louis XVI chose the Maréchal de Broglie to command this army, because of the high opinion his father, the Dauphin, had always had of him. But, being unable to rely upon the two brothers' characters, he did not give the marshal his brother, the Comte de Broglie, as second-in-command, but sent him to Metz. Broglie had outstanding parts, but he also had very strong passions and an odd, devious way of behaving; he was determined to make the king pay heavily for this decision. He succeeded: to begin with Louis XVI told Maurepas, 'I found it very difficult to reply to all his observations . . . He said a great many disagreeable things about my whole ministry. He does not wish to act in concert with M. de Montbarrey; he wants to have his brother with him, and he wants to command the entire coast. I shall certainly not give in to all his whims. He is a most objectionable man – he is a bad citizen . . .' Then, 'The queen is as indignant as I am with the Maréchal de Broglie! He has not asked for an interview with her. He is an ill-natured man, and he has behaved very unpleasantly here.' In the end he managed to settle the matter. Broglie commanded the coast from Dunkirk to La Rochelle and the Maréchal de Mouchy from La Rochelle to Bayonne.

Once this was dealt with, Louis XVI turned his attention to stirring up his uncle in Madrid: the couriers flowed in from Spain, bringing irritating, contradictory letters. The dispatches to Madrid grew more and more frequent, but in vain: they accomplished nothing. To escape from his worries the king took to going to the queen's apartments or the Trianon, where she took refuge in order to rest. In any case there was practically no court in summer, since the journey to Compiègne had been given up. Marie-Antoinette shut herself away in her own part of the palace, dozing or seeing some particular friend, and only going out in the evening.

She fell into the habit of strolling on the terrace every night between eleven and three in the morning, while the musicians of the chapel royal, sitting upon a stand in the garden, played her music for wind-instruments. The terrace remained in the darkness, with only an occasional light from the candles indoors; here and there the bushes and the tall trees were lit up by the musicians' lanterns. The queen, Mme de Provence and Mme d'Artois would come out arm in arm or holding one another about the waist, wearing muslin dresses and immense hats with veils. In the darkness their airy forms could scarcely be made out at all.

It was delightful. But it ended in tears. In order to be admired she allowed the public to come close, to come all round her. Familiarities occured; she was as angry as if they had been gross insults and she closed the garden. Upon this the people insulted her.

Naturally the English propaganda took it up. Attacks against the king would have been preferred, but they had been found to have very little effect. At the beginning of the year *The English Spy* and the *London Chronicle* brought out poisonous articles against Louis XVI, Artois and Provence: in these publications it was said, 'Louis XVI is very tall and thin, but he is so awkwardly built that nature seems to have forgotten the rules of proportion: his head droops upon his breast, he has a waddling gait and he displays such a shocking slovenliness that it is clear to all present that he has never made any sacrifice to the graces.' Yet it was acknowledged that he was religious, pious and intelligent; he also had 'a general wish to promote the public good'. It was impossible for anyone to deny him that, even the queen who, in spite of her scorn, her shabby treatment and her most unkind teasing, had never deceived him.

Yet during those evenings at the Trianon and those afternoons at Mme de Guéménée's she had for some months past grown aware of a feeling hitherto unknown to her. At a ball at the Opéra in 1774 she happened to find herself face to face with the best-looking man she had ever seen: she addressed him, she talked with him, she asked about him. He was Count Axel de Fersen, a gentleman of very good Swedish family, the son of the famous Chancellor Fersen; and everyone joined in his praise. At that time she had felt a certain emotion at the sight of him; and then he had left. But in 1778 he had just come back. She could no longer hide from herself the fact that at last she was in love with someone, and that Fersen was teaching her what no one other than he had taught her. 'Big Axel's' prudence and his noble melancholy, as well as the queen's natural pride, preserved them from any foolishness in 1778 just as it had in 1774; but during the long evenings at the Trianon his was the picture that lit up the twilight, while the king went off to bed so that he could rise early and work.

The king was beside himself with joy at the thought of the baby that would presently be his to love. Most of the time he worked at a furious pace, but he still hunted, and at the end of November he killed a stag so old that its muzzle was completely white; he was very proud of it and in his room he kept a plaster cast, which everyone came to see. But above all his happiness overflowed upon those who surrounded him, taking the form of favours and presents: he gave his two brothers a splendid privateer taken from the English; he had given the queen a golden heart studded with rubies and diamonds at the beginning of the year, and now he overwhelmed her with little presents and treats. When she said to him, 'The carnival will be nothing for me this year, and I shall only see people with their masks off,' he surprised her by asking her, one evening at eleven, towards the beginning of December, whether she would like to see some people dressed up. 'I should be delighted,' she said, 'so long as the king comes in with them, wearing no mask or disguise of any kind.'

He came in wearing his ordinary clothes, followed by Maurepas dressed as Cupid, Mme de Maurepas as Venus, Sartine as Neptune, Vergennes with a globe on his head, a map of America on his cehst and another of England on his back, the Prince de Soubise as a Chinaman, and the Maréchal de Richelieu as a Triton, accompanied by the aged Maréchale de Mirepoix as Aurora: this couple danced a minuet with the light-footed grace of twenty-year-olds. The Maréchal de Biron was dressed as a druid, the Maréchal de Brissac was a dervish, the Duc de Cossé a vizir, Lauzun a sultan, Fronsac a Bedouin, and so on. There were other lords and ladies who made up quadrilles of rabbis, soldiers, hussars, sailors, huntsmen, scouts, etc.; and the pages were dressed as jockeys.

At one in the morning the king led the queen to his room and offered his guests a dish of hot chocolate with iced cream that was thought particularly good. 'This splendid, courtly, spontaneous entertainment,' it was said, 'pleased a great many people and gave the king a reputation as a good host.'

He did not forget to be benevolent as well; and at the same time he sent a hundred thousand francs to the Grand Almoner, to be distributed among the poor after the queen had been safely delivered, and he gave the queen the same amount to send to the chief of the police for the liberation of fathers and mothers of families imprisoned for debts incurred while their children were being nursed, and for other forms of charity. The royal baby's layette had already been brought from Paris, and those who had seen it thought it magnificent. There were already prayers in church for the child that was about to be born, and the rabbi Mardochée Venture even caused his congregation of Avignon Jews in Paris to pray that the child should be a boy – this was something the Catholic priests could not do, for, said they, the teaching of theology was that sex was already determined in the embryo.

Everybody in and around the palace was in a state of agitation, and great numbers of the Versailles servants made vows and said novenas and prayers for the child to be a boy, for a Dauphin had twice as many servants as a princess, and when a son was born their presents were larger and more frequent. The accoucheur alone had a pension of 40,000 francs if he produced a Dauphin and only a gift of 8,000–10,000 if all he could show was a girl. The allied ambassadors and all the king's loyal subjects joined their good wishes to those of the self-seeking domestics. The municipal authorities of Paris decided to find dowries and husbands for a hundred poor and virtuous maidens. The Pope sent to say that he would present the child with blessed swaddling-clothes and that one of his nephews should bring them. As for the Empress, it was reckoned at court that her gifts would be worth more than three million!

There was no household that did not echo this happy expectation, except those of the king's two brothers. If the queen were to have a son, Monsieur would no longer be the next in succession, and the idea of being heir apparent had been dear to his heart ever since 1771. And the Comte d'Artois' two sons would no longer be the *enfants de France*. Artois made jokes about the whole matter; but Monsieur, although he was more discreet, found it difficult to hide his ill-temper and distress.

The king did not choose to notice it and went on with the preparations. He appointed quarters in the queen's wing for her chief physician and her accoucheur. He also wanted to summon the Chancellor Maupeou, who was by custom a necessary witness at royal births. Louis XVI was very happy to take this opportunity of being reconciled to a man of worth. The queen would not hear of it. She did not understand how much hatred she drew down upon herself by hating people thus.

At last the child was born. At eleven-thirty in the night of 19–20 December the first pains began: she passed a trying but not excessively disagreeable night. The full labour started at eight and the child was born at eleven. The king, the princes and princesses of the blood and the whole court had been up since two. The bedrooms, the drawing-rooms and the Œil-de-Bœuf were crammed with people when the doors were opened wide.

The crowd rushed forward. Two Savoyards climbed on a table to see better. The child had been born, but it did not cry. At last it uttered a sound, and all the courtiers clapped their hands. The queen thought she had had a son and with the emotion, the joy and the heat she fainted away. The child had been carried into the next room and the king had followed, delighted at seeing such a vigorous baby. It was found to be a girl, and the greater part of the courtiers went away, disappointed. Meanwhile the queen was looking very poorly; she said, 'I am dying: make haste.' And indeed she was growing cold and lifeless. The accoucheur did not lose his head; he at once asked the surgeon to bleed her at the foot, and a few moments later she came to herself.

As soon as he was reassured about the queen, the king went to hear mass: then he sent off all the necessary messengers and wrote the countless tedious but essential family letters that were so important for keeping up traditions as well as ensuring the unity of his house. Paris hurried to light itself up: the Hôtel de Ville, the Invalides, the Palais Bourbon and the Luxembourg were outstandingly brilliant. The polite, benign Monsieur returned thanks to God, who had seen fit to preserve his rank, and congratulated his sister-in-law, setting lights in all his windows and at every corner of his roof. There was only one building in Paris that remained dark. 'Oh,' cried Mme de Rostaing, as she went by the Palais-Royal, 'Oh, Lord above, here is one illumination that looks as though it were in a sulk . . .' Her remark was bandied about all over the town.

Throughout the country and at court the main feeling was in fact disappointment; but people made the best of it in a good-natured way, if only by writing indifferent verse. For that year the people of France were in a good temper.

So was the king. He was very pleased with his daughter. And at last news had come in from America: it was not very good, but it was by no means bad. Although d'Estaing had done nothing brilliant he had pleased the Americans, and that was of the first importance. He arrived in the Delaware on 7 July: he was made thoroughly welcome there and left for Newport, where he did not manage to accomplish anything and where he met with adverse criticism from American officers and newspapers. Some offensive articles, and a brawl at Boston in which French officers were insulted reminded the French soldiers and sailors that there was not only a military victory but also one over public opinion to be gained.

Such was the indifferent result of the first year of war; but all failures had been avoided, and when the French ships had met the

English they had been very clearly superior to them. The nation was behind the king, and the spirit of patriotism ruled throughout the land.

Leaning over the cradle the king and queen rejoiced in their happiness, and in an innovating mood they determined not to make the baby listen to speeches from the city corporations.

The decision met with approval, but it was thought uncommonly daring.

Chapter IX

The industrious King

IN THOSE EARLY DAYS OF 1779 VERSAILLES REMAINED
empty, and the winter storms finally stripped the gardens and the
park. Every day the king came to the queen's bedside: he spent
part of the morning there and he often came back in the afternoon
and stayed for the evening. He never tired of watching his
daughter.

On 8 February they went to Paris with great ceremony, to
thank God at Notre-Dame for the birth of the child. They
scattered money as they went, but there was little cheering. On
the Pont-Neuf the orange-women complimented them in a
manner that was much remarked upon: they praised the king for
having had an ancestor, since it was thanks to this fact that they
were able to sell oranges in the shadow of his statue. The Provost
seemed to talk rather too long and the market-women were somewhat too free; but everything went off quite well.

The king had arranged everything with the utmost care. Maria-
Theresa of Austria was god-mother and Charles III of Spain godfather. As a lying-in present he gave the queen a hundred and
twenty thousand livres. Since he was fully aware of her inexperi-

ence in politics and of the violence of her political passions he fell in with the practice adopted these five years past by Maurepas and summed up in the words 'give her frivolity free rein'. He went with her to the ball on the last Sunday before Lent, and he let her go by herself to that on Shrove Tuesday. She had cause to regret it: her coach broke down, she had to get into a hired carriage and she arrived very late and alone. Once there she found Fersen and her usual set of friends, who took great care of her. Nevertheless, a little while later she came down with measles. She was obliged to live in isolation from the king and the whole court; but moved by an absurd whim she begged her husband to allow her male nurses in the form of Coigny, Besenval, Guines and Esterhazy. Their number ensured their proper behaviour and he was too delighted with his daughter to refuse: but it caused a great deal of adverse comment.

During this time the king could work, and the business was too important for him not to devote all his attention to it. During September 1778 Bouillé had taken the island of Dominica in the West Indies, but at about the same time the English took Saint-Pierre-et-Miquelon, in the North Atlantic, the islands being scarcely defended at all. It was clear that preparations would have to be intensified and all hopes of a short and easy war abandoned.

England was reacting, equipping new fleets and assembling armies. She tried to make use of Spain, who was pleased with the idea of playing the mediator, against France: she brought pressure to bear to bring Holland over to her side, and the Stadhouder, who was married to Frederick the Great's sister, did his utmost to accomplish this. He did not succeed, however, for La Vauguyon, the French minister at the Hague, had a decisive influence with the western trading provinces, which were jealous of the English and in favour of the Insurgents. But this whole business had to be followed with the utmost attention, and the king had to work in conjunction with Franklin, whose propaganda network in the Netherlands was unusually efficient.

Affairs in Germany began to take a happier turn. Ever since a fifteenth-century charter that invalidated the rights of the Haps-burgs to Lower Bavaria had been discovered, and Maria-Theresa's confessor had told her that her son's claims were unjust, she wanted peace and she did her best to secure it. On his side, Frederick II dared not keep his troops in Silesia and Bohemia during the winter: he withdrew them to his own country. A note from Catherine II to Joseph II completed his discomfiture: it was clear to him that from now on he was isolated in Europe, and he accepted mediation and the holding of a conference at Teschen. France and Russia acted as peace-makers. Austria was represented by Baron Thugut, who had long been an agent in French pay (winter 1778–1779). Everything seemed to be going well.

M. Necker announced that everything was going well in his department too. His administration was that of a thoroughly capable businessman, an experienced banker, and not that of a reformer or a theoretician like Turgot. His first care was to fill the treasury. He thought of a lottery, and it accomplished his purpose; but naturally it was denounced by M. Turgot and his friends and those *philosophes* who did not dine with the Neckers as a wretched method that was unworthy of the King of France and that was also both immoral and calculated to deprave the people. The king paid no attention, and he subscribed to the lottery himself.

But M. Necker had still more daring plans in mind. He annulled the contract for the posts, which had been farmed out, and brought them under state supervision. He did away with the receivers of crown lands; he abolished the posts of *intendant des finances*; he reduced the number of administrators of the lottery to six. He sent Pélisséri, who had criticized these measures, to the Bastille. M. Trudaine, one of the dismissed intendants, had a great many friends, and they made a great deal of noise. Sartine did not conceal the fact that he looked upon M. Necker as a cad; and M. de Vergennes, whose opinion was even harsher, kept it to himself solely in order to do him more harm. In the vexation his choice caused him, Maurepas consoled himself by saying that he had lapsed from Turgomania into Neckromania. The Parlement of Paris watched for its chance, and some hot-headed members such as Duval d'Espréménil made their thunderbolts ready. But the edict for the loan that Necker had drawn up was registered, and as all the bankers supported his administration they subscribed to it at once. They then speculated with their holdings and made as much money out of the public as they possibly could – an entirely natural and customary practice in all periods.

In 1778 Necker set about two other undertakings, bolder ones this time. He induced the king to consent to the setting up of provincial assemblies, the first of which came into action in Berry. These gatherings of distinguished men of the three estates, nominated by the king, and in which the third estate had as many seats as the two others combined, were in the first place to deliberate on the apportioning of the taxes and to make suggestions for the improvement of local administration. According to Necker's intentions they were gradually to take over that share in the country's life which the parlements had unjustly arrogated to themselves; but unfortunately for him he talked about it too much, and the parliamentarians were aware of his views. Nevertheless he conspired with them to bring back the Protestants and to draft a statute in their favour. The king did not set himself against it, for he looked upon the Protestants' position in France as one that could not be tolerated in the long run: yet he did not wish to force the clergy's hand, and in 1778, when the bishops begged him not to undertake anything, he refrained from adopting the measure. He supported Necker, who worked in an orderly manner and whose services he could not dispense with in the midst of a great war that called for massive and regular supplies ... He put up with him.

He preserved a serene equanimity in all circumstances. With equal kindness he welcomed d'Estaing, back empty-handed from the West Indies; Lauzun, who had made a brilliant conquest of Senegal; and La Fayette, home from America. To begin with the king put La Fayette under house-arrest (a civility that was owing to his charming wife, who had been left alone far too long) and then he received him with great honours at Versailles. Louis XVI listened to his long and enthusiastic accounts and to his wild suggestions. The young hero asked for a fleet for the United States – they could not do without one if they were to win – and as the French navy was wholly taken up with France, the West Indies, the Levant, India, etc., he suggested that eight men-of-war should be hired from the King of Sweden. But this by no means suited either the King of France or the King of Sweden. La Fayette then wanted to mount an expedition against the English coast with the 'Knight of the Seas', that strange and wonderful being John Paul Jones, the most splendid corsair of the century. But it was difficult to work out the arrangements.

All the arrangements were difficult to work out. Now that Spain had made up her mind to join France, Lord North pretended that Spain was not really waging war against England by giving France the support of her fleet – Spain was merely conforming to the requirements of the Family Pact and he saw no reason whatever for recalling the British ambassador from Madrid. This was stepping back only to spring the farther. For his part, Charles III was willing to collaborate with his nephew at Versailles, but he did not choose to have his fleet sail to join the French at Brest: he insisted that the rendezvous should take place at the island of Sisargas, off Corunna. All this provided material for endless arguments that were made even more interminable by the slowness of the couriers between Paris and Madrid and Madrid and Paris. The courtiers cursed the Spanish alliance, and M. de Vergennes needed all his patience not to be driven mad by his official dealings with Aranda. In order to soothe him, Vergennes took Aranda home, where his family made much of him. He also spent many hours in drawing up the King of France's manifesto on the subject of the American war: the king would not allow it to contain anything that was contrary to the truth, to good breeding or to the civility that he wished to preserve towards the King of England. His manifesto was therefore well received by the neutral powers, and it was of such a kind that it might draw over those who were wavering in their opinion.

Now, at the beginning of 1779, Louis XVI was beginning to reap the rewards of his prudent conduct. He neither wanted the *philosophes*' crusade that La Fayette and a very small group of gentlemen longed for, nor the annihilation of Great Britain. He wished to give France back the standing she had lost in 1762 and 1763, to increase her trade and to provide her with a new, active and well-placed ally. Those were his aims, and nothing more.

Yet he was obliged to fall in with the Spanish plan, which had the support of public opinion: it was a plan that called for dealing England a mortal blow by means of a great naval victory and the invasion of the British Isles, and that was the reason for the junction of the two fleets, the assembly of an army of forty thousand men at Saint-Malo and various other manœuvres.

There were certain black clouds that worried him: the total lack of sympathy between the Spaniards and the Insurgents, their conflicting territorial ambitions, points of view and states of mind. Gérard had not been successful with Congress: finding this to be the case he had tried to buy the members of that body. Some were willing to be bribed, without carrying out their side of the bargain: all the others burst out in a fury against him. Vergennes was obliged to bring him back to France.

The darkest of all these clouds was the impossibility of discovering any man of genius to take command of the navy. Apart from that the realm was being managed by the most efficient administration that France had ever known. A series of painstaking ministers had entrusted the main departments to permanent civil servants of a greater ability than those of any other country whatever. At the foreign ministry Gérard, his brother Gérard de Rayneval, Hennin and Genet (the head of the translators) formed a staff of exceptional quality; and the many paid agents they had in the foreign administrations, such as Thugut at Vienna, Samuel Cooper at Boston and Jean Luzac at Leyden, provided them with the fullest intelligence. At the treasury Necker was no less well supplied – Coster's ability was famous throughout Europe. At the Admiralty the Chevalier de Fleurieu preserved Sartine from all blunders; and so it went on in all the other branches of the administration. In spite of the hidden rivalry that always affects important men, the ministers themselves got on well together and made up a well-knit team, particularly those who were in immediate contact with the war: they were Maurepas, the co-ordinator, Sartine and Montbarrey, who carried out the plans; Vergennes, who day by day took over a little more of the Mentor's office, though without angering him, and who drew the broad lines of the warlike operations, for this war was never anything more than diplomacy's handmaiden. It was therefore a polite, logical and rational war.

When it is remembered that the main theatre lay some two thousand miles from the staffs and that communication with the forces engaged took place by means of frigates, which needed between thirty and a hundred days to reach the West Indies and as many to return, it is easy to see how carefully operations had to be mounted and how flexible all the plans had to be. In spite of her immense superiority over the Insurgents England had suffered the humiliating failure of Saratoga: this arose from the lack of co-operation between the British armies in America and of under-standing between the British ministries. George III, like Louis XVI, was an upright, patriotic man, and, in spite of all that has been said about him, an intelligent one, but he had neither the knowledge nor the ability to create what Louis XVI had brought into being in four years of concentrated work – a well-balanced, well-tuned, smooth-running machine.

What Louis XVI lacked was a leader of genius. With the help of Sartine, Montbarrey and Maurepas, who knew innumerable people, the king had searched everywhere. He found neither a Tourville nor a Duquesne. He had able, conscientious, brave and prudent seamen – Orvilliers, Guichen, La Touche-Tréville, La Motte-Piquet. At a lower level there were two heroic figures, Suffren, the fiery Provençal, and John Paul Jones, the Scotch-American, a commodore under Congress but serving in France. In 1779 he bewitched the public with his victories. La Fayette longed to attack Liverpool with him. But Jones sailed alone, and by the light of the moon he fought a strange, mirage-like battle within sight of the port of Hull.

All this did not compensate for the lack of a great admiral. For want of a great naval commander, it would be necessary to win by means of method – by means of striking hard at the right moment and at the vital place. Louis XVI hoped for nothing from any landing in England, and he therefore attended to La Fayette's urgent requests for French troops in America. He sensed that the path to victory lay there, but he kept the secret for himself and Vergennes.

M. Necker could not bear anything being hidden from him. But Sartine concealed all operations, current or planned, from the finance minister. Necker, red and puffed up with fury, cried out that in these circumstances he could no longer carry out his functions: that was the great problem of the summer of 1779. The Genevan found that he was both more attacked and more popular than ever. As he believed himself to be the ablest, the most clear-sighted and intelligent man in the ministry, he thought it his duty to defend himself. 1779 was therefore a stormy year. The court attacked him with all its power, the bankers defended him in a hidden but efficacious manner, and the papers, the *Mercures* and *Nouvelles*, gave him their support. The heart of the battle was the conflict between Necker and Sartine: Necker let it be known that the navy cost fourteen million a month, while Sartine had it put about that Necker was more English than French and that he was overlooking nothing to bring the war to an end as soon as possible in favour of His Britannic Majesty.

The king was angered by all this, yet at the same time he was deeply attached to his navy: he did his best to pacify both sides. He put up with the abolition of many offices in his household – the treasurers of the king's and the queen's household, the three posts of controller-general, etc. He even allowed the suppression of the place of Grand Master of the Royal Household, which was held by the Prince de Condé. All this gave pleasure, but it undermined the power of the crown; it is always dangerous to isolate a sovereign in the midst of his people. Yet on the other hand a top-heavy state can ruin even a wealthy country. The king therefore agreed with Necker in these matters. He was more reserved about the provincial assemblies, however. When Necker told him that people complained of the intendants, he replied, 'In every age there have been very loud complaints against the form of administration in the *pays d'Etat*.[1] The hereditary presidents, the councillors, the members, all those pillars of the *pays d'Etat* who make up their establishments, do not make the Frenchmen in the provinces they administer any happier than the others. It is quite

[1] Those provinces that were governed by Parlements and by their own Estates, as opposed to the *pays d'Elections*, which were ruled by intendants.

certain that Brittany, with its Estates, is no happier than Normandy, which has none.' When Necker pointed out his private advantage in no longer being personally responsible for the administration, but rather the intermediary ('the arbiter') between the Estates and his people, the king indignantly replied, 'The essence of my authority lies not in being intermediary but at the head.' He allowed the experiment of these assemblies to be proceeded with, but he did not yet allow them to be set up all over the country.

It was impossible to do without Necker in 1779. Human nature is so constituted that men will more readily put up with the loss of their children than with that of their money. Glory is a consolation for the one, but not for the other. Now Necker produced money for the war without insisting upon too much from the people. Public opinion was in favour of him. With the king's permission he did away with mortmain and announced the fact in a high-flown preamble. The more sensitive souls were moved even to tears. More often than not, those who were subject to mortmain were very sorry that the measure had ever been adopted, for it confronted them with difficulties that they could not overcome.

All this took up the attention of the public, which was very excitable that summer, for the people were waiting for the news of a decisive victory and the end of the war. Nothing came: everyone grew impatient. The French and Spanish fleets had indeed joined, but too late. They swept the Channel without meeting any English ships. A sudden storm scattered them. There was a disorderly return to Brest, and no victory. The Spanish fleet took back a great many sick men and a great deal of ill-feeling. So costly and so indecisive a campaign caused intense vexation.

Meanwhile in the West Indies the Comte de Bouillé's military brilliance had secured Saint-Vincent and Grenada for France (August 1779). For his part, d'Estaing helped the American armies in the north, and then failed in an attack upon Savannah, where he was wounded. He came home crestfallen but glorious. And so the campaign of 1779 came to an end.

There were discontented murmurings at court. People fell into their bad old ways. They forgot the distant war. That is the worst of sea-battles: they do not stir the people in the same way as fighting by land – people watch them as though they were at the theatre. Such was the case with the American war, that 'charming war' as La Fayette and his friends called it, but a tough war for Louis XVI and Vergennes. Mentor was no longer to be relied upon: his gout, his weariness and his irony were all increasing. When news was brought in, good or bad, he hummed a mocking tune. If the king asked him for advice he would reply, 'Sire, it is time for you to manage on your own.'

As if that were possible! The king had to know everything. All problems were brought to him. France carried on an important trade with the Levant: it had to be protected against the English privateers. This was done successfully. Another success was required, and that was the winning of the war. The failure of the 1779 campaign did not greatly surprise Louis XVI; but he particularly wished to ensure the victory of the United States. In 1779 this was thought to be doubtful. Their currency was depreciating; Congress could not wring any more money out of the country. In spite of his courage Washington accomplished nothing with his rapidly diminishing army; and British intrigues in Philadelphia were encouraging a party that called for the whole of Canada, Louisiana, and the West. How could the Canadians bear to become American in the event of a French victory? The alliance would fall to pieces.

It would also fall to pieces if the plots in Congress against Franklin were to continue. The deputies were businessmen; they could not bear to see Franklin as the sole occupant of that lucrative position, where it was possible to speculate so profitably on foreign exchange. The French court stood up for Franklin, whom it liked very much, and showed the strongest aversion for John Adams, who had been sent to help him, but whom Vergennes considered a thoroughly undesirable person – indeed, he refused to see him. The king let Philadelphia know that he would receive no one but Franklin and that Adams would have to be sent elsewhere. Franklin was all the more needed in Paris since he was invaluable in helping France to fob off Austria and Russia, both of whom wanted to thrust their mediation upon Louis XVI.

Maria-Theresa was not particularly eager to do so, but her son, ashamed of the pitiful part he had played in Bavaria, was in search of balm for his pride, and he looked forward with delight to being the arbiter between Louis XVI and George III. The same hope filled the bosom of Catherine II, who was much attracted by the idea of playing an important role in the West, and whose trade was much disturbed by the naval operations. Now it was of great importance not to anger Joseph II, who was already ill-disposed and whose entire court openly displayed its anglophilia; and it would be insane to offend Catherine II, for Vergennes had hopes of winning her sympathy and good offices.

In time of war it is essential to be on good terms with everybody, above all with one's allies. Even when they start to blockade Gibraltar, as did Louis' Spanish friends, saying that the town was short of provisions and that its fall was imminent. Without believing them, Louis XVI gave his approval. It was a family matter.

It was a difficult question to deal with, but it was by no means the most difficult, for that was the problem of Marie-Antoinette. She no longer refused herself to the king, but she would not take the slightest care of herself, and the result was a series of miscarriages. Nothing amused her, apart from her own little band. Even there she quarrelled with Guines, who had tried to lecture her. Her one idol was Mme de Polignac. In this way the king had a hold over her. But he had to pay highly for it – thirty thousand francs a month for Vaudreuil, Mme de Polignac's particular friend, for the duration of the war (his estates were in Santo Domingo, and he no longer received the income from them), as well as a great many favours.

In October, when the court moved to Marly, the king gambled, as a compliment to Marie-Antoinette. He lost 59,394 livres, and understood what it was all about. The same day the queen lost 1,200 louis and Chartres 11,000. During this one stay the man who held the bank won 19,000 louis. The king reflected that Soldini must have been mistaken in recommending gambling to him as a proper means of uniting families by providing them with amusement. He resolved to set matters right.

Meanwhile he was obliged to pay countless debts for the queen, whom motherhood had made even more extravagant: 20,000 francs for gambling debts, 14,250 for her jeweller, 15,000 for her favourite Esterhazy. At the end of the year, 100,000 francs to start her afresh.

1780 began with renewed demands from the queen, whose privy purse had to be doubled (400,000 francs a month, though she agreed not to draw more than 300,000 so long as the war went on).

It also began with a cold that was caught by everyone in Versailles and Paris – a cold which only d'Estaing's return put out of their heads. Crowds gathered in the drawing-rooms of the palace to see the hero of Savannah, Dominica and so many other battles. The king's welcome displayed so much grace and kindness that the papers were obliged to speak of it: 'In the king's reception of M. le Comte d'Estaing we beheld the man who is responsive to gallant deeds, the prince who is devoted to those who serve him well, and the friend of our country's brave defenders; but no less shiningly apparent was the extreme goodness of his heart. His replies and observations were often those of a man of great wisdom and always those of one rich in common sense.' When the Comte de Broglie saw fit to criticize d'Estaing in his presence, the king exclaimed, 'Yes, he was wrong to keep my ships and their crews safe, and to bring them back to me in good condition: you only showed your face in Alsace, and you caused more than twenty thousand men to desert from my armies.' In this way Louis XVI tried to bring back a little of that good French common sense that he possessed in so eminent a degree to his court, in which showy, empty witticisms so often took the place of reason.

This did not prevent all setbacks. In January 1780 the Comte de Vergennes had a most disagreeable one – one that did not fail to reflect upon the king to some extent. Both the king and Vergennes had a weakness for Beaumarchais, whose sound head, whimsical heart and delicate hand had been useful to them on more than one occasion; so when they had to reply to the English proclamation, which was well written and superficially convincing, the king let Beaumarchais display his wit at the expense of the British ministry; for he did not choose to compromise the dignity of the crown or of his ministers in this polemic. The author of the *Barber of Seville* called his work *Observations sur le Mémoire justificatif de la Cour de Londres.* He wrote with all the brilliance of which he was capable, and he was not displeased with the result. Nor was Vergennes: but that more than ordinarily careful man, who read and reread all his subordinates' productions, allowed his watchfulness to doze this time: or did he perhaps believe that in time of war it was useful to tell the truth? He was mistaken. In his pamphlet Beaumarchais described the way in which 'he had felt his courage revive at the thought that his country was to be revenged for the humiliation to which she had been subjected by the way the treaty of 1763 had fixed the small number of ships it still deigned to allow her'.

Choiseul reacted instantly: the offensive words touched him to the quick. Writing to Vergennes he reproached him with allowing the circulation of a falsehood, for the treaty of 1763 contained nothing of the kind. 'There can be no sort of difficulty,' wrote Choiseul, 'in making the falsity of the fact put forward by M. de Beaumarchais evident to the public; but I have the honour of pointing out to you, Monsieur, that this false fact, recorded in a document that is thought to have the ministry's approval, may have dangerous consequences.' He accused it above all of slandering the late king, who would never have tolerated such a clause in a treaty. And he insisted that Louis XVI should be informed of the discussion. Vergennes regretted his carelessness bitterly; he reproved Beaumarchais, and he raised the matter in the council, which decided to put an end to the affair by suppressing the pamphlet. For its part the Parlement took the same decision.

Choiseul had won a point. But this did not bring him back into the king's good graces, for Louis XVI did not forget his father's indignation at the 1763 treaty, and he was waging this war, as Beaumarchais had hinted, in the hope of wiping out the wrongs and the humiliations of 1763.

Louis XVI felt more resentment against Choiseul than he had before. But resentment was a waste of time at a moment when all his forces were barely enough to deal with the current emergencies: Nassau had been beaten in his attack on Jersey; so had the Spanish fleet before Gibraltar; and a French convoy from the West Indies had been taken within sight of its home shore.

All this brought to mind the necessity for winning the war quickly by striking England a crippling blow. Louis XVI decided to carry all the effort overseas – to send Guichen to the West Indies with eighteen ships and four thousand men to reinforce Bouillé, and to make a secret gathering of an army of picked men under Rochambeau in Brittany. Four ships escorted the Spanish fleet, which left for Cadiz on 13 January 1780, and Sartine hurried on with all the other naval preparations.

This news and an infinity of speculation upon it, to say nothing of the flood of untrue, inexact or made-up information, kept Versailles in a fever; and in the case of Marie-Antoinette the tension was increased by the grief of seeing Fersen leave for Rochambeau's army. She hid her sorrow as well as she could, but for the sake of one she felt obliged to show great kindness for all. At this period the king made a great series of promotions in the army so that the land forces, which had not hitherto been engaged but which had been by no means useless, should not grow discouraged, and he did his best to pay as much attention as possible to the queen's wishes. Mercy wrote to Maria-Theresa, 'The queen's protection has had a great deal of influence upon the choice of the field officers who are to be employed during the coming campaign, either in Europe or in America, particularly in favour of the Marquis de La Fayette, the Vicomte de Noailles and the Prince Emmanuel de Salm . . .' These were all very regular attendants at Mme de Polignac's salon. The king took a pleasure in sending the most brilliant young officers to America, so that they should become seasoned and accustomed to fighting against the English.

They were sent to America, and all the others asked to leave for abroad, for everyone knew that although the invasion of England was still spoken of, it had in fact been given up, and that the invasion of Ireland, which Franklin still advocated, had little chance of success. All these plans received their last blow when one fine morning, just as he was about to step into his coach, the

Comte de Paradès was arrested (4 April 1780). This Comte de Paradès, who was neither Comte nor 'de' nor Paradès, but the son of a pastry-cook in Colmar, seemed a charming man, the finest flower of international espionage, of those intelligence agents who then lived in such a grand style in France. Like his hermaphroditical colleague the Chevalier d'Eon, Paradès had been required to prepare the invasion of England. He had been trained from his youth to be a secret agent for the foreign minister: Vergennes, who was on very good terms with Sartine, transferred Paradès to him for missions to England. These journeys, which were well paid, bold and successful, won him a fortune, very important contacts and the protection of the Comte d'Aranda, who still dreamt of the conquest of England. The Duc de Croy valued him highly too – he spoke so well and he had such innate nobility! He was about to become a grandee of Spain with the right of riding in the king's coaches, when the king, moved by a fortunate inspiration, caused inquiries to be made. It transpired that Paradès had been detected by the English in 1778, that he had been acting as a double agent since that date, and that in all events he was wanting in discretion.

So he went to the Bastille. Aranda, who had had no hesitation about making him a grandee of Spain the day before, now declared that he was a traitor. But Vergennes, who beneath his dull exterior was both percipient and witty, made no bones over acknowledging that Paradès was an intelligent, cultivated, courageous man, and in spite of all his thoughtlessness, an honest one, who had not been of the least use to England. Paradès might therefore have had a fresh start if his health had not broken down, sending him to rest for all eternity from a brief, brilliant and broken life. France lost a very valuable tool in him, but nothing more. Yet Vergennes' enemies and Sartine's blew up the affair out of all proportion; and as it was picturesque there was a great deal of talk about it. But it was of little importance, and Vergennes was vindicated by his own well-earned fame.

He had just gained a diplomatic victory that must have made Louis XIV turn in his grave. It was a victory that owed as much to Louis XVI's wisdom as it did to Vergennes' skill. Catherine II,

impressed by the king's personality and anxious to draw closer
to France at a time when that country possessed an intelligent
and hard-working ruler, had already made advances through
Lauzun, an amateur diplomat, a volunteer who hoped in this way
to secure an ambassador's post for himself. These advances failed,
for Catherine and Lauzun had chosen to make use of Marie-
Antoinette, whose flighty mind was incapable of following this
delicate business and whose Austrian heart could take no pleasure
in helping to bring about better relations between France and
Russia. But Vergennes took particular care of his contacts with
Russia, and ever since 1778, when he had reconciled Russia and
Turkey, Catherine had had a very high opinion of him. This was
the state of affairs when it was learnt, in March 1780, that she
had just made a declaration to each of the belligerents: she would
look upon those powers engaged in war who insisted upon searching ships wearing the Russian flag as enemies. At the same time
she fitted out her fleet and suggested to the other European maritime powers that they should form a kind of league for the defence
of the freedom of the seas.

Vergennes hastened to agree with her. In fact this League of
Armed Neutrality threatened England alone, for France recognized the principle and applied it. Thus at sea there were grouped
against England all the powers that accepted Catherine's invitation – Austria, Spain, Prussia, Portugal, Holland, the Two Sicilies,
etc. Never since 1700 had England suffered such a diplomatic
reverse.

Vergennes made the most of this victory: he wrote to La
Luzerne, Gérard's successor in the United States,

> The object of these conversations is directly contrary to the
> interests of the court of London; as for us, not only have we
> applauded them, but confidentially I may tell you that we
> have advanced them as far as possible; and the result of our
> conduct has been that all the powers have done justice to the
> principles that guide the king's council, while at the same
> time they look upon the English more and more as the
> tyrants of the sea, as an ambitious nation that thinks all the
> others are tributary to it.

Vergennes' subtle mind had induced him to put all the resources of French diplomacy in all the courts of Europe and even in America behind Catherine's plan, without depriving her of the glory that she would derive from remaining at the head of this league, which was there in principle to ensure the freedom of the seas and which was in fact directed against the intolerable claims of the English and their even more intolerable practices. If the war were to last, the members of this league might very well be brought into the struggle against Great Britain; meanwhile they threatened her prestige and limited her navy's freedom of action. This diplomatic victory was therefore very timely. It reassured public opinion, which was beginning to grow weary of the war.

Throughout France and the whole of Europe public opinion unanimously hailed the operation as a master-stroke on the part of Vergennes. In the United States it acted as a stimulant for patriotism, at a moment when the country was struggling with a full-scale financial crisis, and when its army was wanting in unity and enterprise.

It also allowed France to urge Spain to greater efforts, and Louis XVI sent d'Estaing to that country. The Spaniards were preparing a fine fleet of forty ships at Cadiz, and they were to be joined by a French fleet that was being fitted out at Toulon.

It was put about that this great armament, carrying fifty thousand soldiers under Maillebois, was to attack Ireland, Scotland and England.

The truth of the matter was that Guichen and his convoy sailed and reached their destination, while La Motte-Picquet, escorting a convoy from Martinique to Santo-Domingo, beat a British fleet superior in number. And lastly on 2 May 1780 the Chevalier de Ternay sailed with his very large convoy, carrying five thousand of Rochambeau's men, his staff and money for the United States, the whole under the escort of seven ships of the line.

He carried France's hopes with him; and with him too there were the country's finest names, all volunteers – the Baron de Montesquieu, the Duc de Lauzun, the Comte de Charlus, the Chevalier de Chastellux, the Vicomte de Noailles, the Comte de

Fersen, the Duke of Zweibrücken . . . There had been furious competition to go.

Nevertheless, they still had to get there over that ocean patrolled by British fleets and lashed by violent storms. The king grew uneasy; Sartine slept no more; Vergennes turned a disagreeable yellow; Franklin's appetite abandoned him. Only Montbarrey remained calm, for his mistress was in the best of moods. Everything turned out well. On 11 July 1780 Rochambeau reached the United States. On 17 April 1781 Guichen beat Rodney off St Lucia; then off Cape St Vincent the Spaniards took an English convoy of fifty-seven ships carrying troops, stores and money to India and the West Indies, while at the same time, in American waters, the Insurgents seized a convoy of twenty-five sail on the way to Quebec.

In spite of the fall of Charleston in May the campaign was beginning well.

Chapter X

The patient King

THE CAMPAIGN WAS NOT LOUIS XVI'S ONLY CARE. HE WAS
conscious of the country's weariness: it was said that the French
losses at sea were greater than those of the English; the men
in command were blamed for their slowness and their lack of dash,
and no credit was given for their skill and humanity. Above all it
was thought that the whole concern was costing too much; and
there was a great deal of discontented, factious mockery. The
king was accused of 'weakness', the ministers were criticized.

Yet Louis XVI kept his ministers under firm control; in May
1780 he dismissed Bertin, who had given good service but who
was now growing dull. The king did not replace him but shared
out his duties among the other ministers. Necker inherited the
most important – mines and factories.

The Genevan was carving out a place for himself that grew in
importance day by day; and as he was a hard worker, thoroughly
conversant with his subject, he gave the country's finances an
appearance of ease and plenty that suited everybody. In fact he
was mortgaging the future. His repeated loans were obliged to
carry very high interest. He concealed this by showy tactics, by

small, comparatively unproductive reforms that he announced with a great deal of noise, the abolition of four hundred and six posts in the royal household, and so on. But compensation had to be paid – that is to say seven million laid out at once for a yearly saving of two million. Foreign countries, the provinces and the *philosophes* applauded. Paris became filled with discontented people. Everywhere adverse criticism of Necker was to be heard; the princes of the blood were angry with him because of the suppression of the receivers-general of the treasury; Sartine accused him of wanting to save England by 'strangling the war', that is to say by refusing him the necessary funds for the navy. There was a scandal brewing.

Another burst out first. During the afternoon of Wednesday in Holy Week the Prince de Lambesc, the Master of the Horse, together with his brother the Prince de Vaudémont and his wife were coming back from the country; as they went along the rue Saint-Antoine in their coach and six, the coachman reined in; Lambesc told him to push on, and the result was that the coach ran straight into a procession formed by a priest carrying the viaticum and the choirboys who were attending him. They were all knocked over, and the priest was hurt. At this spectacle Lambesc burst into laughter and ordered the coachman to whip up his horses. He almost paid dearly for his action, for the angry crowd hooted him and ran after his coach. The horses' speed saved their masters.

But the whole quarter was in a tumult. When the Comtesse de Brionne, the mother of Lambesc and Vaudémont and quite as much of a libertine as her sons but more prudent, heard their ludicrous account of the affair and received a letter from the parish priest she fully realized its gravity. She dismissed the coachman, hastily informed the police and the public prosecutor, and hurried off to the curé's house with a deed guaranteeing a pension of two hundred livres for the wounded priest, to whom she also promised her protection. She would have liked her children to apologize to him, but they found this too distasteful, and the matter was settled without its being done. The priests proved humble and circumspect; but the more religious people criticized the curé's weakness, and even the *philosophes* cried out in indignation against the barbarity of the act – they called for the punishment of the arrogance of those in high places. A little later the king made Vaudémont and Mme de Brionne aware of his displeasure.

The scandal affected Marie-Antoinette, for Mme de Brionne, Lambesc and Vaudémont were princes from Lorraine and friends of hers; her protection had gone to their heads and they had an equal scorn for God and the king. The whole group made an ostentatious display of scoffing impiety. The king and the people felt the same anger welling up, and Louis realized the urgent necessity of making these dissolute and unruly members of the nobility see reason; ever since Choiseul's ministry they were to be seen flaunting themselves everywhere, and Artois was copying their foolishness.

But the clergy could not defend themselves. Their leaders openly displayed their vices – Jarente, the Bishop of Orléans, for example, whom the king forbade to appear before him; Thémines, Bishop of Blois, the acknowledged lover of Mlle Colombe, the dancer at the Opéra, and Cardinal Louis de Rohan of Strasburg, whose magnificence, mistresses and extravagance were the scandal of the town.

Louis XVI was angry with them all, but he was even more angry with the *philosophe* priests. He made use of a trick to punish one of them, the Abbé d'Espagnac. This abbé, who was an ambitious man, was to preach Lenten sermons at Versailles: in his mind this was a step towards a mitre. But on 22 March 1780 the *Gazette de France* said, referring to him, 'There was no sermon in the king's chapel on Holy Thursday, because the Abbé d'Espagnac, canon of the Church of Paris and vicar-general of Sens, who was to preach the Last Supper sermon before His Majesty, felt unwell just as he was about to go into the pulpit, and in no condition to deliver his discourse.'

That was the official account. In reality, at the moment the abbé, puffed up with zeal and vanity, was preparing to climb up to utter a fine philosophical sermon the usher told him that the king knew that he was unwell and excused him from carrying out his duties.

LOUIS XV, BY VAN LOO. GRENOBLE MUSEUM *(Photo Giraudon)*

THE DAUPHIN, FATHER O
LOUIS XVI, BY NIVELO
VERSAILLES MUSEUM
(*Photo Musées Nationaux*)

MARIE-JOSÈPHE OF
SAXONY, BY NATTIER.
VERSAILLES MUSEUM.
(*Photo Musées Nationaux*)

THE APARTMENTS OF THE DAUPHIN UNDER LOUIS XV,
THE BEDCHAMBER, THE DRAWING-ROOM
(*Photos Musées Nationaux*)

LOUIS-AUGUSTE, THE DAUPHIN   (*Photo Musées Nationaux*

ERZ.HERZOGIN.ANTONIA.

THE ARCHDUCHESS MARIE-ANTOINETTE, BY WAGENSCHOEN   *(Photo Bulloz)*

THE DUKE DE CHOISEUL, BY VAN LOO. LÉONINO COLLECTION
(*Photo Hachette*)

THE SIGNATURES ON THE MARRIAGE CONTRACT OF THE DAUPHIN AND MARIE-ANTOINETTE. ARCHIVES OF SEINE-ET-OISE

FÊTE GIVEN FOR THE MARRIAGE OF THE DAUPHIN AND THE DAUPHINE

(*Photo Giraudon*)

THE KING   *(Photo Musées Nationaux)*

THE QUEEN, BY MADAME VIGÉE-LEBRUN   (*Photo Musées Nationaux*)

THE LITTLE APARTMENTS OF THE KING AT VERSAILLES,
THE LIBRARY OF LOUIS XVI   (Photo Musées Nationa

THE BEDCHAMBER OF MARIE-ANTOINETTE AT THE PETIT TRIANON (Photo Archi

LOUIS XVI RECEIVING HOMAGE FROM CHEVALIERS
OF THE ORDER OF THE HOLY SPIRIT *(Photo Musées Nationaux)*

DANCE ON THE SITE OF THE BASTILLE. WALL PAPER. CARNAVALET MUSEUM
(Photo Josse-Lalance)

THE RETURN FROM VARENNES   (Photo Bulloz)

20 JUNE 1792. CARNAVALET MUSEUM   (Photo Josse-Lalance)

THE ROYAL FAMILY'S MASS AT THE TUILERIES, 9 AUGUST 1792, *(Photo Bulloz)*
BY HUBERT ROBERT

CAPTURE OF THE TUILERIES, 10 AUGUST 1792, BY PRIEUR *(Photo Bulloz)*

THE TOWER OF THE TEMPLE IN 1793. ANONYMOUS PAINTING.
CARNAVALET MUSEUM
(*Photo Musée Carnavalet*)

LOUIS XVI AT THE BAR OF THE CONVENTION, 26 DECEMBER 1792

THE EXECUTION OF LOUIS XVI. ANONYMOUS GERMAN. CARNAVALET MUSEUM

The amazed preacher declared that he was perfectly well, and that even if he were at the point of death he would think it an honour to preach before His Majesty. The usher, who knew very well what was afoot, replied firmly that His Majesty was aware of it and that nevertheless he sent to say that he, the abbé, was unwell and unable to preach. The abbé, now thoroughly sick and embittered, went away in his post-chaise.

Like the people, the king loathed the *philosophe* priests. What is more, the clergy did nothing to make themselves popular. The assembly of the clergy, which met in that summer of 1780, did its utmost to contribute as little as possible to the war; and from all parts it received complaints from the truly Christian members of the church about their far from Christian shepherds. A pamphlet protesting against the corruption of the priest – *The Petition of the Faithful of France to our Lords of the General Assembly of the Clergy of France* – was handed about. In his pamphlet the author pointed out all the germs of perdition that he saw present in the people and in the clergy; and he went so far as to prophesy that the kingdom itself would come to harm from it all.

Meanwhile, without reforming themselves, the clergy asked the king to proceed against wicked books and to protect religion – things that he never stopped doing, but that were of little use so long as the clergy gave a bad example. But the most intelligent of them, those whose example others would follow, were doing their utmost to become worldly and 'philosophical', just as in other periods they have tried to involve themselves in social questions. It is always this same question of going along with the world and of adapting oneself to it!

The king on the other hand was faithful to his ancestors' traditions, and he tried to call the clergy back to their spiritual vocation.

In the same way, within his own family he tried to live a family life. His eight-month-old daughter's three teeth enchanted him, and he was never tired of being with her.

The queen, on the contrary, went back to her former habits. She started new fashions: in order to conceal the fact that she was losing her hair, she launched 'flat buns, ending in a

H

sausage-shaped curl, rather like an abbé's wig'.

For his part Artois danced upon the tight-rope, and he was very good at it. And they all went to the Princesse de Guéménée's Arcadian party, packed with shepherds and shepherdesses and crowned with a fire-work display, an illumination and a play.

This delighted the queen; but from this time on, seeing that she was unpopular, she avoided Paris. She had the idea of giving a play at home, and of being both the producer and the star. Together with her in the cast there were the Comtesse de Polignac, the Comtesse de Chalon, the Comte de Polignac, the Comte d'Adhémar, who was particularly good in the simple-minded parts, being far from simple-minded himself, and the Comte Esterhazy. No spectators were allowed, except the king. In this way no one would hiss the performance.

Far from hissing, Louis XVI did his best to be on better terms with his wife whenever he could, and 1780 gave him the opportunity of making her happy. Maria-Theresa never let any throne, however small, lie about without trying to get her hands upon it; and for her fourth son Maximilian she wanted the place of coadjutor (with succession) to the archbishopric of Cologne and the bishopric of Munster. At Versailles many looked upon this plan with disfavour, as one that would add thirty thousand soldiers to the Austrian army. Vergennes, in agreement with the king, caused the Hapsburg candidate to be supported by all the French diplomats in Germany, and in August 1780 he won the day. Louis XVI did this as much for the alliance as for the queen. But it did provide him with domestic peace.

In his ministerial cabinet it was war. Sartine and Necker hated one another, attacked one another, tore one another to pieces. A print of those days shows Necker poking about in the filth with a stick: he rakes up crown pieces which are instantly seized upon by Sartine, who uses them to play ducks and drakes with. This picture was part of Necker's propaganda. He did better than that, however. One day in full council he forced his colleague to admit that he had incurred debts to the extent of ten million over and above the sixteen million that he had acknowledged and his yearly budget of a hundred and twenty. Sartine swore that it was a question of the good of the service. Necker replied that the offence was glaringly obvious and that if that kind of thing were done the state was heading directly for bankruptcy. Louis XVI and Maurepas acknowledged that Sartine was in the wrong. Necker had been waiting to catch his enemy out for a long while, and he did not spare him. With the queen's support he pressed the matter strongly with the king and Maurepas. In a long letter to Louis XVI he explained that he could not carry out his functions if departments made such important loans without his know-ledge: he ended by submitting his resignation (September 1780). In fact he was saying 'Either Sartine or me.' The king would have preferred to dismiss Necker, whom he distrusted; but he could find no one to take his place. As Maurepas put it, 'Only a fool or a knave would want the post.' Sartine was far more liked and respected at court than Necker; but nothing could be done against a minister of finance who showed a balance-sheet in which (by cheating) he proved that the navy had cost a hundred and eighty million in 1780. Finally the king came to Paris on 11 October 1780 to work with Maurepas, and they decided upon the dismissal of Sartine. M. Necker was triumphant.

M. Necker was triumphant; but he had longer views as well. Secretly advised by Choiseul, who found in him a useful tool for the destruction of the ministry in power, and firmly backed by the queen, he proposed one of his friends as Sartine's successor: this was the Marquis de Castries, whom the queen had also recom-mended to him at a secret interview on Sunday, 8 October. Then Necker, making use of a stratagem that was more cunning than decent, went to discuss the names of several officers who might succeed Sartine with Maurepas: he mentioned d'Estaing, who did not seem possible; he mentioned Castries, who did seem possible; he mentioned various others who seemed either possible or ill-chosen, as the case might be. From Maurepas he went, without delay, to see the king and told him that he advised the choice of the Marquis de Castries, of whom M. de Maurepas approved. The king, strengthened by this assurance and in any case full of esteem for Castries, signed immediately: Necker at once went to find

Castries and presented him to the king. Later, talking to Maurepas, Louis XVI learnt what had happened and understood the trick. M. Necker had not said anything absolutely false, but what he had told him had not been absolutely true either; and in any case it was an offensive piece of behaviour. As neither the king nor Maurepas wished to humiliate Castries, who did not deserve such treatment, they remained silent; but it occupied their minds, none the less, and the other ministers, particularly Vergennes, who professed a distinct aversion for Necker, looked to their defences.

M. de Montbarrey set about it badly. Two events that happened in quick succession were the ruin of him. To begin with he recommended a lady to Artois as a companion for his wife: very soon it became quite obvious that the lady was a whore. The king at once insisted upon his making Artois a public apology.

Then there were two candidates in direct competition for a post: the one was a most deserving officer who was supported by the queen; the other was a good officer, and he was supported by Montbarrey's mistress. Montbarrey appointed the second – first stroke of imprudence. The lady boasted of it – second stroke of madness.

Armed with the relevant papers, Marie-Antoinette went to see the king, angry and full of complaint. Louis XVI comforted her and abandoned Montbarrey.

This time he personally discussed the choice of the successor with Maurepas: they spoke of several generals, particularly of Vogüé, Ségur and Puységur, and Maurepas swayed the king in favour of the last. Yet Mme de Polignac and the queen supported the Maréchal de Ségur, a very respectable man, a good soldier and quite as worthy of the post. In this difficulty the king fell in with the wishes of the queen and the opinion of several advisers. Maurepas, who had thought he had persuaded the king, thereupon wanted to resign, and he went to see the king and the queen for that purpose. It so happened that the king had just received a message from Ségur excusing himself and saying that as he was in the grip of a violent fit of the gout it was impossible for him to come to Versailles at once. This confused state of affairs gave rise to a scene that was in the first place engaging and then pathetic.

The queen suggested that they should change their minds about the appointment of Ségur, since he could not carry out his functions. In tears she begged Maurepas to stay, and the king joined his voice to hers. Then Maurepas, also in tears, promised to remain and begged them to keep Ségur, who was a valuable, clear-thinking man. So everything ended happily. But Maurepas did not forget Necker.

Supposing that Maurepas would presently die, M. Necker now looked upon himself as the master of the situation. He had the backing of the queen, the financial world, Choiseul's party and the *philosophes*, and he was supported by anyone whose good will it seemed to him worth his while to acquire. The *Nouvelles à la main* and the foreign diplomats said that the queen had just made two ministers and that henceforward the government of France was in her hands. All this seemed plain, logical and reasonable. It appeared to be confirmed by a fresh incident.

At the beginning of December there arrived a dispatch that was instantly brought to the king: the Empress Maria-Theresa had died on the afternoon of 29 November, with great courage and great piety, in her palace of Schönbrunn, where for so long she had worked and held her court. The king was exceedingly distressed at this news; Maria-Theresa had always been a respectful and kindly mother-in-law to him, and she was the most ardent friend of France and of the alliance in Austria. And then how was he to tell the queen of this loss? In spite of his repugnance, he sent for the Abbé de Vermond, and giving him the letter, desired him to prepare the queen for the terrible news and not to give it to her until she was capable of bearing it. It was an appalling blow to her. In spite of her mother's severity towards her, Marie-Antoinette loved her more than anyone else in the world. The king did his utmost to draw close to her and to comfort her, and her little daughter helped her to recover. And presently the everyday routine of living, her trivial of amusements and the pleasure of being first in everything made her forget that she was unhappy, so that in the end she was less so. The court went into the full appropriate mourning for six months; the courtiers, who were thereby deprived of a great many diversions, looked sour;

and the sellers of costly little toys and other objects – *articles de Paris* – were heartbroken, for this period of mourning, coming just before the New Year and the carnival, meant ruin for them.

For the king this sorrow was made all the worse by a great many other cares. The most worrying of them all was the failure of the 1780 campaign. In spite of France's immense efforts, nothing was accomplished. In America Washington and Rochambeau began by quarrelling in secret. Now a good understanding was essential, for each was too weak to act on his own. There was talk of laying siege to New York and of liberating Georgia. The summer went by, taken up by discussions with the Americans and skirmishes with the English. The most helpful thing was the rapid friendship that sprang up between the troops and the civil population. The officers liked their life in the United States; they liked the ladies of America, and the ladies of America liked them. Here bases of agreement were to be found. The husbands were with the army, leaving the field clear. The French troops took particular pride in showing that they were highly disciplined, and this earned them general esteem; while the officers behaved in so agreeable a manner that among the upper classes the alliance became popular once more.

Yet the Spanish minister was visibly anxious for peace, and this caused disquiet. The English might take advantage of his attitude. But George III would have none of it. He was proud of having done so well with a war that had seemed hopeless at first, and he was too conscious of the superiority of the British position: he refused to negotiate. He prepared an expeditionary force from which he expected a great deal and he placed it under one of his most trusted generals, Earl Cornwallis, a young, bold and fearless commander.

Louis XVI could only set a few favourable results against all these discouraging facts; and even these were owing more to Vergennes than the army or the navy. Holland, after a great deal of hesitation, had just carried out a vote in which the French argument prevailed; Holland would therefore join the Armed Neutrality, in spite of the Stadhouder's opposition. The Duc de

La Vauguyon defended the French interest at The Hague, and he did so with a great deal of subtlety; but his best ally was George III and the British sailors, whose arrogance and greed, when exercised upon the richest prey afloat, the Dutch merchant navy, finally aroused the fury of the shipowners in Rotterdam, Amsterdam and Friesland. With each side provoking the other, England ended by declaring war upon Holland (20 December 1780). Holland was not at all prepared for this, and from the beginning she was in a thoroughly disagreeable position; nevertheless, she did make one ally more for France, one that would attract part of the English forces and occupy them far from the United States.

Faced with this balance-sheet, Necker, the ministers and almost the whole of the court wanted peace. Louis XVI determined to go on with the war. He fixed upon America as the place for his main effort and for the attempt at the decisive victory.

At the same time France prepared a diversion in India, to be commanded by the keenest fighter in the navy, the Bailli de Suffren.

Louis XVI and Vergennes worked day and night; and writing about them on 5 November 1779 Linguet said,

> At present our navy is stronger than it has ever been before, both in power and in that emulation which is the source of heroism, and this is one of our good king's miracles; for when he came to the throne he found a navy as divided as the nation, with ships that were almost rotten and a morale that had in the nature of things been brought very low by the discord within the service, disorder in the finances and distrust on the part of the public; yet in this short time he has succeeded in creating a formidable navy, with which, despite sixteen years of dull, listless peace and men who for the most part had never been under fire and had rarely been to sea, he has on all occasions beaten an enemy who was proud and elated with his first successes – an enemy, furthermore, who had kept in perfect training by four years of war against the Insurgents.

With the opening year 'the court went along gently and quite quietly' said M. le Duc de Croy, who knew what he was talking about, for he had the soul of a concierge, together with the intelligence of a learned man and the wisdom of a grandfather. M. de Maurepas, racked by the gout, scarcely ever appeared. The king did not change at all – family, work, hunting, with a little locksmith's work for a treat and prayer as his secret source of strength. Furthermore he was growing more and more reticent, as the weight of state secrets bore more and more heavily upon him, and more and more solitary, with the departure of those who had hoped for high places and who saw the reign taking its definitive form without their being called for. As this hopeful mist dispersed, so everything seemed harsher, the surrounding hatred more inveterate and the king's life more bitter. But he was too busy to suffer from it and he had too well balanced a mind to take notice of it. There was where his strength lay – and the danger.

Meanwhile perils and scandals started up all around him. In her mind the queen was already deceiving him. Her whole heart was turned towards Fersen, far away on the American battlefields. She told Mme de Polignac, and Mme de Polignac provided her with the information that she was able to gather from all those correspondents who hurried to give her news so that she might pass it on to the queen. This scandal was still hidden, but it was whispered abroad.

The scandal concerning La Fayette was shouted from the housetops, if only out of a desire to be revenged for his unheard-of successes, his triumph at the Opéra and his universal popularity. His mistress, Aglaé de Hunolstein, who was so ready to yield her lovely person to the highest bidder, gave only too much occasion for scandalous gossip. It was said that when he was leaving she persuaded La Fayette that he was responsible for her sudden unexpected pregnancy; in these circumstances he owed it to the young lady's honour to produce an allowance for this untimely, unlooked-for descendant. So La Fayette paid months and months of nurse's fee, only to discover on his return that the baby had lived for no more than a few weeks. The story spread, and it seems that Monsieur, who had never been able to forgive certain impertinences on the part of La Fayette, had a ballad written upon the subject, as well-turned as it was unkind. It was much hummed at court.

When pretty Lise the other day
I met with, coming here,
I thought the maid was far from gay,
In her eye there stood a tear.
You think that once more Cupid may
Her tender heart oppress:
Oh no indeed, you're quite astray
For the cause of her distress . . .
Not long ago within a grove
The guileless charmer strayed
To pick the glowing flowers of love;
But I am much afraid,
That with the flowers she plucked the fruit,
And that I must confess,
Beyond all cavil or dispute,
Is the cause of her distress . . .

The tune crossed the Atlantic, and the indignant La Fayette wrote to the Vicomte de Noailles and the Prince de Poix, who repeated what he had said in the Polignac salon. 'I am told of a wicked unkindness that society is good enough to inflict upon a person I love; I will talk to you about it, but it is difficult to deal with it in writing.' The licentious story travelled to and fro between the continents.

The king knew about La Fayette's misfortune and he was sorry for him: it would have been better if the hero of America had not been a simpleton, but being one was in itself punishment enough. On the other hand Louis XVI was hard on M. de Voyer, a good officer but a hardened *philosophe* and a notorious miser who did not blush to make money out of everything that could possibly be turned to profit. In front of the whole court the king told him that it was unworthy of a gentleman and of a lieutenant-general in the king's army to turn himself into a hard-bargaining horse-coper and to keep an inn and a posting-house at his estate of Les Ormes. The courtiers gaped and Voyer was left in a pitiable state.

Louis XVI was no kinder to Radix de Sainte-Croix, who was in charge of the Comte d'Artois' finances and who had swindled him. 'Parlement is there to sit in judgment upon rogues,' said the king. 'And justice must be left to take its course.' He was more angry still with the worldly priests, and after the Lenten sermons preached by the Abbé Maury, who overflowed with 'philosophical' reflexions and flatteries of the ministers without even mentioning the name of Christ on Easter Day, the king complained to the Grand Almoner and refused the preacher the customary reward.

Above all he was indignant at the excesses of organized gambling, which allowed the ruin of a family in a few hours, without the family's being aware of it. There had recently been a striking example of this – the son of the Comte de La Haye lost eighty thousand livres at M. de Genlis' house. The king was of the opinion that these abuses had to be stopped, and that the exploitation of gambling by those who made a business of it should be prohibited: he let the Parlement know that he would look favourably upon measures taken in this sense.

Parlement did not need pressing. On 21 April 1781 it met and debated this public curse. The king's brothers were not there, which caused a good deal of comment. One of the most zealous speakers was of course the Duc d'Orléans; indeed his zeal seemed to cause his son a certain amount of uneasiness – for with his usual lack of shame Chartres was present. The debate ended with the drafting of an exceedingly severe decree against all those who held a bank and all householders who allowed gambling. Parlement did its best to prevent the foreign ministers from acting as protectors to those who wished to gamble, at the same time neither vexing nor offending the diplomats in any way.

Parlement sent the decree to the king. He retained its prescriptions as a whole: this document renewed the former edicts, ordinances, decrees and regulations on the subject; it defined prohibited games as all those in which the chances were unequal and in which one side had an advantage over the other; it forbade all persons, of whatever degree or quality, to assemble in any place, privileged or unprivileged, in order to play at the said prohibited games. It laid down fines and penalties involving imprisonment and loss of civil rights. The king strengthened the Parlement's decree; the people were grateful to him for doing so and so were all that were sound in the nobility, that is to say virtually all those who lived in the country. The decree caused all the more stir since it taught even the queen a lesson.

She was much vexed, and therefore she took to playing lotto; while Chartres turned to building. He played at it furiously, rebuilding the Palais-Royal in order to make a profitable thing of it. He completed his intense unpopularity with the middle and lower classes of Paris by destroying splendid roads and walks. The whole of the spring, summer and autumn was filled with these road-blocks, which turned the first prince of the blood into the Parisians' particular aversion; but he did not care in the least nor would he deign to delay the carrying out of his plans for a single week. Those who had thought him feeble had to eat their words. But the public took their revenge in the papers, in the broadsheets and upon the walls of the Palais-Royal itself, which they placarded with insults. The town and the court turned against the house of Orléans. Louis XVI took no part in this, but he knew exactly what he thought.

He was perfectly aware how the ministerial changes had caused a great stirring of ambition and a fresh weaving of intrigue; it was said everywhere that from now on the queen was ruling, that the other ministers would soon go and Maurepas would soon die; it was rumoured that Vergennes wanted to resign and that presently Choiseul would come back and negotiate a peace, since that was the royal will.

The truth of the matter was that Maurepas still had the king's confidence and affection, and that the king professed the utmost esteem and respect for Vergennes, an opinion that he made evident by giving him the order of the Holy Ghost. Ségur and Castries were carrying out their functions well, Ségur more modestly and Castries with more worldly wisdom – he saw a great deal of M. Necker and he was often at the queen's private receptions. Both of them proved hard-working and competent. M. Necker kept at a certain distance, but he was convinced that this made him more important, and he worked with ostentatious zeal.

There was a popular song about all the ministers:

> *Maurepas drools and talks nonsense,*
> *Vergennes of the English is scared . . .*
> *Necker he boasts like an angel . . .*
> *And Amelot is friendly with all;*
> *Soubise is fond of the apple*
> *That provided original sin;*
> *D'Estaing is brave and unlucky;*
> *D'Orvilliers – there's nothing to him;*
> *And Guichen is dashing and bold . . .*
> *So Frenchmen, there are the pictures*
> *Of our generals and ministers all.*

This ill temper was smouldering all over the country. The Parlement of Brittany rebelled in order to assert its right of electing deputies freely. It sent delegates to Versailles. The commoner-priests rebelled against the bishops and published *Remarks by the Second Order of the Ecclesiastical Chamber.* They all had to be brought back to a sense of obedience.

A stricter discipline, a stronger rule, was necessary in the army. For this purpose the king set up a Council of the War Ministry. (M. de Pozanne for the cavalry, M. du Châtelet for the infantry, M. de Besenval for the foreign infantry, M. d'Esterhazy for the hussars.) The young men had to begin to learn their responsibilities and to exercise them.

That was how 1781 began, and with these events the first pieces of news came in: the Chevalier de Luxembourg had just been beaten in his attempt on Jersey, and Rodney in trying to retake St Lucia.

This impartiality on the part of Fate seemed unkind.

Chapter XI

The hard-working King

NECKER PROVOKED LOUIS XVI BEYOND MEASURE. THE
question of money can haunt a king just as much as it can a
footman. In order to win a decisive war, gold was essential. And
gold meant Necker. The king could find no way out of this
dilemma and it infuriated him.

He spent nothing on himself; he possessed no new clothes and
in particular no fine garments at all, except for the one made of
swansdown, which he liked although it was old now; and yet he
continually had to pay for the extravagance of others.

For the queen he paid 13,500 francs to the jewellers Böhmer
and Bassenge in January 1781, and in February he gave her
24,000 francs for her gambling – on his own he spent sixteen
francs. He paid Artois' debts, Elizabeth's debts and so on. The
whole family milked him.

The state budget provided a torment of an entirely different
kind. Both the French navy and the United States Congress
seemed quite insatiable. It was in vain to change ministers: the
situation remained unaltered. It was in vain to look forward with
the utmost care at the beginning of each year, neglecting no

detail, weighing the cost of everything with the greatest accuracy: the year never came to an end without the navy having run into debt and without the United States Congress pleading poverty. In Congress there were two opposing parties – that of the friends of the alliance and that of the champions of the nation's dignity. The first were so fond of France that they had not the least hesitation in asking her for the most prodigious sums; the second liked her so little that they thought it essential that she should make herself useful by producing the said sum. France had to pay.

Now for France to be able to pay she needed Necker. And Necker was growing unbearable, both because of his loutish conduct and because of the number of enemies he had roused up against him. The Neckers never stopped blowing their own trumpet. On 20 January 1781 he caused the council to adopt a decree requiring the lords who occupied crown lands to pay rent. Malicious tongues called it 'fool's gold' and asserted that the great families would never pay anything whatever. For her part Mme Necker made it known that she was setting up an 'office of pity' to look after the almshouse she had founded in the parish of Saint-Sulpice. The news caused open-mouthed astonishment.

Finally, on 19 February, he published his *M. Necker's Report to the King*, a little book with the royal printing-house's blue cover, which was sold for a crown at Panckoucke's, the proceeds to go to Mme Necker's good works. The first printing of three thousand was bought up at once, and presently there were more than twenty thousand copies in circulation. What a pleasure it was to see the kingdom's finances displayed openly for the first time – 'The king rendering account as it were – and a very exact account – to his people'! There was an extraordinary craze for it: the little blue book was to be seen in the cafés and the drawing-rooms, at Versailles and the Palais-Royal and even in the ladies' beds, for at all times women have adored what they cannot possibly understand. Necker's book enchanted them. It was very clear and utterly incomprehensible, wholly exact and entirely untrue.

But then it was a well-judged stroke of policy to make an open show of so favourable a result at the moment he was opening a loan of sixty million based on annuities, and after three years of costly war. It was useful to the country, for it discouraged the English, whose public debt was greater than the French and who had been asserting that France was at the end of her tether; it raised the king's standing and credit once more; and it was valuable propaganda for Necker. At this time Necker was overflowing with patriotism and with enthusiasm for what he had accomplished. He said, 'France is grateful both for what the beneficient ministers are doing and for what they want to do; and she longs to be allowed to help in the promotion of the public good, if only by a genuine and sensitive effusion of spirit.' M. Necker was bursting with zeal and fine feelings.

M. de Maurepas, who had not forbidden him to publish his report, behaved as though he wanted to apply the pin that would make the swollen balloon explode. He called the little book *un conte bleu*, a fairy-tale, and he civilly added, 'This book is as full of truth as it is of modesty.' After all, he had allowed Necker to come right out into the open only in the hope that this would rally all his enemies.

Such was the event: all those he had expelled from their places, threatened, taxed, set aside or overlooked united against him for the worst and for the best reasons: the great lords, the intendants, the men of the Parlements, jealous financiers, the former government's friends, Monsieur's officers together with Monsieur himself, those of the Comte d'Artois and Artois too, all joined against M. Necker. Criticisms, mockeries and rude songs flowed in from every side. Pamphlets signed with real names, no names or false names appeared all over Paris: there was one by M. de Bourboulon who was in charge of the Comte d'Artois' finances, and it pierced Necker to the quick; then came a flood of lampoons – *A Friend's Letter to M. Necker*, *A Citizen's Remarks*, with *Further Remarks by a Citizen* and *Still Further Remarks*, which were followed by many more and which sold like hot cakes. A small, illegally printed pamphlet of twenty-two pages was hawked from door to door. It sounded the alarm. 'Having begun like Law, do you want to end up like Cromwell?' exclaimed the author.

M. Turgot died on 22 March, and in his grave he must have

chuckled at the sight of his successor being tripped up in just the same way he had tripped Turgot. The campaign against him led by the royal family and in particular by Monsieur, an old hand at dirty tricks, gave Necker particular uneasiness, for the king attended to the views of his own people when they happened to be reasonable or to have sound arguments behind them.

But the most dangerous was the blow struck by his colleague Vergennes, who at the royal command provided the king with a *Minute on Necker's Report* (3 May 1781) in which he said,

> Sire, you have ordered me to speak without restraint, and I obey Your Majesty's command: a struggle between the régime of France and the régime of Necker has begun. If his ideas prevail over those sanctioned by long experience as did those of Law, Mazarin and the Lorraine princes, then, with his Protestant, Genevan plans, M. Necker is perfectly prepared to establish a system within the finances in France, or a League within the state or a Fronde against the established administration ... In the last resort his *Report* is an unqualified appeal to the people, and its pernicious effects upon this monarchy can as yet be neither felt nor foreseen ...

So Louis XVI was directly aware of the danger that Necker was causing to his dynasty and his crown. No argument could have touched him nearer home. From that time on he distrusted Necker, and although he kept him it was only in order to bring the war to a victorious end. But victory meant so much to him and the moment was so critical that Necker, supported by two ministers and backed by the queen, might have maintained his hold, if only he had made use of a little caution and a little modesty.

But M. Necker had left his modesty at the bank: he was saturated with the vanity of courts. The queen's remark, when she saw a courtier at Marly reading Necker's *Report*, 'Ah, Monsieur, that is the work of a man who is full of zeal for the king's glory and the people's happiness,' went to his head. She said it loudly enough and publicly enough to be sure that it would reach Necker, and he never wearied of repeating it. Counting on her, on his banking friends, on the Noailles, who remained deeply attached to him, on the literary men, above all those who dined at his house, particularly the Abbé Raynal, Loménie the Archbishop of Toulouse, and the famous Abbé de Vermond, and counting also on the Protestants, a more numerous and influential body in France than they seemed, on Choiseul and his party, on Castries, on du Châtelet, Beauvau and Adhémar, ambitious men deeply committed to him, and lastly on the brilliant, dashing light squadron of the ladies, those tireless promoters of his fame – the imperious Duchesse de Gramont, the proud Comtesse de Brionne, the charming Princesse de Beauvau, the seductive Comtesse de Montesson, the enthusiastic Comtesse de Tessé, the exquisite Comtesse de Simiane, the dangerous Marquise de Coigny and so many others: counting upon all these, then, and backed up and strengthened by this phalanx of men and above all of women who admired him, Necker no longer hesitated before the risk of a bold manœuvre. He went to see M. de Maurepas. Once the civilities were over he complained of Bourboulon's attacks and asked for his slanderers to be punished in an exemplary fashion. Maurepas politely fobbed him off. He went to see Artois, but that prince asked him whether, when he had brought out his *Report*, he had not wished people to discuss it? Bourboulon was the public; and he was discussing it.

At the same time Necker found himself attacked on another flank. Parlement dug up one of his minutes dated 1778, in which he suggested provincial assemblies to take the place of the Parlements, whose vices he exaggerated. Now the Parlement protested, and with great difficulty the king insisted upon the matter being dropped.

Yet Necker listened to nobody but his admirers: his *Report* had been translated into every language on earth, and those about him never ceased their flattery. Intoxicated with all this incense he did not pause. He went to see Maurepas again on the pretence of asking his advice. He told him that he could not go on with his work after so much criticism unless he were given more authority. He therefore asked the king for a public mark of confidence – for admission to the council and the possibility of working with His Majesty. 'You in the council!' cried Maurepas, 'you who do not go to mass?' It was impossible to make a Protestant a member of the council; the law of the land forbade it. The idea of working alone with the king would offend the other ministers and unite them against him.

Necker listened with dignity and then observed, 'Sully, who did not go to mass, was a member of the council.' He refused any other solution whatever and cut the interview short. He said no more, but with a Roman air he handed Maurepas a letter, begged him to give it to the king, and withdrew.

Maurepas had behaved in a straightforward manner, but he was charmed with this decision. Was Necker unaware of the fact that his speeches bored the king to tears and that he was heading straight for the answer 'No' by insisting upon this kind of intimacy? When Maurepas handed him the letter, Louis XVI was exceedingly vexed with such a degree of self-importance. When the queen, playing her part, came to beg him to agree to M. Necker's request, he brusquely sent her away. In council all the ministers, except for Castries, made their eagerness to see the departure of M. Necker quite obvious; they distrusted him equally as a minister, a financier and a patriot. Everybody and everything combined against the Genevan, and the king's decision had only been held back by caution and a sense of justice. Necker's ridiculous letter decided the matter. 'Sire,' said the minister, 'my conversation with M. de Maurepas no longer allows me to delay placing my resignation in the king's hands. I permit myself to hope that Your Majesty will retain some recollection of the years of happy but arduous work and above all of the unbounded zeal that I have devoted to Your Majesty's service. Necker.'

The king read these lines carefully; then he asked Maurepas to convey to Necker the news that he accepted his resignation. Meanwhile Necker, counting on the queen's support, had no doubt of success. He appeared at Maurepas' door next day. Maurepas asked him in at once, welcomed him with his usual amiability, and with a mild expression on his face informed him that the king had deigned to accept his resignation. Necker staggered. For a few moments he remained dumb and motionless, apart from a few convulsive twitches. Maurepas had to call his servants and tell them to let M. Necker's men know that he would be leaving directly. That was how they parted.

The noise this made at court and in the town was prodigious. The queen wept; a great many highly-placed and charming women had hysterics and a great many lords told themselves that they had played the wrong card and that in spite of his great age Maurepas was still a profoundly crafty player. M. de Choiseul was thunderstruck, and this time the king's steadiness overwhelmed him: he immediately wrote to his confederate, 'Chanteloup, 22 May 1781. So it is over, Monsieur, and you are leaving us; you will take your glory with you, and leave us the regret. You have done a great deal of good for us, and you would have done more; your withdrawal delivers us up to the most tormenting anxiety, which will perhaps be justified by the gravest calamities . . .' And the poets joined in: one of them drew up a long piece against Maurepas and the king, ending with these elegant lines:

> *Triumph, old monster, but too ripe in years!*
> *Emboldened by poor Sully's sad mischance*
> *England comes to beat us, for she hears*
> *That Henri Quatre no longer lives for France.*

This nonsense went on for some little time; Necker turned into a kind of literary myth, and the narrow circles of 'public opinion' did not drop him, for he had not yet played out the part they desired him to play. At the Comédie-Française, on the following Sunday, there was the play *La Partie de chasse de Henri IV*; in this the king, having pardoned Sully, spoke of his ministers' enemies and said, 'The wretches deceived me.' At this moment a voice in the pit cried out, 'Yes, yes!' and immediately a great many others took up the cry. The tumult went on right through the performance. When M. de Bourboulon appeared at the Palais-Royal he was hooted, booed, chased by a threatening crowd and obliged to withdraw. And as everything ended in songs in those days, they sang,

> *Both North and Necker in their powerful hands*
> *Upheld their countries' fortune and their fate:*
> *In this the likeness stands.*

Triumphant North has raised the English high
But falling Necker drags the Frenchmen low:
The difference here doth lie.

There were other circles in which, on the contrary, everybody was very pleased – at court, and in the financial and parliamentary world. As Necker's successor the king chose a financier whose reputation was that of a prudent, methodical and experienced man – M. Joly de Fleury, the son of the attorney-general of that name. He had no hatred for Necker, and he was friendly and conciliating with all the other ministers. There could be no question of imposing fresh taxes in time of war, so he made the most of the well-filled treasury left by his predecessor; then he beat about, sometimes using the method of loans, sometimes that of taxation. He had no genius, but no self-conceit either. He did what had to be done and he kept quiet.

With this point settled, the king could turn his mind to the war and to his family, his two principal anxieties.

For the queen was pregnant, and as this was a condition that she found boring and hard to put up with she had to be watched over continually: Louis XVI tried to influence her through her love of gems. He gave her a diamond rivière that Louis XV had ordered for the du Barry, a splendid piece of jewellery worth 750,000 livres. Marie-Antoinette found it one morning on her dressing-table, and she declared that it was 'a very charming attention'.

In his happiness the king made a present to his other mistress, the people of France. The Opéra had just been burnt down. He ordered it to be built again at his expense.

Out of his own pocket he maintained a whole band of poor people and aged servants. He was no less kind to the young. One day when he had been to see his aunts at the Château de Bellevue, where they lived in great splendour and kept an admirable table, there was a noise at the park gates. It was boys from the Collège d'Harcourt who had picked upon Bellevue for their day's holiday. Mesdames, who were kind creatures, brought them in, with the idea that they might amuse the king: he at once made them play prisoner's base, he being the umpire. When it was time for dinner the boys vanished and ate at the inn, refusing the meal the princesses had had prepared for them. But they came back afterwards: The king showed them how to play backgammon, and then he questioned them, wanting to know who each was in turn. They all belonged to illustrious families. 'I know all these names,' he told them. 'They bring to my mind people who have served the country well; I have no doubt that in your turn you will do the same.' Then he chatted informally with them, had them given something to eat and made an appointment for the holiday Monday in June. They went away delighted, and he was even more so.

Was he equally delighted with his brother-in-law Joseph II, during the six-day visit he paid to Versailles in the height of the summer? The emperor behaved charmingly and went away enchanted. Yet he did not tell Louis XVI that in fact he had come to urge his sister to take great care to keep her heart Austrian and to take as large a share as possible in the affairs of government; he was soon going to need her in the great operations that he was preparing. He concealed his brotherly advice under a great deal of affection and his reticences with regard to his brother-in-law under a great deal of cordiality.

These princely games and these childish pastimes were amusing; but Louis XVI had no leisure to spend much time at them, for the naval and the diplomatic wars gripped his attention every morning and never let it go until the evening. At that moment he was defending himself against Joseph II and Catherine, who had united to force their mediation upon him – they spoke now of a congress at Vienna, now of one at Antwerp. But for peace of any kind Spain insisted upon the return of Gibraltar, and France upon the recognition of the United States' independence. Since for her part England did not want peace at all, and since her king, full of confidence in Cornwallis and his new army, had no desire to grant the American colonies their freedom, it was easy to avoid diplomatic negotiations – negotiations which could not have been favourable to France.

Louis XVI and Vergennes were determined to maintain a

central, dominating position in Europe. Vergennes' polite and almost velvety skill rendered all this decent and correct. Then there arose the question of getting rid of a young American officer: this was Colonel John Laurens, a very agreeable young man to be sure, but one quite lacking in experience; he suddenly arrived without a word of warning as General Washington's special envoy, with the mission of telling the King of France about the American troops' extreme shortness of supplies and the urgent necessity of providing them with money, munitions and clothing. Vergennes was out of all patience with these insistent American demands at a time when French finances were so precarious and French needs so great: he sent Laurens on to Franklin, who had just been granted a present of six millions. The unhappy man had been begging for it these months past. Everybody was drawing bills on him, Congress, Congress's representatives in Europe and even the American commissioner in the West Indies, and all this at a time when he had no means whatever of furnishing himself with money apart from the French government. Laurens and he had furious battles over the French gold until finally Vergennes resolved the difficulty by having Franklin's accounts checked by the banker Grand and obtaining from the king a personal loan of ten million for Washington. (How could loans be made to Congress, which no longer had either strength or standing?) Louis XVI was of the same mind as Vergennes, and he approved his declaration, 'France is the necessary and sole support of the United States. Their cause is our cause, and if they succumb we shall of necessity be affected by their fall.'

This fall seemed imminent in the first four months of 1781, and it was the centre of a furious conflict by land, on sea, and in men's minds as well, by means of a propaganda campaign that was as savage as the fighting was violent. The conflict could not be won without Louis XVI's tireless, patient activity, without Vergennes' subtlety and his immense capacity for work, and without the inspired ingenuity of Franklin, whose natural intelligence was capable of making use of his vast experience and of the countless helping hands, the secret aid, the collusions of freemasonry.

The struggle wore an unpromising look, and this was because

the whole of Europe and all the continents inhabited by white people were supplied with news by the English papers, which were read by businessmen, or by Dutch papers written by French Protestants, traditionally hostile to the Most Christian King. Widely-read gazettes – widely read even in France – were also to be found at Geneva, Zweibrücken, Liège and Brussels; and all of them disparaged France, for Geneva Calvinism could not forgive France her Catholicism, and Louis XIV's campaigns had left unpleasant memories in the countries on his borders. During the Seven Years' War Genet, the head of the translation department in the foreign ministry, pointed out this danger to Louis XV and tried to deal with it by the publication of a *Summary of the English Gazettes* for the international public – a very highly critical summary, of course. It had little success.

In 1778–1781 the king and his colleagues treated the question with greater care. Ever since his youth Louis XVI had read the English papers and several Dutch publications, particularly Luzac's, which was the best written; and he read Linguet's journal, for Linguet was the most brilliant and best-informed polemical writer of the day. With all this behind him, the king was well qualified to oversee the *Gazette de France*, as he had done since 11 May 1774 – indeed, he often wrote articles for it – and to superintend this war of opinion.

Louis XIV and Louis XV had lost this particular war, but Louis XVI won it. One of the most brilliant victories was gained in Holland, where the French representative, the Duc de La Vauguyon, managed to conciliate the Dutch journalists, who were already inclined to support the Insurgents and who had been gradually won over by John Adams, with the help of an outstanding agent, Dumas. The Franco-Americans succeeded in reversing the century-old position: instead of invariably presenting the English point of view, these papers, and particularly Luzac's, the most widely read, were now a focus of hostility against Great Britain. At Geneva the work carried out by the French resident ministers, Hennin and Vergennes (the minister's brother), together with Franklin's personal influence with certain distinguished Genevans such as the Cramers, succeeded in changing the tone of the *Journal de Genève*.

There was little possibility of doing the same with the papers published in the Empire, for Joseph II did not approve of the Insurgents any more than did the Viennese upper classes, and it was he who set the tone throughout his possessions. Yet when the Armed Neutrality was set up, from every part of trading Europe, especially the ports, there rose a positive outcry against despotic England.

Faced with this outburst of public opinion in the rest of the world, England's chief response was songs and filthy pamphlets that spattered Franklin, the usual target, his friend Vergennes, and the queen, the French monarchy's weak point. What was there that could be said against the king? They harked back to the old tune of Choiseul's party – 'He is weak, stupid, coarse; he is ruled by his wife; he drinks.' Thus one after another there appeared *La Cassette verte de M. de Sartine*, *l'Histoire d'un pou françois*, and many others.

Franklin replied to them very briskly with some wonderfully amusing pamphlets: the *Remarks to the Hessians* was his master-piece (he created an imaginary German princeling anxious to sell his soldiers to England giving his ministers instructions on how to set about it so that the bargain should be as profitable as possible, and telling him how very important it was that the soldiers thus sold should be killed by the enemy, for in that case England paid more). The pamphlet went all round Germany, England and Europe. If to this there are added the countless verses and the conversations in the salons, directed by Franklin from Passy, it is easy to imagine the whirlwind of propaganda that agitated all European and American minds in 1781.

These minds were wholly taken up with Necker during the first months of 1781, and this lasted until about the middle of June; but then the fine weather and the war-bulletins reminded people that the greatest naval war France had ever engaged in was being fought on the seven seas. To begin with there was a little piece of good news. On 2 May the French fleet retook St Eustatius, which the English had taken from the Dutch, and all Holland was over-joyed. 'Here we are enchanted with our new connexion with

France,' said a letter from Amsterdam at the end of May. 'We extol the reign of Louis XVI, who rules without a mistress, something that has not happened among you for a hundred and forty years. In our public and private gatherings we drink to his health and then to that of M. de La Motte-Picquet. There are perpetual songs to the glory of the French – the common people sing them in Flemish and the better sort in your language.'

It was both a naval war and a psychological or propaganda war, as it is called – the kind that Vergennes waged so brilliantly.

In Europe the Spaniards were still blockading Gibraltar and preparing their attack upon the Balearic Islands, while France kept her fleet at Brest, preferring to concentrate her best ships and her best admirals in the West Indies and the North American waters, where the outcome of this war was to be decided.

Chapter XII

The victorious King

THE NAVAL COMMANDER IN THE NEW WORLD WAS THE
Comte de Grasse-Tilly, a member of the family of the sovereign
counts of Antibes; he was well known for his spirit and enterprise,
but this was his first important campaign. He owed his position
to the friendship of Castries, who had given him orders to deal
briskly with the West Indies so as to make time for supporting the
troops of Rochambeau and Washington on the continent.

To begin with that was of no consequence. After a great deal of
quarrelling Washington and Rochambeau made up their minds to
attack New York, the key to the English possessions. For this to
be successful, surprise was necessary. As Fate would have it, the
English intercepted a messenger and learnt all the plans. In spite
of his cold fury Washington pressed on with them. The two
armies therefore joined forces in the White Plains on 5 July 1781,
and they got along very well together. The Americans thought
the French well-made, disciplined men, quite the contrary of
what they had always heard for the last hundred years; and the
French found the Americans agreeable and active, the reverse of
what they had expected. This was all to the good, but things did

not turn out well. The allies were still too few in numbers to take
so strong a place, held by professional soldiers. This was clear to
Washington when one fine August day he beheld the convoy of
British reinforcements come in from Europe, no French admiral
having cut them off. The attack was impossible. It seemed that the
1781 campaign was a failure; once again he would see the troops
become demoralized and Congress lose all heart; and at last the
King of France would resign himself to peace.

Both the generals and the king (who was kept abreast of affairs
by Rochambeau's dispatches) were in this discouraged state of
mind when they received news that delighted them beyond
measure. De Grasse, who had left Brest on 22 March 1781, had
reached Martinique on 28 April. He was looking for an English
fleet or a convoy to snap up. Meanwhile he was in correspondence
with Rochambeau and Washington. Washington's mind was
fixed upon New York: Rochambeau wanted to attack the British
in the south, on the Chesapeake, where Cornwallis's army was
doing a great deal of damage and threatening to become a serious
danger. The two generals sent their plans and their supporting
reasons to de Grasse, whose opinion was that it was better to
attack on the Chesapeake. He promised to be there at the beginning of autumn, bringing troops. As soon as he knew this,
Washington, with that submission to Fate which is a particular
characteristic of those men who are cut out to command nations,
took all the necessary steps.

This was the 'Chesapeake rendezvous'. The commanding
general did his utmost to conceal his movements, so that Clinton
should not get there before him. But above all he set off at once,
and he carried out the operation with a most uncommon speed and
perfection. The French were pleased with the spectacle of these
unknown regions, and marching past the old gentlemen of
Congress and the pretty girls of Philadelphia delighted them;
they reached the rendezvous tired, but full of determination.

Meanwhile La Fayette, whose light division's task was to
engage Cornwallis and hold him down, had been fighting a
campaign admirable for its flexibility, judgment and daring.

La Fayette was endowed with great wealth and an instinctive understanding of the popular mind: he devoted a great deal of money to maintaining spies in the enemy's territory and behind his lines; he therefore always knew where Cornwallis was and where he intended to go. Cornwallis, unfortunately for himself, was too sceptical, cultured and witty. He looked upon the Americans as so many tradesmen who had been led astray and the French as mere ladies' men, agreeable but empty. He was not on his guard. His troops were weary and he was anxious to fall in with Clinton's general plan, so he led them back to Yorktown on the Chesapeake, with his back firmly to the sea – for he had no doubt that the British fleet was in command of the ocean.

He was mistaken. This time de Grasse behaved brilliantly, and so did Washington. The French fleet sailed in: on the way it met with Admiral Graves' fleet at Cape Henry and beat it – one of the first clear-cut naval victories that France had won in this war; then he steered directly for the Chesapeake. Meanwhile Washington and Rochambeau, making forced marches, joined La Fayette before Yorktown and sent Lauzun with his legion to watch the English bridgehead on the other side of the river.

The French fleet arrived first, and it was soon joined by the allied armies: Cornwallis was not particularly worried, for he was certain that he should soon receive the reinforcements that Clinton had promised (he did not know that Clinton, who was jealous of him, was keeping them back in New York).

Opposite him on the south bank there were arrayed Washington, Rochambeau, Saint-Simon (who had come with the French fleet) and La Fayette, fourteen thousand men in all, and on the north bank Lauzun and his legion of eight hundred. They were in complete command of the situation.

There was a regular siege. Cornwallis, a brave leader at the head of seasoned troops, defending himself well. He was still waiting for Clinton; and Clinton, having noticed Washington's departure, was at last preparing his own. Cornwallis tried to break out on the side of the sea or towards the north: he could not – all the ways were blocked. The allies mounted a first assault and pressed it home vigorously; it cost them a good many casualties, and Cornwallis even more, for his space was very cramped. They prepared another, which they hoped would prove decisive.

At this juncture a curious thing happened. On the north bank Lauzun, having had a few brilliant skirmishes, was growing bored; he wanted to go and ask Rochambeau for instructions and to see his friends on the south bank again. He had the idea of asking Cornwallis whether he would let him pass through his camp blindfolded. Cornwallis, with a well-bred man's civility, invited him to dinner with his eyes unbound. They had an excellent meal, and then, just as Lauzun was about to leave, Cornwallis pointed out a little heap of cannon-balls and observed, 'Those few balls and a very little powder is all I have left: we are going to fire them off, and then tomorrow I shall surrender.'

The next day, 19 October 1781, Earl Cornwallis, the general in command of the British army in Virginia, acting through his second in command, gave up his sword to General Washington, the commander-in-chief of the allied armies, who offered it to Rochambeau. 7,050 English surrendered to 11,200 French and 5,100 Americans. The southern states were liberated; the English troops in America were demoralized: from now on everybody knew that the United States would remain a free and independent nation. The next day de Grasse sailed to carry on with his task and to meet with whatever Fate should have in store. Six days later Clinton appeared, then went away again. The match was won.

Rochambeau hurried to send the Duc de Lauzun and the Comte de Deux-Ponts to announce the victory at Versailles, bearing captured standards and messages from Washington and himself.

At Versailles the summer was wearing along, heavy with expectation. The queen was pregnant; so was Mme de Polignac. The king looked after them, and he even went to see Mme de Polignac at her house in Paris, something he had never done for anyone. They kept the queen amused as well as they could, with visits and with plays acted in her apartments. She took to teasing those around her. She asked Monsieur straight out whether it was true that Madame was pregnant. 'There is not a single day when that might not be the case,' the prince retorted. The queen burst out laughing and said, 'Since you answer so well I shall not ask you any more questions.' So they talked about the trees that Chartres was cutting down, the potatoes that Parmentier was bringing in, the chaos at the Opéra, the notorious charlatan M. de Cagliostro, who gave out that he was three or four thousand years old and that he had talked to Jesus, and about a physician who set a mysterious kind of electricity in motion and who was called Mesmer. But the queen often brought the conversation round to the war in America, where she had so dear a friend: unhappily the troops moved about so much that there was scarcely any news.

Finally, at a quarter to two on the afternoon of 22 October 1781, it was learnt that the queen had felt the first pains. In a moment the whole of Paris and Versailles was upside down, and the king was hurriedly brought to the queen's apartments. This time there was none of the confused tumult of 1778, for Louis XVI had abolished the ancient custom of leaving the door open and letting in all and sundry. Everything passed off well. The physician took the child and brought it to the king. Those who were in the bedroom could hear the queen's panting breath, made louder by her anxiety. Breaking the silence, the king said to her, 'Madame, you have gratified my wishes and those of France to the full: you are the mother of a Dauphin.'

In a moment the news had spread all over the palace and there was an immediate rush to congratulate the king, who, with tears in his eyes, shook hands with one and all. His whole being radiated happiness – he was a new man, gay, affable, overflowing with cheerfulness. Meanwhile the Dauphin was put into his cradle and the visitors filed past; the bells rang out and the guns fired their salutes; at six o'clock the Provost and the municipal authorities marched in procession round a bonfire, to the sound of another salvo of guns. An order was published, calling for a general illumination for three days: the greater part of the town had already lit itself up spontaneously.

On the twenty-third and twenty-fourth an orchestra played on the Place de Grève, and there was a distribution of food and drink: the Te Deum was sung everywhere, at court first, then in the

Chambre des Comptes, and then throughout the whole country.

The prettiest sight was at the palace, when all the trades made their visit. Carrying the tools of their calling they came to the Marble Court, marching behind their bands; then they spaced themselves out as though for a parade. The sweeps lined up side by side, dressed as though they were on the stage; with them they brought a splendidly decorated chimney, and the smallest of their mates perched on top of it. The sedan-chair carriers had a brilliantly gilt chair in which an immense wet-nurse displayed herself, with a delightful little Dauphin. The butchers marched with their fatted ox; and behind them came the pastry-cooks, the masons, the locksmiths, etc.

From his balcony the king watched for a long while, with tears in his eyes. There had been nothing of this kind for his birth: but now he had a son! His life took on a deeper, more delightful meaning, a wider, more far-reaching sense altogether.

These were the most exquisite of days for the king and the queen. The queen felt that she was all that she had ever desired to be. The king returned thanks to God and wondered whether at last he might now look forward to the full accomplishment of the task that his father and grandfather had left him – a heavy task indeed, and one that had often seemed to him overwhelming, beyond all measure. The ladies and gentlemen of the court and all the servants right down to the least important footman hurried eagerly around, looking delighted, so that Versailles, which had too often been empty these last five years, was once more a crowded, glittering spectacle; for every one of them expected to profit from this birth, either at once or in the long run.

The only person not to be delighted was Monsieur, who turned away with an uncontrollable grimace of anguish; for he was no longer the heir to the throne. As for Artois, he took the matter with a song, and told his eldest son, the Duc d'Angoulême, who was six, that he ought to go to see his cousin. That evening Artois said, 'Well, what did you think of your cousin?' 'Very small, Papa. How very small he is!' 'Oh, my son,' cried Artois, 'you will think him plenty big enough, when he is your king!'

The whole of France seemed to be concentrating happily upon

this one cradle. The baby proved strong enough to withstand the floods of eloquence, verse and compliments. A fortnight after his birth he weighed thirteen pounds and measured twenty-two inches in length. He had a fine, flowing nurse called Mme Poitrine. The worthy soul, urged by an irresistible vocation, had assumed the post without ever having been summoned. Now her splendid talents were acknowledged, and she rocked the Dauphin to the tune of *Malbrouk s'en va-t'en guerre*, which she thus brought back into fashion.

The Dauphin's cradle was as it were the very centre and navel of the country; everyone came flocking round it, from the canons of Paris to the fishwives in black silk, wearing their diamonds. Indeed, their speech even contained a witty phrase: 'Now we are quite sure that our children will be as happy as ourselves, for this child will certainly be like you. You, Sire, will teach him to be as kind and just as you are. And we undertake to teach ours how to love and honour the king.'

The locksmiths had the prettily-conceived idea of bringing the king a mysterious lock; he received it with great interest, looked into it and discovered the secret. He was so pleased that he gave the ingenious mechanics thirty louis from his own pocket. The Faculty of Medicine was no less filled with zeal; they drew up a Latin treatise on the *Birth of the Dauphin* and had a Te Deum sung.

During these days there were free entertainments for the people. The Comédie-Française put on *La Partie de chasse de Henri IV*, which had not been performed since Necker's dismissal; and it was wildly applauded. Louis XVI had most decidedly become an Henri IV once more! At the Comédie-Italienne there was *Les Deux Sylphes*, and they sang the impromptu song:

> *I am a fairy, and I want to tell*
> *The news of a lovely boy,*
> *A king's own son who has come with a spell*
> *To fill the whole kingdom with joy.*
> Etc.

The brand-new Opéra gave its dress rehearsal as another of these performances. That evening the coalmen sat in the king's box and the fishwives in the queen's: it was their right, for they were the chief corporations of their kind: footmen in full dress waited for them at the door, and the piece was not allowed to begin until they were present. As the curtain went up the auditorium echoed with the cry, 'Long live the king! Long live the queen! Long live Monseigneur le Dauphin!' Then the show went on in the midst of the most attentive silence. At the religious concert there was a cantata on the birth of the Dauphin. And so for two months on end Paris went on with the unwearying celebration of its Dauphin.

The provinces copied the capital: at Strasburg they celebrated the centenary of the French annexation before a full-length portrait of the king, set under a canopy; at Rouen, when the performance of *La Fête villageoise* came to an end, a booted courier appeared on the stage and began to sing the lines of *Par la P'tit' Poste de Paris*, which the audience repeated with immense enthusiasm, together with the chorus, '*Viv' l'Dauphin, viv' l'Dauphin!*' At Limoges they set up a handsome fountain which received the name 'Fontaine Dauphine', while the square in which it stood was called 'Place Dauphine'.

The Jews of Strasburg wanted to show that they were as patriotic as anybody else, and to the sound of a little cannonade they marched in a body to their synagogue, which was in the house of the famous Cerfbeer, a prominent member of their community; it was splendidly lit up and decorated. There they sangs psalms and hymns of thanks before the open tabernacle with the Tables of the Law displayed, a symbol of the most important feasts.

Of course, in this great outburst of joy there was no lack of verses, ranging from those which praised the king, that able gardener, for having managed to graft 'the Austrian rose on the French laurel', to the Gascon's impromptu:

> *You hear the great news? Rochambeau, La Fayette*
> *Have conquered the British a little while since;*
> *And while we are cheering our splendid new prince*
> *They make the poor English pay for his layette.*

I

There was another, rather more delicate, which congratulated him thus:

> *Monseigneur the Dauphin, how happy your chance,*
> *Not in that you're born heir-apparent of France*
> *But in that your cradle preserves you quite free*
> *From grasping the twaddle we pour out to thee.*

Would he have been any more moved by the homage paid to him by the ladies in replacing the jeannettes, the little gold crosses they wore on their bosoms, by charming dolphins, sometimes set off with diamonds? At least he might have been charmed with the masterpiece that Duval, the king's confectioner, displayed in the window of his shop, Au Grand Monarque, in the rue des Lombards: next to the *Taking of Yorktown (including the Fleets)* there arose the *Splendid Obelisk erected at Port-Vendres in the Roussillon in Honour of Louis XVI's Beneficence* – all made of sugar.

There was not enough sugar or enough honey in the whole of France for the Dauphin, nor compliments enough for his father. Congratulations came in from all over the world; and even the insulting songs about him that circulated were flatteries of a kind, since they proved the chagrin felt by those who first put them about: Monsieur? Chartres? Or the English?

Lauzun, Deux-Ponts and the news of the victory arrived a fortnight after the baby's birth, and to Louis XVI's happiness as a father was added the joy of thinking that he had once more placed France where Louis XIV had left her. For the first time for a great while the Bourbons had beaten England; they had done so with the approval of Europe, and they had found an effectual means both of limiting England's power and of reducing her influence.

Unhappily, at the very moment he was brought the news of the victory at Yorktown and of the taking of Florida by the Spaniards, as well as that of the French successes in the West Indies, Maurepas was dying. On 10 November it was thought that all was over; on the twelfth he was rather better – his head was clear and he was as full of mockery as usual. M. de Choiseul, who had hurried to Paris to be on the spot, looked a fool. But from the eighteenth things took so bad a turn that he was given the last sacraments; the physician found that there was gangrene and even the skill of the famous Barthès of Montpellier could do nothing. Yet his medicines did at least give Maurepas the strength to ask the king to grant his doctor's father a patent of nobility. 'He has chosen the right moment!' exclaimed the king, unable to refuse. This brief recovery was his last flicker of life. At eleven on the night of 21 November 1781 the Comte de Maurepas died. The king heard the news as he was going to bed: the Master of the Wardrobe, the Duc d'Estissac, who was related to Maurepas, gave a sigh of distress, for which he begged the king's pardon. 'You have had a great loss,' said Louis XVI, 'but I have had a far greater.'

In Maurepas he lost the man who had succeeded in giving him heart and spirit and a pleasure in being himself, in carrying out his ideas and realizing his wishes; he lost a man who had a deep feeling for France, a love for her traditions and an understanding of her needs; he lost a man whose suppleness gave him strength, whose comprehension gave him generosity and his scepticism kindness; and above all he lost a man of unshakable loyalty. He was still overwhelmed by this loss when another death occurred, one that took away a second reliable counsellor and a firm support.

On 12 December Cardinal Christophe de Beaumont, Archbishop of Paris, died at eleven at night, having governed the Church in Paris for so long a time and through such great upheavals. The *philosophes* and the Jansenists uttered cries of delight, but the king was bitterly distressed. Beaumont was one of the few remaining truly good and pious prelates. Out of his income of 600,000 francs he gave away 500,000 to those in need. He was buried on 17 December, in the midst of a great gathering of poor people.

At once factions came into being, to obtain the appointment of this *philosophe* priest or that to the key-post of Paris. At one time it was thought that Loménie de Brienne had the place, so strongly did the queen, pushed on by Vermond, urge the king in his favour. But Louis did not yield. He wanted a pious, intelligent, zealous bishop; and he did not find one.

In the end his choice fell upon Juigné, Bishop of Châlons, at the recommendation of Vergennes, who represented him as a most charitable man and quite fit for the appointment. For it was to Vergennes that Louis XVI owed the victory that had restored France to her place.

Chapter XIII

The skilful King

LOUIS XVI, HELPED BY VERGENNES, HAD UNDERTAKEN THE American war in spite of Turgot, in spite of Necker, the greater part of the ministers, the court, the clergy and the army, in spite of the wits and of pro-English public opinion; and by the decisive battle of Yorktown he had won it. Silent and reticent as usual, he kept his joy to himself: yet the people shared it with him.

The people were in an ecstasy: in quick succession there came the Dauphin, a great victory won almost without loss, and magnificent rejoicings. For this time the king did not mean to do things sparingly. He told the Provost, and everyone turned to, doing their utmost to have everything ready for Monday, Tuesday and Wednesday, 21, 22 and 23 January 1782.

Above all there were to be no accidents. 'No deaths because of a birth' was the watchword. The Duc de Biron, in command of the Gardes-Françaises, the Chevalier Dubois, in command of the watch, and the chief of police all consulted with M. Moret, the master of the revels, and took measures against the risk of fire; and they had a meeting with the watermen, all of whom were on duty those days, about the danger of people being drowned. All the chimneys in the neighbourhood were swept, the movement of coaches was controlled; the number of soldiers, constables and patrols was increased, and physicians, surgeons and even midwives were posted at various points, for anything can happen in a crowd.

As the festivities were to take place on the Place de La Grève and upon that of the Hôtel de Ville, the Place de La Grève was masked with a splendid decorative framework, and the courtyard of the Hôtel de Ville turned into an immense, richly ornamented hall. The king and the queen dined in public; they then watched a magnificent display of fireworks and attended a sumptuous ball. The weather was delightful and everything went well; the organizers almost died with weariness and anxiety; the soldiers were terribly hot and the king narrowly escaped being crushed. Apart from that, he was very pleased indeed with the entertainment and the people's warm regard for him – they were charmed with him, and they let him know it.

He was in a most gracious humour all day long. But there were not many cheers for the queen, and she remained grave. A few days later the members of the bodyguard gave a party: it included a full-dress ball in the evening and a masked ball at night. The hall in which it was given shone with countless lights, the music was loud and excellent, the uniforms splendid and the women happy. The king did not dance, but he walked about a great deal, talking with everybody, and he declared that he had never seen a finer ball.

To everybody's great surprise, the death of Maurepas did not alter the king's life at all: he heard mass, he hunted and he worked as his usual times; to help him govern he had not called upon either M. de Choiseul, or M. Necker or M. le Cardinal de Bernis, all thought to be likely candidates for the post of prime minister. He conferred with each minister about his own department, and that alone, never allowing him to go beyond it. Only M. de Vergennes knew whom he consulted in the cases that perplexed him; but M. de Vergennes did not discuss the matter, for he too was a reticent man.

Furthermore the king and M. de Vergennes had too much work and too many worries to prattle. Victory is a fragile, precarious thing that has to be used at once, if one does not wish it to fade away or go bad in one's hands. Vergennes had no doubt that from now on negotiations would be more decisive than the fighting, and his agents informed him of an irresistible wave of opinion in favour of peace in Great Britain. On 27 November Lord Shelburne had moved an amendment in parliament asserting the impossibility of continuing the war; Fox had done the same; and although North was still in power, it could not last. Meanwhile the war had to go on, to force peace upon the enemy: Suffren was fighting in India with heroic and successful determination; de Grasse was preparing to meet the Spanish main fleet, to which he was bringing important reinforcements for their combined attack on Jamaica; Guichen was about to sail with fifteen men-of-war and a large convoy to support them; the Spaniards were besieging Gibraltar, and they had just taken Minorca and Fort St Philip.

To tell the truth Vergennes did not really want any more military victories. He would have preferred each nation to return to common sense. But the leaders of the different countries were reluctant. Since 1778 the courtiers had been whispering, 'The Comte de Vergennes is very proud of his alliances: he will see how much his allies cost him when it comes to peace.' He had been afraid of this himself. Now his forebodings were coming true: the Spaniards loathed the Americans, who repaid their dislike a hundredfold. In the end Madrid received an American ambassador, John Jay, an intelligent, civil man; but he was unable to make any progress whatever in his negotiations.

The Americans, since they were indeed American, meant to have a free hand in America; and the Spaniards, since they had discovered America, meant to dispose of it as they saw fit. Spain would have granted the United States the territory of the thirteen federated colonies, on condition that they did not encroach any farther; but the Americans insisted upon a great deal more. The traders wanted the right to sail upon the Mississippi, a river that the Spaniards asserted to be their property; and the planters, anxious to have fresh land always at their disposition for their tobacco – an exhausting crop – wanted to keep the right to push towards the West, which the Spaniards said belonged to them.

The English made the same statement, claiming that they were the owners of these territories, in which the French had been the first arrivals, so that the usual connexion was with Louisiana and Canada. But the Americans wanted Canada too! There was only one point upon which everyone was in agreement, and that was that not the least notice should be taken of the Indians, the owners of this land in which they had lived for hundreds of years.

Vergennes knew that Spain claimed Gibraltar as an essential condition of peace, whereas the United States refused even to discuss it: yet there had to be combined negotiations, otherwise England would win the peace after having lost the war. He therefore increased his appeals for unity in both Madrid and Philadelphia. His minister in the States, M. de La Luzerne, was quite successful: he arrived at a moment when the Congress secretary, Thomas Paine, with the help of a few others, was causing a scandal by accusing several members of having sold themselves to France – an exaggerated charge, it may be added. La Luzerne at once bought Paine and calm returned; Congress voted that the American delegates should come to an understanding with Vergennes, that they should negotiate in agreement with him, and that they should hide nothing from him. This looked very well on paper, but unhappily the delegates, particularly Adams, whom Vergennes distrusted, and John Jay, whom he did not, were utterly determined to act according to their own notions, or 'according to their conscience', which came to the same thing. This did not make Vergennes' task any easier.

Can it be said that the chaos in the British parliament helped him? The two Whig leaders, Lord Shelburne and Charles James Fox, had at last managed to overthrow Lord North (March 1782) whom they each hated equally. But they disliked one another even more, and the king had the same feelings towards them – he thought Fox a ranter and Shelburne a 'Jesuit'. The pill was politely gilded for him by the selection of Rockingham as premier, although in fact Rockingham was incapable of overriding either Fox or Shelburne; and they cheerfully prepared to negotiate.

Fox, the foreign secretary, wanted to carry out the whole of the peace negotiations and to begin by conciliating the United States with recognition of their independence; he sent Thomas Grenville to Paris, and he also advocated an alliance with France and Holland. Shelburne was in charge of the colonies, and his idea was to negotiate with the thirteen revolted states, which still, in the king's eyes, retained their colonial status: the king therefore supported him in this. Shelburne refused to recognize their independence, so that he might go on treating with them and make them buy it at a very high price. He sent Oswald, an old friend of Franklin's, to Paris. Shelburne's was a reasonable plan; so was Fox's. But as each hid everything from the other, and as their respective envoys made a great affectation of mystery, neither the French nor the Americans could understand what was afoot. In spite of all his great good sense Vergennes was intensely suspicious.

In the meantime he went on with his work; he had several conferences a day with the king (except on hunting days, of course) to try to unravel this entangled skein. By way of putting a little oil into the creaking wheels and to come by information, Louis XVI sent his brother Artois to the siege of Gibraltar: in this way the Spaniards, even if they did not gain Gibraltar in the peace treaty, would see that nothing had been neglected to win it for them. Together with the French fleet and army already on the scene, this constituted an impressive demonstration. There was also an exchange of affectionate letters, full of feeling about Louis XVI's poor aunt Sophie, who had died suddenly at Versailles on 3 March; and about the expectations, the consoling expectations, of the Infanta Louise.

Sèvres porcelain was highly prized in Spain, and this helped to keep up the warmth of the family connexion, for Louis XVI was very generous with it. But relations have to be watched closely: the king was informed that his brother-in-law Joseph was preparing one of his own particular enterprises in the direction of Holland. Joseph II was capable of anything; and although his journey of the previous summer had been very friendly, it augured no good. The Baron de Breteuil would have to keep a close eye upon everything that happened in Vienna and the east.

From the east, magnificently attended, there came M. le Comte du Nord and his wife. This impressive name concealed the

Tsarevitch Paul, the son of the admirable and formidable Catherine II. He was married to a princess of Montbéliard-Wurtemberg, whom he loved dearly, and both of them had seized the opportunity of making a tour of Europe, both to amuse themselves and at the same time to learn. Versailles was there, ready to heap pleasure and instruction upon them. They arrived on 20 May, in a state of 'public incognito', which hindered nothing and allowed everything.

The Tsarevitch was presented as a private person of the highest standing, and only one side of the king's door was opened for him. But the Prince de Poix, who conducted him, bowed very low as he passed through. He was accompanied by his ambassador, Prince Bariatinsky. The king received him in his council-chamber, as usual. The Comte du Nord spoke French well, and he radiated friendliness. He made an equally good impression upon the queen and the king's brothers, whom he visited afterwards. His politeness and his respectful demeanour contrasted with his uncommon smallness and with his face, which was so far from prepossessing that when he passed through Lyons all the women had exclaimed, 'Oh, how ugly he is!' This caused him to observe, 'A country where they do not spoil me at last! What a pleasure it will be to stay here!'

It was, indeed. From the first time they dined together, the king and queen plied them with delicate attentions: they dined at a round table, so that there should be no head, with the Comte du Nord next to the queen and the king next to the Comtesse du Nord, a big, plump woman, very good-natured and witty. In the evening there was a concert and a ceremonial reception. The Comte du Nord found Louis XVI distant at great official gatherings, warm in his own circle, and prudent in political conversations. As for the Comtesse du Nord, she got along very well with the king, for both of them had short-sighted eyes and far-sighted minds, fixed on higher things. The queen appeared in her most splendid clothes; she was as lovely as the day, and she handled the Comte du Nord with great skill. The king too was very fine in his 'apple-green velvet coat, with a rich pattern of embroidery in silver beads and coloured spangles, the waistcoat and facings of white velvet, embroidered like the coat with a very richly and closely worked centre-piece.'

The French court was still the most elegant in Europe: the Russians saw this at the full-dress ball that followed, and they were even more fully persuaded of it during their visit to Chantilly, which they found so wonderful that the Tsarevitch said to the Prince de Condé, 'How I should like to be a Bourbon and a Condé!' 'Oh, Sire,' replied the prince directly, 'it would be too great a loss for you, and an even greater one for your people.' The king gave two more entertainments for them; they went to see the Duc d'Orléans, to a session of the Académie Française, to a concert given by the Comte d'Artois at Bagatelle, a ball at the Opéra, etc. The Duc de Croy, thoughtful as usual, wrote, 'This name of Comte du Nord is somewhat excessive, for the kings of Sweden and Denmark are not mere ciphers – far from it; and it might almost foretell that one day, what with the brisk advances that power is making, they may, in like circumstances, take the name of Comtes d'Europe.' Thus the prophetic M. de Croy.

This did not prevent him from admiring the entertainment on 8 June, the most splendid ceremonial ball of the year, where, under the light of three thousand candles and innumerable diamonds, the queen, wearing a dress like La Belle Gabrielle's, danced a quadrille with the Marquis de La Fayette, to the wonder of all. The young marquis' favour had reached the highest point, and the king and queen showered kindnesses upon him: the day he came back to France the king made him a general, before all his fellows and without his ever having been a brigadier; on the same day, at the end of the Dauphin's festivities, the queen herself conducted him to the Hôtel de Noailles, where his wife lived, and there she found a hundred fishwives besieging the door, with laurel wreathes and branches. The whole country delighted in making a hero of him.

He had deserved it by his courage in battle and still more by his comprehension of the royal policy. He was almost the only man who had grasped that if the French alliance with America were to be effective, it was essential that France should be popular in the States. He was still one of Vergennes' most valuable instruments, and the minister rewarded him by sending him to fight before Gibraltar with all the gilded youth of France. He also paid him this compliment: 'Your name is held in veneration. Although you were not commander-in-chief during this great operation, it was your wise conduct and your preliminary manœuvres that paved the way for its success.' Under a strong government, La Fayette was a shining ornament to his country, a most estimable member of society. He was also a courtier belonging to Mme de Polignac's circle.

As this was a year of glory and splendour, the king invited the whole court to follow him to Compiègne. There all was pastime and amusement: the court rose at eight, and if the weather was fine, everyone went hunting; if there was a danger of rain, the pages were sent for to play leapfrog and prisoner's base and other games in which the active, nimble young delight. Then there would be drives with the ladies, and after that billiards or backgammon; but they took care to keep away from gambling, lest the king should see and confiscate all the stakes for the poor. Then came supper; and very late at night, bed. For his part, the king hunted and worked.

He was now working harder than he had ever worked before. A great effort was still needed to make sure of the victory, for Admiral de Grasse had just put everything in jeopardy by losing the greatest naval battle of the war.

Together with Bouillé (who had distinguished himself in the campaign) he had taken St Eustatius, Montserrat and St Kitt's, and with a convoy of a hundred and fifty sail of merchantmen he was going to join forces with the Spanish fleet. This junction would ensure the allies' superiority over Great Britain in the West Indies and the taking of Jamaica. He was already close to Dominica and the Spanish on 9 April 1782 when he fell in with Rodney's rearguard: he did not attack it, although as the wind lay he might have done so. This was his first mistake. During the night of the eleventh he did not abandon one of his ships, the *Zélé*, which had been damaged in a collision, but had her taken in tow, thus slowing down the entire fleet. This was his second mistake. He was overhauled by Rodney, who was superior to him in number (thirty-five against thirty-two) and in equipment (all the British ships were copper-bottomed but only half the French); yet he accepted battle, and this was his third mistake. He might still have won, thanks to the courage and skill of his officers and men, but a shift in the wind divided his fleet into three, and in spite of his repeated signals, manœuvres now became impossible. He fought well in his flagship, the *Ville de Paris*, but he and his ship were taken, together with four more; and another was sunk. The battle raged for eleven hours on end. The British fleet was too roughly handled to be able to profit by its victory: it could neither pursue the French fleet nor attack a French island.

It was only a tactical victory for the enemy, one that had no strategic consequences: but its psychological repercussions were immense. In England there was a great roar of delight, in France a cry of rage and indignation, followed by a great outburst of patriotic feeling. On every hand the towns organized subscriptions to provide the king with new ships; in a few days they offered him twelve, in place of the eight that had been lost, and he ordered the building to be set in hand at once. And the crowd took its revenge on the admiral, saying, 'If it had not been for de Grasse's action, we should have had a Te Deum.' (This being a pun on *action de Grasse* and *action de grâces*, a thanksgiving.) The Parisians added, 'On the ship Paris is giving the king there will have to be written up *Conquer or die: no mercy at all*.' (Another play on *grâce* – mercy – and Grasse.) The Duc de Richelieu also seized upon this opportunity for a witticism. On being told that d'Estaing was going to command a fleet at Cadiz he cried, 'Having returned thanks to God, we are going to leave it to d'Estaing.'[1] Puns like this were popular at the time; and through these it is possible to make out the revival of the national spirit. The whole country was calling out for revenge for the battle of the Saints.

There was still no want of levity among the French. If there was any one family that had benefited from the royal favour for the last hundred years, it was the Rohans. In spite of his serious

---

[1] In French it runs 'Après avoir rendu Grasse à Dieu, nous allons nous remettre au d'Estaing.' Grasse is the obvious play upon *grâce* again (in the sense of thanks); and d'Estaing sounds like *destin* – fate.

shortcomings, the Prince de Soubise had been Louis XV's best friend, and Louis XVI had a respect for him; a lady of that house had brought up Louis XIV's children, another had brought up Louis XV's children and grandchildren; and still another, the Princesse de Guéménée, was bringing up those of Louis XVI. She was one of the closest friends of the queen, who, in spite of her mother's entreaties and her brother's sarcasms, had never stopped seeing a great deal of her, and had even entrusted her with the care of her only son, the Dauphin. His wife's and his brother-in-law's favour at court brought great advantages to the Prince de Guéménée, and his house was one of the most splendid in Paris.

But one fine day – 30 September 1782 – it was learnt that the most noble and most illustrious Prince de Rohan-Guéménée was bankrupt: he had borrowed so much money, loan upon loan, that now he was utterly ruined. More than three thousand creditors were spoken of, chiefly humble people, menservants, doorkeepers and fiddlers, but there were also literary men, who made a great deal of noise.

All the working people of Paris were up in arms with indignation. They did not scruple to speak of Guéménée as a thief. And that was how the king certainly looked upon him: he at once had Guéménée's man of business and his lawyer arrested, and desired the prince to remain in the country, upon his estate in Navarre. The princess had to give up her place as governess of the Children of France and withdraw to one of her father's estates, where, it was said, she indulged herself in a very wild and wanton manner. Everybody turned against them, the great nobles and the court, who were jealous of the Rohans' good luck, the shocked middle classes and the furious common people. The dancer Vestris said to one of his sons who was running into debt, 'I will not have any Guéménées in my family!' The scandal grew prodigiously: to prevent it growing even more the king gave the Guéménées three months' respite, so that the liquidation could be carried out by agreement, without the intervention of the lawyers, who would have eaten up everything that was left. The Cardinal de Rohan and Mme de Marsan handed over great sums to pay the poorest creditors; and it was even said that Soubise renounced his little mistresses from the Opéra, but it seems that rumour flattered him.

It is impossible to exaggerate the king's anger. How could he ever manage to make these people understand their duties when they did not even know how to make a proper use of their privileges? Guéménée was raising all Paris and Brittany against him; and at the same time Chartres, with his financial speculations, was cutting down the city's finest trees and turning the Palais-Royal, the most delightful place in Paris for a stroll a little while before, into a kind of showy prison. And now he had hit upon the idea of putting his children into the care of his mistress, the Comtesse de Genlis! There was one shout of hostile derision from Paris to Versailles: there were rude songs about her and people hooted her in the streets; but she held her head high, for to a total lack of shame she added brazen effrontery. She was not the only one. Closer to him still the king saw the Comtesse d'Artois, between two pregnancies, lie with Desgranges of the bodyguard, who boasted of it. The Bastille taught him to hold his tongue. All this very open, public disorder troubled the people's mind.

The parlements, of course, made an abusive use of it. That of Bordeaux would not sit in judgment any more, on the pretext that the king was trying to force the Président Dupaty upon them; that of Besançon refused to promulgate the decree for the tax of the third twentieth part, and its stubbornness was driving M. de Vau, the governor, out of his wits. In Brittany the Estates, led by the nobles, grew more outspoken, and in December they sent the king a respectful letter in which they termed him 'Father of your people', but a daring one, for it accused him of infringing the rights of Brittany, always respected by his ancestors, by preventing the Estates from choosing their delegates freely and by compelling them to register the decree of 4 November 1780, which they did not approve of.

They even presumed to send delegates to Versailles. Louis XVI wrote to them very sharply:

> There is nothing that can dispense my subjects from the obedience they owe me. In 1780 the Estates of my province

of Brittany should have begun by electing deputies in the manner laid down by the decree of my Council of 11 February of the same year, and this act of submission would have allowed me to see in their representations only an outburst of zeal rather than resistance to my wishes, a resistance that justice and the maintenance of my authority make it impossible for me to suffer . . .

The Estates listened meekly, more alarmed than convinced.

The king had need of a great deal of patience.

After some excellent boar-hunting at Fontainebleau, where the court had been numerous and the rain steady, he moved to Versailles for the winter, and once again there were the intense anxieties of the peace negotiations. The Spanish ministers in Madrid, the American delegates in Paris, the English ministers in London and all their quarrels turned into a Chinese puzzle for Louis XVI and Vergennes. Day and night the importunate messages came in: no one could reproach the Spanish minister with a lack of steadfastness, for they never stopped crying out for Gibraltar. They did not want anything else to be dealt with; they wanted everything to be held up for Gibraltar. The Americans would have none of it. Mr Jay reached Paris from Madrid in August 1781 filled with a settled hatred for Spain and a profound suspicion of M. de Vergennes – a suspicion that was extended to his colleague Mr Franklin, accused of weakness with regard to the French minister. After a great deal of discussion Adams and Jay called upon Franklin to accept their point of view – to negotiate directly with the English without consulting Vergennes, or at least without telling him everything that happened between Oswald and them. They reproached Vergennes with having deceived them by secretly sending the best of his high officials, M. Gérard de Rayneval, to London for direct discussions with the British minister. The fact was true, but the interpretation false: Vergennes had sent Rayneval to London to see Shelburne, the leader of the British government since Rockingham's death (1 July 1782) and Fox's resignation. His wish was not to harm the United States in any way, but to clarify the situation. He was suspicious of Shelburne, who had just sent a fresh negotiator, Fitzherbert, whose head might well have been turned by the battle of the Saints. Rayneval was to tell Shelburne that France insisted upon the recognition of American independence and that she left the Americans to settle everything else with the English; for her part all she wanted was the restitution of all her establishments in India, with the right of fortifying them and of setting up others; of Senegal and Goree, which Lauzun had retaken; and of the Ile Royale; a just settlement of the Newfoundland fisheries, compensation for the captures made before the beginning of hostilities; and the complete restitution of Dunkirk. France was already in possession of almost everything she was asking for. The essence of the matter was to find out whether Shelburne was sincere or not. His obscure, involved negotiations cast doubts upon it. But this arose from the attitude of the King of England, who was doing his utmost to prevent or to delay the peace.

Shelburne, who was in fact quite sincere, was very happy to be suspected. What an advantage in diplomacy, when the other side does not know what you really want! So Vergennes was mistaken in suspecting Shelburne, and the Americans in suspecting Vergennes. Oswald, the British negotiator, made the most of it; he goaded the Americans by showing them the intercepted letters of the French chargé d'affaires in Philadelphia, which criticized the United States' graspingness in the matter of territory. And he pushed on with his negotiations at a great pace.

Shelburne and the leading Whigs (representing the British commercial interest) longed for a commercial treaty with the United States and for an early restoration of their economic supremacy in the New World. In order to succeed in this, Oswald yielded everything – free navigation of the Mississippi, rights over the western territories, fishing rights in Newfoundland, the expulsion of all the American Loyalists without compensation, etc. Between the end of September and 30 November the treaty was hurried into shape, and on the thirtieth it was signed.

The American delegates then entrusted Franklin with the task of carrying the document to Vergennes and also of asking him for twenty million, which Congress happened to be in need of. In the course of his career Vergennes had experienced a great many shocks, but this one really staggered him, for he had believed in Franklin's friendship. He did not conceal from the doctor that the French language had a word to describe conduct of this sort, a far from agreeable word. Franklin bowed his head; then gently, in a quavering, grandfather's voice, he pointed out to Vergennes that the signing was not definitive, that the American treaty would only come into force on the day the French peace treaty was signed, that the English thought themselves very clever for having divided the French and Americans, but that it only depended on Vergennes and Louis XVI for this to be untrue, and that finally a quarrel would mean giving the English the victory when in fact they were beaten. Vergennes breathed deeply, thought awhile, and recovered his serenity, if not his trust. What Franklin said was true. Vergennes remained perfectly civil for the remainder of the interview, which was not long. But for all the rest of that day he remained very pensive: had not M. de Montesquieu said that virtue was the characteristic of republics? At all events, M. de Vergennes, profoundly experienced though he was, had learnt something.

He at once informed the king. From his childhood Louis XVI had known all that there was to be known under the heading ot disappointments; he acquiesced in Franklin's views. There was to be no outward mark of displeasure; only a letter to the French minister in Philadelphia instructing him to tell France's friends in Congress that the king was surprised by this action, as impolite as it was unjustified; and then a loan of twelve million, six being provided by Spain, at five per cent, since they could not do without it. Of course Congress was angry with its delegates, passing a motion censuring them and repeating its assurances of fidelity to the King of France. The English manœuvre was thus circumvented: it was thwarted still more by George III, who distrusted Shelburne even more than the French did, and who would have nothing to do with any commercial treaty with the United States. So France extricated herself from a disagreeable situation in the best possible circumstances; but the fact remained that England, having divided her enemies and having made concessions to

America that she regretted, was going to try to obtain compensation at the expense of the other allies.

Those powers were by no means willing to be a party to anything of the kind. Charles III had not the least intention of reducing his claims; he reminded Louis XVI that in 1759 his grandfather had drawn him into a disastrous war, and he reminded George III that this time England had forced him into the conflict, in spite of his peaceful intentions. Sure of being in the right, therefore, he claimed western Florida, Minorca, and the bay of Honduras, which he had retaken, as well as the Mosquito coast, and he insisted upon Gibraltar as a *sine qua non*. George III, whose indignation was aroused by American independence, acknowledged Spain's obvious rights to Gibraltar; he would willingly have given it back to Charles III, but Shelburne and the Whigs were bitterly opposed to this course. 'Come and take it,' said Shelburne to the Spaniards: France had sent troops, ships and floating batteries, but all in vain; the English ended up by setting fire to the floating batteries and the Spaniards completed their destruction. Paris said, 'The Trojans have burnt the Trojan horse.'

On 20 October 1782 the king sent d'Estaing to Madrid to see the King of Spain before assuming the command of the Franco-Spanish fleet that was to attack Jamaica. D'Estaing was to hint that Gibraltar was not worth the deaths that another year of war would cause. Charles III returned an affectionate and stubborn reply – since peace was indeed an entirely necessary blessing, their first duty was to press on with their warlike preparations.

By return of post Louis XVI replied to these observations of 2 December 1782. He dwelt upon France's need for peace and produced his most telling passage: 'Great Britain's latest proposals seem to offer a real hope of this desired end, and to do so in a manner honourable for the glory of our house, which will always be one of my chief preoccupations.' Then he prayed to heaven that Charles III would understand the situation at last.

During this period Aranda declared that he was bogged down, stuck in the mud: Vergennes' temper was beginning to crack, and in his exasperation he privately told his close friends that 'the Spanish ambassador was a very contemptible scrub indeed'. The one gleam of hope amidst all these complications was Shelburne's obvious haste. Shelburne knew very well that there was an eager desire for his downfall, shared by the king on the one hand and by parliament on the other. He had to take more care of them than of the French, the Spaniards and the Americans. He was particularly anxious for the profitable fame of a peacemaker, and he wanted to put an end to this foolish war by rapidly concluded peace – a desire that he shared with Vergennes and with Louis XVI.

Louis XVI toiled on, stimulated by his people's love. The courtiers said that he could not possibly be more highly esteemed in every respect; wherever he appeared he was cheered; the tragedy *Zorai* had been on the stage since October, and the public never tired of applauding its many flattering allusions to the king. When his bust was unveiled on 7 December, M. Girard de Lourmarin produced some impromptu lines that were so much to his hearers' liking that they made him say them again:

> *A father to his people, wise and strong*
> *In striving for their welfare, righting wrong,*
> *Reproving evil, setting nations free,*
> *Restoring order, calm and liberty,*
> *The years to come shall hold him up to sight*
> *As Louis of France, the friend of truth and right.*

At the same time Nogaret brought out a print that showed him, followed by Prudence and Justice, unbinding Plenty with a sweep of his hand.

Peace had to be made at once. Suffren was fighting furiously, but everywhere else there was the danger of a disagreeable surprise. Shelburne might fall; the war might break out again and last for years and years. Catherine had to be watched carefully, for she and Joseph were preparing a great coup at the expense of Turkey – the creation of a Dacia (Bessarabia, Mondavia, Wallachia) which Catherine would be so kind as to take under her protection, while Joseph would sweep up Dalmatia and Belgrade. Greece was to be made into philosophical republics. Joseph had an iron constitution but a brain of straw, and he was all aflame with enthusiasm for this project.

Louis XVI knew that it was becoming urgently necessary to throw a bucket of water on his head. The best bucket of water would be peace, for once that was signed, England would join France to preserve Turkey.

So long as he was flattered and made to feel important, M. le Comte d'Aranda was quite manageable. Louis XVI and Vergennes sat down to a regular siege (October 1782), and as M. d'Aranda was a *philosophe* Vergennes treated him to a proof in three parts. On Thursday, 18 November, they tackled the Gibraltar question. Vergennes observed that the Spaniards were holding everything up with their Gibraltar. 'You insist upon it; the English will not give it to you. What can we do about it?' 'We can take it,' retorted Aranda, with a long harangue. Vergennes, raising his arms to the sky, asked him if he were acquainted with the means of taking the place and whether he approved of them. Aranda replied that he did not, but that he supposed that they existed, since his court did not despair.

Vergennes listed them:

'Men swimming under the water wearing leather garments called *scafandres* – the Abbé de La Chapelle had used them. These men are supposed to get into the harbour, set fire to the ships and break open the gates of the citadel. Or else hydraulic bombs to flood Gibraltar. Or again catapulted mortar bombs, containing stifling vapours. Or mines that eat into the rock by means of a mysterious water or a vinegar that consumes stone and turns it into sand.'

Aranda said that mines had already been used, but they went forward very slowly and that it was a difficult kind of work to keep going. As for the disease-bearing or asphyxiating bombs, he had heard them spoken of for months, but neither the Catholic King's religion nor his, Aranda's, humble opinion could tolerate such means, which would endanger families sitting peacefully at home if their use became general. The diving-suits, which he knew well and which he had tried, seemed to him usable in rivers, but certainly not in the sea; with this the noble Spaniard had no more to say, and he talked about other matters. He acknowledged that they did not possess weapons capable of taking Gibraltar, and he had the fairness to write to his king to this effect. That was the first part of the proof.

The second had to do with the English. Vergennes once more sent Gérard de Rayneval to London; he was well acquainted with Shelburne and the right people in England, and his mission was to try all the possibilities and send the minister a report. Thus provided, Vergennes employed the honourable stratagem of showing everything to Aranda. What never-ending sessions they were! One lasted from ten in the morning until five o'clock in the afternoon. Aranda began to weaken; the Americans' manœuvre made a deep impression on him; it gave him a measure of Shelburne's skill and his cunning in getting himself into a good position with respect to the French and the Spaniards. Vergennes patiently pressed his point, Louis XVI coaxed Aranda, and both of them flattered him, making it clear that he was the figure upon whom the whole operation hinged.

Finally he yielded, and since his king had given him full powers, Vergennes heaved a sigh of relief – peace was going to be signed! Louis supported the manœuvre by affectionate, peaceable letters to his male and female cousins in Spain. At last, at the beginning of January, Charles III replied. He approved of the peace, so long as he was given back Gibraltar.

'Do not let us allow an opportunity that may never return escape us,' he wrote; and he added that as he had not looked for this war, he was ready to go on with it, if necessary, to win a just and lasting peace. He ended thus:

> Although my ambassador, knowing my heart's tender affection for you, may have gone beyond his orders in continuing the peace-negotiations without insisting upon the giving up of Gibraltar, I should like it to be seen whether there is still any possibility of remedying this situation. But if it is wholly without remedy, and if Your Majesty's *home affairs* do not at present allow you to fulfil all your engagements, I shall not so urge the matter as to bring Your Majesty to extremes that may be unfortunate for yourself and your subjects. This will be no more than the exertion of my tender affection for Your Majesty's person.

This letter, prepared by Floridablanca and corrected and signed by the king, contented Vergennes; but it left Louis XVI with a painful impression. He had had to go to the utmost limit of his credit to obtain the renunciation of Gibraltar in spite of Floridablanca and public opinion. His uncle was soothing his own wounded pride by humiliating his nephew: as a nephew, Louis XVI accepted the lesson; but conscious of his dignity as a king, he promised himself that he would reply. First he had to see that peace was settled.

Aranda, won over and in any case delighted at thwarting Floridablanca, could be relied upon; the Americans were firmly held because of the loan, because of an oversight in their treaty (they had forgotten to settle a point concerning the date of the cessation of hostilities), and because of the instruction of Congress. At last the treaty was going to be signed. Louis XVI then answered Charles III. He did so with the strength and the prudence that he brought to everything he set his hand to.

> Sir, my Brother and Uncle, I am deeply moved by Your Majesty's mark of confidence and by the manner in which Your Majesty does justice to the constance and steadiness of my intention of maintaining the glory of our house and of contributing to Your Majesty's personal satisfaction. The peace is no doubt necessary for both our respective nations; they need relief after a war that has been more costly than any that have gone before it: nevertheless I should have been prepared to continue it if I had been better informed of Your Majesty's intentions and if I had supposed that an outcome happier than that which we experienced in the last campaign would have made our enemy more inclined to agree to the cession of Gibraltar. Your Majesty is aware of the very important sacrifices to which I consented in order to bring about the recovery of this fortification for Spain; to this end I devoted not only all my conquests in the West Indies, but I also gave up one of my most profitable dominions. The English, far from being satisfied by this, insisted upon other concessions that would, by depriving me of very considerable possessions, have compromised the security of those of Your Majesty in the Greater Antilles.

Your ambassador became aware of this peril, and it was then that he decided to make use of Your Majesty's orders of 23 October last. From that moment on the aspect of the negotiations changed, and the English ministers, who, it seems, only displayed so unreasonable an attitude on the cession of Gibraltar because they doubted the possibility of carrying it out, offered such advantageous terms that Your Majesty's ambassador thought it his duty to accept them. Nothing induced him to take this decision other than his own conscience; for since I was resolved to fulfil my engagements to Your Majesty, I did not allow myself so much as a hint that might have lessened their force. This being the present state of affairs, it appears to me that it is now impossible to alter the draught of the negotiations; indeed, I think any such attempt would be attended by very serious disadvantages. The British cabinet would no longer be a party to it, and we might, by thus reawakening the nation's opposition, induce that ministry to bind its government never to treat upon this subject again at any time. If a different set of circumstances should subsequently make it possible for us to engage in this matter, Your Majesty will always find me very willing to agree with your views and to support them; but the experience of this war teaches us that it is not in Europe that Gibraltar is to be won. It will be with pleasure that I shall listen to all that Your Majesty's ambassador may be desired to suggest to me, and I shall cooperate in everything that is within my power. It is my wish to make our union ever closer and ever more sacred. I beg Your Majesty to be as persuaded of this as of the lively and heartfelt friendship with which I am . . .

Louis XVI, winning the greatest war ever won by France, was generous to all, even to M. d'Aranda.

Chapter XIV

The happy King

THE AMERICAN WAR CAME TO AN END AT VERSAILLES WITH
the signature of the peace preliminaries in M. de Vergennes' office
on 20 January 1783. From this moment there was a fresh outburst
of joy.

Out of economy, Louis XVI did not want any great official
rejoicings, but the people drank and sang to their hearts' content.
The news was expected, for some days before Artois had been
unable to prevent himself from giving a hint of it to his partners
when he was playing tennis. The nation was none the less delighted;
and the news was also interpreted as a possible reconciliation
with England, 'the ambitious views of the North' (or rather of
Catherine and Joseph) bringing England and France closer together. That was also the king's impression.

Even Charles III was pleased, and he wrote Louis XVI an
affectionate letter (6 February 1783). He went so far as to praise
him for having been a 'good peacemaker and one who has
laboured for the welfare of our two crowns'. Catherine and
Joseph did not attempt to hide their vexation – a fact that showed
how very timely the peace had been. Joseph II wrote to his

brother Leopold, 'The peace has come at a bad time . . . The great power that had hitherto counterbalanced France is now wholly and finally brought low.' At Schönbrunn, Florence and all the Hapsburg palaces there was weeping over England's sad fate. Louis XVI and Vergennes saw this as an additional plume to their victory.

The best was the people's joy. Throughout the course of the negotiations Paris had been in a state of great excitement; examples had had to be made, the police had raided various cafés and had taken away over-eager newsmongers and people who opened their mouths too wide. Now they were let out of the prison of La Force.

The people went to cheer La Fayette or to call out greetings to Franklin. Above all they sang the song *Malbrouk*, which had been brought back into fashion by Mme Poitrine, the famous nurse to the Dauphin, that child so beloved of all the French that the old courtiers could not set eyes on him without weeping and that the cloth-merchants of Lyons had produced a silk of a colour called *caca Dauphin* – Dauphin's excrement.

Because of Mme Poitrine, then, the king and the queen liked singing Malbrouk; they taught it to the courtiers, and Paris copied them, so that during this spring of 1783, a spring of victory, peace and happiness, Malbrouk reigned supreme. Audinot and the king's company of dancers produced a licentious pantomime called *Malbrouk s'en va-t-'en guerre* that delighted the baker's boys and the chimney sweeps; Nicolet brought out another that was even more ludicrous; and during the carnival the masks followed suit – at every street corner there were funeral hearses for Malbrouk, a hundred different variations on the same theme. And of course there were also Malbrouk hats, bonnets and dresses for the women.

The craze for Malbrouk was so great that the Duchess of Marlborough, his granddaughter, heard of it, and she sent to France for information on all the songs, comic plays and clothes dedicated to her ancestor.

Meanwhile the administration of France could not be left floating in the air. Maurepas had to be replaced. Vergennes seemed to be a right and obvious choice. In spite of his modesty and his retired life, everybody admired him: this was clear from a charade that was much in fashion at the time – 'My first is the name of a crawling creature, my second that of a splendid capital, and my whole that of a great minister. Answer: Vergennes.' (Ver = worm; gennes = Genoa.) All the ministers instinctively gathered round him: the subtle Miromesnil, who not long before had paid sedulous court to Mme de Maurepas and had acted in her plays, brought his zeal with him to Mme de Vergennes' house, playing piquet with her; thus when Vergennes came home he found Miromesnil already there, and they became intimately acquainted. Ségur also understood Vergennes' worth and made advances to him; the foreign minister responded politely by opening the way for the young Ségur as a diplomat and preparing a brilliant career for him. Castries intelligently copied his colleague at the war ministry, and all the others followed his example. Without there having been any official appointment, Vergennes was from now onwards the dominant minister. On 23 February 1783 he took the oath as president of the financial council.

The king was continually obliged to step in; his authority remained as the mainspring of the state at a time when Vergennes was suffering from the agonies of the stone and spending, as he put it, 'whole nights being broken on the wheel'. The negotiations dragged along slowly. 'The Duke of Manchester [the new English ambassador] is as wary as he is weak and, I may say, impercipient. The fault lies with the gods,' remarked Vergennes, who for months had been doing his utmost to win back Negapatam for the Dutch, so that they could sign the treaty with the belligerents and the mediators (the Empress of Russia and the Holy Roman Emperor). He failed.

Manchester did not yield: the peace was signed at Versailles on 3 September 1783 without Holland, which concluded a separate peace some months later, renouncing Negapatam. Vergennes' pleasure was somewhat blunted by this, but nevertheless the impression throughout the world was very great indeed. Vergennes himself, in reply to Croy's remark, 'I do not answer for the honour this peace will do you at present, but I certainly warrant it in a hundred years' time!' said, 'I count on it for at least that period.'

He had attained all the aims that France had set herself in 1778: the independence of the United States; the real and public humiliation of England, which he had even managed to isolate; the recovery of Saint-Pierre-et-Miquelon and the French Newfoundland fisheries; and the conquest of Tobago and Senegal. The clause that gave him most pleasure was this: 'Abrogation and suppression of all the articles relative to Dunkirk from the treaty of peace concluded at Utrecht in 1713, inclusive, to this day.' For the first time since 1715 the whole territory of France was free from any form of English supervision whatever; the humiliation suffered by Louis XIV had been wiped out, just as had those that overwhelmed Louis XV in 1762–1763.

The king, the seamen and the people were overjoyed by this – profoundly happy. Of course the wits and the queen's circle were of the opinion that it would have been possible to do better, that the war had cost too much and that it had obtained nothing solid for France. They forgot that it had cost less than thirty thousand human lives, the smallest losses that France had ever experienced in a great international war, and at the same time it had given France high standing, international authority and the means of enriching herself through a trade that was now supported by bases on the shores of every ocean.

The most splendid result of this war was the moral supremacy that France had gained throughout the world; for the first time for a hundred years all the little nations turned towards France to seek justice and support. The great kingdoms and the empires were forced to reckon with her in all that they undertook.

This was a very great strength, and it was due to the qualities of the king and to the upward surge of the nation.

The king was not less forward-looking than private individuals; and although he looked upon France as an agricultural country, he wanted her to have prosperous trade and industries. In 1782–1783 he caused the great roads, the glory of Louis XV, to be repaired – they had been neglected from 1777 to 1781; and he gave strict orders that the carters and waggoners should not damage them. He sought above all to endow France with a system of navigable waterways, a necessary condition for a thriving industry and flourishing trade.

As it was necessary at the same time to increase the yield of the mines in France and to train a greater number of engineers, Louis XVI, by a decree of the council dated 19 March 1783, set up a School of Mines, a counterpart to the *Ecole des Ponts et Chaussées*, the civil engineering school founded by Louis XV. A programme for the reorganization and improvement of the ports was under consideration: at Le Havre the work of the building of the new town and the royal dock was set in hand without delay, and the same happened at Dieppe. Dunkirk, at last set free from British oversight, was about to rebuild its fortifications, since it was a frontier town, and dig out a dock to replace those whose destruction had been required by the treaty of Utrecht. A beginning was made with low jetties and a quay. Still greater improvements were planned for La Rochelle and Marseilles, and above all for Cherbourg. The nation encouraged the king with its eager rivalry; the papers of the time reported a strong, widespread enthusiasm for trade and business in all the provinces. It was very fine, after a war that had destroyed nothing, to see the French all so zealous to build and to create.

Louis XVI gave orders for pressing on with the work of developing his capital; the lines of the Champs-Élysées as well as those of the present Place de la Concorde could already be seen – the loveliest in Europe.

Luxury was so widespread and the quest for fine clothes so universal that the city presented a very highly-coloured spectacle. A journalist wrote,

> Luxury has even reached the clergy, those men who should seek only the veneration of the public and whose most splendid ornaments ought to be the modesty and propriety of their condition. Formerly the most stylish abbés scarcely went so far as to allow themselves coats of sombre, inconspicuous colours, such as puce or burnt coffee; by imperceptible degrees they went on to reddish-brown and Spanish

snuff, and thence to violet, *prune de Monsieur* and to blue-grey;
I do not despair of seeing them advance, by graduated shades,
as far as pink itself.

This was a time when the civilization of France had its own
taste and its own colour.

It also had a certain indefinable feverish quality that worried
the king. Gambling went on unchecked; every quarter the king's
accounts contained the entry 'Elizabeth's debts'. The princess in
question was neither prudent nor wise, for she allowed herself to
be dazzled by her brother Artois and to be drawn into the queen's
magic circle. It was a little world that was inimical to the king,
and it was filled with intrigue. There was no longer any question
of bringing back Choiseul, who was worn out; but all the king's
choices were criticized, and there was continual support for
Necker and for Loménie de Brienne, that bad priest, whom the
still all-powerful Vermond had never ceased to protect. This
circle was called 'the queen's society', and the ministers feared it;
to gain its good will Ségur appointed Besenval to the command of
the army of Paris and Vergennes sent Adhémar to the London
embassy. The society looked upon Castries with favour, he being
one of Necker's friends.

These manœuvres and these shady compromises were harmful
to the royal power. Yet Louis XVI put up with them as the lesser
evil. He had not chosen his wife. Since he was fifteen he had
lived with her, watching over her and helping her. He thought
that now the influence of the children, who were beginning to
grow, would calm her down. His behaviour was dictated by
affection, kindness, respect for the family and by political prudence. His work consoled him for everything, even for this. But the
sight of the tide of immorality rising on every hand alarmed him.

Freemasonry was becoming a powerful force in French society,
a factor in the movement and orientation of ideas, that is to say
in the struggle against the Church and against monarchical principles; in spite of the allegorical forms in which it was wrapped,
it disturbed the government and the king kept a careful watch
upon its progress.

The king looked upon the French monarchy as something more than a political régime, something more than a great tradition; he saw it as a civilization, and he knew that it would not survive if its bases were destroyed. As king he was at one and the same time guardian of the country's laws, institutions and morals; and for these he was and he remained answerable to God.

Everything that aimed at overturning the Catholic, family order in France affected him deeply, even when it was not directed against his power, as was the case with the freemasonry of 1783. Setting up a system of utilitarian ethics, a 'philosophical' faith and republican attitudes in France meant cutting away the roots of his authority. But being the Most Christian King and not a tyrant he did his utmost to defend the whole of the inheritance that had been entrusted to him not by violence but by intelligent and unremitting work, by a heartfelt love of the people, and by right conduct.

The king found that the enemies of the government would not lay aside their hostility and that they refused it all credit in spite of the victory. He looked for a man who could stand up to this gang of wreckers and who could at the same time retain that good-natured, happy atmosphere in the government and the country that was suitable to a powerful and victorious nation. He rejected Necker, whom the queen's society, the ladies of the court and all the *philosophe* salons were trying to force upon him; nor would he have Foulon, an intelligent but harsh intendant, the candidate of Monsieur and Mesdames.

He had to beware of the old, who were too well known, and of the young, who were not known well enough. His choice fell upon Charles-Alexandre de Calonne, chevalier, Comte d'Hannonville; he was forty-eight, and he came from a northern parliamentary family. He had been married to a daughter of the famous financier Marquet (who owed his fortune to the Duverneys), and although she was now dead he was still intimately connected with her family, which was accused (wrongly, no doubt) of having caused the run on the *Caisse d'Escompte*. Calonne had reached power by means of his work and his personality. He had negotiated with La Chalotais during the difficulties in Brittany and he had obtained certain results, especially the hatred of La Chalotais and the parliamentarians. When he was appointed intendant at Metz he made a success of the post, and he won a great many friends there.

M. de Calonne was attractive: his black eyes, contrasting with a red-headed man's fair complexion, had a particularly striking brilliance; his well-drawn mouth, strong nose and decided chin gave the impression of strength and fineness; the elegance of his clothes, his white wig and his hands strengthened this first idea, and his conversation completed the process. With his quick mind and cheerful heart he was conscious of superior powers and he looked forward to a splendid career; neither work nor difficulties frightened him, but he preferred power to both, and to power he preferred the pleasure of being liked. Generally he succeeded, and he was therefore detested by those with whom he did not or who were in some way jealous of him. There are no resources of hatred, falseness or slander that men will hesitate to use against an enemy who is known to be liked. This was the case with M. de Calonne. But it was of little moment to Louis XVI, who did not listen to the talk of the salons or to backstairs gossip, nor did it matter to Vergennes, who knew nothing about it.

1783 came to an end, a well filled year – general peace, two new ministers, the finances going well ... As a relaxation the king played with the Dauphin; he never tired of watching him in his pretty dark sailor-suit with a broad pale-blue sash round his middle. The Dauphin was a jolly child, pleasant with everybody, and he liked playing with his father, whom he did not find at all imposing. And in this year that was coming to a happy close, it was like a real and living dream of happiness.

Chapter XV

The arbiter of the world

EVERYONE SHIVERED AT VERSAILLES DURING THAT winter of 1783–1784, and the chapel might have been the North Pole. The cold martyred the old courtiers, hindered the king's hunting, and worried Calonne.

The poor wandered sadly about the streets of Paris: the great fires that the princes lit in front of their palaces and the nobles in front of their houses were increased in number, so that the street-porters, the sweeps, the cab-drivers and all those unfortunate people who could not leave the streets should not die there of cold. At the king's command, Le Noir caused the curés to distribute relief. The administration provided work and pay for the labourers and journeymen. All through these two months the one subject of conversation was the general wretchedness, the disasters, flooded villages, bridges carried away, and the hopeless, destitute peasants who gathered into bands to rob their more fortunate neighbours.

To begin with the king granted the sum of three million in lowered taxes for the current year for 'charitable work'; then he set aside another three million for relief in the countryside 'to be

K

employed above all in the purchase of essential food, the replacement of animals or tools needed for cultivation, and as a contribution to the replacement of dwelling-houses.' Another million was added to the highway department's ordinary funds for the carrying out of urgent work. To meet these unexpected expenses, the king cut the outgoings of his household, reduced the building-fund, made savings in the war department and elsewhere, by refusing to grant any new favours for a year and by letting others become extinct, and lastly by stoppages in pensions above 100,000 livres.

The comptroller found this a heavy burden. The people, particularly the poor, were grateful for such humanity in their king. As the Parisians of those days had charming ways in their amusements and all the details of their lives, they built countless ephemeral monuments out of the snow. Upon one such obelisk a passer-by wrote:

To Louis the Man

The fragile pile will not outlast my rhyme,
But Louis' goodness in this evil time
Has raised a monument that draws its source
From gratitude: no bronze has greater force.
Your sword has lately set the New World free,
And England's pride must bow its head to thee;
But on your fame a brighter light is shed
When by your hand the poor are warmed and fed.

He helped the poor to the very utmost of his powers: when it was a question of taking the severest measures against the marauding peasants, he said in council, 'We must help them live, not kill them. Let them be given lawful resources – that is the best way of making them give up the expedient of crime.'

Louis XVI's humanity enchanted the humble people, who were conscious of its depth. During those years the king's popularity shone throughout the country. A foreign diplomat said, 'The King of France has a clear understanding and an excellent heart; he eagerly seizes upon anything that seems to him useful to his people. Peace abroad is as valuable to him as peace at home, for which he makes great sacrifices.' Prince Henry of Prussia said the same (1783), 'This prince has great judgment and magnanimity.'

The Abbé de Véri and Miromesnil, the Keeper of the Seals, rounded off these opinions with a more detailed portrait, though it is more biased, since it comes from those who were close to him and necessarily partial.

> Not the least suspicion of falseness can possibly exist with regard to the king, and yet the outward appearances have not the least relation to the inner man. His heart is gentle and compassionate; he never hears of wounds or misfortunes without an expression of real concern coming over his face; and yet his way of speaking is brusque, his replies often harsh, and his manner far from sensitive. He is firm and bold in all the plans that have to be adopted in council; dread and fear do not affect his decisions in any way.

At this period when every man of wit proclaimed his fine feelings aloud instead of living them, the king saw them clearly and made them part of his daily life; in a country raving with logical unreason, he was a man whose instincts were undamaged. His great strength, the source of his prestige, lay not in a subtle intellectual logic nor in superfine processes of thought, but in those deep, thought-out, active insights that he was the only man of his century, apart from Frederick II and Washington, to make use of. This often made him look something of a bear; but it generally meant that he was right. And it made him a people's king; one who had a clearer knowledge than any other member of his council of the feelings and wishes of ordinary Frenchmen.

The lines that the town of Dôle wished to inscribe on his statue are evidence of this:

To Louis XVI, aged twenty-six

No slavery at home nor on the seas,
Decrees our king; America he frees.
His laws, our blessings, and his plans so sage
Undying fame ensure from age to age.

While Calonne was working with all his might, approved by some and criticized by others, the king took pleasure in searching for information among the working people; dressed as an ordinary gentleman he set off with his captain of the guard, who wore the same kind of clothes, travelling the roads, going into inns and farmyards and talking with those he met. These journeys and visits reminded him of those of his boyhood.

But now he found it easier to converse with people. Sometimes surprising things would happen: one day he was riding back alone from shooting, and when he was in a copse near Versailles a young peasant, who did not know who he was, approached him and begged insistently for alms. 'My father and mother are ill,' he said again and again. 'We have had no bread for two days.' In spite of the biting cold the king stopped; he wanted to find out the truth. 'Are you perhaps deceiving me? Perhaps you are only repeating something you have been taught to get charity out of people passing by.' 'Oh, Monsieur, I am telling the truth!' 'Where do you live?' 'In the next village.' 'Take me there.' They went, and the king discovered an only too genuine wretchedness. He emptied his purse, and then made inquiries about the honesty of the unhappy people he had seen. Back at Versailles he granted them a suitable pension for the rest of their days. These researches among the French people comforted and encouraged Louis XVI. But he could not linger: the court required his presence.

Yet his journeys and his hunting went on. He spent a while at his new château of Rambouillet. A courier arrived with an urgent message; Gustavus III had just arrived at Versailles, incognito, under the name of the Comte de Haga, and he was expected for dinner. Louis XVI galloped at full speed to Versailles and there he dressed hurriedly, helped by a few ushers, for his household was at Rambouillet. When he made his appearance the queen burst into laughter and asked whether he meant to give a ball that evening and had already begun to change into fancy dress, or whether he wanted to show the Comte de Haga an example of French elegance. One of his shoes had a red heel and the other was silver, one side of his head was powdered and the other plain, and so on for all the rest.

He looked upon Vergennes, Calonne and Miromesnil as essential colleagues in the task of bringing about that political and moral renewal of the country which was becoming more urgent every day.

The clergy was sinking in corruption. *Les Lettres secrètes sur la religion*, a wellwritten clandestine pamphlet attributed to the Bishop of Arras, unmasked simoniac priests and free-thinkers. In 1784 the Jansenists no longer concealed their alliance with the *philosophes*, and many of them felt closer to the Protestants than to the 'Ultramontanists', as they called them. They were allied with the parlements, and they openly struggled against the power of the crown and the bishops. freemasonry relied upon them for support. The Parlement had protected freemasonry by refusing to register the bull that Rome had launched against the society. So about 1780–1785, priests flocked into the lodges.

The most deeply compromised of the clerics belonged to the highest classes of society. These classes had no hesitation in sending their younger sons to the seminary in order to obtain a bishopric. So long as these families remained faithful to the Church the bishops behaved well. But from 1760 onwards by far the greater number of people at court were unbelievers and *philosophes*. The noble prelates, ordained without any vocation, lost all sense of shame . . . It was they whom Louis XVI called to order first.

Many nobles therefore thought Louis XVI too 'harsh'. He was trying to halt the spread of scandal. It was known that the Duc de Chartres pushed his financial operations to the point of fraud and his dissolute ways to that of infamy. His suppers with naked girls at his house at Monceau were notorious throughout Europe; the choice of his mistress as governess for his children set him at variance with his wife and aroused a strong and universal disapproval.

Following his example the young nobles heaped folly upon folly, grossness upon misconduct. Above all, they behaved outrageously. Guéménée wanted to return to court at a time when the scandal about his affairs was actually growing worse. The king refused to see him. But he bought Lorient, which belonged to the Guéménées, in order to speed the liquidation. He banished the Marquis de Louvois, a wit who was cheerfully ruining himself, to his country estate. He had the son of the Comte de Choiseul-Meuse, who had killed a cab-driver over a trifle, shut up at

Pierre-Encise.[1] Despite the great fame of his house he sent the Duc de La Trémoille to his province, saying, 'When the Duc de La Trémoille has paid his debts in full, it will be time to think about him again.'

The king was trying to bring these hotheads back to a sense of their dignity and to a respect for their traditions. It was not an easy task with any of them, least of all with Chartres. In March 1783 Chartres wanted to go and live in London, settling there with his wife and children. He came to ask leave of the king. The king acknowledged that he could easily do without him and 'that Mme la Duchesse de Chartres was entirely free to go if the idea of the stay pleased her; and he asked him what his thoughts were with regard to the children. M. le Duc de Chartres having replied that he meant to bring them up in the English manner, the king grew indignant at this most improper suggestion; he said they belonged to the state and that he was opposed to their being taken abroad.'

Nevertheless the king was still kind to Chartres, as he was to everybody else. When Chartres was in need of money to go on with his building at the Palais-Royal, the king advanced him four million on account against the Orléans inheritance, which was to come back to the crown the day there were no more heirs-male. A handsome act. The king was no less gracious with his old enemy Choiseul, whose affairs were growing more and more entangled; he lent him four million, and in the course of these proceedings he had several cordial interviews with him that caused it to be believed that Choiseul was about to return to power. It was nothing of the kind, but merely an example of the king's good heart.

In short, Louis XVI served God at a time when the Devil was in fashion. People doted upon Satan. Monsieur and his gentleman-in-waiting, M. de Modène, used to call him up; the Duc de Chartres had meetings with him in the Montrouge quarries or in the plains to the north of Paris, by means of the spells of the diabolists Chavigny and Beauregard, who also worked for the

---

[1] A castle near Lyons, which was used in the eighteenth century as a prison for members of the privileged classes arrested in the Rhone valley or the Massif Central.

Prince de Ligne and the Duc de Fitz-James. But Chartres' chief contact with hell was the 'Grand Etteilla', who gave him an infernal amulet, promising him the crown. It was a game, no doubt, but even when one is only playing with fire, it still burns.

Among all this philosophical nonsense, Louis XVI retained a lucid mind. He often shrugged his shoulders. People were displeased. But could he be blamed? Even Versailles shared in the general madness from which he was trying to preserve himself. His faithful valet Thierry tried to provide him with a mistress. It was whispered that he had looked with approval at the Comte de Grasse's daughter-in-law. But he filed away at his locks; and he exiled de Grasse to his estate for having spoken too much in London and Paris. He protected the Cardinal de Rohan from the thunders of the Parlement of Paris, which accused him of mismanaging the Quinze-Vingts,[1] and he tried to pacify the Parlement of Brittany, which was ready to set the whole of France in turmoil because the snuff furnished by the government smelt unpleasant!

It was all part of a king's calling.

[1] A hospital for the blind in Paris.

PART THREE

Tyrant or Martyr?

Chapter I

The splendour and the wretchedness of the kingdom of France

JANUARY 1785. EVERYWHERE FRANCE'S VICTORY RALLIED hearts and minds about her and her king. At Berlin the Academy offered a prize for an essay on the Universality of the French Language, and it was won by Rivarol, who demonstrated the superiority of his native tongue.

Louis XVI enjoyed his great popularity, and he wanted to make use of this moment to carry out reforms that had been urgently necessary for the last twenty years. After the services he had just rendered to the country his people would surely have confidence in him and follow him. Yet he was aware of the difficulty of the undertaking, the various kinds of opposition that he would meet with, and the way the upper classes shirked their obligations. It was necessary to act quickly.

There were certain institutions that worked badly – justice and the country's finances among them. They had to be reformed without turning France upside-down and without harming her international authority. Louis XVI would have nothing to do with violence. From his earliest days he had been told about Charles I of England and his terrible example. He meant to reform the administration in full agreement with the best elements in the country, and for the people's good.

The queen felt low-spirited and tender-hearted; she longed for the shade of a sighing grove ... She refused to wear bright-coloured clothes and ordered Mme Bertin to 'banish feathers, flowers, pierrots, shifts, polonaises, Turkish dresses, Circassiennes, etc.' She wanted to look serious, almost solemn.

The king felt the need for this no less than she. Throughout his life he had worked, but now he was living as it were inside his work. It was not very good for him, since he put on weight, and his physicians could find no way of preventing it. His Saxon blood proved stronger than all their measures. He was sorry for it, but it did not worry him, for he had never taken much trouble to please the fair sex and now, although he was said to be having an affair with Mme de Grasse, he gave up the effort altogether. He worked long hours with Vergennes upon all the diplomatic dispatches that had to be sent all over the world on the Dutch question or upon the never-ending Eastern problem, which was once more causing trouble. He hunted less often and he seemed to take less pleasure in it; but he was passionately concerned with all the business that came before the council. It was observed that more than ever he brought forward ideas that had not been adumbrated by the ministers. Carping minds therefore assumed that he once more had a secret source of information, a successor to the late M. de Pezay; more thoughtful men were of the opinion that his personality was growing stronger as his judgment had a greater body of experience upon which to base itself.

The evilly disposed said that that spring brought him another pleasure – the death of the Duc de Choiseul. And La Harpe, who by no means plumed himself upon the possession of a tender heart, celebrated it in these lines:

> Here lies Choiseul. '*Oh what a good thing,*'
> *Quietly murmured the Most Christian King.*

But everyone was obliged to admit that Louis XVI had helped him in his distress. The queen, who had been so fond of Choiseul long ago, soon forgot him.

In the midst of this lovely summer there exploded a most prodigious bomb. At eleven o'clock on 15 August, as Cardinal de
Rohan, about to officiate in his splendid scarlet watered-silk
cassock and his magnificent English point lace rochet, was going
into the king's inner study, at Versailles, the king said to him,
'What is this purchase of a diamond necklace that you are said to
have made in the queen's name?' At this question Rohan turned
deathly pale. 'Sire,' he stammered, 'I have been cheated. But I have
cheated no one.' In a kind tone the king replied, 'If that is the
case, cousin, you must not feel any anxiety. But tell me about it...'
The explanations showed only that Rohan had allowed himself
to be taken in by a woman thief. Louis XVI wanted to stifle the
matter, but the offended queen insisted upon Rohan's being imprisoned and brought to trial.

At once the whole town echoed with talk of the cardinal and the
necklace. But nothing exact was known! At Versailles the queen
displayed a strange, hard, joyful face; Breteuil was scarlet with
delight; and the king hid in his workshop: the courtiers therefore
flooded to see the Rohans, Mme de Marsan and the Prince de
Soubise, and to find out what was afoot. Within a week the whole
court, all the clergy, the greater part of the Parlement and public
opinion were in favour of Rohan. 'Yes,' they said, 'he has behaved like a presumptuous simpleton, but surely that is what he
is? But the queen has acted, as she always does, from motives of
pride and hatred.' This 'Austrian woman' had not hesitated to
throw mud at the finest name in the French nobility and the
noblest prelate in the French clergy!

At the hasty secret council held on 15 August Miromesnil, the
Keeper of the Seals, said to the king, 'It is an unfortunate business.
Let us make the least possible noise over it all.' But he too,
crushed by the queen's stare, was reduced to silence. Vergennes
was much distressed when the king told him about it; he was very
fond of the Rohans and he loathed scandal. He advised the king
to stand aside from the trial and to keep it to the smallest possible
proportions. For his part he set all his sleuths on the trail of La
Motte, who had crossed to England with the necklace to get the
best price he could: Vergennes' agents also tried to silence the

countless pamphleteers in London, who seized upon this excellent opportunity to besmirch France, the king, the queen, the clergy and Catholicism. A thankless task. Even in Paris it was impossible to keep the lampoon-writers and journalists quiet.

The trial at once became a crucial issue. It would be no exaggeration to say that everyone was full of it for the whole of the winter. Through all the flood of scurrilous sheets and public arguments, it did at least clearly appear that the letter signed 'Marie-Antoinette' was a forgery whose author had been found, that the cardinal's interview with the queen in a grove at Versailles – the very essence of the trial – had been a trick elaborated by Mme de La Motte in order to make up Rohan's mind, and that Mlle Leguet had played the part of Marie-Antoinette that evening, perhaps without knowing it. So from this point of view the all-important aspect was safe; but Louis XVI had not been able to prevent the queen from showing herself to be harsh and passionate, without any respect for an archbishop or for one of the oldest names in France.

She was cruelly punished. The Parlement, by a majority of twenty-six to twenty-four, found the cardinal innocent of all charges – a complete acquittal. He shared this honour with Cagliostro, which no doubt moderated his delight. The absent La Motte was condemned to the galleys for life, and Mme de La Motte to be branded with a V (for *voleuse*, thief), to be publicly whipped, and to spend the rest of her days in an asylum. The judgment emphasized the queen's total innocence. Yet because of the cardinal's acquittal it was she who seemed to be condemned, and this was certainly the case with Breteuil, who became one of the most unpopular men in France. All Paris was a in a state of tumult; the delirious crowd, shouting and cheering without a moment's pause, led Rohan back to the Bastille, where he was still to spend another night. 'Long live the Parlement! Long live the innocent cardinal!' was the cry (22 May 1786).

Chapter II

The reforming King

THERE WAS MOUNTING CHAOS ON EVERY HAND, CHAOS IN morals and in family life, chaos in minds and institutions, and an international chaos too, fomented by England and her secret agents, and by Joseph II and his shatter-brained ideas; it was a chaos that seemed to be the spirit of the age, and it had to be resisted. Louis XVI was too clearly aware of it not to wish to react. It was becoming absolutely necessary to restore order in all French affairs; and to begin with he wished to check the strength of the defences facing England, for that was the only side from which danger could come – no European king would dare attack the victor of Yorktown. It was only England that might seek her revenge. The king, who promised himself a visit to Brittany when that province should be calmer and in a better mood, began with Normandy.

He left Rambouillet at five in the morning on 2 June, with the Maréchal de Ségur and the Maréchal de Castries. He had what was no more than a small suite for those days. 'His Majesty will have few people with him and he will travel with only fifty-six horses', said the papers: twenty-five followers altogether, not counting the two mounted equerries and the military escort.

He was simply dressed in a scarlet travelling coat with the rank-marks of a lieutenant-general, interspersed with lilies embroidered in gold. He set off cheerfully, the others in his coach being the Prince de Poix, the captain of his guards, the Duc de Villequier, first gentleman of the bedchamber, and the Duc de Coigny, his first equerry.

He reached Caen the second evening, and there he made his coachman drive at a foot-pace and he dismissed the military escort so that everybody might come near and see him. The mayor and the municipal magistrates made him a speech and presented him with the keys of the city, upon which there could be seen the motto *Apertis cordibus*, with open hearts. He then went on to Cherbourg, the object of his journey. Here the king's delight was perfectly open and unconcealed. He could not be persuaded to remain on land – he had to go aboard a ship. He saw the duty squadron carry out manœuvres before him under the command of Albert de Riom, the picked officer who was in charge of this picked force. The king declared that this, together with the day of his coronation, was the finest of his life. He granted favours right and left. When several workmen were hurt at the moment of setting an upright in the new breakwater, the king plucked a gossiping medical man by the sleeve and sent him to work. He was delighted, and the people no less so; they never tired of shouting 'Long live the king!' and from time to time when the cries were louder than usual, he would turn and call, 'Long live my people!'

He spent the night at Le Havre and saw the beginning of the great works. From Le Havre he went to Rouen. This town welcomed him with the utmost fervour – triumphal arch, vast crowd, endless cheering punctuated by the guns from the *Vieux Palais*, and all the church bells ringing. On the river the ships were all decorated with their flags and pendants. The chapter greeted him with a 'short and elegant speech' that pleased him, and offered him the customary six loaves and twelve bottles of wine: the members of the court of appeal were presented by the Duc d'Harcourt and the Maréchal de Castries. He dined in a room in the archbishop's palace, and the doors were left open so that the people might come in and out and see everything. After dinner he went down the rue Grand-Pont, and when the bridge had been raised he saw a ship sail past him; then late that night he went to Gaillon, where at one minute past twelve the archbishop entertained him to a delightful supper, not a fast-day meal, for now that was over. The next day he returned to Versailles. This was 28 June. The journey had been wonderful. Everywhere he had gone, the king had granted favours and he had had a friendly word for all the important local figures and the officers on duty. People were astonished and delighted by his good nature. He owed a good deal to M. de Calonne and his untiring urbanity. 'With a thought as attentive as it was beneficent he had prepared a map of the route that His Majesty was to follow, based upon the new maps of France, which show, as everybody knows, all the villages, the country houses, the farms and even the thickets. M. de Calonne had had the names of the owners added, with historical notes to give the king an idea of it all . . .'

The courtiers could not understand how the king, who was travelling in Normandy for the first time, behaved as though he had always known all the Normans. He had Calonne's information, and to this he added his own good nature.

His popularity was reflected on to those about him, and particularly on to the Dauphin. In 1785 Louis XVI chose a piece of ground on the terrace at Versailles close to his son's quarters; he had it made into a garden, and every morning he came to dig in it with the little boy, to teach him agriculture, while the public walked by, watching. Everyone was charmed with the sight, and they praised the sovereign for a bringing-up that was so suitable for the future master of a great agricultural kingdom. It was not surprising that a ploughman should have composed these lines:

> *All that comes from our king or our queen*
> *Is good of its kind, if you see what I mean.*
> *Our hearts rejoice and are filled full of joy*
> *If it's a girl or if it's a boy.*
> *Whichever they favour we're equally glad,*
> *It's charming to look like their mum or their dad.*

The aim of this little poem was to comfort the queen, who had had a daughter on 9 July 1786, a very big baby but not well formed, who was called Madame Sophie in memory of the king's aunt. Marie-Antoinette was responsible for her child's misfortune: it had been impossible to persuade her to leave off her corset during her pregnancy. At a time when she was still affected by the disagreeable events of the summer, this was another cause for sorrow: her sister and brother-in-law, the Duchess and the Duke of Saxe-Teschen, governors of the Austrian Netherlands, came to comfort her with a visit that she could have wished longer. The king returned to his work, for he wanted to make an immediate use of the people's confidence – a confidence of which they had just given him such touching proofs.

Of all these worries the most disturbing was the Assembly of the Clergy. These gentlemen had seen fit to set at their head the most ostentatious and the least pious of their whole order, Dillon, the Archbishop of Narbonne. From this moment on the 'administrator-bishops' were in command. Hence there arose quarrels with the government over their feudal possessions; bitter complaints about the small number of teachers and their incompetence; and an obstinate reluctance to increase the country curés' stipends as the king desired.

The fourth subject to be dealt with was the struggle against impiety. Up until that time lay and ecclesiastical writers had been urged to devote themselves to it. 'The administrator-bishops carried the day against the *zelanti*.' There are periods when the clergy lose their sense of vocation. The clergy of the eighteenth century had reached that stage.

Deprived of their help, Louis XVI looked about him for support. He still had Vergennes, that fine mind, manly and judicious in his prudence; but Vergennes was growing old. After Vergennes there was no one but Calonne. The king was very fond of him, but without entire confidence: he had compromising friends – Artois, Besenval, etc. Yet he worked with freedom and intelligence; he retained the urbane ways that few ministers keep up once they are in power, and these seemed to be the result not of any calculation but of his inward being. He was both enterprising and cheerful.

In November, at Fontainebleau, he had a charming idea. Ever since he had been inoculated against smallpox the Dauphin had been poorly; he would not eat or play, and the king and queen were much upset. One day M. de Calonne drew the queen to a window, and plucking aside the curtain he showed her a delightful sight – eight little Siberian ponies of nine hands pulling a charming coach of the same proportions, and behind them a little groom leading a mildly capering riding-pony that matched the others exactly. The coachman, the postillion and the footmen were all of a suitable size, and they wore the Dauphin's colours. Calonne confessed to Her Majesty that he had sent for the ponies from Siberia, that he had had the coach built in Paris, and that he had engaged the children and the young jockeys who had trained the ponies. He begged leave to make this present to M. le Dauphin. The queen thanked him with tears in her eyes, the king was delighted, and the courtiers declared that it was an exceedingly handsome attention. As for the child, he spent hours on end gazing at his dream-like carriage.

The king had no time for dreaming. The country's finances were still in a bad way. The battle with the Parlement in December 1785 had shown Calonne that he could no longer raise great loans. He had been obliged to be satisfied with small-scale expedients, borrowing six million from Brittany, ten from Flanders and twenty-four from the city of Paris.

The treasury's situation was becoming more and more impossible. In spite of his skill, the minister knew that he could not get out of it this way, and since he had the king's confidence, the valuable support of Vergennes and therefore of Miromesnil, he decided to submit a daring plan to the sovereign.

On 20 December 1786 he brought the king a minute upon the work he had accomplished, the resources he had found for the treasury and the orderliness he had managed to introduce into all the state's financial transactions: he added, 'It must be admitted, Sire, that France is only keeping her head above water by a kind of artifice.' With a deficit of a hundred million a year, radical means had to be used, 'and so that they will not distress Your Majesty's feelings it is necessary that they should not increase the burden of taxes; indeed, it must be lessened.'

The king did not want the calling of the States General,

foreseeing that such a gathering would be a mob in which the most unscrupulous would rise to the top; but he did accept an Assembly of Notables as a consultative body. It was a bold policy, but Louis XVI felt in the mood for boldness. The commercial treaty with England, signed on 26 September, had been a bold stroke: it was to open England to French wine and agricultural products, and France to England's manufactures. French manufactures might be depressed by this for a while, but in the long run it would be to their own advantage, for as they would be obliged to reorganize themselves and improve their methods, they would eventually overtake and outstrip the English in the world markets.

At the age of thirty-one Louis XVI made up his mind to undertake the economic and political reform of the country while at the same time he increased his efforts for its moral reformation. The risk was enormous, for the forces that had been kept in check since 1774 seemed to be regrouping in order to make use of the country's financial difficulties to get rid of the elder line of the Bourbons. If the first blow were not struck powerfully and promptly, all would be lost. The royal revolution had to be carried out successfully, and as quickly as possible.

At Fontainebleau he examined the plan once more with Calonne, Vergennes and Miromesnil. Calonne wanted an Assembly of Notables to be summoned without delay. He asked that it should meet at once: this was necessary to avoid bankruptcy, for a great many of the supplies that he reckoned upon arose from taxes in kind, which were slow to collect and to turn into money. 'There is not a day to be lost', he declared.

He also insisted upon 24 January as the date and upon 'the prompt sending out of the letters'. The four chief acts to be ratified by the notables were to be: (1) a plan for a territorial subsidy (a tax on all landed property, even that belonging to the nobles and even that belonging to the clergy); (2) a plan for the setting up of provincial assemblies; (3) the regulation of the corn trade (which was to be freed from all forms of hindrance); and (4) the regulation of forced labour, which was to be abolished. Speed was a most important factor in these plans, and in order to carry them into effect it was necessary to announce the meeting of the assembly and send out the invitations at once. The assembly was to be composed of a hundred and forty-seven members.

The king held a great council on 29 December, lasting for five hours. With the agreement of his three ministers, Calonne, Vergennes and Miromesnil, he accepted the plan. The next day it was announced in the papers.

Then the battle began.

Calonne could count upon several trump cards. The popularity of the king, who was an enthusiastic supporter of the plan (the night after, Louis XVI did not sleep at all: 'I did not close my eyes all night,' he said, 'but it was from happiness.'). Vergennes, who had great standing, a deep knowledge of the court, of the parlements, in which he had relations, and of the journalists, almost all of whom were in his pay; Vergennes at once seconded one of his highest officials to Calonne – this was Hannin, a remarkable mind and a *philosophe* with a very great many contacts. And lastly Miromesnil, who had kept the Parlement in control these last twelve years. He also counted on the younger generation of financiers, Panchaud's friends, who could scent high profits in his scheme, and upon the careful, the wise and the timid, to whom he guaranteed reform without shocks, without wastage and without turmoil. Above all, he counted upon himself.

Opposed to him Calonne had the hotheads; the group that wanted to succeed him; the Parlement, which his plan would reduce to a minor role; those who did not want any reform at all and those who did want reform, but on a revolutionary scale. His opponents tried to make the most of the nation's inborn love for feverish excitement and disturbance. Nevertheless Calonne was to win.

But at first fortune turned against him. Vergennes died (13 February 1787) and Calonne himself fell seriously ill – overwork was having its revenge. Of course his enemies spread the tale that this illness was an excuse to delay the opening of an assembly that had not been properly prepared.

In Vergennes Calonne lost his best supporter, and the guarantee of Miromesnil's loyalty. This delay of a month emboldened the opposition; it allowed them to win over the notables, who had gathered at Versailles and who were eager to see the king, the court, the theatres, the salons, the cafés, the masonic lodges, all the places where the minister of finance was detested. They were urged to be tribunes, leaders, not mere assenters; and their vanity – a very powerful emotion in France – was purposely stimulated.

Calonne defied it all. As soon as he was well enough, on 22 February, he convoked the notables for their opening session in a hastily built addition to the Hôtel des Menus-Plaisirs. It was a magnificent hall, hung with the finest of the royal tapestries with Savonnerie carpets under foot, fleurs-de-lis on the upholstery, the ceilings painted with allegorical scenes and huge stoves at the four corners.

Louis XVI, bearing all the emblems of royalty, was present at this inaugural session, and he spoke first.

> Gentlemen [he said], I have chosen you from the different orders of the realm and I have gathered you about me to inform you of my plans. This has been the custom of many of my predecessors . . . The plans that will be communicated to you upon my behalf are of great scope and importance . . . As they all tend to the public good and as I am aware of the zeal for my service with which you are filled I have no fear in consulting you about their execution . . .

Then the Keeper of the Seals delivered a pompous speech, full of tedious flattery of the king. After this it was Calonne's turn. At the outset he was wise enough and truthful enough to present his plans as the king's wish. He recalled the dismal state of the finances in 1783 and he gave a brilliant, flattering, short account of his stewardship, both from the financial point of view and from that of the country's economic life. Then he came to the heart of the matter – the deficit. He did not minimize it: no, indeed, he emphasized it.

Once he had dealt this blow Calonne changed his tone and stated that it was the king's desire to do everything possible to remedy this state of affairs. He wished to stop borrowing and anticipating; he even wished to stop increasing the taxes; he would continue to economize, as had been his invariable practice; but all this was still insufficient 'and could only be looked upon as a subsidiary means'. The true remedy was to be sought in the elimination of abuses. France swarmed with abuses – financial privileges, exceptions from the general law, unjust exemptions, disproportion between the contributions paid by different subjects and different provinces, and interior customs that hindered trade. The minister asserted that after so many vain diatribes only a 'general operation' could succeed in putting an end to all this.

He proposed not a system, which was always dangerous, nor yet innovations, which always smacked of charlatanry, but an epitome, a synopsis of the plans for the public welfare that had been conceived these many years past by the most able of statesmen, whose execution had never yet been attempted. 'It was reserved,' he added, 'for a virtuous young sovereign with no passion but that of his people's happiness to undertake, after ripe consideration, what none of his predecessors had been able to do, and to carry it out with unshakeable determination.'

It was a magnificent speech: Calonne had a musical voice, a fine presence and noble gestures. The basis of what he said could not be denied; and the king's authority, committed to this plan, made it deeply impressive. Impartial and thoughtful men were of Besenval's opinion – 'That resourceful man, M. de Calonne, has in my view conceived the finest plan that any minister has yet brought forth.' Unhappily, the notables, being an assembly, were neither impartial nor thoughtful: they might have been aware of their own interests, and that would have saved everything; or they might have been frightened, and that would have saved everything; but neither the one nor the other was the case. And on 22 February the surprise that Calonne had relied upon no longer existed, whereas vanity, together with the desire to shine, was working full force upon each individual member and upon the Assembly as a whole. Now the Assembly could only shine at the expense of Calonne. Furthermore every member knew that he was being watched by 'public opinion' and by a secret group. A sheet was being handed about, a sheet that provided a critical and threatening description of each one of them.

One after the other, each of Calonne's schemes was rejected, except for those that had to do with the corn trade and statute labour. The Archbishop of Narbonne, who had been elected president of the Assembly, led the attack: in the name of the clergy he violently rejected every concession. Confronted with such a degree of shamelessness, at the third session Calonne tried flattery. An untoward incident upset all his calculations. Certain speculators whom he had entrusted with the task of supporting the chief government stocks during the sitting of the Assembly abused their position. This became known. Mirabeau, fee'd by Calonne, launched a furious satire against jobbery and against Necker, whom he accused in veiled allusions. The allusions were too veiled altogether: the accusation was thought to be directed at Calonne.

In spite of this scandal Calonne attended the fourth session. There he explained the sacrifices that the king had agreed to make from his own estates. He was applauded. He then ended with a 'warning' that had been drawn up for him by the barrister Gerbier, and which was meant for the whole nation. After summing up the king's plans and refuting criticism of them he said, 'Some privileges will be sacrificed, yes, indeed: justice requires it and necessity insists upon it. Or would it be a better plan to overburden the unprivileged with an even greater load?' The blow went home. The furious notables burst out in protests and insults, and finally into scurrilous lampoons.

Calonne was aware that this had to be brought to an end. The Assembly was turning into a pandemonium and his position was becoming intolerable. Apart from Artois, Besenval and the Polignacs, they were all joining against him. The clergy were doing so with open violence, the Parlement secretly. Then there were Necker, Loménie, Orléans, Monsieur (the leader of the whole plot), his colleagues in the ministry, and lastly the queen, egged on by Vermond and now his inveterate enemy.

Miromesnil proved the most faithless of them all. Taking advantage of the Holy Week vacation, Calonne went to see Louis XVI. He unmasked the stammering Keeper of the Seals in the king's presence and then called for an example to be made. As soon as Miromesnil had left the room, the king promised Calonne to send Breteuil to Miromesnil for the seals at once, to give them to Lamoignon, whose name Calonne had put forward.

'A success at last!' he said to himself.

In fact it was his downfall. When Breteuil and his colleagues saw that the king was sacrificing Miromesnil to Calonne they took fright. They were all implicated up to the neck in the plot against the finance minister. With the backing of the queen and Monsieur they told the king that so long as Calonne remained in power the programme of reforms would never be accepted. The queen had been badgering the king without a pause for the last two months with criticisms of Calonne, and now she let fly with all the violence of which she was capable: for the first time Louis XVI replied in the same tone and then turned his back upon her. Monsieur was more skilful. He told his brother that once Calonne had gone he would be able to have the programme of 22 February accepted. The king sat down at his desk and signed the *lettre de cachet* requiring Calonne to resign: but he expressed his friendship and his loyalty to the programme they had worked out together by asking him to find someone who would carry on his work, continuing it on Calonne's lines. Louis XVI threw over Calonne solely in order to save his programme, being convinced that otherwise the monarchy would fall (8–10 April 1787).

When this news spread in Paris there was a violent outburst of joy: idle fellows and lawyers' clerks in search of noise filled the streets with shouts and songs against the minister, and they burnt him in effigy at the crossroads. The salons were hardly any quieter; they were full of ecstatic praise for these events and for their hero, La Fayette.

The king alone understood what was happening, and he was filled with dread.

Chapter III

The King betrayed by the nobles

THE KING HAD STATED THAT HE DID NOT WANT 'ANY
dirty little Neckers or any dirty little priests', so the queen had not
dared press for Loménie. The ministers, Castries, Montmorin and
Ségur spoke for Necker, but in vain; while Breteuil, violent as
usual, savagely opposed him. So the search went on.

Vermond thought this a favourable time to bring Loménie in.
Mme de Staël was intriguing for her father (who was then in exile,
the king having banished him to put an end to his quarrels with
Calonne). Vermond forestalled her. On his instructions the queen
went to the king and wept. Montmorin and Lamoignon came to
see him and bemoaned the country's poverty. The unhappy king,
supposing that they were asking for Necker, exclaimed 'Well,
let him be sent for, then!' They relieved his mind by suggesting
Brienne. 'He is said to have a restless, ambitious character,' he
said. 'But the latest reports he has sent me are more sober-minded.'
He gave way.

It was announced on 3 May that Loménie de Brienne was to be
at the head of the council of finances and a member of the great
council. Brienne was a bad priest, a frivolous administrator and

an odiously worldly man, as well as a rake devoid of charm. His face bore witness to his debauches, and the skin-affection that covered his person was so unclean that in the end the king would no longer touch papers that had been handled by His Excellency. Public opinion was wholly favourable to him.

For their parts the notables did exactly what they chose and nothing else: letters from the king were handed about all over Paris, confidential papers communicated by the ministers, highly secret documents ... In their opinion Loménie was no better than Calonne, since he was a minister.

He appeared before them, taking no pleasure in it and bringing no programme of his own. He defended Calonne's plan, neither understanding it nor succeeding in his defence. Loménie felt the ground giving way under him, and with Lamoignon's support he obtained the king's permission to dissolve the Assembly.

The king took this as a defeat. He was aware of the underhand, destructive role played by Monsieur, and he did not conceal his knowledge of it. When a courtier was telling him about the Duc de Biron and his pleasure in displaying himself at the review, Louis XVI replied, 'He has always loved parades, just as my brother loves offices.' 'Not me, upon my word,' said Artois, 'they bore me to death.'

The wits said, 'The king may have won the American war, but Monsieur has won that of the notables.' And the people who knew what was going on were of the opinion that he had taken a very skilful revenge for his brother's and Calonne's refusal to admit him to the council.

The Assembly of Notables came to a final end on 25 May 1787.

One day during the summer of that year the king saw a placard posted up on a wall:

> *So long as he was but a fool,*
> *'Forgive the fool' we said,*
> *But now he wants despotic rule*
> *Let's knock him on the head.*

The papers, the handwritten sheets and the lampoons were changing their tone, too. The best known of these publications,

Bachaumont's *Mémoires secrets*, turned into a revolutionary journal. It ceased to be an elegant, stylish miscellany, *philosophe* but respectful to the king, and it attacked the government.

The king hid his indignation behind an unmoved expression. He worked, drew maps, hammered his locks and saw to the teaching of his children. On 1 May 1787 the Dauphin was handed over to the care of men with the customary ceremonies; he had a complete household, without a prelate. The king also had to sit for the portrait that the city of Caen had asked for. The patriotic newspapers cried out against this 'useless expense'.

Meanwhile the king carried on with his calling. He trained Vergennes' successor, Montmorin, a skilful negotiator who had formerly been his companion and then ambassador to Spain, where he had proved his ability; he was a well-bred man, but he was too easily influenced and too diffident. The king also watched over Loménie, whose career promised to be a difficult one.

Loménie de Brienne took Calonne's decrees to the Parlement for registration, and he obtained the acceptance of the complete freedom of the corn-trade without difficulty, as well as the replacement of statute labour by a tax, and the establishment of provincial assemblies. But the Parlement refused the decree increasing stamp-duty (22 July 1787) and insisted upon being shown statements of the financial position (6–8 July). In a passionate speech Duval d'Espréménil, who knew nothing about international affairs, declared that all these fears were groundless and he condemned the decrees as 'contrary to the rights of the nation'. The Parlement agreed with him by eighty votes to forty: Brienne then had to act. On 14 August 1787, the day before the Feast of the Assumption, each member of the Parlement received a *lettre de cachet* banishing him to Troyes.

There were cheers for Provence, the hero of the Assembly of Notables. The *Cour des Aides*[1] called for the States General instead of registering edicts. In Paris rioters were in command of the streets. Biron brought in troops and organized patrols in the city, and with his help Breteuil restored order in six days. This tragedy was cut short. The parliamentarians found life at Troyes boring.

[1] A supreme court dealing with taxation, particularly customs.

With 'a lady' as a go-between Brienne settled everything. The Parlement could come back to Paris, and on 9 September it registered a decree extending one of the disallowed twentieths for five years and the other for an unlimited period. Instead of the measure in favour of the people that the king had proposed, the Parlement maintained a tax that fell solely upon the third estate.

Thus the struggle came to an end, leaving the king's administration in complete disorder. The worst had been feared – a new Fronde, led by Monsieur. One day when he refused to go to the *Chambre des Comptes* Louis XVI said to him, 'Do you by any chance want to renew the unhappy days of Charles VI, or of the League or the Barricades?' And the king's hand made so fierce a gesture that Monsieur obeyed directly. His plot came to nothing. Brienne's had more success. At the most critical moment the queen caused the king to agree that he should be 'chief minister', and that the journey to Fontainebleau and certain posts in the king's and queen's households should be given up. For the sake of a trifling economy the king thus made a void about himself, without thereby pacifying public opinion. The resignation of Ségur and Castries, who could no longer bear Loménie, saddened him very much indeed. At this period everything saddened him, and his only comfort was hunting until he almost dropped with fatigue. But even that gave grounds for slander: he was seen to stagger with weariness, and it was said that he was intoxicated, fuddled with drink. The queen, urged on by Mercy, was angry with him for not entrusting Brienne with foreign affairs, the only department the king refused him. Louis XVI was much distressed by the international situation. Turning the rebelliousness of the notables and the general disorder to good account, Great Britain and the new King of Prussia came to an agreement to supplant France as the most influential power in Holland.

In home affairs Brienne was quite at a loss – he could not tell how to get out of his difficulties. His ministry, whose numbers had been made up by his brother (at the war ministry), Malesherbes and Nivernois (ministers of state), could not tell either. Lamoignon and Breteuil and the others longed for conciliation. The king

was silent, for he did not trust Brienne enough to speak. The
return of the Parlement brought about a clarification. During the
riots the effigies of Calonne, Breteuil and Mme de Polignac had
been publicly burnt; the queen's, though it was insulted for a long
while, was just spared. The more prudent, judicious men in the
Parlement and in freemasonry grew alarmed. The Duc de
Luxembourg and Huguet de Sémonville and after them Duval
d'Esprémenil secretly went to see Brienne and Lamoignon.
Brienne was frightened, and he refused. Lamoignon came to an
understanding with Duval. The Parlement would agree to loans
of five hundred million, spread out; the king would promise to
call the States General.

A majority seemed certain in the event of a vote, but the royal
session did not reach that stage. Murmurs arose, and in the
hubbub Orléans stood up to declare the registration illegal: he required a record of the fact that it was done at the king's direct
command. The king replied, 'Certainly it is legal, since it is my
wish.' As soon as the king had left the 'patriots of the Chambre des
Enquêtes' (a section of the Parlement) proposed that the Duc
d'Orléans' protest should be recorded on the register, and their
resolution was passed; and Sabatier had the form of the session
and the registering declared illegal. Orléans left the Palais de
Justice carried shoulder-high by the crowd. He took Monsieur's
place, and from now on he was the leader of the 'patriots'.

The next day the king banished him to his château at Villers-
Cotterêts, so that he might there reflect upon the dangers of
popularity and spend some of his time hunting. The most violent
of the parliamentarians were imprisoned in the Château de
Doullens and Sabatier at Mont-Saint-Michel. The year 1787 came
to an end in the midst of uproar and bitter disagreement. For
four months the Parlement uttered protests and appeals to the
king for the liberation of the two prisoners. Louis XVI would not
give way nor allow the reopening of the clubs, which had been
closed at his orders in August 1787. The only point of agreement
was the decree of toleration (February 1788), which granted the
'non-Catholics' (Protestants, Jews, etc.) a civil being and a status
almost the same as that of the Catholics. The only thing that

remained closed to them was access to power. This was a step that the public approved.

Their approval was no consolation to Louis XVI for the chaos in which the state was foundering: nothing was being done any more; the Parlement and the monarchy were dealing one another blows that nothing could ever heal; disorder was spreading over the entire realm. The king suffered so much from all this that he came out in a violent bout of St Anthony's fire, with a high temperature; he had to go to bed, and this was some kind of a rest. He was brought from it by the sudden death of Madame Louise in her convent at Saint-Denis. Soubise died on 19 June 1787; Richelieu was on his death-bed; Mme de Marsan was no longer to be seen. Rohan had been forgotten, and even Beaumarchais himself could no longer attract the public eye. The past seemed no more than a dream.

Neither Christmas nor New Year's Day brought about any settlement. On 4 May the Parlement took it into its head to insist that the levying of the twentieths should only be carried out according to the existing registers, without any alterations. The notion came from Goislard de Montsabert, a member of the Chambre des Enquêtes, which was the centre for the hotheads, the leaders of the agitation; the Parlement passed a resolution asssert-ing that the king could not levy taxes without the courts' in-spection and that he could not create new ones with the authoriza-tion of the States General. This was tantamount to a proclamation of the nation's sovereignty.

In reply the ministry ordered the arrest of the two most violent parliamentarians, Duval d'Espréménil and Goislard de Mont-sabert.

Brienne looked upon these measures as the beginning of a great political movement designed to bring the third estate to power and to reconcile him with the *philosophes*. For his part Lamoignon was in favour of the restoration of a strong monarchy. Breteuil, his patience at an end, had gone. La Luzerne was settling down at the Admiralty, not without difficulty, and Montmorin was endeavouring to extricate himself from the embarrassments caused by Catherine's victories and her advances towards France.

The queen's only idea was to help Brienne, who was still protected by Vermond. And the silent king watched over the most important interests of the country as well as he could.

Brienne was at bay. He wanted to carry out his plan of seeking the support of the third estate, and on 5 July 1788 he published a decree of the council anticipating the States General and asking all Frenchmen with any knowledge of the matter to send him information and advice on the manner of holding them, or to publish it for his enlightenment. There was to be no more censorship! The result was a flood, but a flood chiefly of insults directed against the ministry and the royal family. At last, on 8 August he announced the meeting of the States General for 1 May 1789. But he did not have the money to last that long. In their summer assembly the clergy, his last hope, refused him the eighteen million he needed to hold out. So on 16 August Brienne suspended state payments for six weeks, saying that he would resume them partly in cash and partly in notes.

This was bankruptcy. The king appeared to have made up his mind to dismiss Brienne: Mme de Polignac made his task easier by coming to tell the queen that her favourite must disappear immediately if she did not want him to be hanged in the next few days, and herself and Mme de Polignac with him. The queen was furious, but she was terrified too, and she gave way. To console him she gave him her portrait surrounded with diamonds and appointed his niece, Mme de Canisy, lady in waiting to Madame Royale; in any case, Brienne had taken care to compensate himself by exchanging his archbishopric of Toulouse for that of Sens and by some fat abbeys. The king, always open-handed and in this case anxious to make it clear that the present confusion was the fault of the opposition and not of the minister, even granted him a few small guns for the decoration of his château at Brienne – a symbolic present from a Most Christian King to an archbishop who was not a Christian at all.

The crowd wanted to hang him, disembowel him, set fire to his carriage and throw it in the river. They did burn his image, together with the queen's. A kind of rage against her was mounting up from every hand, even from the court.

This violent indignation began to take the name of hatred; for the time of hatred had come.

M. de Malesherbes, who liked to understand events that he had neither the wish nor the power to influence, conversed with King Louis XVI about this stench of hatred that rose on all sides. He was becoming more and more attached to the king, and he was worried about the future for him.

'I know no position more disagreeable than that of a king in your present situation,' I said. 'You say that you have committed certain errors. That is true. But you have one consolation, and that is that you always acted under the persuasion that you were doing right, and that you only followed advice that you were to suppose sound and well-informed. For example, the greatest of them all, and the one that will be the cause of sad difficulties, was that of having convoked the Assembly of Notables ... You read a great deal, Sire, and you are more learned than people imagine. But reading is nothing unless it is accompanied by reflexion. Recently I looked over the piece on Charles I in David Hume's *History of England*. Read it again, reflecting upon it. Your two situations are alike. That prince was gentle, virtuous, devoted to the laws, far from harsh, far from venturesome; he was just and benevolent; yet he died on the scaffold. And this, I believe, was the reason. He came at the moment when the conflict arose between the prerogatives of the crown and those of the nation. If he had yielded his prerogatives he would have seemed ignoble to those who, from lifelong habit and because of the benefits the nobles derived from them, looked upon them as sacred. But on the other hand he was the weaker in the course of that dispute, during which fresh concessions were extorted from him at every turn. If he had been born fifty years earlier, his virtues would have made him a model king; and if he had come fifty years later, when the rights on either side had been settled beyond dispute, he would not have overstepped them and his reign would have been long and happy. Your position is the same. The conflict lies between the earlier customs of authority, and the present demands of the citizens! Fortunately, religious

L

disagreement is not involved.' 'Oh yes, there we are indeed fortunate,' said the king, taking my arm. 'The ferocity will not be the same, therefore.' 'Besides, the gentler ways of our time guarantee you against the excesses of those days. But gradually many of your prerogatives will be taken from you. It is for you in your council to fix upon a thoroughly considered plan as to the concessions that you should make for the general good and as to what points you must never give up. Your firmness alone may be decisive in the success of such a plan. Without firmness on your part nothing certain can be foreseen at all. I will answer for it that things will not reach the stage they did with Charles I; but I will not answer for the absence of any other forms of excess. You must turn your mind to warding them off.'

Thus preached M. de Malesherbes, one of the clearest minds of the eighteenth century and one of those most responsible for the terrible storm that was gathering. The king attended: he was determined not to shed the blood of Frenchmen nor to imitate Charles I; and faced with the terrible march of events he counted upon his wisdom, his prudence and his patience. Above all he counted upon the mercy of God.

Chapter IV

The King betrayed by Orléans

A GUST OF HATRED WAS BLOWING ACROSS FRANCE, AND IT
wafted lampoons in Louis XVI's face. The only advice that the
king received now was that of hatred, and the only thing for
which he was praised was a remark he was supposed to have
addressed to Brienne – 'Well, you shaveling priest, so they refuse
to register! See how you can get out of that!' It was still possible
for him to deflect the hatred from himself by directing it against
the clergy.

In all this Louis XVI recognized the same tone and the same
expressions that he had heard between 1771 and 1774, when the
parlements and the *philosophes* in league had made war upon
Maupeou, Louis XV and the monarchy. But in 1788 a new eagerness and a new delight could be felt. It might have been the joy of
barbarians gazing at a vast, rich city at their mercy which they
were about to sack – all the treasures of the clergy, of their
monasteries and their churches, whose coming confiscation 'for
the nation' was announced! – the monarchy and its palaces, which
were cried down as 'abuses' and which were coveted as booty!
The great shudder of emotion that ran from the as yet unknown

Desmoulins to the barely known Mirabeau and from La Fayette with his untidy wig to Orléans, lurking in his Palais-Royal, was an eager, itching lust for the goods of this world. And all the pleaders for the third estate, all their pamphleteers, as well as all the hotheads of the three orders, shared in this intoxication. But there was more to it than this: Chamfort said to Marmontel, 'To overawe the weak we have that resolute class that sees nothing to lose in a change and that believes it has everything to gain. The strongest of incitements are at hand to set them in motion – poverty, hunger, money, cries of warning and terror, and the mind-shattering frenzy of dread and fury . . . Money and the hope of loot are all powerful with these people . . . We shall have immense forces, and we can obtain an immense following.'

'Everything foretold the storms that were about to break over the monarchy,' said the Duc de Montmorency-Luxembourg, the founder and secretary general of the Grand-Orient de France, the centre of French freemasonry. 'I knew perfectly well what hand was behind the people . . .'

In France Orléans, the grand master of the Grand-Orient and of other lodges, was in control of this society. He assigned one of his secretaries to it, first Leray de Chaumont, Franklin's friend, and then others. Without compromising himself he made use of this powerful organization against the 'simpleton king' Louis XVI, whose place he wished to take.

Louis XVI was perfectly well aware of the danger. When the triumphant Genevan made his appearance at Versailles on 26 August 1788 he looked him full in the face and said, 'Ah, Monsieur, it is many years now since I had a moment's happiness.' Necker, with the broad smile of satisfied appetite, replied, 'In a little while, Sire, you will no longer talk like this.' Necker was incapable of doubting that once he was in power everything would go well, and above all go as he wanted it to go.

Louis XVI did not like Necker, a Protestant, republican and a money-grubber. He had found him to be a good underling and a bad leader. Yet now he was obliged to accept him as his chief minister, in order to pacify threatening public opinion. Since the pick of the country and the privileged classes would not set the house in order, he had to rely upon the support of the people to carry through the essential reforms. Maybe this democratic banker would manage to speak to the people, manipulate them and make use of them. In a few weeks he refilled the empty treasury.

What Louis XVI could count on was his own firmness of mind and his courage; and there was his great popularity among the people. The twenty-two million Frenchmen who lived in the country and the little towns loved him as he loved them. But he could not rely upon his wife, nor upon Monsieur, who was more eager to replace than to help him, nor upon Artois, who was too scatter-brained. Orléans had been his enemy since their childhood, and now he was his direct rival. The clergy, whose support had allowed Hugues Capet and his descendants to become and to remain a national dynasty, was betraying him, joining forces with the *philosophes*. With an income of a hundred and forty million they paid only four million a year by way of twentieths instead of the twelve or thirteen they ought to have produced for the royal treasury: in their assembly, the clergy had refused to lend the king's government the sum that would have allowed the sovereign to settle the date of the States General without constraint or danger. The clergy allied themselves to the 'patriots' (the name assumed by the opposition); and as a body they did not appear, since Christophe de Beaumont's death, to think about anything other than their immediate material interests. The great families copied their example. An enormous pack of private interests had been unleashed.

The country was filled from one end to the other with argument, and the flood of pamphlets mounted high. Almost all of them cried up the third estate. The ladies too lavished their intelligence and their money upon this cause (particularly Mme de Staël, the most vehement of them all). Out of hatred for the privileged classes, the queen joined in the cry for double representation of the commonalty. Mme de Polignac and Artois and their friends were almost the only people who insisted upon the peril of delivering everything up to the mercy of the third estate.

The king saw this danger, but he saw both sides of the question: doubling the third estate meant running the risk of giving lawyers control of the States General; not doubling it meant providing a shield for the privileged classes, who for the past two years had proved themselves to be incurably blind and selfish.

In spite of his daughter's harangues, Necker himself was uneasy. In the cold of that terrible winter, when more snow fell than France had ever known in the memory of man, he summoned the notables to ask their views. Necker had to humble himself and visit Monsieur. Monsieur was a great help, because he understood everything and flinched at nothing, no scheme that might be useful to him and harmful to his brother. With great difficulty he obtained a majority of three in his committee for the doubling of the third estate. He thought that this would mean the fall of Louis XVI, and that the country would at last turn to an intelligent prince. Necker, to his daughter's delight, announced that on the advice 'of an important minority of the notables' the Estates General were to be summoned, with double representation for the third estate.

They relied upon the third estate. It was not to be vexed by being required to meet far from Paris or Versailles, in some place a hundred miles and more from the capital. Would it not be wiser to receive it in the impressive setting of Versailles?

On 8 August there appeared the decree of the council summoning the States General for 1 May 1789.

As soon as they heard the news the people grew turbulent. In Brittany the third estate at once claimed double representation in the States of that province, which were then sitting. The nobles resisted. Blows were exchanged.

Henceforward this was the prevailing spirit all over France. The notables and the men of the parlements had been in a state of turmoil these last eighteen months, and now people were beginning to grow seriously worried. When the curés read M. Necker's imposing lucubrations from the pulpit and announced that representatives were going to be elected there was a great uproar: every kind of vanity sprang to life. In the gilded salons of Paris the sharp-tongued ladies discussed the matter: the Marquise de Coigny was the most furious in her hatred for Marie-Antoinette, the Comtesse de Simiane the most zealous for freedom, and the Comtesse de Beauharnais the most passionate. People talked violent nonsense in the clubs, the cafés, the shops and even in the open street. The continually rising price of bread added its stimulant: in Paris the four-pound loaf rose from eleven to fourteen sous in January 1789,[1] and presently the whole of Provence was in a state of insurrection, so much did the population dread a famine. Everywhere suffering and excitement produced violence.

In the provinces the intendants were out of their minds; in Paris the authorities were overwhelmed.

Orléans spent millions with a lavish hand. He gathered troops and the leaders of the people about him. They all prated of violence, as though the monarchical state were an armed camp! In fact this state had little physical force at its disposal, and it had ruled the country for the last eight hundred years by its moral ascendancy alone.

Philippe d'Orléans was playing a cautious game. When he recalled him from banishment, Louis XVI told Orléans certain unpalatable truths and threatened him with a fresh exile if his adherents did not keep quieter. He therefore discarded Du Crest in favour of the more discreet La Touche and he allied himself with a young parliamentarian, a friend of La Touche's, named Adrien Duport, a quiet, well-bred man, circumspect at the lawcourts and very reserved in private life, who for more than a year and a half had had a 'meeting' at his house in the Marais – a very limited, very discreet, but very effective band. With active members selected from various lodges he gathered together a combat-team numbering at first twelve and then thirty.[2] The Thirty did their utmost to set up an immense network of collusion all over the country, in order to be able to attack the government everywhere at the same time and to send their messages to every corner

---

[1] The livre (20 sous) was 10½d at this time, and a labourer's average daily wage was 19 sous.

[2] For a further account of the political aspect see B. Faÿ, *La Grande Révolution 1715–1815* (Le Livre Contemporain).

of every province. Together with the king's administration and the Catholic hierarchy, the masonic lodges formed the only nation-wide organization at that time. Orléans made what use of it he chose, and every pamphlet that he brought out therefore had a circulation and an influence that no one else could command.

Countless bales of pamphlets left the Palais-Royal and Duport's house. Every meeting of the Thirty Club rejoiced at seeing the temperature rise in France, and above all in Paris. But that was not enough.

The populace only gets really worked up at the sight of blood. Laclos knew this and Orléans understood it. In these circumstances nothing was easier. It was a simple matter to buy it in 1789 – the agitators maintained not so long before by the Parlement were ready to hand. Because of unemployment and the provinces' shortage of supplies Paris was filling with hungry workmen, eager for trouble. On 27 April the crowd set fire to M. Révillon's factory. This manufacturer had the reputation of being a worthy man, a philanthropist who paid his workers well, and a philosopher who had helped the Mongolfiers in their aeronautical experiments. But he had committed the crime of getting himself elected to the States General instead of the candidate protected by Orléans. Furthermore, Orléans paid him the honour of passing in front of his house on the way back from the Vincennes races, to see whether all was going well. All was going very well indeed; the soldiers, summoned in haste but commanded by Besenval, whose prudence was equal to his foresight, avoided action. The second day, when everything had been burnt and the demonstrators had earned the twelve livres a head they were paid for this feat, peace and calm returned. This confirmed Mirabeau's view, 'For a hundred louis you can have a very elegant riot'.

On 3 May the gorgeously dressed heralds proclaimed through-out Versailles that the next day, Sunday, there would be the pro-cession of the States General. It was a very fine spectacle, with diamonds and gold lace blazing under the radiant sun. Orléans, who thought of everything, had not forgotten to hire some women to shout 'Long live the Duc d'Orléans!' as the queen went by. Marie-Antoinette was so shocked that she almost fainted, but then she straightened herself, ashamed of such weakness.

The next day the opening session of the States General took place in the great hall that had been prepared for them. The king, the great dignitaries and then each of the orders took their places with high ceremony: Orléans, instead of putting himself with the princes of the blood, ranged himself among the nobles; and as he came in he thrust a curé from his estate of Villers-Cotterêts through the door before him – the crowd cheered. The king observed it. Then he rose: he had prepared his speech long since, down to the slightest variations of tone. He said, 'Gentlemen, the day that my heart has looked forward to for a great while has come at last, and I see myself surrounded by the representatives of the nation that I glory in ruling . . .' This short, judicious and prudent speech was very well received; it was greeted with applause and tears. Unhappily the Keeper of the Seals' address seemed dull, and Necker's, the chief event of the session, long-drawn-out, involved and pettifogging. For three hours on end he wandered about among details. In any case, the ringleaders had plans other than mere obedience.

Orléans and the Thirty wanted power by means of a democratic constitution in which the third estate should be dominant and in which they should govern. The money was to be found by nationalizing the property of the clergy. Necker's silliness and his daughter's vanity were making the operation easy. The chief obstacle was Louis XVI. Then something happened that quite overwhelmed him: on 4 June, after a cruel struggle, the Dauphin died. The king was shattered, and he wanted to shut himself up in his own quarters for a few days to grieve alone. A delegation from the States General asked to see him and insisted upon it in spite of his refusals; they had prepared their speeches and they were going to deliver them. 'Are there no fathers in this assembly?' cried Louis XVI, and then, with dry eyes, he received them. But for some days he found it very hard to keep himself under control.

During this time the three orders had been fighting a strange battle, which the third was to win. Louis XVI's prudence shows that he had foreseen this. The choice of Necker, which had been dictated by circumstances, in itself implied the predominance of the third estate. The great families were wooing the commonalty and abandoning their own order. The Rohans, who alone might have been relied upon, were still disqualified by the Guéménée bankruptcy and the affair of the necklace, which had been followed by Soubise's death. In this state of destitution the nobles assembled at Versailles replaced their old president, M. de Montboissier, by the Duc de Montmorency-Luxembourg, who was willing to take office. Did they hope to win over the freemasons? Too late: Orléans was abandoning them and the Thirty were pitilessly opposed to them.

Yet Montmorency accepted the invitation: did he do so out of jealousy of Orléans, anxiety about the future, or did he remember, rather late, that he was 'the first Christian baron of France'? It was in this capacity that he went to see Louis XVI. In spite of the long-standing antagonism of the Montmorencys and the Bourbons, the king welcomed him, and they had a series of tragic conversations. When Montmorency was fulminating against the meeting of the orders and the third estate, Louis XVI took him by the arm and said, 'You wanted these States General, you asked for them. And now you have them!' 'No, Sire,' he replied vehemently, 'the States have no existence . . . The States General would have been united to the king and to France by a rightful balance of their powers. They would only have presented you with grievances, which you would have considered wisely and discussed; but you have favoured an assembly whose weight and extent you have not measured . . .' Faced with this flood of words, coming so strangely from an active member of the Thirty Club, Louis XVI declared, 'I shall never abandon my nobles nor my authority; you may rely upon that.'

Chapter V

The revolutionary onslaught

THE THIRD ESTATE, LED BY THE THIRTY, RESISTED LOUIS XVI's orders and set itself up as a National Assembly (23 June 1789).

The king, still overwhelmed by the recent death of the Dauphin, collected himself and realized the danger for the crown and for the country. He did not wish to shed French blood, but to maintain order and to overawe the rebels. He hoped, by gathering great forces around him, to be able to dissolve the Assembly without violence, and on 26 June he gave secret orders for the stationing of twenty thousand men, chiefly foreign troops, in the immediate neighbourhood of Versailles. On 11 July he quietly dismissed Necker and had him unobstrusively taken to the frontier.

None of these measures escaped the notice of his enemies' spies. They were determined to counter force with force; and they were not afraid of bloodshed. A manipulation of the stock-market coincided with the manipulation of the masses; like true patriots the financiers of the capital never stopped lowering prices all through June. For their part, the troops were making ready; the

Palais-Royal was a hive of activity and an overflowing source of vituperation against the ministers. 'Electors' were gathering at the Hôtel de Ville for the preparation of a citizen's militia.

Other patriots set about winning over the soldiers, beginning with the Gardes-Françaises, who were angry at the severe discipline imposed by their new colonel, the Duc du Châtelet. On 30 June a crowd of hangers-on of the Palais-Royal liberated ten Gardes-Françaises who had been shut up in the Abbaye for lack of discipline. The cavalry were sent for to restore order: they refused to charge. At Versailles every barracks was reported to be wavering. The arrival of the regiments on the heights round Paris increased the effervescence. At the Palais-Royal and at Mme de Genlis' house there was open talk of dethroning Louis XVI and replacing him by Orléans. On 8 July the Assembly called for the removal of the troops: the king replied that they were there to ensure its safety, but that he would not refuse to transfer the Assembly to Noyon or Soissons. On 12 July, when it was learnt that Necker had been dismissed, the stockbrokers closed the exchange.

Early in the morning La Fayette and Bailly went to the Palais-Royal, and there they took their last measures.

On 11 July La Vauguyon replaced Montmorin and Broglie Puységur; La Luzerne and Saint-Priest left the government; Breteuil took over finance, and he was to become president of the council, for it was he who mounted the operation. But everything was lost because of the sluggishness of Besenval, the man who was supposed to be in command of the troops in Paris. On the fourteenth the 'patriots' murdered Flesselles, the Provost, and set up a 'permanent committee' at the Hôtel de Ville which asked the governor of the Bastille for his weapons. He refused and opened fire; then he negotiated, and finally he surrendered. Thereupon the crowd tore him to pieces; they killed most of the officers and the old soldiers who did not get away quickly enough, and they paraded others round the streets all day long with their hands tied – the trophies of a bawling procession that marched behind the blood-dripping head of Launay. It was hot: the Palais-Royal was filled with the atmosphere of triumph.

The news reached Versailles, exaggerated by the terror of some reporters and the cunning of others. Neither Breteuil nor Broglie dared attempt the trial of force. The Paris militia was worthless, but street fighting was a perilous business: Artois and the terrified queen begged the king to withdraw to Rambouillet or to Rouen. But that would have meant handing over control to Orléans. The king stayed.

An old friend, the Duc de Liancourt, went to the palace without warning his colleagues and persuaded Louis XVI that he alone could resolve the situation and avoid the shedding of great quantities of blood. He brought the king back to the Assembly, which received him standing, and in silence (Mirabeau had called for this in these terms: 'The peoples' silence is the school of kings.') In a brief, plain, but moving speech Louis XVI said to them, 'Gentlemen, I have called you together to consult you upon the most important affairs of state. There is none more urgent, none that touches me nearer the heart, than the terrible disorder that reigns in the capital . . .' He begged them to send a deputation to Paris and to intervene. It was an essential move, no doubt, and one that reconciled him with the Assembly; but it put the Assembly in the position of arbiter.

The deputies in procession conducted him back to the palace in the midst of the shouting and cheering of the crowd; the anxious queen had come out on to the balcony with the Dauphin[1] to wait for her husband, and they cheered her. But for all that, a woman came close to the king and cried out, 'So you have changed again! Are you sincere, and will you not let yourself be turned around once more?' Another pushed Artois roughly and said, 'Long live the king, whatever you may say!' However, calm returned: but this pacification was expensive – the troops had to be sent back to their garrisons, Necker had to be recalled, Bailly accepted as 'mayor of Paris' and La Fayette as commander of the National Guard, as he had been proclaimed at the Hôtel de Ville.

Thus physical power passed into the hands of the revolutionaries and a new 'patriotism' came into being, a patriotism that had

[1] Because of his elder brother's death, the Duc de Normandie had become Dauphin.

triumphed on 14 July; it was no longer a love of the country's soil and traditions, of the national interests and the King of France, but rather a love for a political ideal incarnated in the people of France. The true hero of this patriotism, which had been shaped by the *philosophes* and the masonic lodges, was not Orléans at all, but La Fayette. Even as leader of the revolutionary party and even as grand master of the Grand-Orient the first prince of the blood was still a prince of the blood – and a sceptic. The disappearance of the monarchic way of life was more harmful than valuable to him; he made the bourgeoisie and the bankers uneasy. Power did not slip from the king's hands to the followers of Philippe d'Orléans; it was transferred to La Fayette's National Guard, backed by the whole of the army and all the fears of the bourgeoisie. The 'hero of America' was too much a member of the establishment and at the same time too keen a political mind not to be aware of this.

As early as 17 July Louis XVI went to Paris, alone and without an escort, to be reconciled with his 'good city', but also to give his countenance to what the rioting had accomplished, for such was the price of the reconciliation. He was well received; his coach, escorted by the former Gardes-Françaises, now the National Guards, drove to the Hôtel de Ville, which he visited. An 'arch of steel' (swords crossing over his head in the masonic fashion) welcomed him as he went in. Bailly handed him a tricoloured sash – from now on these were the city's colours – and La Fayette made him a speech: 'Gentlemen, this at last is the moment the National Assembly has desired above all others: the king was deceived – he is deceived no longer. He has come into our midst today without arms, without troops, without all that display which is so pointless for good kings . . .' Lally, who was a member of the Assembly's delegation, was cheered when he announced peace and the end of proscriptions. 'Long live the king!' cried everybody there, 'Long live the peace!' And that indeed was the wish of the great majority of the country, and of the wealthy bourgeois who had made the revolution in order to turn it to account. With Necker back again, their party settled in to govern.

The king reorganized his cabinet according to the wishes of the victors. He recalled Montmarin, whom everybody liked; he appointed La Tour du Pin, Germaine de Staël's good friend, to the war ministry; Cicé, Archbishop of Bordeaux, and Pompignan, Archbishop of Vienne, both faithful followers of La Fayette, to the Seals and ecclesiastical patronage respectively; he put Saint-Priest, La Fayette's confidential friend, in charge of Paris; and M. de Lambert, who was generally approved of, into the ministry of finance. The Maréchal de Beauvau was minister without portfolio; and they were all ministers without authority. Even Necker no longer counted. The treasury was empty; he wanted to make a loan and he asked for thirty million at five per cent. He was granted only twenty-four million, and a 'patriotic contribution' was relied upon to fill the gaps. The Assembly alone had authority, and it only had it upon condition that public opinion and the conspirators agreed with it. La Fayette caused the Assembly to pass a Declaration of Rights, an idealist, bourgeois document, a symbol of the new patriotism, but one in which private property appeared as an indefeasible right and in which Catholicism retained its supremacy. Not the slightest social right or right of association for anyone. The revolutionaries protested violently. The king refused his consent.

The Breton Club, an essentially Orléanist body, never wearied of attacking the king; and Chapelier, the deputy from Rennes, coordinated his activities in Brittany with those of the Parlement Urged on by him, Rennes protested against the veto; in liaison with him, Mirabeau, the distributor of Orléans' money, stirred up the wards or *districts* of Paris. On 30 and 31 August Camille Desmoulins and Saint-Huruge tried to lead them to Versailles to force 'the people's will' (acceptance of the decrees of 4 August, removal of the king and the Assembly to Paris, etc.) upon Louis XVI. La Fayette and his National Guard had great difficulty in stopping them. He was beginning to experience the disagreeable side of this policeman's calling: he was losing his popularity and he shrilly accused Orléans of stirring up trouble, Lameth of coveting his place, the king of being secretive and Mme de Simiane of not understanding him.

La Fayette's tense excitability alarmed Mounier. He suggested to the king that the Assembly would be better at Soissons or Compiègne. But the king scented the danger and would not agree; the only precaution he would allow was the bringing of the Flanders regiment to Versailles.

Even that was too much. The party the bodyguard gave for the regiment, attended by the king and the queen, who carried the Dauphin, had not the least resemblance to an orgy. But there was the song *O Richard, ô mon Roi, l'univers t'abandonne* . . . and there were some unkind words about the patriots. The king foresaw danger.

He was not mistaken. La Fayette was angry with the king for not having given him warning, and the deputies belonging to the Breton Club claimed that it was provocation. In Paris things were more serious; the town was short of bread and the angry people waited in queues outside the bakers' shops. Marat, the most violent of the pamphleteers, had just founded *L'Ami du Peuple* and Loustalot *Les Révolutions de Paris*. The threatened La Fayette came to tell his woes at Versailles.

On 3 October the Palais-Royal burst out in fury against what it called the plotting of the court, and on Sunday, 4 October, Marat and Loustalot called the *districts* to arms, urging them to march on Versailles with their guns. In the *district* of the Cordeliers an agent of the Orléanists and the English, Danton, summoned the Commune (the new municipality of Paris) to order La Fayette to insist upon the king's sending the troops away. Paris was stirring.

Paris, the capital of all Europe for luxury, saw almost the whole of its earnings cut off by these endless revolutions, which frightened away travellers and shut up the nobles' town houses. It was hoped that the king would bring back order and prosperity, and although the movement in fact worsened the state of which the people complained, it did have a genuine popular foundation. What is more the plan seemed well concerted. In the morning a crowd of women of all classes, but chiefly the lowest – there were men dressed up as women among them – forced their way into the Hôtel de Ville without meeting any resistance. One of the 'conquerors of the Bastille', a certain Maillard, put himself at their head and led them to Versailles. They reached the palace in the afternoon, nobody having stopped them.

A few hours later the grenadiers of the National Guard offered La Fayette the choice of going with them to Versailles or being hanged. He persuaded the Commune to authorize him to go and he took his troops there as quickly as he could. If he were to dawdle he might well find the queen murdered, the king fled and Orléans in charge.

At Versailles Mirabeau had warned the Breton Club, but neither the Assembly nor the court knew anything – the king had gone hunting. When the women reached the entrance gates at five o'clock night was falling. The National Guards of Versailles joined forces with them.

When the king came back from hunting he took counsel with some of his ministers and certain members of the Assembly: they advised him to escape in the direction of Rambouillet and Rouen. Coaches were made ready. The king refused to leave. That would have been playing directly into Orléans' hands.

La Fayette arrived with another disorderly crowd and his National Guards, whom he had lectured on the way; he at once saw the king and begged him to stay; then he went to the Assembly. At midnight he posted men he could rely upon at the outward entrances to the palace. The bodyguard held the inner posts. The soldiers of the Flanders regiment were lying with the Paris whores, who had seduced them from their duty. And everyone was asleep. Except for the agents of Orléans.

La Fayette was snoring when they came to shake him awake. The dawn was showing a first white gleam, no more, in the streets; but in the palace it was red, for the crowd had 'found' an open door and had rushed in, going straight to the queen's apartments. Two bodyguards had been surprised and cut to pieces. The queen fled in haste to the king's room. The king, bitterly distressed and ashamed at finding his people so cruel, had an expression of indescribable sadness on his face.

The whole family and a few faithful courtiers were gathered in the room. The queen, who had pulled herself together, said with a smile, 'M. de La Fayette sleeps soundly . . .' The king ordered the members of the bodyguard to withdraw and conceal themselves. At half past seven the National Guard occupied all the posts. Once again La Fayette was in complete control of the situation. In the courtyard a mob of five thousand, men and women together and all armed, were roaring, 'Bread, or to the gallows!' La Fayette, quite awake now, negotiated with the crowd, which was beginning to tire; he promised that the king and queen should appear on the balcony over the Marble Court and promise to come to Paris directly. At a quarter past eight they obeyed. There were shouts of 'The queen alone!' She persuaded the king to go in and she stood there by herself on the balcony, facing the mob.

At half past one the king was ready and the procession set off. In front there marched the greater part of the National Guard, each soldier carrying a loaf on the end of his bayonet, then came the fishwives, full of joy, passion and wine, carrying branches trimmed with ribbon. Some were too drunk to walk, and they rode astride the guns; others, wearing their spoils, the breastplates and hats of the captured bodyguards, rode in pomp on their victims' horses. They were surrounded by hosts of Parisian workers and patriots, singing, roaring and yelling. Then came carts loaded with wheat and flour taken from Versailles, covered with foliage; the grenadiers marched with them, leading the bodyguard as prisoners, bare-headed and on foot; the dragoons and the Cent-Suisses surrounded the coach in which there rode the king and the queen, who held her son upon her knees. All the soldiers present celebrated the departure by firing their muskets. From time to time there was a halt for fresh volleys. The fishwives made a ring, dancing round and round in the mud in front of the royal coach and singing,

'The baker's wife has golden crowns,
For which she never toiled . . .'

And then they would shout 'Here's the baker, here's the baker's wife, and here's the little baker's boy!' They kissed anyone who came within reach. It was dark and cold; there were sudden downpours of rain. This lasted for six hours.

In Paris they went to the Hôtel de Ville, where M. Bailly made a long speech, praising the king and blaming the ministers. Then he gave Louis XVI a tricolour cockade, which the king put in his hat, bravely saying, 'Relying upon my people's affection and loyalty, I have come into the midst of my subjects with unquestioning trust.' Outside, the people shouted to know what was happening. The windows of the hall were opened at once and the king and queen appeared on the balcony, flanked by two great blazing torches that threw a tawny glare upon their faces. From the square packed tight with people there arose an immense cry, 'Long live the king!' So something at least had been saved.

From the Hôtel de Ville they went to the Tuileries: in the morning a courier from Versailles had brought the order to 'prepare the palace with all speed, to receive His Majesty that same evening'. But the palace was filled with people whom the royal generosity allowed to live there. In twelve hours a hundred rooms had to be emptied, cleaned and furnished. All the court officials followed the king. In that dismal gloom all these splendidly-dressed people, sweating with weariness and dread, quarrelled over their lodgings, for there were far too few – a fresh misery for the king and queen, and one that lasted well into the night.

Chapter VI

The treachery of the lawyers

LOUIS XVI WAS NOT THE ONLY LOSER IN THESE OCTOBER days; through his cowardice Orléans had put himself out of the running, and he did so to such an extent that he had to take refuge in England.

France was becoming a mass of small republics, topped by a muddle-headed Assembly and a prisoner king.

Convinced that this monstrous anomaly could not last, the king behaved with the utmost prudence, in order neither to lose his popularity nor to provoke the least incident. Throughout November, December and January the queen and he lived the quietest, most private life in the Tuileries.

This way of living did at least allow him to come closer to his children than he had ever done before; he took a very deep pleasure in this intimacy – one that was mingled with anxiety, however. When the tension became too oppressive he used to play whist with Monsieur, Madame and the queen. He had returned to his lock-making, but the greater part of his time was taken up with thinking over the means still at his disposal for reviving the monarchy, saving the kingdom from anarchy and preserving the dynasty. Although he was now called 'Louis XVI, King of the French,' he had neither renounced nor disowned his tradition. That autumn he sent the Abbé de Fonbrune to the King of Spain to engage his interest and to disavow in advance any signature that might be extorted from him. He maintained the family bonds and the Family Compact.

On 10 October he entered into alliance with La Fayette, giving him the command of the regular troops within thirty-five miles of the capital. He tolerated the popular leader's supervision of his ministers. Yet La Fayette was unable to come to an understanding with Mirabeau, Duport, Barnave and Lameth to form a new 'patriot' ministry and name Mirabeau as ambassador. Mirabeau slipped out of it, the triumvirs wavered, the king held back, and the Assembly, seized with jealousy, passed a decree forbidding deputies to become ministers.

Then a kind of bourgeois reaction came over the Assembly: now that they no longer had Orléans they attended to the pleas of those who loved order, and the result of this was a great increase in La Fayette's authority – an increase that made 1790 the finest year of his life. The provinces also grew much quieter.

In view of this general calmness, Louis XVI listened to La Fayette's advice; as soon as he saw the left weakening the 'mayor of the palace' felt it necessary to emphasize his unity with the king. This was what was happening now. The king yielded to his persuasion, and on 4 February 1790 he went to the Assembly. He arrived at noon, with no guard, accompanied by the ministers and a few officers of his suite. He was greeted with prolonged applause; he spoke standing, for the Assembly, to mark the rank it claimed for itself, had placed a chair for him at the same level as that of their president.

Without betraying any emotion and speaking in a fatherly tone that did away with any necessity for explanation by wiping out all unpleasant incidents, he said, 'It is time, gentlemen, that I should associate myself more closely and in a still more direct and open fashion with the successful carrying out of all that you have planned for the benefit of France . . .' Then turning to the past he listed the efforts that he had made for reforming the country, and he undertook to support all measures that were intended for the country's happiness. He skilfully disavowed the *émigrés* and the embittered opponents of change: everyone should gather in unity about the Assembly for the public good. 'You who have so many ways of influencing opinion, enlighten the people as to their true interests, the people I love so dearly and who are said by those who wish to comfort me in my distress to love me in return.'

The deputies were enchanted; many of them wept, and Barère exclaimed, 'Oh, what an admirable king ... We must indeed raise up a throne of gold and diamonds for him.' The references to the Dauphin and to his patriotic upbringing delighted these legislators, who were as 'tender-hearted' as they were 'virtuous'; and since they were demagogues as well they took advantage of the opportunity to insist that all citizens appointed to public office should take an oath of the same nature as the king's.

So Louis XVI and Marie-Antoinette once more began moving about in Paris, and there the people, the shop-keepers, the citizens, the men in the street, lavished marks of affection upon them. Once more the queen was cheered at the Opéra: one day, when they were playing *Iphigénie* and the actors reached the line '*Let us sing and celebrate our queen*' there were the same rapturous scenes that there had been in 1774. The king and queen listened to the cheers with a lump in the throat: how could any pleasure be so bitter? Every day filthy pamphlets against them were cried in the streets, and perhaps to protect them, perhaps to honour them or perhaps to supervise them, La Fayette would only allow them to go about Paris surrounded by officers of his National Guard.

This precaution was of no avail against the publication of the *Livre rouge*, the notebook in which Louis XVI had recorded secret expenditure. Between 1774 and 1789 these sums amounted to about two hundred and twenty-eight million, eleven and a half being for the king and his family. The pensions committee, which had gone through it with him, allowed copies to be taken, and the result was an unusually poisonous pamphlet against the king. The worst was that the revelation of the names of all the

German princes who had pensions from the crown offended the country's friends and put weapons into the hands of her enemies. Certain deputies were furious at finding themselves mentioned – the Lameth brothers, for example, for whose schooling the queen had paid sixty thousand francs. These squalid struggles turned life into a perpetual battle.

The king and queen were happy when May came round and it was decided to take the air at Saint-Cloud. The long winter in the turbulent city had been a wearisome trial: Saint-Cloud was not freedom – they could expect a National Guard at the end of every walk in the garden, and in the country La Fayette's horsemen keeping watch – but at least it meant fresh air, a little more room to move, some pleasant memories, and a certain amount of hope. The king was able to return to his long hours on horseback, which he loved; and Marie-Antoinette to her walks with Fersen. He was back from the Russian war, and his attachment remained even after the loss of his pension and regiment. In order to be able to see him she accepted La Fayette's complicity; he allowed Fersen to come in and out of the Tuileries at any hour of the day or night. The result was that La Fayette had a civil contempt for her and she a violent hatred for him.

Since the Assembly had 'nationalized the possessions of the Church' (2 November 1789), the creation of assignats, an interest-bearing paper currency redeemable after the sale of church property, had encouraged speculation, and it quickly reached immense proportions. The wealth of the Church, reckoned at three thousand million, stood as security for the indebtedness of the state, which assumed responsibility for ecclesiastical expenses. With a stroke of the pen the clergy lost their independence and the financial world gained prodigiously. To begin with four hundred million assignats were issued (December 1789), then twelve hundred million (25 September 1790), then six hundred million (18 May 1791) and so on – two thousand five hundred million in a year and a half. The more this currency was issued the more it depreciated and the greater became the gap between it and the louis. This gap left room for every conceivable kind of jobbery. It was one of the great subjects for debate in the Assembly:

the king did not interfere at all, seeing that there was nothing he could do about it.

He limited himself to a passive defence. He only paid Mirabeau in order to avoid his most violent attacks; he neither desired nor expected anything more (end of 1789). The queen, tormented by fear and urged on by Mercy, came to a different agreement with him (June 1790). But in any case, Mirabeau was of little use. He was unable to stop the Assembly depriving the king of the right to decide upon war or peace. He still retained that of proposing either. Mirabeau was heavily paid by Spain, but here again he failed in obtaining French help for that country in its dispute with England over Vancouver Island. The Jacobins won the day every time.

Yet Louis XVI was still popular. La Fayette had prepared a great 'federation' ceremony in Paris to celebrate 14 July and to bring together delegations from all the National Guards in the kingdom. He was ready to yield to his own deification with a good grace, even though it should be at the king's expense.

What happened was quite the contrary. The king scored an immense success; as soon as the delegations reached Paris they wanted to see him. Even the marquee in La Fayette's garden with tables perpetually spread came second. One after another each of the federations came to bring the king expressions of affection and loyalty. On 13 July they came in a body to pay their compliments, led by La Fayette, who did not lose this opportunity for making a speech. 'Sire,' said he, 'in the course of the memorable events that have given us indefeasible rights and in which the people's energy and the virtue of their king have shown the nations and their leaders such a noble example, we delight in honouring the finest of all titles in Your Majesty's person, that of leader of the French and king of a free people.'

In his turn Louis XVI, without hiding his emotion, replied, 'May this solemn day upon which you are all about to renew your oath to the constitution see the disappearance of all dissension; may it bring back calm and cause law and freedom to reign throughout the realm!'

The 14 July was celebrated in the Champ de Mars, which had

been arranged like an amphitheatre, with the altar of the father-land in the middle, tiers of seats all round, a throne for the king and a gallery for the queen. It was raining. The Federates sat on the benches; the king, appointed supreme head of the National Guards of France for this day, appeared once more with all the emblems of royalty; La Fayette, to whom he delegated his com-mand, saluted him and then put the Federates through various evolutions. After this Talleyrand said mass, the king took the oath to the nation and the laws, and the others followed his example. The guns boomed out. Suddenly the sun broke through the clouds, as though in greeting.

A strange ceremony, in which a bishop worshipped a God he did not serve, in which a nation in the persons of its representa-tives glorified a king it had been insulting for the past three years, in which the people were present at a mass without knowing that it was being said and without minding that it was sacrilegious, in which the great and sincere efforts at giving resurgent patriotism a heroic splendour resulted in a ludicrous display under the pouring rain and in the apotheosis of a fallen king.

A dangerous day, one that deceived the lovers of order as to their own numbers, La Fayette as to his strength and the king as to his popularity. The people who cheered him were sincere, but they were passive in a country where only the Jacobins were full of active zeal.

This was seen at once. Ill-received in London, disappointed in his ambitions and tired of Mme de Buffon, Orléans came back to Paris with fresh supplies of money. He feared neither La Fayette, who had not dared push on with his trial, nor the king, who did not want to see him again. He returned at the beginning of July.

He cut a poor figure at the Champ de Mars: people turned their backs. Then he went to pay his respects to the king, who received him courteously. 'Come and learn from your king how to belong to France and how to be worthy of the race of the man who governs the French', Louis XVI had written to him; and now he desired neither a break nor a quarrel. Those about him were indignant. Everyone had looked for a display of hatred, even the queen. Not the king. His duty was to remain as the country's ultimate resource, to endure in the hope that at last the French would understand the harm they were doing themselves. He was told that in two frenzied sessions, on 19 and 23 July, the Assembly had voted for the abolition of all titles of nobility. His expression did not alter in the slightest degree: he signed. There is nothing more trifling than emotion, nothing more empty than the saving of the flag when the fortress is lost. M. Necker was deeply shocked.

The affair of the ministers was very serious. The disorders in the fleet at Brest disturbed public opinion in France and in Europe. France, only yesterday the ruling nation, was now defenceless against England. The Assembly strongly proclaimed responsibility of the 'executive', the king and his ministers – the ministers in fact, for the king was not answerable before the Assembly. 'Charles de Lameth, in his facetious way, says that the executive power is playing dead,' wrote La Fayette at the time; but Lameth would have been wiser and less facetious if he had observed that 'the executive *was* dead.' What remained was a dictatorship of the Assembly with a praetorian guard commanded by La Fayette. The Jacobins were infiltrating all the regiments and setting up cells, and any officer who wished to maintain order had to take his life in his hands, as Bouillé did at Metz and Nancy. Not many had the courage to do so.

Mirabeau took advantage of the situation to indict the ministers, whom he hoped to overthrow and replace. On October 20 1790 he failed. But they saw how the wind lay, and one after another they disappeared – La Luzerne on 28 October, La Tour du Pin on 16 November, Champion de Cicé on 22 November. The only one to stay was Montmorin, the king's intimate friend and La Fayette's 'watchman' on the council. La Fayette put forward the names of his friends to fill up the ministry, thus forcing them upon the king. A straightforward, uninteresting but quite intelligent man had the Admiralty; a Jacobin, Duportail, the war ministry; and one of Montmorin's friends, Duport-Dutertre, the Seals. Saint-Priest remained at the ministry of the interior until the end of the year. Louis XVI had so little confidence in this motley gathering that he spoke as little as possible at meetings of the council and pretended to be asleep whenever dangerous subjects were broached.

Yet the time came when withdrawal was no longer possible. All his functions had been taken from him, all that he had inherited from his forefathers; their work had been destroyed, together with his own, and he had been unable to prevent it. Now he feigned indifference, although he could not but be bitterly distressed, horrified, at the sight of France hacked into eighty-three *départements*, the finances given over to speculation, the army's strength vanishing for want of discipline and the finest navy France had ever seen condemned to rot in harbour. Yet all that counted for nothing compared with the Civil Constitution of the Clergy, a monstrous piece of liberal idealism and canonical ignorance. The bishops, once so proud and now so humble, wanted to accept it and begged the Pope to allow them to do so. The Nuncio had written to Rome on these lines. The two bishops appointed by the Pope to advise Louis XVI on religious matters, the Bishop of Pamiers and the Bishop of Langres, had told him not to refuse his sanction, and he gave it on 28 July. Ever since, he felt that he had been misled.

He was haunted by the slow, slow negotiations with the Pope, and by the mounting anger of the Assembly, in which the Jansenists, Protestants and atheists competed to see who could be most zealous in subjugating the clergy, insulting the Pope and scandalizing the faithful. The annexation of Avignon to France made everything worse. When the deputies decided to compel all the clergy to take the oath to the Civil Constitution without waiting for the Pope's reply, the king's conscience revolted. 'This law', he said to those around him, 'is contrary to my religious opinions: I see it as the signal for endless persecution in my kingdom.' To induce him to sign, his two ecclesiastical advisers had to show him that if he refused it would mean giving over the priesthood to the pitiless vengeance of the clubs and the mob. But this time his whole being turned from it in a convulsion of anguish and disgust. All his life he had followed the precepts of his tutor, Mgr de Coëtlosquet, and then those of the Abbé Soldini, the confessor who had formed his moral conscience and had brought his spiritual life to its full development. He was ashamed before them.

This particular distress was too deep and too personal for anyone to be able to comfort him. And it was that which made him see the urgent necessity for escaping from the bondage of the Assembly. Here his friends could help him: in the autumn there had already been question of a journey to Compiègne, with La Fayette's agreement, and the king would have gone from there to Metz, there to meet Bouillé. The public heard of the plan, and he dropped it. But with the help of his real friends he went on preparing his escape. He had to beware of La Fayette, who was never to be relied upon, because of his need for popularity, and of Montmorin, who was too weak to bear the weight of such secrets.

The king was certain of Arnaud de Laporte, a man of the utmost loyalty who was in charge both of finance and of intelligence. Through him and Talon the subsidies were distributed to the deputies, who accepted them willingly, even the Jacobins; and it was Laporte and Talon who saw to the help given to the royalist papers. Montmorin also made use of part of these funds, with La Fayette's consent. Through the Abbé de Fonbrune, whom he sent to England, and through Breteuil, whom he sent to the friendly courts (Austria, Sweden, Sardinia) at the end of October 1790 to look into the possibilities of international intervention in France to restore order and re-establish the monarchy, he sought support outside France. D'Agost, the Bishop of Pamiers, who had come back from Switzerland to see him and to urge him to decisive action, was given a mission of the same nature. And favourable articles were published in some of Panckoucke's periodicals. All this amounted to little, and it cost a great deal.

Since the Assembly had ordered the taking of the oath, the great mass of the good priests in France had refused to submit to it; and in its sectarianism the Assembly had thus succeeded in doing what the king, with all his earnestness, had never been able to accomplish – the Church of France purged itself of its bad priests, the Loménies, the Talleyrands, the Fauchets, all of whom took the oath. This sorting out ensured that the Church of France should rise again, but for the moment it caused very great upheaval: the Assembly deprived the non-juring priests of their functions, their ecclesiastical rights and their civil rights. This campaign revived the active wing of the revolutionaries, filling them with zeal and ardour. The notion that the Church might not bow to the revolution, that it might refuse to break with the past, and that it might be in itself a continuing tradition, seemed to them intolerable. 'Liberals' such as La Fayette and La Rochefoucauld reminded them that the Declaration of Rights guaranteed freedom of religion and worship, but in vain; they replied with the rights of the people and the usurpations of the Pope, a foreign ruler. Mesdames de France did not want to have anything to do with the 'bad priests'; they would rather leave. They asked the king's advice, and they held over their decision from 21 January to 15 February. At last, with his agreement, they decided to go to Rome, to see the Pope and to be with their friend Cardinal de Bernis again.

The king helped them. He had their passport prepared by the foreign minister and the minister of the interior informed the important municipalities that they would be passing through, asking that they should be treated kindly (9 February 1791). A campaign led by the Jacobins at once burst out against them; they were accused of meaning to take the Dauphin away; and the market women made a great commotion. Adélaïde understood what was afoot. She announced her departure for a given date and left the day before. All the hostile preparations fell to pieces. There were attempts at catching them, but they got through, and they experienced the unspeakable sadness of standing free and happy on foreign soil!

In Paris the whole thing made an unbelievable hubbub. The slumbering civil war sprang to life again. On 28 February 1791 his informers told La Fayette that a great riot was being prepared against the castle of Vincennes – the castle was said to be connected to the Tuileries by a tunnel! It was rumoured that the Orléanist clan had laid an ambush to kill La Fayette, or that it was a royalist plot.

On 4 March 1791 Louis XVI had to take to his bed with a fever:

he stayed there for a month, coughing, spitting blood, unable to get over his illness. Although he was innocent he could not forgive himself for having accepted the Civil Constitution. His tender conscience yearned for atonement without being able to find the road to it. He wanted to escape, but Leopold II, whose help was essential, either did not reply or refused to commit himself. Yet Louis XVI could not do without the support of the Austrian army if he were to take refuge at Malmédy with Bouillé. Gustavus III, warm-hearted and clumsy, had settled at Spa, but his attempts at setting his great neighbour Catherine II in motion were fruitless, for she was too busy preparing the annexation of Poland. The English did at least promise him their neutrality (Champcenezt's mission). The most dangerous aspect of it all was that the mob was beginning to get to know about the plans and to cry out against the king's escape.

He tossed feverishly in his bed: Lent had begun, and presently it would be Easter. Would he dare take Communion after what he had done? Would he accept the sacrament from the schismatic hand of a priest who had taken the oath? His confessor, the Abbé Poupart, curé of Saint Eustache, had taken it in February. The king would no longer consult him. He prayed to God. He called upon the Sacred Heart, a form of devotion much loved by the simple people, and one that he had adopted. His father had raised an altar to the Sacred Heart in the chapel at Versailles, to the amusement of the *philosophes*. He himself had been taught the lessons of Saint John Eudes, one of the apostles of the Sacred Heart.

These childhood images rose to his mind's eye. He wrote, 'Oh God, You see all the wounds that tear my heart, and the depth of the abyss into which I have fallen.' To obtain the help of the Sacred Heart he made the vow 'to revoke as soon as possible all the laws that were pointed out to him, either by the Pope or by four bishops chosen among the most virtuous in his kingdom, as being contrary to the purity and the integrity of the faith, to the discipline and the spiritual jurisdiction of the holy Roman and Catholic faith, and particularly to the Civil Constitution of the Clergy.' At the date he wrote this the Pope had not yet officially given his decision, and prudence obliged the king to include the Constitution among the fundamental documents of the Church of France. The king placed himself and his kingdom under the protection of the Sacred Heart and promised to build a church and institute a solemn feast in its honour as soon as he was in a condition to do so.

> I solemnly promise [he said] to go myself, in person, within three months after the day of my deliverance, to the church of Notre Dame in Paris or to any other principle church in the place where I may be, on a Sunday or a feast-day, after the offertory and delivering my oath to the celebrant, and to utter an act of dedication to the Sacred Heart of Jesus, promising to give all my subjects an example of the worship and devotion due to that Heart we should all adore.

This decision gave him back the spiritual energy to get over his illness. He left his bed.

Chapter VII

Louis XVI between God and the Supreme Being

ON APRIL 14 THE NEWS OF THE POPE'S CONDEMNATION OF the Civil Constitution of the Clergy reached Paris. The Pope had spoken: from now on Louis XVI knew the task that lay before him – he was to bring about the abrogation of this schismatic document. In order to act in spiritual unity with the Church he looked for a confessor other than the Abbé Poupart, whom he had consulted these fifteen years past. He was determined to compromise no one and to give his trust only in full knowledge of what he was about, since for him his confessor was his spiritual father; and he chose a monk in whose work and personality he had been interested as early as 1786–1787: this was Father Hébert, a Eudist who combined a manly heart with a mind turned wholly to spiritual things. Louis asked his advice about his plan for escape and for the subsequent restoration of religion in France. He asked him whether he might communicate in spite of his share, his involuntary share, in a heretical law.

> Monsieur Hébert, I am acquainted with the full purity of
> your Catholic principles, which are mine too, and always will

be. Judge from your own heart the anguish that mine feels at the wrongs done to religion. It is the cruellest of all the pains that afflict me: everything that has been done against religion has been done in spite of me, and if God should see fit to give me back my authority you may be sure that the first use I shall make of it will be to solace the Church and to build up the ruined sanctuary once more . . .

Father Hébert replied that he was of the opinion that these views were enough: the king might perform his Easter duty. But as Louis XVI wished to give no spiritual offence whatever to the faithful, he wrote to M. de Bonal, Bishop of Clermont, on 15 April 1791.

I write to consult you with full confidence, my lord bishop, turning to one of the members of the clergy who has steadily shown the most enlightened zeal in favour of religion. The subject upon which I seek your advice is my Easter duty: may I perform it, and should I perform it in the next fortnight? You know the unhappy position in which the acceptation of the decrees on the clergy has placed me: I have always looked upon their acceptation as an act of compulsion, for as far as I am concerned I have never hesitated to remain unalterably united to the Catholic leaders, and I am firmly determined to restore Catholic worship if I regain my power. A priest I have seen thinks that these opinions are sufficient and that I may perform my Easter duty; but you are in a better position to see what the Church in general thinks and to view our present circumstances, whether on the one hand this would cause offence to some, and on the other I find the innovators (though indeed this is not a reason that should have any weight in the balance) already speaking in an almost menacing tone. In this matter I beg you to consult those bishops whose advice you think valuable and whose discretion you can wholly rely upon. I also wish you to reply before midday and to return my letter.

LOUIS.

The Bishop of Clermont answered the next day, returning the king's letter and telling him that it would be better not to

M

communicate, since 'without very great objections' he could not publicly retract.

Louis and Bonal gauged the peril. The Revolution was bogging down. The only thing that was prospering was speculation; the only men who were growing bolder were the Jacobins. No one knew how to give the Revolution a fresh impetus.

The answer was a religious war.

Unpleasant incidents began: the soldiers of the guard, permeated by the Jacobins and thoroughly indoctrinated, refused to attend the king's mass. La Fayette compelled them to go. Once there, they insulted the chaplains. There were all the signs of approaching violence. The king gave up the idea of going to Saint-Cloud; La Fayette strongly urged him to return to the plan. He wanted to make it look as though the king were free. The Jacobins spread the rumour that the king intended to take Communion in secret.

At eleven o'clock on 18 April – the Monday of Holy Week – the king stepped into his coach with five gentlemen of his household. At once the National Guards mutinied and closed the gates, shouting and roaring threats. When La Fayette tried to make them obey they insulted him too. After two hours of this uproar the king left his coach and returned to his apartments. He did not want French blood to flow for so foolish a cause. Nor was he altogether displeased that this shameful rebellion should make it perfectly obvious to the world in general that he was being kept a prisoner.

La Fayette was angry with the king for this attitude: he said that Louis XVI had encouraged the mutiny. Yet the National Guards and the mob who had searched the palace during the afternoon, looking for non-juring priests, had by no means been asked in by the king. This operation was explained by the approach made by the Paris Directory[1] that same day: an address composed by Talleyrand was read to the king – the people of Paris were uneasy because they saw him surrounded by non-juring priests, whom he protected. In order to reassure them what was needed was 'a

[1] A departmental body, not the national Directory of 1795–1799.

frank and positive initiative that should remove all who might be looked upon as hostile to the Constitution from his person and thus demonstrate to the nations of Europe that he had sincerely adopted the Revolution, since he was surrounded only by its friends.' At the same time posters and pamphlets foretold a general massacre of the priests and aristocrats if the king did not yield. A tragic situation for the king! An exceedingly disagreeable position for La Fayette! Orléans was having his revenge.

On Father Hébert's advice Louis XVI went to the Assembly on 19 April. He said, 'I come into your midst with the trust I have always shown you. You are acquainted with the resistance that prevented my leaving for Saint-Cloud yesterday. I did not wish it to be stopped by force, because I was afraid that rigour might be used against a mistaken crowd of people who supposed that they were acting in support of the law, whereas in fact they were breaking it.' Then he stated, 'It is in the nation's highest interest to prove that I am free', and he declared that for this purpose he should go to Saint-Cloud but that in any case he would keep all his oaths, including that to maintain the Civil Constitution. He ended by reminding them that his only wish was 'the people's happiness'. This skilful speech alarmed the Assembly: if they let it be said that the king was a prisoner they would lose face. They replied by denouncing the Jacobins, and then they compelled the king to sign a letter to the foreign powers asserting that he was free. He even had to attend a mass said by the conforming curé of Saint-Germain-l'Auxerrois, his parish. But he refused to take Communion there or to receive Poupart as High Almoner.

By these sacrifices he obtained a truce for the non-juring clergy and the orthodox Catholics. On 7 May the Assembly passed a motion acknowledging and ratifying religious tolerance – a tolerance that the Paris Directory had already admitted and regulated. La Fayette had worked very hard to get this passed: his pious wife insisted upon it no less than the king, and his friends La Rochefoucauld and Sieyès, who were devoted to the notion of freedom, made his task easier in the departmental directory. Talleyrand also helped, seeing that this coincided with his plan.

The queen overcame her anxiety and tension by seeing to the

preparations; she sent her diamonds to Brussels, her travelling-case to Vienna, trunks of belongings and linen for the children and herself to Brabant – in short everything that a good mother would like to take away with her and everything that could betray her.

The king remained calm. It was agreed with his brother-in-law Leopold II that he should find a body of troops close to the north-eastern frontier and that he should have fifteen million francs as soon as he was free; now he secretly gave his last orders, wrote a letter intended for the Assembly, and warned his advisers, Laporte and Father Hébert. Since it could not be avoided, he signed everything that the Assembly sent him. As for the rest, he prayed to God.

He had settled 19 May as the date for leaving for Malmédy; Monsieur left the same day for Belgium. It had to be postponed until 20 June, to avoid the most dangerous of the Dauphin's maids. There were none but completely loyal people in the design. They left through the Duc de Villequier's apartments, which had remained empty and whose door opening on to the courtyard was never guarded.

Towards eleven at night Mme de Tourzel went out, taking Madame Royale and the Dauphin, dressed as a girl. They got into the carriage, a kind of old cab in which Fersen, dressed as a cab-driver, was waiting for them. He drove round a little so that they should not be noticed and so that the king, the queen and Madame Elisabeth should have time to come. At about half past eleven Madame Elisabeth appeared, and at midnight the king. Bailly and La Fayette had attended him to bed, which had delayed him. The queen arrived a quarter of an hour later, having lost her way in this part of Paris which she did not know; and La Fayette's coach had brushed by without her being seen.

Fersen did not know Paris well and he drove by way of the rue Saint-Honoré and then the boulevards – slow progress. At last they found the berlin with the Swedish postillion and the three bodyguards beyond the Saint-Martin gate. The royal family were supplied with Russian passports and they passed without difficulty; one of the men in charge of the barrier was celebrating his marriage in style.

Then they set off as fast as they could and Fersen went back into Paris. In spite of the horses taking a fall and broken traces that had to be hastily repaired, the coach travelled on towards Malmédy: they obtained horses everywhere, and nobody asked to see their passports. They reached Châlons at about four in the afternoon of the twenty-first, and everything passed off well.

In the carriage they talked. 'So here I am,' said the king, 'out of that city of Paris, where I have had to endure so much bitterness. Believe me, once my breeches are in the saddle, I shall be a very different man from the one you have seen until now.' He delighted above all in the idea of being able to speak freely to his people and of re-establishing religion.

'At this moment,' he said, 'La Fayette certainly does not know what to do with himself.' That made the queen smile: for her part she was more inclined to dream of a regency in which she should show the French how energetic she could be. Madame Elisabeth thought that Artois, her dashing, knightly brother, would save them all, entirely by himself. So each one of them dreamed on separate lines. The hours went by.

The first reaction in Paris on the morning of the twenty-first was stupefaction; nobody had thought that Louis XVI would have the initiative to leave. Then, whipped up by the Jacobins, fury spread all over the town. La Fayette, the unfortunate gaoler, was threatened. He turned the threat aside by a reply that might be described as brilliant, so crammed it was with fiction and so fully did it satisfy both the mob and the Assembly; though it was dull and hackneyed enough if one remembers that for the last fifty years people had been repeating the same formula – 'The king has been deceived and kidnapped.' It saved him. He at once sent messengers to catch Louis XVI and bring him back. The Assembly was much more nonplussed, than furious,

In the afternoon the king's declaration was brought to the Assembly: in it he protested against all that had been done and all that had been forced upon him since 6 October 1789. He declared all his signatures since that date void, since they had been made under compulsion. The only thing that obliged him to go and to speak out was the anarchy now devouring France. He then ran over all the sacrifices to which he had agreed since May 1789 and which had ended in his captivity and in the chaos which was the outcome of the Constitution. It had been drawn up to please the revolutionary clubs, and it was bringing about the destruction of France. He promised a general pardon, a freely accepted constitution, peace and freedom, the re-establishment of religion and the safety of property. In the meantime he forbade the ministers to sign anything whatsoever in his name.

The Assembly listened to the reading of this in silence. Far from bursting out in rage, all these bewildered tribunes felt a kind of relief: this revolution that was leading them to the abyss – was it at last going to be halted? If the king were to accomplish this, they would flock over to his side. There was confidential talk of sending him a great deputation of sixty members. If La Fayette had not sent messengers after the king, no one would have thought of it.

Only the Cordeliers, a Jacobin and Orléanist group, sent out their people to tear down the emblems and the fleurs-de-lis of royalty; Paine and Duchâtelet wrote a poster calling for a republic; Condorcet published a sheet demanding the king's removal. And Laclos made ready for the regency of Orléans. At the Duc de La Rochefoucauld's house the republic was the one topic of conversation.

In the evening of the twenty-second the Assembly heard of the king's arrest at Varennes. Bouillé had under-estimated the ill-will of the people living in the Meuse, who had already been worked upon by the Jacobins: when the king reached Sommevelles he did not find the expected troops.

He pushed on; but was recognized by the son of the master of the posting-station, Drouet, and he was arrested at Varennes. A grim, threatening, continually increasing crowd pressed round the carriage. There were also some of Bouillé's cavalry there. But Louis XVI did not want any bloodshed. He gave up.

Then came the return journey. They were spared no humiliation, but their lives were preserved. Escorted by members of all the clubs of the neighbourhood and fifty sappers, and preceded by a hundred and fifty dragoons, the berlin set off. In the stifling heat the horses were pushed on to a gallop; crowds gathered in the villages to insult the royal family, and as they passed through the municipal authorities presented their keys, in mockery.

At the sound of his son and his daughter crying, Louis XVI smiled with an unbelievable joy. Until this time he had never been anything more than a king; but now he was suffering a God-like agony.

Chapter VIII

The King defeated

AN OPPRESSIVE SUN BEAT DOWN ON PARIS. A VAST CLOUD
of stifling dust came slowly along the Champs-Élysées. Nothing
was to be heard but the soldiers' marching feet and the horses'
hoofs. Not a single shout. The innumerable crowd that lined the
avenue watched the sight in silence. There were posters upon the
walls reading 'Any man who cheers the king will be beaten:
anyone who insults him will be hanged.' This was clearly La
Fayette's hand, for the Jacobins would have hanged anyone who
cheered and rewarded any who shouted insults. When the procession neared the Tuileries the forest of bayonets surrounding
the two carriages could be seen. On the seat of the first, three disarmed members of the bodyguard. There was blood on the
wheels. When they were still nearer the palace insults, curses and
the most appalling threats burst out like the explosion of a firework jetting filth. Everyone in the two carriages was conscious
of mortal danger. With their arms reversed the National Guard
formed a triple line of dishonour. Yet the queen's courage touched
Barnave, one of the Assembly's commissioners, and he watched
over the prisoners' safety. Two other members of the Assembly,

the Vicomte de Noailles and the Duc d'Aguillon, had also made a point of being there – the last insult of two inveterate enemies, or the obscure atonement of two faithless friends? The king, soaked with sweat, his clothes filthy, stepped out with his eyes blazing and his head held high: he said to the deputies, 'In thinking it proper to remove myself from Paris, I had no intention of leaving France. I wished to settle on one of the frontiers of the country and to become the mediator in the disputes that grow every day more frequent in the Assembly; I wished above all to work in complete freedom and without distraction for the happiness of my people, the unceasing object of my care.' Then, a prisoner from now onwards, he walked into the palace.

Thirty-six National Guards chosen by La Fayette watched the king and his family; they were kept under close surveillance, and they only saw those visitors whom La Fayette looked upon as safe – the Crillon brothers and Liancourt. The king would not allow the guards to take the Dauphin away; he had him carried into his quarters by Hue, his valet. The child said to him, 'As soon as we reached Varennes we were sent back. I do not know why. Do you?' 'Hush,' whispered the valet. In fact the child did know. When he got up he said to the guards, 'I have had a horrible dream: I was surrounded by wolves and tigers and wild animals that wanted to eat me . . .' The groups that came from the *sections* to see that the king was there certainly had that appearance. Louis XVI openly and calmly busied himself with reading the life of Charles I.

The republican party was taking shape. There were endless meetings at La Rochefoucauld's house: Condorcet urged the plan forward, but La Fayette held back. He would not have a republic dominated by Orléans. Barnave, Duport and the Lameths, those implacable enemies of the monarchy, were now clinging to it. They joined with La Fayette to prevent Orléans from becoming the leader.

They then induced the Assembly (16 July 1791) to vote for keeping Louis XVI on the throne. The king's skilful and sincere report helped, but it was above all the result of the deep feeling of guilt that pervaded this Assembly, defenceless before a Europe in arms. Fear is a powerful divinity. They relied upon Louis XVI to save France much more than they did upon themselves. They therefore came to this decision, in spite of the bellowing of the Jacobins, the threats of the Cordeliers and edifying lectures of Robespierre.

As soon as the mob of the clubs learnt of the decree of 16 July, on Friday evening, the Orléanists and the republicans united in their fury, which burst out in the cafés, the clubs and at the Palais-Royal.

During the morning of Sunday, the eighteenth, La Fayette dispersed the first gathering of the 'brigands'. In the evening the commotion began again; the municipality declared martial law, hoisted the red flag and sent La Fayette and his men to the Champ de Mars. The crowd flung stones at them and fired some shots. After some time the National Guards lost their temper, levelled their muskets, and brought down fifty people. The cavalry charged: the rebels fled. That night the whole town was lit up.

The rash yet crafty La Fayette supported a law that entirely changed the high command of the National Guard: henceforward each chief of a legion would command in turn. This meant cutting off the head of the Parisian National Guard. La Fayette was also thinking of getting himself elected mayor of Paris. His steward told him that his income, which was two hundred thousand in 1788, had fallen to forty thousand. The riots at the beginning of the States General had cost a great deal; so had 14 July; and so had all the rest.

He was less diappointed than anxious, and he thought about the future: if the king were to refuse the constitution, that would be total disaster. He therefore went more and more often to the Tuileries, boring the king with studied compliments in which the threats were partially hidden behind deference. Every time he came in the queen felt a violent start of horror and the king offered this sacrifice to God.

The whole of his strength was in God. His misfortunes had deepened this without changing his essence in any way. Ever since his childhood he had been told that the revolution was coming. He looked upon it without hatred, but with an ever-increasing pain: the work of nine centuries lost; France fallen lower than the other nations, and defenceless. He did not leave himself out of the great shame he felt for those who were guilty of all this. He was determined to persist in his efforts to save his crown and the country, and he prayed and meditated. The queen grew indignant, and at the same time she drifted farther and farther from him, for her love for Fersen occupied her entirely. Elizabeth was wholly devoted to Artois, and she blamed the king's 'weakness'. All that remained to Louis XVI were his two children, Madame Royale, who was plunged into something like a mad, wordless death-agony, and the delightful, laughing Dauphin, who skipped along through the filth and the blood, asking his father 'Why?' as children do at that age. When grown men are seen to be raving, what can children be expected to understand?

The strange spectacle ran on, with its sudden violent changes. Muguet de Nanthou, a deputy and one of Barnave's friends, who was in charge of the report on Varennes, put the blame on Bouillé. The king and queen were whitewashed. The tension slackened a little at the Tuileries. On 3 September La Fayette made a ceremonious visit to the palace: when he had been ushered into the council-chamber he said to the king, 'Sire, the fact that the constitutional instrument will very shortly be presented to you allows me to remove the guards who have been placed about your person.' The king replied, 'The Assembly put them here; it is for the Assembly to take them away.' La Fayette withdrew, abashed. He could never understand that a gaoler, even a grand and imposing gaoler, remains an odious figure. The guards were removed that same day.

The next day, 4 September, a deputation from the Assembly led by Thouret appeared at seven in the evening, bringing the king the constitution with great solemnity. With torches marching before them, they walked in procession between two lines of National Guards, entering the palace by the Carrousel gate: the king received them, surrounded by his ministers and the high court dignitaries. 'Sire,' said Thouret, 'the representatives of the nation have come to offer the constitutional instrument for Your Majesty's acceptance; it enshrines the indefeasible rights of the French people; it gives back its true dignity to the crown; and it regulates the government of the empire.' Once again the country's fate lay in the hands of this king whom everyone had wanted to hang or burn only six weeks before.

'I shall examine the constitution that the National Assembly has charged you to present to me' he replied, 'and I shall inform the Assembly of my determination in as short a time as the close study of so important a document allows. I have decided to remain in Paris, and I shall give the general officer commanding the Parisian National Guard the orders I think proper for the guard-duty here.'

From that day on the king once more had his royal guards and it was he who gave them their orders. A frail privilege, and one that depended upon his firm-mindedness. Now Montmorin, urged on by Morris and Pellenc, pressed the king to accept only a modified version of the constitution. The other ministers and the queen, influenced by Barnave, advised a prompt and unconditional acceptance.

The king therefore accepted; on 14 September he went to the Assembly to inform that body of his decision. They received him with cheers, but with no politeness – he and the president were on the same level. This did not prevent him from making a carefully-considered speech, in which he did not conceal the document's faults but in which he accepted it as it stood; he promised to respect it while at the same time he would try to improve it. He called for a general reconciliation and he obtained an amnesty for all who had been imprisoned because of Varennes. Once again he had overcome a most terrible situation.

While the world in general was in a state of violent agitation, a studied calm reigned at the Tuileries. As much from a sense of dignity as to see his friends and not to forsake his faithful courtiers, the king kept up a court that was rendered more numerous by the diplomats and the bravest of the Parisians. The king's levee and his morning audiences took place in the usual manner of Versailles. There was no more hunting, but if the weather and the circumstances allowed it he would leave at half past nine to take a turn in the Bois de Boulogne. At noon he came back for mass, which was celebrated in the very dilapidated Tuileries chapel; he heard it in a side gallery in the choir, and he would usually appear in his 'collarless myrtle-green coat, edged with a narrow green embroidery'. His white silk waistcoat, embroidered in white, his black silk breeches, his white stockings and his gold-buckled shoes showed how very little attention he paid to dress. He went there to pray, and he did pray. Then came the day's work, the long interview with the ministers, the stealthy exchanges with his real friends . . . At half past nine, supper. After dinner and after supper the king played billiards with Elisabeth, so as to take a little exercise. At eleven everyone went to bed, though very often the king worked far on into the night.

He was working for France, which was assailed on every hand. He worked alone, with two loyal helpers, Breteuil abroad and Arnaud de Laporte in France. He knew that he was threatened with death, and he openly made ready for it. He was no longer linked to the queen by any sort of intimacy whatever, for she was obsessed by her love for Fersen and politically she was entirely under Mercy's domination. Fortunately Vermond had fled. Yet she remained a stranger to her husband, whom she despised; and she hid her own personal policy from him – friendship with Barnave, collaboration with the triumvirs, appeals for violence against France in her letters to Gustavus III, Leopold II, etc.

His brothers were working against him, too, and so were the émigrés, who dreamed of nothing but revenge and the reconquest of France.

Louis XVI had to beware of everybody. His slightest movements were spied upon, and the least imprudence might be his ruin. His attitude towards the constitution would be judged by his choice of ministers. They were to anger neither the majority nor the minority; they were also to remain loyal to the king, and they too were to be wary in all their proceedings and suspicious with regard to their subordinates. The Jacobins had succeeded in introducing their spies into the highest reaches of the civil service; there was a certain Bonjour, for example, in the Admiralty, a most notorious informer. In order to butter up his minister he would begin work every day by drinking a bottle of capital wine with him, sitting on the corner of his desk.

The king wanted to make a good beginning with the new Assembly. He let Montmorin go, for the minister was too weak and too deeply compromised, and in any case he wanted to leave. He would have liked Moustier, a wholly reliable man, but Moustier was rejected as an aristocrat; he wanted Barthélemi, but Barthélemi would not come; and Ségur, but Ségur refused because of the queen. They would not even have Montmorin as minister without portfolio. In the end he took Lessart, whom he knew and valued.

For the Admiralty, he called upon Bertrand de Molleville, who declared himself incapable. 'Where am I supposed to find my ministers?' said the king to him angrily. 'And what is supposed to become of me, if the people who are on my side refuse me their services and abandon me?' Bertrand accepted.

In this group he had only one friend of whom he could be quite certain, Arnaud de Laporte, the minister of the civil list. Sickened by all he saw around him, he had begged the king to allow him to resign; but at the sight of the tears in his master's eyes he threw himself at his feet, promising to remain at his disposal until the end. Louis XVI was of those leaders who cannot be served without being loved and admired.

Louis XVI relied upon a secret service; he helped the Feuillants (the club that supported the monarchy and the constitution), subsidizing their publication *Le Logographe*; and he obtained information about the Jacobins by means of thirty-five spies, who were paid from three to ten francs. These men attended the sittings of the Assembly and the clubs, visited the Palais-Royal, the Tuileries, the cafés and the taverns. They cheered or hissed or presented motions in the clubs, and they drew up a report for the king. Their leader was named Clermont. Durand was at the head of another network; he tried to buy Brissot, Isnard, Vergniaud, Guadet and Fauchet for six thousand livres a month, just as Danton had been bought for a hundred thousand écus[1] in 1790. Lessart thought them too expensive. It was easy enough to buy politicians, but hard to get value for one's money.

Let it not be supposed that Louis XVI was reduced to corrupting innocence. Through her agent Miles, England was distributing gold among the Jacobins; so was Prussia, by means of the Jew Ephraïm. Danton had been and Lebrun was in English pay. Talleyrand received bribes from every side on every occasion. Some courtiers could point out how to purchase whole blocks of deputies, as did Brémond with Gouverneur Morris, the minister of the United States. Louis XVI, La Fayette and Robespierre took nothing from anyone. This was known; and it had its weight.

There were also magnanimous people to be found: the banker Laborde edited a royalist paper and distributed it among the masonic lodges, to bring them over to the monarchist side!

[1] The écu or crown was three livres.

Chapter IX

The King brought low

NO ONE THOUGHT MUCH OF THE DEPUTIES, AND THEY KNEW it: the easiest way of raising themselves in the public eye was to debase the king, the most highly respected man in the nation. At the very beginning the Assembly decreed that it was to be 'independent of the king's will when he was present, and that therefore they should be seated before the king sat down, that he should have a chair no different from that of the president, and that when he was spoken to he should no longer be called by the title of Sire or Majesty but always as King of the French.' These were not trivial measures, for men always end up by acting according to their thoughts and thinking according to their actions.

Once this point was dealt with, the seventy conforming priests in the Assembly launched their campaign against their non-juring brethren. Everyone was in favour of this, the Jacobins out of hatred for Christianity, the Feuillants out of love for the constitution, and the royalists out of the hope that it would make the people rebel. The Assembly faced the non-jurors with the choice between a new oath and exile. Now the oath was schismatic. The non-juring bishops met in Paris and urged the king to refuse. 'It is quite certain that I shall not agree to that!' replied the king warmly. On his ministers' advice he vetoed the law, without explanation. Cahier de Gerville advised him to take conforming chaplains in order to silence the evilly disposed. 'No, sir,' cried the king. 'No. Do not talk to me about it; let me be left in peace upon that matter. When the freedom of worship was established it was made general; I must therefore have a right to it.'

The year was ending badly; the king knew that in the event of a foreign or a civil war all was lost for him, for his family and for tradition. Yet everybody wanted war – the émigrés in order to smash the Revolution, the Jacobins to take over power, the Fayettists to bring forward their hero, whose victories would raise him to the highest summit . . . The only ones to hold out against the madness were Lameth, Barnave and Duport, all intelligent men, and Robespierre, acting upon the impulse of a brilliant instinct. Unhappily the Assembly looked upon a conflict as the necessary way out of a situation which had become hopelessly entangled by six years of upheaval.

The same kind of madness was spreading among the rulers. Catherine II, in the act of swallowing up Poland, wanted to see the other powers busy elsewhere. Frederick William II had too fine an army not to take advantage of it: England subsidized the Jacobins, the revolutionary leaders and the deputies, and at the same time she claimed not to be interfering in France's affairs in the least. What luck for Pitt if the French were to rid him of his most dangerous enemy, Louis XVI! Leopold, the most intelligent of the sovereigns, preferred peace. He signed it with Turkey, and he handled France with great care, but he could not remain unmoved by his sister's appeals. At one time he took measures to expel the émigrés from the Rhineland, as the Legislative Assembly asked; then he announced that he should protect the German princes with possessions in France who had been deprived of them by the French laws (10 December 1791); he informed France that his troops in the Low Countries would protect Treves should the necessity arise (21 December), and he stigmatized the Jacobins. In this way he satisfied no one, delaying the war without avoiding it.

During the long winter evenings the king revolved these

problems in his mind. Peace was the greatest of blessings; but could there be peace in Europe so long as France, too powerful for her wild disorder not to make her neighbours anxious and too wealthy for her disarray not to attract greedy eyes, had no peace at home?

In this perilous state of affairs the king alone was qualified to carry on the country's foreign policy. Condorcet and the well-informed men in the Assembly knew this. But the jealousy of the deputies did not allow him to do so. He was perpetually hampered. In September 1791 the émigrés published a violent protest against him and his decision to accept the constitution. He at once replied by a proclamation calling for peace between all Frenchmen, inviting the émigrés to return and praising the harmony and tolerance that reigned in France. Monsieur took no notice, but laid claim to the regency, lest Orléans should grasp it by sudden violence. Calonne, who was henceforward Monsieur's 'minister', never ceased working against Breteuil. Meanwhile the Assembly, on 30 October, required the princes to return to France within two months and sequestrated their property. On 9 November it published a decree ordering the émigrés to disperse. The feelings of the nation were being roused against them.

In view of the mounting tumult, the king needed a guard that he could rely upon. The Constituent Assembly had voted him one, but as a measure of prudence he decided to make up its numbers half from the army and half from the National Guard – each department was to send him four men elected by their comrades. There was a flood of requests. In order to be able to spy on the king more effectively, the Jacobins, who controlled the departments, had Jacobin soldiers elected. The Paris National Guard, which had been guarding the king since October 1789, declared that its feelings were wounded. The king gave way, leaving them the palace duty, to be carried out together with the new guard. He even had to make an appeal to their better feelings to induce them to obey. Yet he had every reason to feel doubtful of their affection: one day towards the end of November a corporal had taken it into his head to shut the king and queen in their apartments from nine in the evening until nine in the morning for two

days in succession, without a word. Accustomed to harsh treatment and too proud to protest, they remained silent; it might have
lasted a great while, if a good-hearted grenadier had not told the
captain. The corporal had acted without orders, and he was
court-martialled.

It was hoped that the king would make changes in his court,
and it would have been a shrewd stroke; but he had neither the
time nor the heart. 'The queen really cannot be asked to mix with
the wives of Pétion or Condorcet or women of that kind,' he
said. 'As for me, most of the men whose attendance I liked most in
my former household have abandoned me, and among those that
have remained there are some who make my life a torment . . .'
He was thinking of Chauvelin, who was always about him,
acting as a spy: the only way he could get rid of him was to send
him as ambassador to England, where Talleyrand was lurking.
People looked askance at Talleyrand in London, and Chauvelin
acted as a screen for him; everybody was pleased, particularly
Louis XVI.

The ministers urged him to appoint the officers of his household. They were filled with longing at the thought of all these
lucrative places! He made use of craft to gain time, asking each to
write a report that could be discussed in council. Meanwhile
Narbonne was plotting to become minister of foreign affairs or
indeed chief minister, and he was backed by Mme de Staël and
La Fayette, whom the king had just appointed commander of one
of the three French armies, together with Rochambeau and
Luckner. Furious at his lack of success, Narbonne revealed his
colleagues' plan for providing the king with a majority in the
Assembly. This caused a quarrel with Bertrand, who was supported by Duport. Brissot intervened with a violent attack upon
Bertrand and the generals came out in favour of Narbonne. The
king settled the confusion by dismissing first Narbonne and then
Bertrand (9 March).

On 10 March the king's reply to the Assembly, stating that in
spite of the Assembly's denunciation he did not find Bertrand
guilty, arrived at the same time as the news of Narbonne's dismissal. A storm blew up immediately. Brissot and the Girondins

passed a motion stating that Narbonne carried the nation's regrets with him. At the same time Narbonne denounced Lessart in the most violent and damaging terms, and the Assembly passed a decree for his arrest. The unfortunate Lessart was at once sent to Orléans, there to appear before the national high court. This galvanized the other ministers with alarm, and they instantly resigned.

They were so afraid that as they left they agreed together to advise the king to form a Girondin ministry. This was the undoing of the triumvirs, their protectors, and a fresh set-back for Louis XVI. Yet he was not without weapons against Narbonne, for he held proofs of his plots and his corruption. During his short career in the ministry, this young man had paid all his debts, which were heavy. But the king refrained from making these papers public, for he did not wish to complicate an already very difficult situation. On the contrary, he hoped to bring about a general easing of tension.

He knew an intelligent, dynamic, well-informed officer, M. Dumouriez, who had at one time been employed by Louis XV in his secret service. He was an adventurer, but he was not a democrat; his heart was royalist (it was also somewhat given to straying). His clear-sightedness and his links with the Jacobin leaders made him exceedingly valuable. On 30 October 1791 he had persuaded Laporte to show the king a daring plan that Louis XVI had thought very wild at first, but circumstances bore out Dumouriez' reasoning, and the king called upon him to form a ministry rather than attempt the high-handed methods suggested by the triumvirs. No longer having any weapons with which to fight his enemies, he hoped to win them over by means of Dumouriez.

The lively spirit of this officer accustomed to military discipline, the clarity of his opinions and the sharp distinction of his reports delighted the king, who had a profound knowledge of men. The first candidates who came to mind were Danton and Collot d'Herbois; but the first had been an agent of the British and the second's mind appeared to be unhinged. Clavière was therefore chosen for finance and Roland for the interior, Duranthon for justice, Lacoste for the Admiralty and the Chevalier de Grave for war, while Dumouriez, the strong man of this ministry, had foreign affairs. He promised to silence the pamphleteers who insulted the royal family and to provide adequate protection against such outrages.

For some days past the wild insults and threats had been breaking out again. 'The time has come for terror to go into that palace from which it has so often issued,' said Vergniaud in the Assembly (10 March). 'Let everyone in it tremble; there is not a single one of them who is inviolable.' There was a rumour that the queen was to be denounced, the king suspended and the Dauphin proclaimed. Without waiting for a moment, Dumouriez set about changing the tone; wearing a red cap, he went to the Jacobins' club and gave them proofs of his brotherly affection. To keep a hold upon his friends he found jobs for the noisiest and the neediest: Bonne Carrère, the former president of the Jacobins' correspondence committee, became a high official in the foreign ministry, together with the journalist Lebrun (who was in the pay of the English agent Miles) and Danton's friend Noël, who had less important posts, while Pache and Lanthenas were given places in the ministry of the interior. It seemed that from the point of view of retaining the central position for himself, Dumouriez had picked the ministers well, but he had forgotten the wives, particularly Roland's (who was also attached to many others). Very soon she came to the fore as the deciding force in this cabinet. She entertained all comers, keeping open house; and she was always ready to talk. Her husband was a dull, pompous man, but he did not stand in her way at all. She was a fiery democrat and she was jealous of Marie-Antoinette: she was the moving spirit of the group.

The Girondins plunged both hands into the royal and the national treasury. In the council Roland uttered improving lectures and Dumouriez carried on with his manœuvres. He wanted a war – a victorious war, of course – to liquidate this wild and raving Assembly. The king attended to what they said; and as he alone understood his calling, he explained the business that came before the council, translating the English and German dispatches. The ministers listened to him, charmed yet suspicious.

Then they would go and sup with Roland and listen to his wife's enthusiastic politics, or with Dumouriez and a band of wenches.

They felt Robespierre pressing them hard, and they wanted war quickly. In the autumn of 1791 he alone had held true to their doctrines and their organization. Since then his standing had grown every day. By means of his friend Couthon he was trying to induce the Assembly to suppress without compensation all feudal rights that were not based upon written documents. His following among the countrymen was therefore increasing. He now came before the Jacobins as the critic of the Girondins, as the defender of peace and as the implacable enemy of royalty. 'They want to make you agree to a transaction that will provide the court with a greater extension of power,' he said. 'What they want is a feigned war that will make a capitulation possible.' Brissot replied, 'Do you want to crush the aristocracy, the rebels and the malcontents all with one blow? Then destroy Coblenz.' Both for the one and the other it was a question of saving the Revolution. For Louis XVI it was a question of France herself. In September 1791 he wrote to his brothers,

> Force can only be brought to bear by foreign armies, and this method means nothing less than having recourse to war. Can a king allow himself to bring war into his own country? And is not the remedy worse than the disease? . . . I know that kings have always prided themselves upon using force to regain what had been taken from them; I know that fearing these disasters in such circumstances is called weakness. But I confess that a reproach of that kind touches me less than the misfortunes of the people, and my heart rebels when I think of the horrors of which I should be the cause.

On 1 March Leopold II suddenly died. This was unfortunate for Louis XVI, whose plan the Emperor had approved. His son Francis had the reputation of a violent, ruthless man. The murder of Gustavus III did away with the Revolution's one determined enemy, at a time when Austria and Prussia were slowly working out the lines of an expedition against France. Much heartened, the Assembly called for war, and the members of the clubs came and roared under the king's windows to insist upon it. Under this pressure, Louis XVI used delaying tactics, questioning the council, listening to the Dumouriez' report in favour of war, requiring each minister to give his opinion in writing. They all wanted war. He gave way. On 20 April he went to the Assembly and speaking in a toneless, muffled voice he proposed the declaration of war against the King of Hungary and Bohemia. Without paying any attention to the Feuillant Becquey, the only man who dared protest, the Assembly voted for war.

In spite of all the boasting of Narbonne, who had claimed that the French armies were well trained and disciplined and that the arsenals were full, the war began with disasters. The army that attacked Flanders, which was expected to rise, was unable to deploy; and at Quiévrain and Tournai the troops fled in causeless panic, murdering their commander, Theobald Dillon. On 6 May the Royal Allemand regiment went over to the enemy, and on 12 May the 4th Saxon Hussars and Berchenyi's regiment did the same. In spite of Custine's taking of Porrentruy these early days revealed the powerlessness of the French army and laid France open to invasion.

The hundred thousand men of the French army were unable to beat forty-one thousand Austrians. The generals distrusted the soldiers, and the soldiers the generals. In Flanders Rochambeau had only reluctantly obeyed the minister's order to attack. La Fayette, so brilliant in America, was hesitant. Many officers deserted. Rochambeau sent in his resignation post-haste. An army without discipline is nothing more than a mob. But the revolutionaries had been preaching undisciplined conduct to the soldiers since 1786. In 1792 not one of them wanted to get himself killed for a war decided upon in Paris by powers that he did not respect, for aims that he did not understand.

Dumouriez was taken aback: he had reckoned upon the Frenchman's fighting instinct. But Louis XVI had foreseen this rout, whose disastrous results were very quickly felt. The factions burst out, all seeking to put the blame for the failures on others. Robespierre cried, 'No, I have no trust whatever in the generals; and making a few honourable exceptions I say that practically all of them regret the former state of affairs and the favours that a court has at its disposal: I base myself upon the people only, the genuine people.' Like Louis XVI he knew that a constitutional monarchy, an intellectual masterpiece, can only live by means of peace; it can bear colonial, but not national wars. To save a country at war what is needed is a clear, distinct idea, a violent passion. He held up the Jacobins and their bands to France, crying 'Behold the people!' And since the troops were no longer to be kept in order by their former devotion to the king, he advocated and planned the Terror, the only efficient means of fixing a general idea into the mass-mind.

Robespierre had formerly been a barrister given to high-flown verbiage; from this time on he appeared as the incarnation of the Enlightenment, pitiless but creative. He was more solitary than the other popular leaders; he grew less involved than they and he went further. In this tragic hour his aim was to bring an ideal France into being, using blood and logic as his means. Marat helped him in this task: the Swiss, misshapen and gifted for cruelty, roared out accusations of treachery at the Cordeliers' club. The Chevalier de Grave, overwhelmed by his responsibilities, resigned from the war ministry. Mme Roland had him replaced by Servan, a furious Girondin who was determined to force the victory. At this the generals rose in protest, among them La Fayette. Brissot's supporters tried to soothe him, sending Marat before the high court and Royou to prison, passing a law upon military discipline and prosecuting Dillon's murderers. La Fayette would have none of it.

Ever since September 1791 La Fayette had suffered too many affronts; the appointment of Servan had been made without consulting him and it was directed against him. Conscious of this, and resenting the insult, he turned against the Jacobins. He became reconciled with the Lameths and Duport, whom he took into his army (May 1792). In agreement with them he sent the Jesuit Lambinet to Mercy, who was then at Brussels, to ask the Emperor for a suspension of arms and a declaration of neutrality so that he might march on Paris with his army, silence the Jacobins, dissolve the National Guard, recall the émigrés and set up a true constitutional monarchy. The moment was most unfortunately chosen. Seeing France's weakness, the allies meant to beat her; and Mercy, Marie-Antoinette's adviser, shared her hatred for La Fayette. He desired La Fayette to address his request to Vienna.

The three commanding generals then decided to halt this disastrous offensive. But Roland did not see matters in this light at all; since he could not use compulsion against the generals, he did as his wife told him and turned against Louis XVI. Persuaded by the Girondins, the Assembly merely filed the notification in which the king informed them that he had chosen M. de Fleurieu as the Dauphin's tutor and asked for their approval. There were violent diatribes against the 'Austrian committee', which was said to be preparing for the victory of the enemy and to be headed by the queen. This attack – which was justified, for the queen kept Mercy informed about the intentions of the French leaders – was repeated all over the town with unbelievable vehemence.

On 27 May, the Assembly, in order to strike at the king, passed a new decree against the non-juring priests, a decree meant to replace that which he had vetoed in December. On 29 May it disbanded the king's guard and handed over its commander, the Duc de Brissac, to the high court. To hit La Fayette, they persecuted the king.

Since the king was now without power over his generals, the stratagem did not answer. Servan thought of a better one – the setting up of a camp of twenty thousand departmental Federates outside Paris to defend the capital against the enemy or against La Fayette. The bill was passed on 8 June. Judging from his agents' information, Louis XVI saw this as the beginning of a *coup d'état* and as a certain cause of grave disorders. On the advice of Duport, who had been seen by Laporte, he vetoed it.

He felt the temperature rising and he wanted to hold on at all costs, so that he might be there when France, recovering from her fever, should look about for support. By way of counteracting the Jacobins and their paid agitators, he succeeded in setting up an organization of his own. This he did with the help of Bertrand and his agent Buob, formerly a magistrate in Alsace and now a judge of the first instance in the Poissonière *section*; the organization saw to the denunciation and condemnation (by Buob) of the most dangerous Jacobin agitators and the ringleaders of the Cordeliers. The judge Larivière was brave enough to condemn Carra, a journalist and one of the most notorious Orléanist agents, who had insulted the king, the queen and the members of the 'Austrian committee'. Larivière also had the courage to issue summonses against Basire, Chabot and Merlin, the three extremist Jacobin leaders, who had spoken in the same terms.

This unexpected blow reconciled all the Jacobins; joining forces once more, they carried a motion sending Larivière to Orléans to be brought before the high court, and then another dissolving the king's guard – he was unable to defend them, for he could find no minister to support him. Dumouriez alone reacted violently when he learnt of the planned camp before Paris, which Servan had decided upon without consulting him. In his anger he at once attacked Servan, giving Louis XVI his endorsement (constitutionally necessary for the king's signature to be valid) for the veto of the bill. Duport and his officials confirmed the gravity of the danger.

Outraged by this obstinacy, Roland sent him a grossly insulting homily, written by his wife (10 June). At the same time the king learnt that there was a plot to seize him and keep him in the Languedoc under the supervision of Protestant National Guards. Very strongly moved, he dismissed Roland, Clavière and Servan, though at the same time he desired Dumouriez to remain, together with Lacoste and Duranthon. The Assembly was furious; it passed a motion stating that the three dismissed ministers 'took with them the nation's regrets' and it hooted Dumouriez; he took fright, and begged the king to sign the decree, otherwise there was a danger of his being killed. The king scorned death. He held out and replaced the resigning Dumouriez and the Girondins by four Feuillants introduced by Duport (Lajard, war; Chambonas, foreign affairs; Terrier de Monciel, interior; Beaulieu, finance). Lacoste, Duranthon and Laporte remained. The rage of the ousted Girondins burst forth in senseless, slanderous rumours – the king was preparing for peace with Austria (16 June), the king was insisting upon an amnesty for the émigrés, and so on. Meanwhile La Fayette, meaning to support the king, sent him and the Assembly a diatribe against the dismissed ministers, Dumouriez and the clubs. The letter was read in the Assembly on 18 June, and there it aroused a smothered fury. The Girondins, who had long been La Fayette's accomplices and the recipients of his pay, dared not turn against him when he was out of their reach, in the midst of his troops and in possession of innumerable proofs of their venality. Since they could not get at him, they would give him a terrible lesson by trampling on the king.

As early as 16 June the *districts* of Saint-Antoine and Saint-Marceau were stirred into excitement, on the pretext of commemorating the Oath of the Tennis-Court and protesting against the flight to Varennes. The Girondins made up their minds to go armed to the Tuileries on Wednesday, 20 June, to present the king with petitions to that effect. The departmental council forbade it, but the mayor gave his encouragement. Three municipal officials came to ask the king's permission for the procession to march past through the garden. The king told them to direct it along the Terrasse des Feuillants. In spite of the orders that had been given, the gates into the garden were opened, and at three in the afternoon the rioters tried to force the main door – and it was opened for them by the municipal officials. A flood of sansculottes and women swept into the palace. Throughout the entire building there was the sound of smashing doors.

Acloque, the commander of the National Guards on duty, advised the king to show himself alone. Louis XVI therefore went into his first anteroom and stood upon one of the chests near the windows, surrounded only by the old Maréchal de Mouchy, M. d'Hervilly, Acloque and a dozen grenadiers. A little farther off, pushed up against the panelling, Elisabeth was protected only by the group of ministers and a few guards. In a moment the sansculottes and women filled the room: they threatened the royal family with their pikes, belching out insults and threats against the king and calling for the reappointment of the ministers and the acceptance of the Federals' camp.

'What is it that you want?' Louis XVI asked them. He was so calm, he looked so great a man and so serene that these armed people all fell back before him. Once again the king's gaze caused hatred to withdraw.

He wanted to take advantage of this to speak to them, but the ringleaders broke in. 'Down with Veto! Down with Madame Veto and all their gang!' they shouted. 'Where is he, so that I can kill him?' roared a pikeman, pointing his weapon. 'You swine,' replied a grenadier, pushing the pike aside, 'that's your king. How dare you look at him?' Another called to the king, 'Sire, you trust in us and never be afraid . . .' 'Afraid?' cried the king, 'Put your hand on my heart and see if it beats any faster.' The first crowd to get in, impressed by the king's firmness, were growing calmer. But a fresh swarm armed with pikes rushed in, howling and brandishing their weapons. The grenadiers replied with a 'Long live the king!' that was lost in the incessant insults. There were phrases that kept returning, like the burden of a song – 'Recall the ministers' and 'Agree to the Federals.' The procession lasted four hours. As a challenge or perhaps as a form of protection the king and Madame Elisabeth had been thrown red caps, which they put on their heads. The slightest clash would have meant instant death. But the king's serenity and Elisabeth's courage inspired everyone with respect. Vergniaud and Isnard came and harangued the crowd, telling them to go away: nobody listened. Finally Pétion made his appearance. He congratulated the mob upon the orderly dignity with which it had marched and called upon it to withdraw. Since he was the paymaster, they obeyed. The palace emptied.

Louis XVI had dominated the crowd by his majestic bearing; many of the sansculottes had felt pity for him, and many women had cried. He was able to rejoin the queen, who had been besieged in another part of the palace, much more agitated than her husband. But she was soothed, and a group of two hundred grenadiers protected her. So it all came to an end without any massacre; but this riot was certainly to be the precursor of others. This could be felt from one end of the country to the other, and now public opinion seemed to be rising up against it. The Department of Paris, made up of Feuillants, expressed its indignation by suspending Pétion and Manuel. Some deputies came to the Tuileries on 21 June to ask the king to remove to the Assembly as soon as he saw any danger, and they promised him their protection. Addresses expressing devotion to the king came flooding into the palace from the provinces, and the Assembly was overwhelmed with petitions calling for the closing of the Jacobins' club. In Paris one of these petitions, deposited with the notary Guillaume, received more than twenty thousand signatures. Many of the departmental assemblies censured Pétion and his hordes. In the Ardèche and in Lower Brittany the royalists raised their heads and gathered together in armed troops.

La Fayette himself came to Paris on 28 June to call upon the Assembly to dissolve the Jacobins and to punish those responsible for 20 June. He was greeted with tumultuous applause by the deputies, who rejected the censure motion set up against him by 339 votes to 234. Fate seemed to be rewarding the king's patience and to be bringing the hearts of his people back to him. Once more he found it possible to hope to win by force of endurance, by clinging to the people's love. Would they be mad enough to let themselves be swept along by this terror which the revolutionaries saw as the only remaining means of democratizing France, now that they had ruined the country, brought it low and led it into defeat? Or would they recover their senses? Thus the king's prayer rose towards heaven.

Yet once again faction ruined everything. La Fayette was planning a sudden violent stroke: he intended to raise the National Guard against the Jacobins in the course of a review. Pétion was told by the queen, who hated her former gaoler, and he cancelled the ceremony. That evening only a hundred men appeared at the general's rendezvous at the Champ de Mars. An abortive attempt. All it accomplished now was to compromise the king, who was looked upon as his accomplice, and to reunite the Jacobins and Girondins.

The Girondins, more eloquent and greedy than intelligent, wanted to compel the king to give them back their ministerial posts. On 28 June Brissot and Robespierre, both speaking at the Jacobins' club, called for the punishment of La Fayette. In the Assembly the Girondins turned to the most deadly methods; they threatened the Feuillant ministers with impeachment, and they subjugated all the administrative bodies by forcing them to hold nothing but public sessions which the clubs would dominate. And lastly on 2 July they authorized the provincial National Guards to come to Paris for 14 July and granted them their travelling expenses and billeting orders. Thus the king's veto was circumvented. This mobilization was completed by orders sent out to the departmental clubs.

To the turmoil of politics was added the fever of war. The Prussians were massing on the Rhine. Luckner, having attempted an offensive in Belgium, took Courtrai, lost it, and then fell back before Lille: France was invaded. On 6 July the king told the Assembly of the peril; he had gone there to announce the advance of the Duke of Brunswick and the King of Prussia with an army of Prussians, Austrians and French émigrés. On 3 July Vergniaud had openly threatened the king as the man responsible for the generals' inaction; and finally on 10 July the Assembly proclaimed 'the country in danger'. All the administrative bodies were to remain in permanent session and all the National Guards were called up. Batallions of volunteers were raised and in Paris fifteen thousand men enlisted in a few days. The whole of France was in a fever.

The king saw the danger. At the end of June he wrote to Father Hébert, 'Come to see me today: I have done with men and I look only to Heaven.' He did not fear death, but nevertheless he struggled. He sent the Swiss Mallet du Pan to his brothers and the allied sovereigns, to tell Artois and Provence to hold back and leave everything to him, and to ask the powers to display strength and moderation and to publish a declaration promising to respect the integrity of the kingdom, the nation's independence and private property, to state that they were opposed only to an 'anti-social fraction', but that the Assembly, the clubs or individuals guilty of violence against the king or his family would be punished and lastly that they undertook to treat only with the king and to insist upon his freedom. An intelligent plan. Words of this kind might have had a decisive influence at this moment, when the French nation was deep in weariness.

The king was speaking to people who could not or would not hear. The émigrés, feeling themselves supported, burst out in threats; the queen encouraged them in her wild letters to Fersen; the same kind of fury, but in reverse, reigned in France; addresses drawn up by the Jacobins reached the Assembly from all the great towns, threatening the king and calling for his deposition. The ministers tried to persuade him to denounce faction in the Assembly, but he would not, and they resigned in a body on 10 July. Every day Paris was filling with little groups of Federates, whom the clubs enrolled at once. The Cordeliers adopted the men from Marseilles and worked them up to a white heat of enthusiasm. On 13 July the Assembly revoked Pétion's suspension and restored him to office, thus setting up the king's most inveterate enemy against him once more.

In the face of so many dangers, La Fayette and Luckner suggested to Louis XVI that they should bring about his escape on 15 July. The cavalry would cover his flight in the direction of Compiègne. After that the army would protect him and peace would be made with the foreign powers. The queen opposed this plan out of hatred for La Fayette, and in the end the king renounced it, not thinking it sufficiently well worked out. He therefore confronted the Federation entirely by himself, with no other support than his faith in God.

On that day the king once more dominated a monstrous uproar. As his guard he had the monarchist battalion of the Filles-Saint-Thomas, which gave him unwavering protection. Furthermore, his calmness, Elisabeth's charm and the Dauphin's beauty inspired universal respect. Only the anxious little face of Madame Royale and the queen's trembling gave the crowd a certain hold. They had to go to the Champ de Mars, as they had done in 1790. The long march-past of a bawling mob, the pompous, meaningless ceremony, the dreadful, barren oath, joined to the din of fifty-four guns all firing at once would have been nothing without the shouts of 'Long live Pétion! Long live the beggars! Long live the brigands! Down with Madame Veto! Down with the Austrian woman!' which went on and on for an hour. The king took the oath; but when he was asked whether he wished to set fire to the tree loaded with red and blue ribbons, coats of arms and crowns that symbolized feudalism, he looked the president straight in the face and replied, 'There is no feudalism any more.' Then he walked back to the gallery where his wife and children were waiting for him. During the march-past the troops alone, but all the troops, displayed their respect for him. They all shouted 'Long live the king!' as they saw him coming back safe into the courtyard of the military school. They were amazed at his safety, as if it had been a miracle.

The next day came the reaction: the Assembly decreed that the regiments of the line and the Swiss should move away from Paris; petitions came in calling for the suspension of the king and the impeachment of La Fayette; one deputy suggested impeaching the whole army, and he was cheered.

However, the resignation of the ministers had made the Girondins monarchist once more. The worthy Thierry, who had some very odd connexions, and the painter Boze brought the king letters from Vergniaud, Gensonné and Guadet, to whom the king and queen granted an interview. In the Assembly the Girondins turned against the factious members; Brissot called for 'the sword of the law against those who wanted to violate the constitution and set up a republic.'

Too late! Robespierre was in control of events. It was hot, the Federates drank, and Robespierre, the Incorruptible, held forth against the traitor La Fayette and the weak and flabby Assembly. He called for the deposition of the king, the dissolution of the Assembly and the election of a constituent body chosen by all the citizens to make a democratic constitution. He was wildly cheered; the *sections* remained in permanent session, organizing a central committee. A violent seizure of power was being openly prepared.

Brunswick's manifesto, drawn up by Fersen, came like a thunder-clap in this stormy atmosphere. Its arrogant tone, its harsh threats, its presumptuous claim to re-establish an absolute monarchy in France and to punish the guilty 'with fire and sword' could not but arouse furious anger in the minds of the French and provide the revolutionaries with a powerful weapon. The indignant Louis XVI could not understand how his thoughts could possibly have been so distorted. As early as 3 August he wrote to the Assembly to disavow this intolerable publication and to remind them of his behaviour in the whole affair.

France finds herself threatened by a great combination of forces. Let us all acknowledge the need for unity. Calumny will find it difficult to believe the pain my heart feels at the sight of the dissensions that exist at present and the misfortunes that are being prepared for the future. But those who know the value I set upon the life and the happiness of the people will believe in my feelings and my sorrow. I brought a love of peace to the throne, because peace, which is the most important need of nations, is the most important duty of kings.

Having recalled all that he had done to avoid this war, he ended,

'My duty was to work for the happiness of the people, and and I have done my duty; that is enough for the heart of an upright man. No one shall ever see me compromise on the glory and the interests of the nation, nor bow to the dictation of foreigners or a party. It is to the nation that I owe myself, and the nation and I are one; there is no interest of any kind that can separate me from it; the voice of the nation alone shall guide me, and to my last breath I shall maintain the nation's independence. Personal dangers are nothing in comparison to public misfortunes; and in any case what do personal dangers mean to a king from whom certain interests wish to take his people's love! That is where my heart has been most cruelly wounded . . .'

Louis XVI raised his voice above the tumult, and his last cry to the mob that insulted him was a father's appeal.

Those about him thought that all was lost and they wanted to get him into safety. La Fayette kept his cavalry as near to Compiègne as possible and once more he sent an agent to Brussels – Masson de Saint-Amand, who was charged with asking first for a truce and then for Spanish mediation with a view to peace. Duport bought Pétion, Santerre and Delacroix for a million. Danton had been paid fifty thousand écus. Fabre d'Eglantine obtained his neutrality by negotiation, and Brémond, helped by

N

Morris, raised a kind of royal army, recruited from the most violent of the revolutionaries, to cover the king's departure, or, when the king had once again refused to leave, to do battle with the rioters. The sum of 550,000 francs in louis was put up in little purses to be distributed in this way.

Through his spies Robespierre knew everything: on 4 August he denounced a conspiracy on the part of the court for the king's escape. A secret directory was set up to lead the assault. This also became known. Trembling with fear, the Assembly hurriedly brought about a reconciliation among its members: on 7 August they all gave one another the kiss of peace. The next day the Assembly wholly acquitted La Fayette of all the charges against him. Its voting was the effect of fear and nothing else. In every part of Paris the extremists were preaching rebellion.

The inhabitants of the palace could no longer go out. Huge placards had been set up, the one on the Terrasse des Feuillants reading 'The land of freedom' and the other, in the garden of the Tuileries, 'The land of Coblentz.' As soon as the royal family appeared they were hooted from all sides. The terrified queen wrote imploring letters to Fersen: 'It is clear that the king's life is threatened . . . and the queen's, too.' 'The band of murderers is perpetually increasing.' 'A single day's delay may cause incalculable misfortune . . .'

Countless rumours filled the town on 3 August. It was said that the people were going to compel the Assembly to declare the king deposed, and that all Paris was about to rise in rebellion. An astonishing noise was heard on the night of 4-5 August. The king was told. 'What do they want of me now?' he cried. 'Let them come! For a long while now I have been ready for everything.' He forbade his people to wake the queen and he went back to sleep. It was the Federates changing their quarters.

The days of 7 and 8 August were scorchingly hot and calm. Was the disorder going to burn itself out? If so, there was no doubt that the monarchy would revive. Or would it destroy the king? Each side made preparations. With the military leaders the king examined the palace's means of defence. It was the Jacobins who moved the faster. During the night of 9-10 August Cara,

Chaumette, Santerre and Alexandre raised the Federates.

The tocsin rang out. A revolutionary municipality replaced Pétion and his gang. Mandat, the commander of the National Guard, was summoned to the Hôtel de Ville and quickly tried and found guilty – he was a royalist. Then, as he was being led to prison, they murdered him. The defence of the palace no longer had a chief. The Commune appointed Santerre head of the militia.

The king, warned by his agents, informed the Department of Paris, pointing out that if they were to order the National Guards to attack, the Federates, more noisy than courageous, would disperse, and the suburbs would return to order. The members of the Department, having consulted the National Guard, replied that they could defend, but not attack.

The Assembly carried on with its discussions, without reaching any decision. In the palace no one slept; the ministers spent the night there; the queen, in a state of great tension, paced from room to room. Having said his prayers, the king rested in his bed-chamber. He took care, however, to send a messenger to the Assembly, asking for some representative members to be sent to him. There was no reply.

At five o'clock the children woke, and at six the king came out on to his balcony: a great cheer from the loyal troops greeted him. He went down into the courtyard and passed along their ranks. When he was opposite the Carrousel gate the Federates saw him and shouted, 'Down with the king! Long live the nation!' A savage tumult spread throughout the whole neighbourhood.

Roederer, the departmental public prosecutor, harangued the troops, calling upon them to defend the king, the law and themselves. A small minority of the National Guard seemed determined to do so; but the artillery-men, as their only reply, unloaded the guns. In the Assembly the petrified deputies stood waiting.

Surrounded by his loyal friends, the king meant to die with them; he was told of Mandat's murder; a little later Roederer came back with a deputation from the departmental directory. 'Defence is impossible,' he said. 'To save yourself, your family and all these good people, take refuge in the Assembly. Leave this palace – there is not a moment to be lost.'

N 2

Louis XVI would have preferred death, but the sight of his children, his friends and his servants decided him. Once again his humanity took precedence over his other feelings. Followed by his ministers and a score of the gentlemen of his court, he crossed the Terrasse des Feuillants, protecting his wife and children as well as he could.

In the Assembly he said, 'I have come here to avoid a great crime, and I think I could not be in a safer place than among you, gentlemen.' Guadet, the president of the Assembly, replied with a pompous, kindly speech. He had the king and his family led to the box reserved for the editor of *Le Logographe*. Gentlemen dressed as National Guards stood at the doors. Outside, there was the sound of battle.

The rioters wanted blood. The National Guard, the sections and the artillery had left the palace: nevertheless, the Federates attacked it. The Swiss and the gentlemen put up a good defence. The Tuileries flowed in blood.

The reign of Louis XVI was coming to an end in an apotheosis of horror: that of the Terror was beginning.

Chapter X

The King a prisoner

SHUT INTO THEIR NARROW BOX IN THE FULL SUN, THE
royal family sat suffering there in a daze. The sound of gunfire
brought the king from his hidden prayers. He had already given
orders for the fighting to stop. Once again he wrote the order,
commanding the Swiss to leave the palace and their officers to
take refuge with him. The Federates had burst into the Tuileries
and they were killing everyone they met – guards, Swiss, menservants, maids, kitchen-boys, more than nine hundred people –
and the whole place was sacked. Throughout Paris the statues of
the kings were thrown down, all the emblems of royalty destroyed,
the names of the streets changed and suspects arrested. In the
Assembly a third of the members remained in session: one after
another 'patriots' appeared at the bar of the house, bringing the
broken remnants of pillage, jewels, silver, assignats and papers,
and over and over again they denounced the king. Pain and
physical weariness overwhelmed the refugees in the *Logographe*
box. From time to time some faithful friend would bring a
little water, a glass of orgeat, something to eat, or news of the
situation.

This lasted for fourteen hours. A little after midnight Vergniaud, speaking in the name of the extraordinary commission, announced that there would shortly be a meeting of a 'National Convention', the mouthpiece of the people's will; he also announced the 'provisional suspension' of the head of the executive, who would receive a salary but not his civil list. The defeated Legislative Assembly was abandoning the crown! France, with neither a legislative nor an executive authority, was submitting to the dictatorship of the Jacobins, who ruled through fear. It was fear that put the words into Vergniaud's mouth, and it was fear that obliged the deputies to have placards posted up at every cross-roads reading 'The king has been suspended: he and his family are held as hostages.' Only the king was not afraid. Shut up for the night with his family in four communicating cells in the Feuillants' convent, he said to Tourzel and Aubier, 'Some people regret that I did not have the rebels attacked before they broke into the Arsenal; but apart from the fact that by the terms of the constitution the National Guards would have refused to be the aggressors, what would such an attack have gained? The plan was too well laid for it to have been possible for my side to have won without even leaving the Tuileries. It must not be forgotten that the moment the factious Commune had M. Mandat murdered it made all his arrangements for the defence of the palace useless.' He was certain that he had always obeyed his conscience, and he regretted nothing. Indeed, he took a pleasure in this fate, as in a terrible gift from God. *Amor Fati.*

Outraged Europe recognized the divine hand in these terrible events. Louis XVI, the only Bourbon apart from Henri IV always to remain popular, to work only for the people whom he loved, never allowing himself to be distracted or sullied by the life of a court, and the only one never to have experienced anything but victory – this king received a horrible punishment. He was the prisoner of an Assembly itself the prisoner of the Jacobins, and he was denounced as being guilty of the people's rising 'provoked by his own infractions'. Yet he was the only man in the country who obeyed that raving constitution whose ruin the Legislative Assembly had just accomplished by confirming the revolutionary

Commune, by summoning a Convention elected by universal suffrage, and by suspending the king until the meeting of the Convention, which would decide upon the matter! They were not yet too frightened to repudiate nine hundred years of history.

From now onwards the King of France was at the mercy of the dregs of the population, an outlaw with no money to buy bread, no linen for himself or his children. Out of pity the officers of the Cent-Suisses sent him a few shirts, and the Duchesse de Gramont and the English ambassador's wife provided clothes for the queen and the Dauphin.

For three nights they slept at the convent, spending the day in the *Logographe* box, enduring perpetual insults. Ministers were appointed: Roland (interior), Clavière (finance), Monge (navy), Danton (justice) and Lebrun (foreign affairs) – the last two had been in the pay of England. The real power remained with the Commune, which was controlled by Robespierre; it insisted upon keeping the royal family, that token and trophy of its victory, an invaluable weapon for making fear radiate in every direction!

The Assembly wanted to intern the king in the Luxembourg palace and then in the Chancellerie; the Commune fixed upon the Temple. By the Commune's order the king was refused the half score of servants whose names he mentioned. Yet his insistence over-awed his gaolers, and he was granted six attendants for his whole family. The mayor and the Commune's attorney, who led the royal family to the Temple, ostentatiously kept their hats on before Louis XVI and only called him Monsieur. His coach was stopped for a moment in the Place Vendôme so that he should see the statue of Louis XIV overturned, broken and trampled under foot by the crowd. 'This is how tyrants are treated,' shouted the sansculottes. The vast demolition of France was beginning in its palaces and its churches. The new religion allowed only civic beauty – no other kind at all. At the Temple, Louis XVI still imagined that he would live in the palace, where the Contis and after them Artois had dwelt. In order to make the blow all the harder they did not undeceive him. The apartments were full of sentries, who never took their eyes off the royal family for a moment. At ten they had a little supper and the representatives of the municipality withdrew. At eleven the king and all his family were taken to the tower, which was to be their lodging. The king's room was on the second floor; it was lit by a single window and its furniture consisted of three chairs and a miserable bed. A verminous old hurdle lay in an uncurtained alcove. The king displayed neither surprise nor ill-temper. Having said his prayers he took the prints down from the walls, for he thought them unseemly, and went to bed. He slept well. Every hour, outside the door, there was the heavy tread of the sentries relieving one another. They looked in, keeping watch on him.

From the first day Louis XVI made an orderly arrangement of his life. As soon as he was dressed (six o'clock) he said his prayers and read in the little tower that opened out of his bedroom. At nine, breakfast. Then he went to see his family, walked with the children in the garden between one and two, and supped with them. Then he went back to his tower and read. At eleven, bed. He was reading the *Imitation of Christ*. The day was spent in the queen's room, on the first floor, looking over the garden.

Every day their treatment grew harsher: hoods over the windows, continual supervision, etc. Yet the palace catering service still prepared their meals and the queen obtained a new wardrobe, thirty seamstresses working upon it: Louis XVI was voted a civil list of five hundred thousand francs, which he was not paid! Sometimes Pétion would write to him as 'Sire'. Often a soldier would show his sympathy for them, or a voice outside would sing a royalist song. But the guards presented arms with the butt in the air as a mark of dishonour, and if they were seen from outside there were shouts of 'Long live Pétion!' or 'Down with the Austrian woman!' The captive's greatest suffering is the total loss of privacy.

During the night of 29 August their last servants were taken away from them and imprisoned, except for Hue, who managed to remain in the king's service. The Revolution was becoming more frenzied: the Assembly voted for a new oath for the civil servants and the priests; they voted for delegating the duty to search for suspects and arrest them to the municipalities, for the arrest of the ministers and of the administrators of the departments of the Rhône-et-Loire, Moselle, Somme . . .

As France was invaded, so the fear mounted higher: the allies surrounded Thionville and took Longwy (27 August). To bring terror to bear, the Assembly set up the extraordinary tribunal that the Commune insisted upon. The situation grew worse: Verdun besieged, a rising in the Vendée, a royalist movement in Dauphiné, ferment in Brittany. Roland and Servan wanted to retreat behind the Loire; Danton wanted to stay in Paris. The crowd was his element and his strength. And if the worst came to the worst he had friends among the allies! However, he ordered domiciliary visits as a reply to the arrival of the uhlans in the Argonne and by way of stimulating the threatened capital.

Hue managed to get the news from the more trusting sentries and from the cries of the newspaper-sellers in the streets. He repeated what he learnt to Madame Elisabeth, who was less closely watched than the king; and when her brother came to her in the embrasure of their window he heard of the tremendous happenings – La Fayette's desertion, the votes in the Assembly, the military defeats, the beheading of Laporte on 24 August . . . Everything was as ominous as the manner in which he was living: he was pitilessly searched, they took his sword away, they refused to bring a physician for his children, they threatened to separate him from them. On 2 September, while priests, nobles, suspects and innocent people were being massacred in all the prisons in Paris, they took his faithful Hue from him.

An officer of the municipal guard came into the room and said, 'Monsieur, you do not know what is happening. The country is in the utmost danger. The enemy has entered Champagne and the King of Prussia is marching upon Châlons. You will be answerable for all the evil that may come out of this. We know that we shall perish, we and our wives and children; but the people shall be revenged and you shall die before us. Yet there is still time, and you can . . .' The king broke in energetically, but without harshness, 'I have done everything for the people; I have nothing to reproach myself with.'

A little later the king caught sight of a bloody head on the end of a pike at the window: with its blond hair, still in curls, it retained a hideous beauty. He recognized Mme de Lamballe. The queen did not see it. But the growing tumult outside went on; and indoors there was a great turmoil that made the king think that they were making ready to kill them. The guards told him that the crowd wanted to see them at the window, but that it should not be so. One of the members of the municipality, who was walking about the room, said to the queen, 'They are trying to hide the woman Lamballe's head from you – it was brought to show you how the people take vengeance on their tyrants. I advise you to show yourself, if you do not want the people to come up here after you.' Hearing this, the queen fainted. The king did not allow any barbarity to shake him: a chance conversation informed him of the abolition of the monarchy. Neither his expression nor his behaviour changed. On 20 September Cléry, who had succeeded the arrested Hue, learnt from an officer of the municipal guard that the king was going to be separated from his family. He was greatly distressed and he thought it his duty to warn his master: he did so with a great deal of holding back. 'You could not give me a greater proof of your attachment,' said the king. 'I must insist that in your loyalty you hide nothing from me; I am prepared for everything; try to discover the date of this painful separation and tell me of it.' It took place on 29 September, after the king's papers and writing materials had been seized.

September 1792: elections for the Convention. They were dominated by fear: the only people to vote were the Jacobins, their friends and those whom they had terrorized. The seven hundred and fifty elected members were determined to carry on in the spirit of 10 August. The situation forced this upon them: the currency was collapsing, unemployment spreading, the ports emptying, bread growing scarce and rising in price. Disorder everywhere. Throughout France life was growing so difficult and the incompetence of the government so staringly obvious that the country was ready to give itself up to the first authority who should dare to rule.

If he had been able to prevent the disaster of 10 August, now would have been the moment for the king; the voluntary surrender of the eastern towns was a certain mark of this, and the harsh treatment inflicted upon him was the proof. If he had not been a dangerous rival nobody would have thought of imprisoning him, persecuting him and perhaps killing him. They began by executing men who had worked with him, such as Laporte and his supporters – du Rozoi, Cazotte and d'Angremont, for example. But the Gironde, which had come back to the Convention in great numbers, did not appear to have the least desire for this solution for Louis XVI. Their leaders were men who profited by the Revolution rather than revolutionaries. They knew the king, and he filled them with respect. After all their negotiations, deals and bargains with the court they were afraid of revelations that would be their ruin. Garat, the minister of justice, therefore delayed the king's trial as much as he possibly could. The question was brought before the legislative committee on 16 October, and it appointed Mailhe chairman of a committee to inquire into it; on 7 November he presented his report to the Assembly: yes, they had the right to judge the king, since he had violated the constitution that declared him inviolable. Besides, the meeting of the Convention had rendered that constitution invalid. Since 10 August Louis had once more become an ordinary citizen, liable to judgment under the penal code like any other. He should be judged by the whole nation: the Convention, which was the epitome of the nation and which represented it, should judge him. Mailhe ended by asking that three commissioners should collect the evidence for the crimes of which Louis XVI was accused and draw up the indictment. By a vehement harangue Saint-Just carried the day. But Buzot and Danton began their manœuvres by requiring that all the Bourbons should be brought to judgment.

Returning from London, Théodore de Lameth enlisted Danton's greed for money on the king's side (October 1792). Danton swore to do everything possible to prevent the trial; for, he said, 'Once the trial begins he is dead.' He was preparing a plot when on 20 November he was stopped by another: Louis XVI's papers were produced. They were said to have been handed over by Gamain, his locksmith, and to have come from some mysterious hiding-place. The documents relating to Mirabeau, Talon, Talleyrand and others proved the venality of the men behind the Revolution. Once more they whipped up the highest degree of hatred. On 21 November the Convention appointed a commission of twelve members to make an inventory of these documents. The Montagnards roused the sections, which came to protest against the slowness of the proceedings and to denounce Roland. The terrified Girondins gave way; on 3 December Barbaroux demanded that the king should be brought to trial. Robespierre at once called for the death penalty.

> A dethroned king in a republic is good only for two things, either to disturb the peace of the state and imperil its freedom, or to strengthen both the one and the other at the same time ... Now which is the choice that a right-thinking policy calls for to consolidate a republic that is just coming into existence? The right choice is one that will engrave contempt for royalty ineradicably in the citizens' hearts and stun all the king's supporters ...

He was calling for a ritual crime to strengthen the republic.

This time the Gironde was too frightened. Replying to the Incorruptible, Buzot said that no doubt those who wished to rush on with the king's trial had an interest in preventing him from speaking. Finding the Girondins so stubborn, Marat thought out the method of subjecting them to the mob. At his suggestion the Convention decreed that all the votes on the trial should be made individually, by roll-call, under the eyes of the crowd. So on 9 November Robert was able to place the commission's report on Louis XVI's crimes before the Assembly.

The king, entirely shut away, without newspapers, without contacts with the outside world, knew nothing of these discussions. He had been reunited with his family, and his great happiness was to give his son, his *chou d'amour*, his lessons. Most of all he took pleasure in teaching him geography and drawing maps for him. The harsher an imprisonment becomes, the more intense are its remaining joys.

On 7 December Cléry's wife sent to tell him how close the

danger was and in what conditions the king would be examined. As he undressed his master, Cléry told him that his trial would begin in four days and that he would be separated from his family. The next day Louis XVI spoke of it to Marie-Antoinette, who rebelled against this fresh burden. She was less strong than he, and she still had hope: she counted upon Brunswick. His mysterious retreat threw her into despair. Louis XVI, who expected no more from mankind, could not be alarmed by any intrigues.

At five in the morning of 11 December the drums beat to arms in Paris and guns were brought into the courtyard of the Temple. At eleven, when the king was playing the game called Siam with his son, the boy was taken away from him; at twelve the mayor, the prosecutor of the Commune and some other municipal officers came and conducted Louis XVI to the Convention, where Barère examined him. Out of care for himself and others he replied with negations and doubts. The Montagnards tried to confuse him, but in vain; his calmness and good humour inspired everyone with respect. In spite of his four days' beard and his dirty clothes he dominated the interrogation and the Assembly. The tribunes and the deputies were completely taken aback. Once the examination was over he asked for counsel, a copy of the indictment, and communication of the documents. He was led back to the Temple. Alone in his filthy tower, surrounded by watchful hatred, he gave Cléry a pale smile and said, 'I do not expect any consideration or any justice; but let us wait and see.' He was surprised, therefore, to receive a delegation from the Assembly during the afternoon and to learn that he was granted a counsel. (The Convention feared the words of a barrister less than those of the king.) He said that he chose Target or Tronchet, or both if the Convention agreed. On the morning of the thirteenth he was told that Target refused, but that Huet, Sourdet, Guillaume and Malesherbes proposed themselves as his defenders. Nicolay, Lally-Tollendal, Malouet and Mounier also sought for this honour and this deadly peril.

Malesherbes' offer filled him with joy; he respected him and liked him. They were outwardly very unlike and in some ways their natures were opposed, but they resembled one another in countless traits of character, in their liking for the old ways, their contempt for trifling graces, their love of tradition combined with a kindly regard for the new things of the mind and for young people, their grave intelligence and their good-nature; and lastly they both took the same pleasure in doing good. To these qualities that united them the king added a practical common sense, a courage in action and a deep love of God that were lacking in Malesherbes – a lack that made him seem light-minded, inconsistent and visionary. The king's danger roused Malesherbes' hereditary virtues. As soon as the Assembly's permission had been obtained he hurried to the Temple. His appearance gave the king fresh life. The baseness of his gaolers and the degradation of his people were a haunting, ever-present unhappiness for him, close to despair. The sight of an affectionate man of integrity showed him that his memories and his struggle had a meaning. With tears in his eyes he said to his old friend, 'Oh, it is you, my friend. You see where it has brought me, my extreme love for the people and the self-denial that made me agree to the sending away of the troops intended to defend my power and my person against a factious Assembly. You have come to help me with your advice; you are not afraid to endanger your life to save mine. But it will all be useless.' 'No, Sire, I am not endangering my life, and I even presume to think that Your Majesty is in no danger. Your cause is so just and the defence is so decisive!' 'No,' replied the king, 'they will put me to death. It does not matter: leaving a memory without a stain upon it will be victory for me. Let us look into my means of defence.'

Together they examined the defenders, Tronchet and de Sèze, whom he had chosen and whom the Convention had accepted. Carried along by the king's personality, they proved worthy of him. One day during the trial Treilhard heard his lawyers calling the king 'Sire, Your Majesty.' He sprang up in indignation. 'What makes you so bold as to use words in this place that the Convention has proscribed?' he asked Malesherbes. 'Contempt for you,' replied Malesherbes, 'and contempt for death.' With such men Louis XVI could open his mind; he expected nothing from the war that was being fought. 'If the throne were reconquered by force it would be shaken afresh every day . . . It would be happier for me and far safer for the quietness of the state that I should owe the return of my authority to the love of the French.' Even when he was faced with death his love for his people prevented him from wishing for anything but being loved by them.

The life of the accused king was more cruel and less harsh. No contact with his family, apart from furtive notes by Cléry and the valet Turgy. But he was given back writing materials and his razors . . . Every evening from five to nine he saw his counsel in private, and they brought him newspapers and information; every morning Malesherbes came to see him. His natural fortitude, sustained by constant prayer, armoured him against his own sufferings, but not against those of his wife. He defended her and he was intensely anxious about her. 'These factious men,' he said, 'only decry and denigrate her with all this passionate intensity to prepare the people for the spectacle of her death: her death is decided upon. If her life were spared they would be afraid that she might take her revenge. Unhappy princess! Marriage with me promised her a throne: what future does it offer her today?'

In his catastrophe he was grieved for the sufferings of others, not for his own. At thirty-eight, an age when a man's delight in living becomes sharper and more intense, Louis XVI no longer clung to anything of this world. When Malesherbes attempted to reawaken the pleasure of ruling he replied, 'Out of pleasure, no; out of duty, yes.' And even then he set two conditions – 'that the Catholic religion should continue . . . to be the religion of the state . . . that the usurping power . . . should declare a state of bankruptcy.' That he did want. As early as the first day he saw Malesherbes he begged him to find out whether Father Edgeworth de Firmont, a good and holy priest who had been pointed out to him by Madame Elisabeth, would agree to attend him in his last moments; he gave Malesherbes a letter for Edgeworth in which he asked him as a favour and a 'last token of his atttachment for him' to do him this last service, though at the same time he gave him permission to name another priest if his heart should fail.

In spite of his destitution the king retained his pride. He had no resources, but he would not allow anyone to help him or work for him for nothing. He left a note for the Convention begging that assembly to pay his debts; it was painful for him to be unable to give de Sèze anything. He was resigned to death and he knew that he was innocent. He saw himself referred to as a tyrant in a paper. 'Me, a tyrant!' he said to Malesherbes with calm forcefulness. 'A tyrant sees everything with reference to himself; have I not invariably seen everything with reference to my people? Is it they or I who loathe tyranny most?' His charity forbade him to feel hatred, and his disgust at the spectacle of his persecutors retained that touch of astonishment that is the courtesy of contempt. Yet it all mattered very little to him, for he was already living in death. He asked Malesherbes whether he had seen a white lady. 'So you do not know the legend that whenever a prince of my house is about to die a woman dressed in white wanders about the palace?' he said. Yet he was touched when Malesherbes read him songs that were being sung in Paris in his honour. The first, to the tune of *Pauvre Jacques*, ran:

> *My people, what have I done to you?*
> *Virtue I loved, and justice was my breath,*
> *Your happiness my only aim,*
> *And now you drag me to my death.* (twice)

The second was called *The Complaint of Louis XVI in his Prison*.

> *To Thee, great Lord, my heart looks with a sigh!*
> *Beneath the headsman's axe prepared to die*
> *I yield a guiltless soul to Thee, and tread*
> *To the scaffold from the throne with little dread.*

Yet he never indulged in self-pity, nor would he allow anyone else to be moved for him. When de Sèze read him his speech to the court, which contained certain passages that had stirred him, Louis XVI said, 'These must be cut out; I do not wish to appeal to their emotions.'

Might he have succeeded by doing so? Valmy, Jemmapes and the withdrawal of the invading forces worked in his favour. It was rumoured that Brunswick had left because of Louis XVI's secret intervention. Everyone considered him innocent; and the Gironde wanted to save him. The Girondins attacked Philippe-Egalité in order to divert attention from the king; Chabot stepped in with a speech reminding them that the constitution forbade the banishment of a deputy – and Egalité was one. The Convention protected him. The Gironde, compromised and defeated, was once more overwhelmed with fear.

There were others who wished to save the king. Godoy, the King of Spain's prime minister, tried to interest Pitt in Louis XVI's safety and in a combined effort at buying Danton, who was willing. The Whig leaders begged him to take action to preserve Louis XVI, and Noël, Danton's agent, arranged a meeting between Pitt and Talon, who was handling the business. Danton asked for £40,000. Pitt refused.

The Spaniards then attempted direct negotiation: the Chevalier d'Ocariz, their chargé d'affaires in Paris, was ordered to do everything possible to avoid a death-sentence, and, if it were pronounced, to bargain for a reprieve in exchange for peace and Spanish mediation. On 26 December 1792 he wrote to Lebrun to point out the irregularities in the trial, to remind him that the great mass of the French still retained their love for Louis XVI and to beg him to send the royal family into foreign exile. On 31 December he repeated the offer. It was all in vain, just as the countless plots to free the king by force were in vain.

On Christmas Day Louis XVI prayed for a long time, finished his will and read in Tacitus. In his will he forgave everyone, his enemies, his false friends, his wife 'if she felt she had any cause to blame herself', and the whole of France; he asked forgiveness of those he had offended without meaning to do so, and he said,

> I charge my son, if he should have the misfortune to become king, to remember that he owes himself entirely to the happiness of his fellow-citizens, that he must forget all hatred and all resentment, most particularly that which has to do with the misfortunes and the sorrows that I now experience; to remember that he cannot make the nation happy except by

ruling according to the law, but that at the same time a king cannot make the law respected or do the good that his heart desires unless he has the necessary authority, and that otherwise, being hampered in his operations and inspiring no respect, he is more harmful than useful.

His experience showed him what disasters await both a country that will not accept authority, and a leader who possesses none. Once he had said this, all that remained for him to do before dying was to turn towards God.

I firmly believe and I confess all that is contained in the symbol and the commandments of God and the Church, the sacraments and the mysteries as the Catholic Church teaches and has always taught them. I have never set up as a judge of the different ways of explaining the dogmas that rend Christ's Church, but I have always relied, and I always shall rely if God grants me life, upon the decisions that the ecclesiastical authorities united in the Holy Catholic Church give and shall give in accordance with the discipline of the Church that has been followed since the days of Christ . . . I end by declaring before God, being ready to appear before Him, that I do not hold myself guilty of any of the crimes that I am accused of.

Done in two copies in the tower of the Temple,
25 December 1792.

LOUIS.

He made ready for the second hearing with more serenity than confidence. 'What we are doing here,' he said, 'is Penelope's work; my enemies will very soon have torn it all to pieces. Let us carry on, neverthelesss, although I am not accountable for my actions except to God.' He defended himself neither in the hope of being acquitted, nor in the belief that he was answerable to the nation, but in order not to be guilty before God of suicide.

On 26 December, at ten in the morning, he was brought to the bar of the Convention. He was not afraid of all these pallid faces, alive with a hatred that arose from morbid exaltation or from fear. His calmness irked the Convention. M. de Sèze defended him with talent, zeal and that barrister's skill in uttering empty words

nobly. He showed the illegality of the trial, which was too flagrant
for anyone to deny. But it was right that a speech for the defence
intended for posterity should record that truth, which men forget
when it is a question of the strong oppressing the weak. He proved
that all the accusations brought against Louis XVI either did not
come home to him or were untrue. For the last three years the
king had had no power whatever; it was ridiculous to impute this
mass of crimes to him! The only conservative among all these
revolutionaries, he had obeyed a constitution that they had drawn
up without believing in it and without adhering to it.

Ending his speech he said,

> Listen to History repeating its verdict to Fame: 'Louis came
> to the throne at the age of twenty; and at twenty he gave an
> example of moral conduct upon that throne; he brought no
> guilty weakness to it nor any corrupting passion; upon the
> throne he was frugal, just, and strict; he proved himself
> the people's steadfast friend . . . He anticipated the people's
> wishes by countless acts of self-sacrifice.' And yet it is in the
> name of this same people that today the prosecution asks . . .
> Citizens, I shall not finish! I halt before the face of history.
> Consider what your judgment will be, and reflect that this
> will be the verdict of the centuries.

The Assembly shuddered, then pulled itself together.

Louis XVI rose and said,

> Speaking to you perhaps for the last time I declare to you
> that my conscience does not reproach me in any way and that
> my defenders have told you nothing but the truth. I have
> never feared a public examination of my conduct; but it
> wounds my heart to find in the indictment the charge that I
> wished to shed the people's blood, and, above all, that the
> misfortunes of 10 August were attributable to me. I confess
> that the often repeated pledges that I have at all times given
> of my love for the people and the way in which I have always
> behaved seem to me an evident proof that I had little fear
> of endangering myself in order to spare their blood, and
> that these pledges and this behaviour should preserve me for
> ever from any such imputation.

The independents and the Girondins seemed entirely overcome. The king had denounced no one to defend himself! Lanjuinais wanted to take advantage of this to have the charges withdrawn. In his enthusiasm he attacked the ringleaders of 10 August. A rash stroke! In a fury the Montagnards protested. Lanjuinais was forced to withdraw his words. Vergniaud put forward the king's inviolability; Brissot and Salle spoke of Europe's indignation and called for an appeal to the people. Lebrun himself read Ocariz's letter. His proposal was referred to the diplomatic committee. There remained the hope of an exile to the United States, which was advocated by Paine, Genet and the Rolands, with the backing of the United States government. They were afraid. Meanwhile at the Jacobins' club itself Louis Robert argued that political wisdom insisted upon delaying the condemnation of Capet.

Robespierre was above all these weaknesses. Urged on by the spirit of the Enlightenment and by his Jacobin ardour, he had made a decisive speech on 2 December; knowing that a popular vote would save Louis XVI he used every means of avoiding one, and his chief weapon was fear. 'Victory will decide whether you are rebels or the benefactors of mankind, and it is your strength of character that will determine the victory.' In the name of the nation's peril and of virtue, 'of that virtue which has always been in a minority upon this earth', he wanted blood. His Montagnard colleagues completed his work: Gasparin revealed that Vergniaud, Guadet and Gensonné had been in negotiation with the court from 5-9 August 1792; and when Boze was called to the bar he was an utterly damning witness. The next day, 4 January, Barère, who was compelled to be zealous because of certain revelations from the Iron Chest, mildly explained, 'The trial is in fact an act of public safety or a measure of general security; and an act of public safety is not subject to ratification by the people.' After that there was nothing left for the thoroughly frightened Girondins but silence.

As he left the hall Louis XVI said to Malesherbes, 'Are you not now really convinced that my death had been decided before ever I was heard?' Malesherbes, visionary as usual, told him that on the contrary after the Assembly had been asked to appeal to the people, he and the two other counsel had been quite surrounded, and many deputies had said, 'He shall not die; or at least he shall only do so after us and our friends.' Louis XVI replied, 'Do you know these men? Go back to the Assembly, try to see them again and find out who they are: tell them that I shall never forgive them if there is a single drop of blood spilt for me. I did not want any to be shed when it might perhaps have preserved my throne and my life; and I do not regret it.'

Public opinion was openly for him. At the Théâtre-Français, where they were playing *L'Ami des lois*, there was wild applause for everything that had any resemblance to an allusion in favour of the king's safety. At the Vaudeville there was *La Chaste Suzanne*, and the audience made the actors repeat the incident where a character says to one of the elders, 'How can you be prosecutors and judges at the same time?'

Louis XVI received the new year's wishes of the queen, the children and Elisabeth through a guard. 'What a New Year's Day!' he said to Cléry, returning to his book. Cléry was his only companion, but the valet's presence was warm, pious and unburdensome; he never allowed himself any word or action that might be disagreeable to the king. The soldiers, warders and municipal guards had gone back into that dream in which gaolers always live for their prisoners; from now onwards they had no more existence for him than the mud, the darkness, the evil smells and the physical wretchedness. He no longer even asked to see his family, being of the opinion that he would be granted a last interview when he had been sentenced to death.

The voting started on 14 January; it went on and on, for it was done individually and every deputy could explain his views for as long as he wished. Now all of them, with dread behind them, wanted to make the most of this opportunity, and they all uttered the standard, formal declamations. Guilt was voted unanimously, with a few abstentions; the appeal to the people was rejected by 424 votes to 287. When the penalty was to be decided, 334 deputies voted for chains, imprisonment or conditional death, 26 for a suspended death-sentence, and 361 for death without any reservations. Louis XVI was condemned to death by the majority of one vote. If they had been free there would not have been a hundred deputies to vote for the death-sentence; but the roaring of the mob whipped up by the Jacobins that besieged the Convention, and the intimidation tactics of the Montagnards, directed by Robespierre, left them no freedom whatsoever.

Chapter XI

The King's death

THAT EVENING THE KING WAS SITTING AT HIS TABLE,
deep in meditation, with his back turned to the lamp on the
chimney-piece, his elbows on the table and his face buried in his
hands. He heard Malesherbes come in, raised his head and said,
'For the last two days I have been searching through my reign to
find whether I have at any time deserved the least reproach from
my subjects. Well, Monsieur de Malesherbes, I swear to you in all
sincerity, and as a man who is about to appear before God,
that I have invariably desired the welfare of the people and that
I have never once wished for anything that could be contrary
to their happiness.'

Malesherbes agreed, and then in a muffled voice he told him of
the sentence of death. Without agitation or distress the king embraced him, comforted him and listened to his detailed account
of the vote. Then they drew up the request for a stay of execution:
might it not be possible to circumvent so trifling a majority?
Lastly Louis XVI thanked him and begged him to summon the
Abbé Edgeworth with all haste: Malesherbes withdrew to carry
out these missions.

Some of the Girondins, paid by him, supported the request on the grounds of the country's relations with foreign powers. Barère replied that this would mean prolonging a painful and dangerous situation. They were beaten by 380 votes against 310.

Meanwhile, sitting by the meagre fire in his tower, Louis XVI pondered over the list of deputies who had voted for his death. 'I am not looking for any hope,' he said to Cléry, 'but it does grieve me very much that Monsieur d'Orléans, my own relation, should have voted for my death . . .' Cléry told him that Dumouriez' coming to Paris showed it was the army's wish that he should live; in any case, a riot might break out. 'I should be sorry if that were to happen,' said Louis XVI, 'there would be fresh victims . . . I can see the people, given over to anarchy, becoming the prey of every kind of faction; I see crime following upon crime, and France rent by lasting discord.'

So the hours went by. Malesherbes did not come to see him on the eighteenth or the nineteenth. To pass the time Louis XVI did a word puzzle and found that 'sacrifice' was the answer; then he read over the death of Charles I again. On Saturday 19 January, his two rooms were searched through and through. That evening he complained that he was being separated from his advisers and he wrote a note to the Commune also asking that he should no longer be kept under constant surveillance. 'It must be evident that in my present situation it is exceedingly painful for me not to be able to be alone and not to have the necessary peace to turn my thoughts to God.' The continual importunate presence of an inimical watcher is like filth weighing on a captive's heart.

As soon as he got up on 20 January he asked for the reply to his letter but without result: the morning dragged by in waiting. At two o'clock the door was flung open. The whole executive council, the mayor and the departmental authorities crowded into the room, fifteen men in all. As soon as he heard the noise the king stood up; he faced them without perturbation or anger. Garat, the minister of justice, read the Convention's decrees declaring him guilty of conspiracy against the nation's freedom. Louis XVI listened without a muscle of his face moving; he smiled slightly at the word 'conspiracy'. Then with an untroubled gaze he looked them all firmly in the face. Unhurriedly he put the death-sentence away in his letter-case, and then in his pocket.

He then read and handed them a letter to the Convention in which he asked for three days in which to make himself ready to appear before God, for the attendance of his confessor, the removal of the perpetual supervision and the right to see his family. He recommended those who had been attached to him to the nation. Garat took the letter and promised to deliver it promptly to the Convention. At the last moment the king gave him the Abbé Edgeworth's address.

At dinner his knife and fork were taken from him, as is done to convicts. He ate little and returned to his reading. At ten o'clock a great deal of noise; Santerre entered the room, walking in front of Garat: the Commune granted all the king's requests except the delay. He listened, unmoved. A bitter disappointment for the gaolers, who had come 'to see what kind of a face he would put on it'.

Garat and his colleagues, on the other hand, were red with shame; and Garat therefore eagerly announced Edgeworth's arrival as soon as the king asked for him. Then the abbé himself appeared: as soon as he saw him Louis XVI made a gesture and the ministers left.

The moment they were alone the abbé, in tears, fell at the feet of Louis XVI. For the first time the king was overcome; then, mastering himself, he begged the priest's pardon. He was so accustomed to living among enemies that the sight of a loyal subject was exceedingly moving to him. He led the Abbé Edgeworth into the little tower, gave him a chair, showed him his will and asked him to describe the present position of the French clergy. At about half past eight the news that his family was there interrupted them. He went to see them at once; and at the sight of his own flesh and blood he was at first moved to tears – they all sat down together, mingling their sobs. Then with a calm mind he told them about the trial; he reminded the Dauphin of his religious duties and of his duty to forgive his father's executioners. He blessed his two children, spoke gently to them and comforted them. But he would not let the family spend the night with him.

He had too great a need for calmness of mind. However, he promised to see them again in the morning. As she left, the queen fainted.

He sent them away at a quarter past ten, to devote his last hours to God. 'Ah, Monsieur,' he said to the priest, 'what a meeting I have just undergone! Is it right that I should love so and that I should be so tenderly beloved? But it is over: let us forget all the rest and think only of this one concern, our salvation – it is upon that alone that I must now concentrate all my affections and all my thoughts.' He therefore confessed. Then, at about eleven, he ate a light supper and obliged the abbé to do the same. The priest, whom the king's confession filled with the deepest pity, proposed giving him communion. This was a difficult, perilous undertaking, but Louis XVI's joy was so great that the Abbé Edgeworth did not hesitate to see the commissioners in charge of the king at once, and in the end he persuaded them to give him permission to say mass, and the means of doing so.

Edgeworth brought his good news to the king. Comforted, and full of spiritual happiness, he talked with the abbé until far into the night; then he went to bed, telling Cléry to wake him at five. It was he who woke first. 'I slept well,' he said to Cléry, who was lighting the fire. 'I needed it; yesterday was a tiring day.' Cléry dressed him and did his hair in silence. At six o'clock the abbé said mass, using a chest-of-drawers set up in the middle of the room. The king followed the service on his knees and communicated with great piety.

When the mass was over Cléry begged the king to bless him. He did so, thanking him for his loyal service. He gave him a seal for his son, a ring for the queen and a lock of his hair. He put his other things, watch, letter-case and so on, on the mantelpiece.

Since five o'clock the drums had been beating to arms; troops of cavalry were coming into the Temple courtyard. The king longed most ardently to see his family. The priest advised him against doing so, for the queen would be unable to bear it. 'You are right; it would be a mortal blow. It is better for me to do without that sweetest of comforts and to let her live a few moments longer in hope.'

From seven o'clock onwards there were knocks on his door – the persecution of zealous officials. At nine a great din announced the coming of Santerre. The king was warned that the fatal hour had come. 'I am busy,' he replied. 'Wait for me there. I shall be with you directly.' Shutting the door, he knelt before Edgeworth. 'It is all over, Monsieur; give me your last blessing, and pray to God that He may sustain me to the end.'

Then he went back into his room, took his hat and followed the guards, less distressed than they. In the second courtyard he was put into a hired coach, together with the abbé and two gendarmes. No one spoke: he read in Edgeworth's breviary. There was the sound of the soldiers' feet, the beat of the drums. The slow, interrupted march lasted for two hours.

The king's thoughts looked back towards the past. How great had been his need to love! How he had loved this people! But how much hatred had risen against him! Choiseul, the man of the *philosophes*; the parliamentarians and the sectaries; then Orléans, the Thirty and the Jacobins. They were triumphing today; France was repudiating her traditions, her civilization and her faith. She was refusing that world supremacy that his family had desired and that he had won. What would become of her with neither anchor nor compass, even if her people were to retain their heroic qualities and their wonderful spirit? He regretted nothing. Better die than kill his subjects.

Meanwhile in every corner of Paris the royalists were seeking an opportunity: the day before one of them had killed Lepeletier de Saint-Fargeau. But on 21 January 1793 the great numbers of eager, watchful police prevented action. And so the coach reached the Place Louis XV. There they got out. Before this, speaking in his uniformly calm, firm voice, he had required them to respect the abbé after his death. Three executioners came about him to remove his clothes. He thrust them back and undid his collar and his shirt. They made as if to tie his hands. 'Tie me!' he replied indignantly. 'No. I shall never consent to it. Do what you are ordered to do, but you shall not tie me: give it up, I say.'

The scene might have become utterly appalling: in a low voice the Abbé Edgeworth said to him, 'Sire, in this fresh outrage I see yet one more likeness between Your Majesty and the God that is about to be your reward.' This was like the lash of a whip in the king's face. He raised his eyes to heaven – eyes that now for the first time showed a reddish light. 'Indeed,' he cried, 'I need nothing short of His example to bear such an insult.' Then, to the executioners, 'Do what you wish: I shall drink the cup to the dregs.'

His hands were tied behind his back. He walked up the steep steps of the scaffold without hesitating. Then at the top he escaped from the executioners; he moved forward towards the crowd, and in a thunderous voice he cried, 'I die innocent of all the crimes I am accused of. I forgive the authors of my death and I pray to God that the blood you are about to spill may never fall upon the head of France . . .'

There was a wavering among the lines of troops; some of the soldiers were weeping. Santerre[1] ran to order the beating of drums to drown his voice. Amidst this din the executioners hastily did their work. The plank tipped over. One more great cry was heard. Louis XVI's head fell into the basket.

A group of men and women rushed forward to dip handkerchiefs and cloths into his gore. Louis XVI's blood spurted a great way off.

Since then the whole history of France has born its stain.

[1] He boasted of having done so, at least, as long as the Revolution lasted.

Index